SOCIALIST ESCAPES

Socialist Escapes

*Breaking Away from Ideology
and Everyday Routine
in Eastern Europe, 1945–1989*

Edited by

**Cathleen M. Giustino,
Catherine J. Plum,
and
Alexander Vari**

berghahn
NEW YORK · OXFORD
www.berghahnbooks.com

Published in 2013 by

Berghahn Books

www.berghahnbooks.com

© 2013 Cathleen M. Giustino, Catherine J. Plum, and Alexander Vari

Library of Congress Cataloging-in-Publication Data

Socialist escapes : breaking away from ideology and everyday routine in Eastern Europe,
1945–1989 / edited by Cathleen M. Giustino, Catherine J. Plum, and Alexander Vari.
   p. cm.
   Includes bibliographical references and index.
   ISBN 978-0-85745-669-4 (hbk. : acid-free paper) — ISBN 978-0-85745-670-0
(ebook)
   1. Europe, Eastern—Social life and customs—20th century. 2. Europe, Eastern—
Social conditions—20th century. 3. Europe, Eastern—History—1945–1989.
4. Escape (Psychology)—Europe, Eastern—History—20th century. 5. Amusements—
Europe, Eastern—History—20th century. 6. Leisure—Europe, Eastern—History—
20th century. 7. Socialism and culture—Europe, Eastern—History—20th century.
8. Social psychology—Europe, Eastern—History—20th century. I. Giustino,
Cathleen M. II. Plum, Catherine J. III. Vari, Alexander.
   DJK50.S63 2012
   947.0009'045—dc23
                                                                                        2012001677

British Library Cataloguing in Publication Data

A catalogue record for this book is available from the British Library

Printed in the United States on acid-free paper

ISBN 978-0-85745-669-4 (hardback)
ISBN 978-0-85745-670-0 (institutional ebook)

Contents

Figures

Preface

Cathleen M. Giustino

This book grew out of questions about possibilities for the existence of "fun places" in post-war Eastern Europe. For our authors, this theme served as a starting point for sharing insight into what it was like to live under communist single-party rule in the East Bloc—to grapple with the "*Ding an sich*" ("thing in itself") of everyday experience behind what Winston Churchill called the Iron Curtain in his 1946 Fulton, Missouri speech. In the early stages of this project, it became clear that the concept of "fun" can be challenging for historians and other social scientists to study or discuss in objective terms. It is an emotional category, the borders of which can be vague, unbounded, and difficult to define. Furthermore, experiences of this subjective state can leave evidentiary traces that are hard for scholars to locate and analyze, especially in societies that were heavily censored like those of Eastern Europe during the Cold War.

Important discoveries emerged in the early stages of our exchange of research and ideas about "fun places" in Soviet-styled states. Among others, we identified a more concrete path for the pursuit of experience in the East Bloc. This path derived from the second word shaping our initial inquiry, namely "places," a spatial category that is more material in nature than fun and more amenable to objective analysis. Places can be mapped or drawn, and they leave substantive evidence including buildings, signs, advertisements, brochures, souvenirs, legal regulations, police reports, business records, and media accounts that can be amassed and analyzed. All of the participating scholars always treated place when seeking to understand experience in the East Bloc. Moreover, we always tended to treat a specific type of place—ones to which people went or traveled while engaging in leisure, entertainment, and tourism.

Our shared attention to free time destinations and distractions soon led us to change the volume theme from "fun places" to "getaways." This latter category proved useful for advancing our insights into everyday life in

Eastern Europe because it raised deeper questions about popular motivations and experiences. Above all, we asked: What were Eastern Europeans "getting away from" during the Cold War period? When many think of getaways, they think of destinations where one leaves behind the sometimes dull everyday routines of work, school, and home, while enjoying uncommon pastimes which are often rejuvenating but sometimes tiring. These departures from mundane routines were an important aspect of the leisure, entertainment, and tourism that we were examining, but there was something in the context of post-war Eastern Europe that made the theme of getaways too limiting. By itself, getaways did not sufficiently highlight official Communist Party ideology embedded within East Bloc free time activities. Thus, at this point in our collaborative endeavor, we embraced the idea of socialist escapes, a more illuminating category for our analysis. Socialist escapes helped us to appreciate that when inhabitants of post-war Eastern Europe engaged in leisure, entertainment, and tourism, they could be motivated by conscious and unconscious desires to experience at least relative autonomy from the party and its ideology, in addition to seeking breaks from mundane responsibilities. It is here with the notion of socialist escapes where the conceptual refinement of our volume's analytic theme finally rested. The results of our intellectual group journey are the articles here, which contribute to more nuanced and accurate understandings of state power in the East Bloc as well as other contexts with single-party rule where inhabitants experienced some opportunities for agency and *Eigen-Sinn*.

Acknowledgments

Many people were involved in the completion of this volume and the co-editors wish to acknowledge them. Above all, we thank the authors of the articles contained here for their hard work and patience during the long process of transforming numerous drafts into published works. In addition to participating in numerous stages of refining their own contributions, they all participated in valuable peer reviews of one another's evolving essays. We are very grateful to the anonymous peer reviewers who provided excellent suggestions for the improvement of this collaborative work. We also thank the many wonderful people at Berghahn Books for bringing this volume to fruition, especially Ann Przyzycki DeVita, Melissa Spinelli, Elizabeth Berg, and our copyeditor.

Cathleen M. Giustino acknowledges T. Mills Kelly for the wonderful ideas that he brought to this volume during its early stages, including first suggesting the notion of "socialist escapes." She appreciates the knowledge about edited volumes and friendship that Nancy M. Wingfield shared. Her department chair, Charles A. Israel, gave her generous latitude to pursue this publication. She thanks both her co-editors for their excellent contributions and many hours of hard work, including Catherine J. Plum for her very careful editing of the first manuscript. Cathleen's biggest thanks go to her husband, Garth Stauffer, and son, Christopher Parsons, for their patience and love.

Catherine J. Plum thanks the dean of arts and science and her colleagues at Western New England University for the generous leave time necessary for work on this project. Her husband, Russell Tessier, demonstrated patience and constant encouragement while interlibrary loan books multiplied like Stasi files in the 1980s and work on this book intersected with their courtship, engagement, and first year of marriage. Her co-editors and fellow contributor, Caroline Fricke, offered valuable support and friendship during the time spent on this volume.

Alexander Vari thanks Karl Brown, William Conlogue, his co-editors, and several contributors to the volume for the critical reading and very helpful suggestions and comments that they provided during various stages of writing and editing.

Introduction

Escaping the Monotony of Everyday Life under Socialism

Alexander Vari

It is November 1955. Gyuri, a young Hungarian basketball player, is on a train traveling to a provincial city south-east of Budapest. The incessant sound of a man snoring in his compartment bothers him so much that he decides to step out. The connection between the passive state of sleep and his decision to leave the scene unexpectedly triggers in Gyuri the desire to put behind him the whole experience of living under communism by "sleep[ing] through the entire thing, only [to] wake up when everything ha[s] changed." What bothers Gyuri most is the boredom of life under communism. He muses that the "[d]ictatorship of the proletariat [in Hungary], apart from the abrasive and brutal nature of its despotism, was terribly dull." One train of thought leads to another, and Gyuri concludes that socialism was simply "not the sort of tyranny you'd want to invite to a party."[1]

Although Gyuri is a fictional character from Tibor Fischer's *Under the Frog*, a 1992 British novel inspired by the experiences of the author's parents in Stalinist Hungary, his thoughts on that train ride in November 1955 might have well been shared by many Eastern Europeans who experienced everyday life under communism. In the case of the communist regimes established in Eastern Europe after World War II, the issue of controlling citizens' everyday lives turned into a matter of both ideological and political imperative. One's day was supposed to be shaped by an internalization of the communist ideology, expressed through a denial of subjective agency in favor of an unconditional embrace of collectivist ideals. In this sense, the individuals' everyday thoughts and actions in the newly Sovietized satellite states were supposed to overlap with and conform to a reality shaped by ideological expectations and precepts. As historian A.E. Rees writes, "Stalin spoke of the Soviet state as a 'monolith' with every person acting as a cog (*vintik*) in a great machine, exemplifying what Engels had characterized as 'barracks socialism' with its *étatisme*, regimentation and uniformity."[2]

The authors of this volume argue that attempts to achieve a monolithic control of the everyday under Stalinism gave birth to attempts to evade its overbearing pressure. Recent scholarship on Stalinist societies has emphasized that even at the height of post-war attempts to impose ideological uniformity and conformity in the states making up the Soviet Bloc, and in spite of the continuous use of violence and coercion by state officials, there was room for popular dissent, grassroots resistance, and differences of opinion.[3] It is important for students of Eastern European history to understand that people living under communism constantly sought ways to challenge the system from within on an everyday basis. Visitors to castle museums in late 1940s–early 1950s Czechoslovakia could, for instance, laugh at the jokes museum guides told, instead of listening attentively to their propagandistic preambles. In another geographic context, that of Stalinist Romania, party officials could leave the stifling halls of power in Bucharest in order to practice nudism and carve out a bohemian lifestyle in a remote village located on the Black Sea coast. It is true that such domestic diversions and pastimes fit more in the context of the thaw, a concerted effort made between the mid-1950s and the early 1960s by Nikita Khrushchev and reformist party officials to open up the Soviet Union and its Eastern European satellites to more interaction with the West—a policy that was paired with an unprecedented emphasis on socialist consumption and improvements in people's living standards.[4] But even when the strong ideological pressures and controls characteristic of the hardcore Stalinist period weakened in the more liberal and emancipated atmosphere of the thaw, the fundamental tension between a conformist everyday dominated by ideology and an escape into individual expression and enjoyment continued to characterize life under socialism. However, the intensity and ability of people to escape into a different realm of experience varied according to the impact of domestic and international developments on everyday life within the Eastern Bloc as a whole (such as the events of June 1953 in East Germany, those of 1956 in Poland and Hungary, the building of the Berlin Wall in 1961, the 1968 Prague Spring in Czechoslovakia, the spread of intellectual dissidence in several Eastern European countries and the Soviet Union, the rise of the Solidarity movement in Poland, and the continuous rivalry between the United States and the Soviet Union during the Cold War), as well as country by country.

Discussions of any attempt to transgress officially established boundaries need to take into account such chronological and regional discrepancies. At the same time, as post-Stalinist regimes became more permeable to ideas, forms of consumption, music, and fashions originating in the West, and more responsive to the needs and the desires of a new generation of people that came of age two decades after World War II, the nature and content of people's leisure pursuits turned into a hotly contested field. While officials were interested in regulating the way people spent their free time, members of the post-war generation saw leisure venues as opportunities for expressing themselves more freely. During the late 1950s and 1960s, new mass leisure practices, such as tourism, hitchhiking, wild camping, listening to jazz, dancing to beat and rock and roll tunes, and the wearing of tight-fitting jackets and jeans, symbolized the youth's quest for everyday pleasures, adventure, and nonconformism, not just in the West, but in the Eastern Bloc as well. These leisure pursuits and countercultural ways of life allowed people to "escape" socialism "without leaving it."[5] This escapist mindset persisted even as the last two decades of socialism brought with them new challenges. In a period of economic and political stagnation and new repressive measures in the cultural sphere, the 1970s and 1980s witnessed the revival of a stronger ideological stance and renewed controls over free time and some leisure activities; however, a new youth generation's quest for its own ways of expression (exemplified, for instance, by the embrace not just of rock and roll, but punk and heavy metal lifestyles) continued to simmer underneath the cauldron of socialist party politics.[6]

Framing these developments from the perspective of the impact they had on people's everyday lives and their relationship to politics can tell us more about the nature of living under socialism. The study of everyday life has an illustrious lineage in historiography. From Anglo-Saxon practitioners of history written "from below" and German *Alltagsgeschichte* historians to Italian practitioners of microhistory, and historians belonging to the fourth generation of the Annales School in France, scholars have examined the subversive and emancipatory potentials of everyday life in various historical and geographic contexts.[7] In spite of this, and until very recently, research on everyday life under socialism was scarce. The most important recent breakthroughs concern the early years of the Soviet Union and post-Second World War East Germany and Czechoslovakia.[8] The study of everyday life in the German Democratic Republic (GDR) has been especially fecund and inspiring lately.[9]

Taking cue from these studies, this volume bridges an important gap by offering coverage of more than just one socialist state in Eastern Europe. We hope that with its focus on East Germany, Poland, Czechoslovakia, Hungary, Romania, and Bulgaria, this volume will encourage further comparative interest in the study of everyday life under socialism. In order to achieve this, we have adopted a narrower focus. Instead of considering the sites of everyday life broadly by visiting important locales of people's socialization under socialism such as the factory, school, and domestic spaces,[10] or by looking at the important issue of gender relations[11] or socialist fashion and consumption,[12] we examine it from the perspective of people's attempts to acquire their own agency in the field of culture, leisure, and entertainment and the state's attempt to control, monitor, and shape—in turn—these escape venues.

As a growing literature suggests, struggle and resistance were important components in both the building and dismantling of socialism. People resisted socialism in various ways. In their recent collection of essays, *Revolution and Resistance in Eastern Europe,* Kevin McDermott and Matthew Stibbe identify national communism, intellectual dissent, armed peasant resistance, and popular protests against communist rule as four different types of resistance against the socialist system.[13] Unlike the well-known cases of popular protest that occurred in East Germany in 1953, and in Poland and Hungary in 1956, or the spread of intellectual dissent and civil disobedience predominant in the events of the Prague Spring in 1968, and later in the activity of underground groups such as the Czech Charter 77 and the Polish Solidarity movement, escapes from the dull everyday life of socialism represented a softer (and therefore less examined) form of dissent against the socialist system.[14] The paradox of many of the escapes discussed in this volume is that initially they were "socialist" escapes in the sense that they were often initiated by communist officials and only later embraced and turned into escape venues by the masses living under socialism. Authorities did not organize breaks and excursions solely to control, indoctrinate, and pacify the masses, but also to entertain and provide pleasure. State socialism did not question whether or not one should be able to escape, but rather how one should escape, with whom, and to what purpose. Through state-sponsored escapes, communist officials sought to both secure political legitimacy and fulfill the socialist promise of the so-called "good life" as a reward for labor, albeit often within the context of what bureaucrats deemed "productive leisure." The attempt made by party officials in Poland and Bulgaria to teach workers how to enjoy relaxation in a natural setting could be considered relevant in this regard. Even daily escapes that groups and individuals initiated in spite of and against the teachings of the party, such as nudism, excessive smoking and drinking, the wearing of jeans, and listening to and dancing to Western music, could still be described as "socialist" because they developed in a spirit of defiance to state prohibitions, and as such they would be less meaningful if examined in a different context.[15]

Overall, the concept of an escape is useful in understanding socialist leisure, entertainment, and recreation for several reasons. Whether physical or cognitive, escapes are conscious actions. They often involve planning and goal setting, both in the case of typical weekend activities and escapes of a more extraordinary variety that included travel. As highly intentional acts, escapes are a useful tool for investigating state, group, and individual goals and motivations, as well as conformity and resistance. It is important to keep in mind that even in cases where state authorities expected nominal participation or planned escapes for employees or children, individuals were capable of independent action and had the ability to attach different meanings to leisure, recreation, and travel. Ultimately, the various escapes discussed in this volume commonly share breaks from labor, factory, office, or domestic duties, which also strengthened people's individual agency under socialism.

Through the lens of people's attempts to escape the boredom of life under socialism, we can better understand how average people experienced and reacted to state policies in their everyday lives. The escapes offer us new avenues to explore the effectiveness of state efforts to engineer society and win legitimacy among average people through leisure, entertainment, and related forms of cultural programming and consumption. They help us identify ways in which some Eastern Europeans found opportunities for enjoyment, agency, and self expression while living under repressive rulers in poorly managed shortage economies. While state-controlled escapes integrated political ideology with play, the development of parallel, non-sanctioned escapes provides a window into popular dissatisfaction, subcultures, and a degree of autonomy and independent identity formation in Cold War Eastern Europe. These escapes can also be described as reactions to the stifling processes of ideological routinization imposed from above and expected to be adhered to on an everyday basis. The very imposition of such everyday routines played a very important role in causing the population to develop a set of particular reactions to them. As sociologist Don Slater writes, "discourses on routine should be considered as performative, and processes of routinization (whether successful or resisted) centrally involve participants in taking an attitude to routinization itself: that is to say, the notion of 'routine' is topicalized by actors themselves, and this is consequential in the production (or the flouting) of routine."[16] In addition to their performative and cultural dimension,[17] however, people's escape from meaningless socialist rhetoric and routine into the world of meaningful leisure activities also had a strong spatial component. As the essays in this volume document, the escapes that people engaged in under socialism unfolded along a spectrum of multiple spatialities: space between the past and the present, geographic space, space to be travelled through, space to be discovered and incorporated, space to be enjoyed, space to be lit up, and space to be controlled. Their broader context can thus be defined along a continuum that stretched from the cultural realm to the spatial, kinetic, and physical components of everyday living.[18]

Concert Halls and Estate Museums

In addition to the enforced policies of industrialization, collectivization, and state management of the economy, the Sovietization of Eastern Europe in the late 1940s led to the adoption of the Stalinist concept of *kul'turnost'* (culturedness) as an ideal to be attained by workers. *Kul'turnost'* was a model for the "inculcation of [socialist] disciplines" that, according to Vadim Volkov, "proceeded without recourse to open violence or terror."[19] As the socialist parties of Eastern Europe called upon the working class to replace the dominance of old elites with its own cultural hegemony, cultural sophistication required workers to master a broad body of knowledge and engage in specific practices that were meant to become routine. In addition to paying attention to personal hygiene, taking care of their personal appearance, and reading Soviet literature, socialist regimes also required workers to take trips to museums and attend cultural events.[20] The emphasis communist parties in Eastern Europe placed on the latter is well-documented.[21] The gap between desire and reality, however, was often considerable.

Creating a socialist culture required not just the self-education of the masses, but their adoption of a socialist spirit.[22] Therefore, in the sphere of arts and culture, writers, painters, sculptors, and musicians were expected to write, paint, sculpt, and compose music according to the guiding principles of socialist realism, a literary and artistic style that was supposed to be easily understood by the masses, and thus forge a strong bond between intellectuals and the working class under the auspices of the party. Socialist realism had a strong propagandistic content.[23] While works of art and literature painted glorious portraits of working class heroes, the regime asked musicians to collaborate and rally the masses through the production of a large amount of "sonic propaganda."[24] In Stalinist Romania, for instance, as Joel Crotty writes, Matei Socor, the President of the Union of Composers and Musicologists "and his supporters worked for the total Sovietization of Romanian music and promoted text-based music over symphonies and chamber works because the propaganda element was easier to promote."[25] This propagandistic element also played an important role in the case of the music festivals organized during this period in East Germany and Poland, as David Tompkins posits in his chapter in this volume. While escaping the ideological grip of the party was difficult for East German composers, the situation was better in Poland, where, as Tompkins argues in his chapter, "Instrumentalizing Entertainment and Education: Early Cold-War Music Festivals in East Germany and Poland," music festivals—especially after1953—afforded an escape from the ever-present pressure of Stalinist ideology. Whereas in the GDR the tight control of the party over cultural programming periodically estranged both composers and audiences, in Poland, authors of choral and symphonic music were able to forge their own festival culture by going against the grain of official expectations.

Unexpected escape venues can be found in other contexts as well. For instance, after World War II, socialist regimes nationalized the castles, chateaux, and palaces owned by members of the aristocracy in every Eastern European country and turned many of them into museums to educate the public about the luxurious lifestyle of former elites.[26] However, visits to the newly opened castle and chateaux museums in Czechoslovakia did not always fulfill their intended educational role, as Cathleen M. Giustino's chapter entitled "Open Gates and Wandering Minds: Codes, Castles and Chateaux in Socialist Czechoslovakia before 1960" in this volume reveals. Throughout the 1950s, estate museums, such as the one at Ratibořice with displays celebrating Božena Němcová's "beloved Czech novel" *Grandmother,* lacked signage that could bear the ideological imprint that the state required as part of its takeover of every aspect of Czech public life. State officials' expectations for ideological correctness were repeatedly violated by improperly trained tour guides and continuously failed to be implemented to their letter. Visitors to Czechoslovak estate museums were thus often able to appropriate the meaning of exhibits on display through their own creativity and imagination.

As another example of ideological expectation gone awry, recent research on neighboring Poland (and the more distant Yugoslavia) shows that even workers, who, in broad educational terms, benefited from having access to the high culture foisted upon them by the party, often came up with their own version of it.[27] In this respect, reading classic works of literature, listening to contemporary music in Poland, or visiting museums in castles and chateaux at the height of Stalinism in Czechoslovakia afforded an escape from the ideological expectations imposed in other areas of everyday life by the party state.

Cabins in the Woods

The party tried to educate workers not just through museum displays and music festivals, but also by teaching them how to make better use of their leisure time in nature. As field research in Poland in the late 1940s demonstrated, this goal was all the more important since workers in many Eastern European countries did not know what to do with their free time. Padraic Kenney points out that when "state-organized and -subsidized paid vacation[s] (*wczasy*)" in mountain resorts were offered to Polish workers in 1947, to the "consternation of union and party officials," they did not take advantage.[28]

On the one hand, workers preferred to spend time with their families after long hours of work in the factories, while on the other hand, they felt awkward in the presence of social superiors even after they had demoted them from their former positions of power.[29]

Notwithstanding, the party wanted workers to not only embrace new leisure opportunities made possible by a more egalitarian society, but also to participate in mass socialist tourism in rural and urban settings. Socialist tourism was a concept quite distinct from middle-class and elite tourism which had dominated historic tourist industries. Although traveling to foreign destinations was generally out of the question, there was a lot to discover at home in the first two decades following World War II, particularly in natural settings, both traditional leisure destinations and untamed pastoral locales.

The Soviet model of diverting interest in traveling to foreign countries into exploring domestic destinations also became the norm in Poland.[30] As Patrice M. Dabrowski argues in her chapter on "Encountering Poland's 'Wild West': Tourism in the Bieszczady Mountains under Socialism" in this volume, the Polish regime presented the Bieszczady Mountains, located in the southeastern corner of Poland, as a veritable terra incognita that was ripe for socialist citizens' discovery and exploration. By the early 1960s, the region was opened for mass tourism after a highway was built to penetrate this natural setting and make it more accessible. Workers from the industrialized regions of Poland traveled to the villages dotting the Bieszczady area, where they were encouraged to escape into nature by taking strenuous hikes through the surrounding mountain ranges. Thus by the 1960s and 1970s, the Bieszczady mountains became a site for mass tourism. Socialist authorities, however, could not keep up with tourists' demand for services and accommodation. In the end, escaping into the wilderness of the Bieszczady came to symbolize the failure of the socialist system to adequately address their needs. Instead of supporting the state in its attempt to create proletarian tourism, Poles turned away from it, finding in the wilderness of the Bieszczady, as Dabrowski argues, the opportunity to escape the oppressive strictures of the socialist quotidian.

The connection between nature, leisure, and children also played an important role in socialist ideology and practice. Twin goals of healthy recreation in nature and political education came together in the central Pioneer camps the communist youth organization sponsored in East Germany. Similar to their counterparts across the Eastern Bloc, the East German Pioneer camps were situated in beautiful natural settings. However, the lack of basic amenities and, in some cases, polluted waters near the site left something to be desired, as Catherine J. Plum argues in her chapter in this volume, "Summer Camp for Socialists: Conformity and Escapism at Camp Mitschurin in East Germany." The Pioneer camps offered a temporary escape into nature, particularly for children used to crowded mass housing, but not a respite from political education and other ideological unpleasantries and challenges in socialist East Germany. Communist youth leaders were most successful when they fused politics with fun, for example, by using a campfire setting for the singing of ideological songs, or organizing paramilitary adventure games in the woods. By the 1980s, the case study of Camp Mitschurin/Matern reveals a decline in political education, as nonpolitical activities expanded and Western influence increased based on the interests and prerogatives of Pioneers and camp employees.

Beach Parties

While the party initiated many of the state-supported escapes in nature described above, there were also escape sites that came into being as a result of private initiative and regimes' occasional toleration of rebellious social groups or subcultures. Some dissenters challenged ideological orthodoxies regarding the human body, and sometimes socialist regimes made minor concessions. In East Germany, for instance, visual representations of the human body in party-sponsored journals and magazines represented an area where censors were willing to relax certain ideological taboos and satisfy popular demands. *Das Magazin,* a new journal the SED approved in 1954, published a female nude picture on a monthly basis during the first decade of its existence. This obvious concession was one of many efforts to make the 17 June 1953 worker's uprising in the GDR fade from public memory by shifting attention to people's material and erotic desires. By the 1960s and 1970s there was a veritable boom in nude photographs in various East German publications.[31] A similar effort was underway in Hungary as well, where, after the 1956 uprising, humoristic publications such as *Ludas Matyi* offered readers both jokes and nude photographs.

While erotic representations of the human body gained acceptance under socialism, public nudism continued to stir controversy and resistance. The gamut of official responses stretched from tolerance to periodic moral outbursts (followed by interdictions) against it. Comparing East Germany to Romania is instructive in this regard. As Irina Costache discusses in her chapter, "From the Party to the Beach Party: Nudism and Artistic Expression in People's Republic of Romania," practicing nudism on the beaches of the Romanian Black Sea coast during the 1950s was limited to a small group of individuals closely connected to the upper echelons of the party. These well-connected artists and intellectuals established a tightly knit community in a remote village close to the Romanian-Bulgarian border, where their nudist practices were tolerated by the authorities. During the late 1960s, the bohemian life-style of the early nudist settlers assumed even more of a counter-cultural bent through the arrival of a younger generation of students and intellectuals who, in addition to nude bathing, brought with them a keen interest in Western music and practices. The case of Romanian nudists illustrates the existence of important chronological discrepancies between socialist policies regarding public nakedness within the Eastern Bloc. While Stalinist Romania, a rather prudish Eastern Orthodox society, tolerated nudism, in East Germany through the mid-1950s, the regime fought vehemently against this practice, which had significant roots in working-class culture during the Imperial and Weimar period. The passage of time witnessed a reversal based on popular reception; beach nudism became extremely rare in Romania in the 1970s and 1980s, and progressively more accepted and widespread in the GDR.[32]

As mentioned above, while loosening the grip that party officials kept on people's everyday lives, the period of the post-Stalinist thaw produced new tensions and expectations, which allowed for experimentation in new types of escapes. Socialist governments played a role in their genesis by trying to compete with the West and providing entertainment and consumer goods to their citizenry. In spite of persisting Cold-War enmities, in the freer intellectual atmosphere of the thaw, socialist state officials encouraged a broad expansion of citizens' leisure and consumption practices.[33] They no longer based their models primarily on old Soviet practices,[34] but rather on recent developments in Western Europe and North America.

Thus, the socialist world of the late 1950s and the 1960s was marked by an attempt to catch up and compete with the economies of the United States and Western Europe.[35] Encouraging consumption and leisure became state-supported goals. As Eli Rubin writes in reference to the GDR, in that country "along with the emphasis on consumption, the SED regime also realized that it had to offer leisure opportunities to East German citizens, especially for vacations and weekends, to be able to construct an alternative to the kind of 'good life' rapidly opening up for the middle classes in the post-war West."[36] The post-war economic success of the United States, Britain, West Germany, Italy, and France,[37] and the global turn towards a consumer society,[38] enticed socialist states to provide not only leisure opportunities for their citizens, but also the mass consumption of cars, household goods, music, sports, and services.

The tourism industry served as an important bridge in this respect. The goal now was not just to build socialism, but to market it both to foreign and domestic consumers.[39] During the 1960s and 1970s, many Eastern European countries outperformed the Soviet Union in this respect. While the Soviet Intourist had a difficult time figuring out how to market socialism and deciding what to sell foreigners,[40] the Czechs and Romanians attracted more and more tourists from the West.[41] The socialist countries with access to the Adriatic and the Black Sea also promoted sun and beach tourism.[42] Soviet tourism officials advertised the city of Sochi as a getaway from the harsh Russian winter as early as 1946.[43] The Black Sea resorts became a favorite destination not just for Soviet citizens, but those from Eastern European socialist states and, progressively, for Western visitors as well.[44] By the 1960s, Bulgarians became experts in advertising their golden beaches and a variety of entertainment options to both domestic and foreign visitors. Socialist authorities in Bulgaria found no contradiction in their adoption of capitalist market practices and the building of socialism.[45] The situation, however, was compounded by the fact that the Bulgarian state also wanted to sell a natural and naturally addictive product, namely tobacco. This led, as Mary Neuburger perceptively notes in her chapter, "Smoke and Beers: Touristic Escapes and Places to Party in Socialist Bulgaria, 1956-1976," to the emergence of parallel discourses that constantly contradicted each other, one promoting a cure for smoking through physical exercise in natural settings, and the other marketing tobacco to foreign and domestic tourists in mountain and sea resorts.

Roadside Adventures and Bright City Lights

Geographic and chronological idiosyncrasies also existed between different socialist countries in the field of personal mobility. Many of the communist regimes that emerged in Eastern Europe during the late 1940s inherited a weak road infrastructure that precluded easy communication and transport between different areas within national borders. The use of horse carriages was widespread in Hungary, Poland, Romania, and Bulgaria, and it was mostly through rudimentary public transit that workers could reach their workplace even in the more developed Eastern European countries.

However, the virulently "viral" effects of automobility and rising individual car ownership in the West[46] could not be prevented for very long from spreading to the Eastern Bloc. The pressure to modernize came from the Soviet Union as well. Soviet leaders emphasized the importance of automobility in shaping the socialist society of the future as early as the late 1920s. Indeed, a future innovator in the Soviet automobile industry, Valerian Osinskii, wrote in November 1928 that the working class in the Soviet Union was "a class on wheels, the most revolutionary class in history, the class that forged an 'iron party,' and a class that will travel to socialism in the automobile."[47]

Although Stalinist party officials continued to pay attention to automobility, the results obtained by 1953 were meager. After 1945, for instance, the size and quality of the Soviet auto stock and supply increased not because of internal developments (such as the creation of a Soviet automobile industry during the 1930s), but as a result of American and British wartime deliveries and looting in Eastern Europe.[48] The Sovietization of the latter area also brought into the hands of the communist party officials new industrial resources for making automobiles, such as the Škoda factory in Czechoslovakia. Soon after socialist leaders founded the Council for Mutual Economic Assistance (COMECON), a market for cars was born.[49] By the 1960s and 1970s, the old Soviet Pobedas and Moskviches gave way to a new generation of socialist cars such as the Wartburg and Trabant (produced in the GDR), the aforementioned Czech Škoda, the Dacia (made in Romania), the Yugo (a Yugoslav version of the people's car), the Polski Fiat (a proud Polish achievement), and the Russian-made Lada and the Zhiguli, emerging from the conveyor belts of new car factories built in the Soviet Union.[50]

The road, repair, and refueling infrastructure necessary for the use and maintenance of these cars, however, was rudimentary in many parts of the Eastern Bloc. According to a Western observer writing in 1968, although the Soviet Union was by then "a highly industrialized country, [...] its private sector" appeared as if only "on the threshold of the gasoline age."[51] This observation could be extended to other countries of the Eastern Bloc as well. Moreover, practices such as refusal to wear a seat belt and the bribing of policemen and drivers that historian Lewis H. Siegelbaum found so prevalent in his research on the car culture of the Soviet Union[52] infused the automobility culture of all of the other socialist states in Eastern Europe.[53]

This lack of resources, however, encouraged innovative approaches to scarcity as illustrated by the national hitchhiking program introduced in Poland in 1957, which the Polish socialist state supported up until its demise.[54] In his contribution to this volume entitled "Hitchhikers' Paradise: The Intersection of Mass Mobility, Consumer Demand and Ideology in the People's Republic of Poland," Mark Keck-Szajbel maintains that the popularity of hitchhiking in that country transcended its borders, drawing in foreigners from both socialist and non-socialist states interested in taking advantage of this mode of travel. Indeed, authorities in both Czechoslovakia and the Soviet Union sponsored short-lived attempts to imitate the Polish hitchhiking program. In a country such as Poland, where the production and distribution of automobiles never satisfied popular demand, hitchhiking was a useful alternative for those who lacked cars. Moreover, hitchhiking held out the promise of both social and sexual encounters, while allowing those who engaged in it to reach remote rural destinations (not serviced by the railway), and learn more about the different regions of the country. Most importantly, however, as Keck-Szajbel argues, private transport offered an alternative to organized group vacations. By allowing youth to periodically escape the dust of industrial cities, hitchhiking was a prized getaway tactic, which gave its users a sense of free-dom and control over their own lives and everyday itineraries. In this latter sense, it was an escape that was more rewarding to people than many of the other socialist escapes discussed in this volume.

The increase in people's mobility and the advent of mass tourism in the Eastern Bloc prompted other important developments as well. Instead of be-ing just centripetal (allowing people to make it to the woods, lake and sea shore beaches, and the mountains), socialist mobilities were also centrifugal bringing people from abroad and from the countryside to the metropolitan areas of Eastern Europe and the Soviet Union. Turning the latter into desti-nations included in international tourist circuits became especially impor-tant to socialist authorities all over the Eastern Bloc. In order to achieve this they were willing—as we have seen—to allow surrogate capitalist enclaves to come into being in the very midst of the socialist economic system. These endeavors, however, caused new domestic cleavages that opened up oppor-tunities for other types of escapes. Indeed, during the 1960s, as Alexander Vari shows in his chapter "Nocturnal Entertainments, Five-Star Hotels, and Youth Counterculture: Reinventing Budapest's Nightlife under Socialism," tourism officials in Hungary engaged in a sustained campaign to make the capitals' nocturnal offerings more attractive to foreigners. Ranging from im-proved and more varied menus and evening entertainment in restaurants to luxury accommodations provided in new five-star hotels, what Budapest of-fered its visitors became more similar to what they could expect to find in Western locations. From a domestic perspective, however, the escapes into a surrogate capitalist world were reserved for party officials and the politically well-connected in Hungary. The majority of the Hungarian population had to enjoy nightlife in locales tightly controlled by the Communist Youth Al-liance (KISZ); their escape route from socialism to capitalism did not lead through five-star hotels and fancy restaurants. It was rather in places such as the *Ifipark* (The Youth Park), a restaurant and concert venue located in Budapest, and dingy suburban Houses of Culture, where average Hungarians embraced pop, rock, and punk music. These musical venues created a paral-lel and non-party sanctioned route of escape for many young people, that culminated by the 1980s in the emergence of constantly policed and highly marginalized subcultures.

Sports and Stadia

The rise of such youth subcultures was a phenomenon to be noticed in every country of the Eastern Bloc in the 1980s.[55] The youth groups varied from punk rockers and heavy metal enthusiasts to often violent sports fans. The rise of underground subcultures challenging the mainstream orthodoxies of the socialist systems was especially noticeable during the last years of the GDR's lifetime. As historian Mike Dennis writes: "At the beginning of the 1980s, Western skinhead music, dress and militancy began to appeal to young East Germans, including the violent-oriented football supporters, as an alternative to the dominant political and ideological system and its institutional instruments such as the Free German Youth."[56]

These developments and the domestic disturbances they triggered were particularly worrisome to East German authorities who had capitalized on the international sporting successes of the GDR as a way of legitimating not only the socialist way of life, but its very existence as a separate German state.[57] Sport had played an important role in the building of socialism.[58] Throughout their existence, the Soviet Union and its satellites in Eastern Europe utilized sport in order to unify multi-ethnic populations, sustain a healthy and productive workforce, and attain international respect and recognition—in short as essential building blocks in the process of socialist nation-building.[59] Therefore, as sports historian James Riordan has argued, sport under communism played "the quite revolutionary role of being an agent of social change, with the state as pilot."[60]

Between the 1950s and the 1980s, only the US, the Soviets, and select nations of Western Europe could challenge Eastern European teams in various international Olympic sporting competitions such as swimming, weightlifting, and canoeing.[61] Many Eastern European countries were also strong in handball and football. Communist regimes both during the Stalinist period and after actively supported footballers and hoped to gather mass support from victories on the soccer field. The Hungarian soccer team, for instance, earned its most brilliant international successes before 1956.[62] Moreover, the East German victory against the West German team at the FIFA World Cup games held in West Germany in 1974 turned many GDR citizens into supporters of their national team in spite of any personal grudges that they might have had against Honecker and his regime.[63]

As an "artificial nation" in the crossfire of Cold War politics, the GDR needed sports as a common source of national identity and pride.[64] The East German regime, however, with its priorities set high to support swimmers, ice skaters, and bobsledders, was slow in recognizing the importance of soccer in promoting state propaganda. While the Honecker regime heavily funded certain sports, it neglected others. Some of the most neglected and underfunded sporting events in East Germany were the highly popular motorcycle races.[65] As Caroline Fricke shows in this volume in her chapter "Getting off Track in East Germany: Adolescent Motorcycle Fans and Honecker's Consumer Socialism," the lack of funding stems from the fact that similar to soccer, motorcycle races produced a considerable amount of internal opposition against the regime in the form of unruly fans influenced by Western models. Instead of co-opting them, East German authorities further estranged rebellious youth by keeping them off of the race tracks at Bergring in Teterow, the site of one of the most popular motorcycle races in the GDR. Their decision backfired, however, since it created an unofficial campground and private escape site near the race tracks for motorcycle and heavy metal fans, and also prompted East German heavy metal enthusiasts to escape official interdiction by participating in yearly pilgrimages to the motorcycle races held in Brno, in neighboring Czechoslovakia.

While East German motorcycle fans protested against their marginalization by engaging in violent clashes with the police, the reaction of soccer fans to their surveillance and oppression was much more muted in Romania during the 1980s. There were several reasons for this. In his chapter "Power at Play: Soccer Stadiums and Popular Culture in Ceaușescu's Romania" in this volume, Florin Poenaru explores the important dual role that stadia fulfilled in socialism. The regime used stadiums both as arenas for sports competition and as venues for large popular gatherings convened by the party to celebrate its successes building socialism. The latter were indeed extremely popular in all of the Eastern European countries during the height of Stalinism.[66] Although by the 1960s and 1970s they were discarded as dull rituals symbolizing the power of the party in countries such as Poland, Hungary, and Bulgaria, they survived relatively intact in East Germany, Czechoslovakia, and Romania.[67] In Romania in particular, they played an important role in propelling the revived personality cult centered on Nicolae Ceaușescu, the country's all-powerful leader since 1965.

Party sycophant and court poet Adrian Păunescu orchestrated festivities known as *Cântarea României* (The Singing of Romania) in Romanian stadiums to celebrate Ceaușescu[68]—one occasion among others when people were taken from their workplaces to sing the praise of the Conducător.[69] While many of these events certainly contributed to the strengthening of the party's ideological grip on people's everyday lives, they could also serve as escapes from it. As Poenaru shows in his chapter, at the mass gatherings organized in the stadiums celebrating Ceaușescu, many people read books and magazines, gawked at each other, and even took photographs in the short intermissions between mass choreographic movements. People challenged the party during soccer games as well, when many of them chanted slogans that contained indirect criticisms of Ceaușescu's all-powerful arm, the Securitate (the Romanian State Security). Together these two types of behavior served as escapes from the harsh daily reality of increasing state repression and shortages in

Romania. The smell of change was in the air. In the wake of popular discontent in December 1989, which led to urban rioting and ultimately the disintegration of the regime, citizens all over Romania celebrated the execution of Ceaușescu and his wife in Bucharest as the people's final escape from the repression they endured under communism.[70]

Conclusion

A similar celebration, with even more symbolic portent, took place just a month before, in East Berlin. The fall of the Berlin Wall was, as historian Joe Moran has recently stated, one of those rare moments when the continuum of history is disrupted through the "disturbance of the everyday, [and] the transformation of unthinking routine into new moments of awareness … For a few, extraordinary days in November 1989, Berliners shook off the monotony and predictability of their daily lives. They danced around in night shirts, let off fireworks and kissed strangers, with whom they exchanged the single word: '*Wahnsinn!*' (Crazy)."[71] Numerous observers in other Eastern Bloc capitals witnessed and described the carnival atmosphere occasioned by the fall of communism.[72] In fact, the whole late 1980s unfolded in Eastern Europe under the sign of the carnivalesque.[73] For millions of people, the fall of communism was the big escape that they had dreamt about for decades.

Twenty years after the event, there is agreement among scholars that communism in Eastern Europe collapsed in 1989 because of a variety of reasons, ranging from the impact of Mikhail Gorbachev's reforms in the Soviet Union to the economic and moral exhaustion of the socialist system itself.[74] Seen from a macro-structural point of view, this is certainly true. If one extends one's perspective to the microscopic fissures in the system caused by millions of individuals' dreams and desires for a better life, the role played in it by the continuous breaks away from ideology and everyday routine are worth pondering. Examining the role of states-in-between in the life experience of the last Soviet generation, anthropologist Alexey Yurchak argues that from the perspective of the actors living under socialism, "the reference to 'fun life' refer[red] to a kind of 'normal life' in everyday socialism, a life that had become invested with creative forms of living that the system enabled but did not fully determine."[75] In spite of the illusion of normality that it provided to the regime, the quest for a pleasurable and creative life under socialism was an erratic variable embedded in the system. As many of the socialist escapes examined in this volume suggest, once people invested it with their wishes and desires, the variable also put pressure on the Eastern European and Soviet regimes' many internal fissures and cracks leading, together with a host of macro and global developments, to their ultimate implosion.

Notes

I would like to acknowledge Catherine J. Plum's contribution to the content of this chapter, and thank her and Cathleen M. Giustino for their suggestions and comments.

1. Tibor Fischer, *Under the Frog* (New York: Henry Holt, 1992), 159.
2. A.E. Rees, "Introduction: The Sovietization of Eastern Europe," in *The Sovietization of Eastern Europe: New Perspectives on the Postwar Period,* ed. Balázs Apor, Péter Apor, and E.A. Rees (Washington, DC: New Academia Publishing, 2008), 6. The French term *étatisme* refers to state control.
3. For the Soviet Union, see Sheila Fitzpatrick, ed., *Stalinism: New Directions* (London and New York: Routledge, 2000), and Juliane Fürst, ed., *Late Stalinist Russia: Society between Reconstruction and Reinvention* (London: Routledge, 2006) as well as her recent book *Stalin's Last Generation: Soviet Post-war Youth and the Emergence of Mature Socialism* (Oxford: Oxford University Press, 2010); while for Central and Eastern Europe in general see Eleonore Breuning, Jill Lewis, and Garett Pritchard, ed., *Power and the People: A Social History of Central European Politics, 1945-1956* (Manchester: Manchester University Press, 2005).
4. See Anne Gorsuch, "From Iron Curtain to Silver Screen: Imagining the West in the Khrushchev Era," and Susan E. Reid, "Who Will Beat Whom? Soviet Popular Reception of the American National Exhibition in Moscow, 1959," in *Imagining the West in Eastern Europe and the Soviet Union,* ed. György Péteri (Pittsburgh: University of Pittsburgh Press, 2010), 153–71 and 194–236; and the essays in *Soviet State and Society under Nikita Khruschchev,* ed. Melanie Ilič and Jeremy Smith (London: Routledge, 2009).
5. I borrow this expression from Michel de Certeau. See the introduction to his book *The Practice of Everyday Life,* transl. Steven Rendall (Berkeley: University of California Press, 1984), p. xiii where the author discusses the significance of escaping the internal traps of a culture "without leaving it" in reference to the Spanish conquerors of the Aztec empire, on the one hand, and the Aztecs and the Mayans, on the other.
6. See See Uta G. Poiger, *Jazz, Rock and Rebels: Cold War Politics and American Culture in a Divided Germany* (Berkeley: University of California Press, 2000); Sergei I. Zhuk, *Rock and Roll in the Rocket City: The West, Identity and Ideology in Soviet Dniepropetrovsk, 1960-1985* (Washington, DC: Woodrow Wilson Center Press, 2010); William J. Risch, "Soviet Flower Children: Hippies and the Youth Culture in 1970s L'viv," *Journal of Contemporary History* 40, no. 3 (2005): 565–84 and *The Ukrainian West: Culture and the Fate of Empire in Soviet Lviv* (Cambridge, MA: Harvard University Press, 2011); Mark Allen Svede, "All You Need is Lovebeads: Latvia's Hippies Undress for Success," in *Style and Socialism: Modernity and Material Culture in Post-War Eastern Europe,* ed. Susan E. Reid and David Crowley (Oxford: Berg, 2000), 189–208; and the essays in David Crowley and Susan E. Reid, ed., *Pleasures in Socialism: Leisure and Luxury in the Eastern Bloc* (Evanston, IL: Northwestern University Press, 2010).
7. We cannot offer here a comprehensive coverage of this extensive literature. For some seminal works, however, see E.P. Thompson, *The Making of the English Working Class* (New York: Pantheon Books, 1964, 1st ed.1963); James C. Scott, *Weapons of the Weak: Everyday Forms of Peasant Resistance* (New Haven: Yale University Press, 1985); Alf Lüdtke, ed., *The History of Everyday Life: Reconstructing Historical Experiences and Ways of Life* (Princeton: Princeton University Press, 1995); Carlo Ginzburg, *The Cheese and the Worms: The Cosmos of a Sixteenth-Century Miller* (Baltimore: The Johns Hopkins University Press, 1980); and Daniel Roche, *A History of*

Everyday Things: The Birth of Consumption in France, 1600-1800 (Cambridge: The University of Cambridge Press, 2000).

8. Sheila Fitzpatrick, *Everyday Stalinism: Ordinary Lives in Extraordinary Times. Soviet Russia in the 1930s* (Oxford: Oxford University Press, 1999); Christina Kiaer and Eric Naiman, ed., *Everyday Life in Early Soviet Russia: Taking the Revolution Inside* (Bloomington, IN: Indiana University Press, 2006); Mary Fulbrook, *The People's State: East German Society from Hitler to Honecker* (New Haven: Yale University Press, 2005); and Paulina Bren, *The Greengrocer and his TV: The Culture of Communism after the 1968 Prague Spring* (Ithaca: Cornell University Press, 2009).

9. Katherine Pence and Paul Betts, ed., *Socialist Modern: East German Everyday Culture and Politics* (Ann Arbor: University of Michigan Press, 2008); Jan Palmowski, *Inventing a Socialist Nation: Heimat and the Politics of Everyday Life in the GDR, 1945-1990* (Cambridge: Cambridge University Press, 2009); and Paul Betts, *Within Walls: Private Life in the German Democratic Republic* (Oxford: Oxford University Press, 2010).

10. See, among others, Sandrine Kott, *Le communisme au quotidien: les enterprises d'état dans la société est-allemande* (Paris: Belin, 2001); Jeanette Z. Madarász, *Working in East Germany: Normality in a Socialist Dictatorship, 1961-1979* (London: Palgrave Macmillan, 2006); Sándor Horváth, *A Kapu és a Határ: Mindennapi Sztálinváros* [The Gate and the Border: Everydays in Stalin City] (Budapest: MTA, 2004); Sándor Horváth, ed., *Mindennapok Rákosi és Kádár korában* [Everydays under Rákosi and Kádár] (Budapest: Nyitott Könyvműhely, 2008); John Connelly, *Captive University: The Sovietization of East German, Czech and Polish Higher Education, 1945-1956* (Chapel Hill: The University of North Carolina Press, 2000); Andrew I. Port, *Conflict and Stability in the German Democratic Republic* (Cambridge: Cambridge University Press, 2007); and Esther von Richthofen, *Bringing Culture to the Masses: Control, Compromise and Participation in the GDR* (New York: Berghahn Books, 2009).

11. See Malgorzata Fidelis, *Women, Communism, and Industrialization in Postwar Poland* (Cambridge: Cambridge University Press, 2010); Mark Pittaway, "Retreat from Collective Protest: Household, Gender, Work and Opposition in Stalinist Hungary," in *Rebellious Families: Household Strategies and Collective Action in the Nineteenth and Twentieth Centuries,* ed. Jan Kok (New York: Berghahn Books, 2002), 199–229; Gail Kligman, *The Politics of Duplicity: Controlling Reproduction in Ceaușescu's Romania* (Berkeley: University of California Press, 1998); and Shana Penn and Jill Massino, ed., *Gender Politics and Everyday Life in State Socialist Eastern and Central Europe* (London: Palgrave Macmillan, 2009).

12. Djurdja Bartlett, *FashionEast: The Spectre that Haunted Socialism* (Cambridge, MA: MIT Press, 2010); Ina Merkel, ed., *Wunderwirtschaft: DDR-Konsumkultur in den 60er Jahren* (Cologne: Böhlau Verlag, 1996); Paulina Bren and Mary Neuburger, ed., *Communism Unwrapped: Consumption in Cold War Eastern Europe* (Oxford: Oxford University Press, 2012); Mark Landsman, *Dictatorship and Demand: The Politics of Consumerism in East Germany* (Cambridge, MA: Harvard University Press, 2005); and Patrick Hyder Patterson, *Bought and Sold: Living and Loosing the Good Life in Socialist Yugoslavia* (Ithaca: Cornell University Press, 2011).

13. Kevin McDermott and Matthew Stibbe, ed., *Revolution and Resistance in Eastern Europe: Challenges to Communist Rule* (Oxford: Berg, 2006). For more on intellectual dissent and grassroots protest see also the essays in Vladimir A. Kozlov, Sheila Fitzpatrick, and Sergei V. Mironenko, ed., *Sedition: Everyday Resistance in the Soviet Union under Khrushchev and Brezhnev* (New Haven: Yale University Press, 2011).

14. Scholars vary in their definitions of resistance, from broad to narrow applications of the term. While the authors of this volume accept broad definitions of resistance and opposition, the narrower concept of dissent, as used by Ian Kershaw, is also useful in characterizing a variety of forms of everyday opposition this volume discusses, from spontaneous verbal challenges such as telling a joke critical of a regime, to cultural practices which might include the adoption of Western forms of entertainment, fashion or sports heroes. For a discussion of the scholarly

debates regarding these terms see the preface to the second edition of Kershaw's text, *Popular Opinion and Political Dissent in the Third Reich, Bavaria 1933-1945* (New York: Oxford University Press, 2002), x–xiii.

15. The distinction between "officially sanctioned" and "private methods of evasion" proposed by Štěpán Kaňa, in his discussion of the Czech musical underground of the 1970s, is a relevant one in this respect. See Štěpán Kaňa, "Rock the State? The Czech Musical Underground versus the Normalization Regime," in *Socialist Realism and Music,* ed. Mikuláš Bek, Geoffrey Chew, and Petr Macek (Prague: KLP, 2004), 108–14.

16. Don Slater, "The Ethics of Routine: Consciousness, Tedium and Value," in *Time, Consumption and Everyday Life: Practice, Materiality and Culture,* ed. Elizabeth Shove, Frank Trentmann, and Richard Wilk (Oxford: Berg, 2009), 217.

17. For an excellent analysis of the performative dimension of living under socialism, explored from the perspective of the late Soviet period, see Alexei Yurchak, *Everything Was Forever Until It Was No More: The Last Soviet Generation* (Princeton: Princeton University Press, 2005).

18. The cultural imaginary of socialism is explored richly and creatively by Susan Buck-Morss in *Dreamworld and Catastrophe: The Passing of Mass Utopia in East and West* (Cambridge, MA: The MIT Press, 2002). Another important work on this topic is Anne White's *De-Stalinization and the House of Culture: Declining State Control over Leisure in USSR, Poland, and Hungary, 1953-1989* (London and New York: Routledge, 1990). Research on the connections between space and everyday life under socialism, however, is still in its infancy. For a few important contributions in this area, see David Crowley and Susan E. Reid, ed., *Socialist Spaces: Sites of Everyday Life in the Eastern Bloc* (Oxford: Berg, 2002); Victor Buchli, *An Archeology of Socialism* (Oxford: Berg, 2000); Juliana Maxim, "Mass Housing and Collective Experience: On the Notion of *Microraion* in Romania in the 1950s and 1960s," *The Journal of Architecture* 14, no. 1 (2009): 7–26; and the chapter "Living in Common Places: The Communal Apartment," in Svetlana Boym, *Common Places: Mythologies of Everyday Life in Russia* (Cambridge, MA: Harvard University Press, 1994), 121–67.

19. Vadim Volkov, "The Concept of *Kul'turnost'*: Notes on the Stalinist Civilizing Process," in *Stalinism: New Directions,* 211.

20. It should be noted that the roots of such practices go back to the late nineteenth century when social democrats and socialists in Germany, England, and Russia were actively engaged in activities whose aim was to raise the cultural level of the workers. For more on this see Andrew Bonnell, *The People's Stage in Imperial Germany, Social Democracy and Culture, 1890-1914* (London: I.B. Tauris, 2005); Lynn Abrams, *Workers' Culture in Imperial Germany: Leisure and Recreation in Rhineland and Westphalia* (London: Routledge, 1992); Chris Waters, *British Socialists and the Politics of Popular Culture, 1880-1914* (Manchester: Manchester University Press, 1990); and E. Anthony Swift, *Popular Theater and Society in Tsarist Russia* (Berkeley: University of California Press, 2002), especially Chapters 2 and 5.

21. See Norman Naimark, "The Sovietization of Eastern Europe, 1944-1953," in *The Cambridge History of the Cold War,* vol. I: *Origins,* ed. Melvyn P. Leffler and Odd Arne Westad (Cambridge: Cambridge University Press, 2010), 195.

22. For a more detailed discussion, see especially the chapter on "The New Student," in John Connelly, *Captive University,* 205–25.

23. For a recent exploration of the tenets of socialist realism, see Evgeny Dobrenko, *The Political Economy of Socialist Realism* (New Haven: Yale University Press, 2007), and for an engaging transnational perspective discussing its artistic and social impact in various socialist countries and beyond, see Thomas Lahusen and Evgeny Dobrenko, ed., *Socialist Realism Without Shores* (Durham: Duke University Press, 1997).

24. Joel Crotty, "A Preliminary Investigation of Music, Socialist Realist, and the Romanian Experience, 1948-1959: (Re)reading, (Re)listening, and (Re)writing Music History for a

Different Audience," *Journal of Musicological Research* 26, no. 2–3 (2007): 151–76, quotation from p. 154.

25. Ibid., 155.

26. Taking workers to castle museums and thus educating them about the lifestyle of other social categories was not limited to Eastern Bloc countries. In France, for instance, the French Communist Party and the CGT implemented a similar set of vacation activities through their leisure organization called Tourism and Work. For more on this, see Sylvain Pattieu, "La 'vie de château' ou les gains symboliques du tourisme populaire, 1945—années 1980," *Revue d'histoire moderne et contemporaine* 56, no. 2 (2009): 52–78.

27. Boleslaw Janus, "The Politics of Culture in Poland's Worker Paradise: Nowa Huta in the 1950s," *Jahrbücher Geschichte Osteuropas* 56, no. 4 (2008): 542–53; and Igor Duda, "Workers into Tourists: Entitlements, Desires, and the Realities of Social Tourism under Yugoslav Socialism," in *Yugoslavia's Sunny Side: A History of Tourism under Socialism (1950s-1980s),* ed. Hannes Grandits and Karin Taylor (Budapest: Central European University Press, 2010), 33–68.

28. Padraic Kenney, "Remaking the Polish Working Class: Early Stalinist Models of Labor and Leisure," *Slavic Review* 53, no. 1 (1994): 1–25, quotation from p. 19.

29. Ibid., 19-23. See also Duda, "Workers into Tourists," 50–52.

30. For the Soviet Union see the discussion in Anne E. Gorsuch, "'There's No Place Like Home': Soviet Tourism in Late Stalinism," in *The Business of Tourism: Place, Faith, History,* ed. Philip Scranton and Janet F. Davidson (Philadelphia: University of Pennsylvania Press, 2006), 165–85.

31. Josie McLellan, "Visual Dangers and Delights: Nude Photography in East Germany," *Past and Present* 205, no. 1 (2009): 143–74; and "'Even Under Socialism, We Don't Want to Do Without Love': East German Erotica" in *Pleasures in Socialism,* 219–38.

32. See Josie McLellan, "State Socialist Nudism: East German Nudism from Ban to Boom," *The Journal of Modern History* 79, no. 1 (2007): 48–111; and *Love in the Time of Communism: Intimacy and Sexuality in the GDR* (Cambridge: Cambridge University Press, 2011).

33. There has been a spate of recent academic works on this topic. See, among others, Susan E. Reid and David Crowley, ed., *Style and Socialism: Modernity and Material Culture in Post-War Eastern Europe* (Oxford: Berg, 2000); David F. Crew, ed., *Consuming Germany in the Cold War* (Oxford: Berg, 2003); Mark Landsman, *Dictatorship and Demand: The Politics of Consumerism in East Germany* (Cambridge, MA: Harvard University Press, 2005); Judd Stitziel, *Fashioning Socialism: Clothing, Politics, and Consumer Culture in East Germany* (Oxford: Berg, 2005); Eli Rubin, *Synthetic Socialism: Plastics and Dictatorship in the German Democratic Republic* (Chapel Hill: University of North Carolina Press, 2008); and Susan E. Reid, "Our Kitchen is Just as Good: Soviet Responses to the American Kitchen," in *Cold War Kitchen: Americanization, Technology and European Users,* ed. Ruth Oldenziel and Karin Zachmann (Cambridge, MA: The MIT Press, 2009), 83–112.

34. For research on consumerist practices in the Soviet Union under Stalin and before see Marjorie L. Hilton, "Retailing the Revolution: The State Department Store (GUM) and Soviet Society in the 1920s," *Journal of Social History,* 37, no. 4 (2004): 939–64; Jukka Gronow, *Caviar with Champagne: Common Luxury and the Ideals of the Good Life in Stalin's Russia* (Oxford: Berg, 2003); Amy Randall, *The Soviet Dream World of Retail Trade and Consumption in the 1930s* (Basingstoke: Palgrave Macmillan, 2008); and Julie Hessler, *A Social History of Soviet Trade: Trade Policy, Retail Practices, and Consumption, 1917-1953* (Princeton: Princeton University Press, 2004).

35. For a discussion of Eastern European consumerism in a slightly later chronological context, and connected to the politics post-1968 normalization in Czechoslovakia, see Paulina Bren, "Mirror, Mirror on the Wall … is the West the Fairest of them All? Czechoslovak Normalization and Its (Dis)Contents," in *Kritika. Explorations in Russian and Eurasian History* 9, no. 4 (2008): 831–54.

36. Eli Rubin, "The Trabant: Consumption, Eigen-Sinn and Movement," 37–38. The SED refers to the Socialist Unity Party, the communist party in East Germany.

37. On France see Jean Fourastié, *Les trente glorieuses, ou la révolution invisible de 1946 à 1975* (Paris: Fayard, 1979); while on West Germany see Hanna Schisler, ed., *The Miracle Years: A Cultural History of West Germany, 1949-1968* (Princeton: Princeton University Press, 2001).

38. See the essays in Shelley Baranowski and Ellen Furlough, ed., *Being Elsewhere: Tourism, Consumer Culture, and Identity in Europe and North America* (Ann Arbor: University of Michigan Press, 2001).

39. For more on this see Anne E. Gorsuch's book *All This is Your World: Soviet Tourism at Home and Abroad after Stalin* (Oxford: Oxford University Press, 2011).

40. Shawn Salmon, "Marketing Socialism: Inturist in the Late 1950s and Early 1960s," in *Turizm: The Russian and East European Tourist under Capitalism and Socialism,* ed. Anne E. Gorsuch and Diane P. Koenker (Ithaca: Cornell University Press, 2006), 186–204.

41. Evidence for this development can also be seen in an increase in interest among French visitors in Czechoslovakia, Romania, and Bulgaria as opposed to the Soviet Union. For more on this, see Sylvain Pattieu, "Voyager en pays socialiste avec Tourisme et Travail," *Vingtiéme Siécle. Revue d'histoire* 102, no. 2 (2007): 63–77. It should be pointed out though that when seen from an East-West comparative perspective, the developments described above still did not match the scale of what was going on in Western, Northern, and Southern Europe. For more on this, see Thomas Mergel, "Europe as Leisure Time Communication: Tourism and Transnational Interaction since 1945," in *Conflicted Memories: Europeanizing Contemporary History,* ed. Konrad H. Jarausch and Thomas Lindenberger (New York and London: Berghahn Books, 2007), 133–53.

42. For more on this, see Judith Palloth and Dennis J.B. Shaw, *Planning in the Soviet Union* (London: Croom Helm, 1981), 204–5; Christian Noack, "Coping with the Tourist: Planned and 'Wild' Mass Tourism on the Black Sea Coast," in *Turizm,* 281–304; Igor Duda, "Adriatic for All: Summer Holidays in Croatia," in *Remembering Utopia: The Culture of Everyday Life in Socialist Yugoslavia,* ed. Breda Luthar and Maruša Pušnik (Washington, DC: New Academia Publishing, 2010), 289–312; Kristen Ghodsee, *The Red Riviera: Gender, Tourism, and Postsocialism on the Black Sea* (Durham, NC: Duke University Press, 2005); and the essays in *Yugoslavia's Sunny Side.*

43. See Anne E. Gorsuch, "'There's No Place Like Home': Soviet Tourism in Late Stalinism," 180.

44. See Allan M. Williams and Vladimír Baláž, *Tourism in Transition: Economic Change in Central Europe* (London: I.B. Tauris, 2001), 100, 225.

45. See Mary Neuburger's chapter in this volume. On the role of marketing campaigns in neighboring Yugoslavia see Patrick Hyder Patterson, "Truth Half Told: Finding the Perfect Pitch for Advertising and Marketing in Socialist Yugoslavia, 1950-1991," *Enterprise & Society: The International Journal of Business History* 4, no. 2 (2003): 179–225; and *Bought and Sold.*

46. For a discussion of the system of automobility as an unstoppable virus see John Urry, "The 'System' of Automobility," in *Automobilities,* ed. Mike Featherstone, Nigel Thrift, and John Urry (London and Thousand Oaks, CA: Sage Publications, 2005), 25–39.

47. V. Osinskii, "Itogi I perspektivy avtomobilizatsii," (Kharkhov, 1929) quoted by Lewis H. Siegelbaum, *Cars for the Comrades. The Life of the Soviet Automobile* (Ithaca: Cornell University Press, 2008), 4.

48. On the Soviet looting of the car park in Eastern Europe see Bogdan Mieczkowski, *Transportation in Eastern Europe: Empirical Findings* (Boulder, CO: East European Quarterly and Columbia University Press, 1978).

49. On the connection between car making and private consumption in the Soviet Union, see Nordica Nettleton, "Driving Towards Communist Consumerism: AvtoVaz," *Cahiers du monde russe* 47, no. 1–2 (2006): 131–51; and Lewis H. Siegelbaum, "Cars, Cars and More Cars: The

Faustian Bargain of the Brezhnev Era," in *Borders of Socialism: Private Spheres of Soviet Russia,* ed. Lewis H. Siegelbaum (New York: Palgrave Macmillan, 2006), 83–103.

50. It should be noted though that the Polski Fiat, Lada, and Zhiguli as well as the Dacia were slightly changed versions of the Italian Fiat and respectively the French Renault, and were made in Poland, the Soviet Union, and Romania as a result of mutual agreements between these countries and France and Italy. On the symbolic meanings attached to the Lada as a "socialist car," see Peter Hamilton, "The Lada: A Cultural Icon," in *Autopia: Cars and Culture,* ed. Peter Wollen and Joe Kerr (London: Reaktion Books, 2003), 191–98, while for more on the Yugo see Jason Vuic, *The Yugo: The Rise and Fall of the Worst Car in History* (New York: Hill and Wang, 2010).

51. Hans Koningsberger, *Along the Roads of the New Russia* (New York: Farrar, Strauss, and Giroux, 1968), 176, quoted in Siegelbaum, *Cars for the Comrades,* 212.

52. Siegelbaum, *Cars for the Comrades,* 7–8.

53. Research on this topic is still in its infancy. Regarding the GDR, see Jonathan Zatlin, "The Vehicle of Desire: The Trabant, the Wartburg and the End of the GDR," *German History* 15, no. 3 (1997): 258–380, Eli Rubin, "The Trabant: Consumption, Eigen-Sinn and Movement," *History Workshop Journal* 68 (Autumn 2009): 27–44, especially page 37, while on Hungary see the essay by György Péteri, "Streetcars of Desire: Cars and Automobilism in Communist Hungary, 1958-1970," *Social History* 34, no. 1 (2002): 1–28. The recent book edited by Lewis Siegelbaum, *The Socialist Car: Automobility in the Eastern Bloc* (Ithaca: Cornell University Press, 2011) is an important work attempting to redress this situation.

54. Hitchhiking could be contrasted to another method of dealing with economic scarcity: the role fulfilled by professional Hungarian truck drivers (one of the few categories of socialist workers allowed to travel abroad) in transmitting ideas about and smuggling in goods from the West in the 1960s and 1970s. For more on this, see Ferenc Hammer, "A Gasoline Scented Sindbad: The Truck Driver as a Popular Hero in Socialist Hungary," *Cultural Studies* 16, no. 1 (2002): 80–126.

55. See Mark Fenemore, *Sex, Thugs and Rock 'n Roll: Teenage Rebels in Cold-War East Germany* (New York and Oxford: Berghahn Books, 2007); Gregor Tomc, "A Tale of Two Subcultures: A Comparative Analysis of Hippie and Punk Subcultures in Slovenia," in *Remembering Utopia,* 165–98; and Karin Taylor, *Let's Twist Again: Youth and Leisure in Socialist Bulgaria* (Wien and Berlin: Lit Verlag, 2006). For precedents going back to the Stalinist period see Mark Edele, "Strange Young Men in Stalin's Moscow: The Birth and Life of the Stiliagi, 1945-1953," *Jahrbücher Geschichte Osteuropas* 50, no. 1 (2002): 37–61; and Katherine Lebow, "Socialist Leisure in Time and Space: Hooliganism and *Bikiniarstwo* in Nowa Huta, 1949-1956," in *Sozialgeschichtliche Kommunismusforschung. Vergleichende Beiträge zur sozialen Entwicklung in der Tschechoslowakei, DDR, Polen und Ungarn, 1945-1968,* ed. Christiane Brenner and Peter Heumos (Munich: Collegium Karolinum, 2005), 527–42.

56. Mike Dennis, "Soccer hooliganism in the German Democratic Republic," in *German Football: History, Culture, Society,* ed. Alan Tomlinson and Christopher Young (London and New York: Routledge, 2006), 61.

57. Molly Wilkinson Johnson, *Training Socialist Citizens: Sport and the State in East Germany* (Leiden, Brill, 2008).

58. See James Riordan, ed., *Sport under Communism: The USSR, Czechoslovakia, the GDR, China, Cuba* (Montreal: McGill-Queen's University Press, 1978); and Robert Edelman, *Serious Fun: A History of Spectator Sports in the USSR* (Oxford: Oxford University Press, 1994).

59. James Riordan, "The Impact of Communism on Sport," in *The International Politics of Sport in the Twentieth Century,* ed. James Riordan and Arnd Krüger (London and New York: E & F Spon, 1999), 48–66.

60. Ibid., 49.

61. For scholarship on the politics of the Olympics, see Alfred Erich Senn, *Power, Politics, and the Olympic Games* (Champaign, IL: Human Kinetics, 1999). On the medal count of the Soviet Union, Hungary, East Germany, and other socialist states at the 1968 Mexico City Olympics and the ones held in 1972 in Sapporo, Japan, see James Riordan, *Sport in Soviet Society* (Cambridge: Cambridge University Press, 1977), 370–71.

62. Andrew Handler, *From Goals to Guns: The Golden Age of Soccer in Hungary, 1950-1956,* East European Monographs (New York: Columbia University Press, 1994).

63. See Markus Hesselman and Robert Ide, "A Tale of Two Germanys: Football Culture and National Identity in the German Democratic Republic," in *German Football: History, Culture, Society,* ed. Alan Tomlinson and Christopher Young (London and New York: Routledge, 2006), 36–51.

64. For more on the ideological stakes of the competition between the two German states in the field of sports, see Uta Andrea Balbier, "'A Game, a Competition, an Instrument?' High Performance, Cultural Diplomacy and German Sport from 1950 to 1972," *International Journal of the History of Sport* 26, no. 4 (2009): 539–55.

65. It is interesting to note that while neglecting motor sports, the East German regime was keen to use bicycle races for a propagandistic purpose as early as the 1950s. For more on this, see Molly Wilkinson Johnson, "The *Friedensfahrt*: International Sports and East German Socialism in the 1950s," *The International History Review* 29, no. 1 (2007): 57–82.

66. Petr Roubal, "Politics of Gymnastics: Mass Gymnastic Displays under Communism in Central and Eastern Europe," *Body and Society* 9, no. 2 (2003): 1–25. For a discussion of May parades (another type of public ceremony boasting the power of the party) especially in reference to Czechoslovakia, see Roman Krakovsky, "Continuity and Innovation: Itineraries of the May Day Ritual in Czechoslovakia," in *The Sovietization of Eastern Europe,* 135–48.

67. On Czechoslovakia see Petr Roubal, "A Didactic Project Transformed into the Celebration of a Ritual: The Czechoslovak Spartakiads, 1955-1990," *Zeitschrift für moderne europäische Geschichte* 4, no. 1 (2006): 90–113.

68. See Lucia Dragomir, "Poésie idéologique et espace de liberté en Roumanie," *Terrain. Revue de l'ethnologie de l'Europe,* no. 41 (2003): 63–74. Available online at http://terrain.revues.org/index1635html (accessed 10 April 2010).

69. *Conducător* (leader) was one of the many epithets Ceaușescu adopted to enhance his megalomaniac quest for absolute power. For more on this, see Adrian Cioroianu, *Pe umerii lui Marx. O introducere în istoria comunismului românesc* [On the Shoulders of Marx: An Introduction to the History of Romanian Communism] (București: Editura Curtea Veche, 2005), 418–21. See also Vladimir Tismaneanu, *Stalinism for All Seasons: A Political History of Romanian Communism* (Berkeley: University of California Press, 2003), 213–15.

70. On the broader context, see Peter Siani-Davies, *The Romanian Revolution of December 1989* (Ithaca: Cornell University Press, 2005).

71. Joe Moran, "November in Berlin: The End of the Everyday," *History Workshop Journal,* no. 57, no. 1 (2004): 216.

72. See Timothy Garton Ash, *The Magic Lantern: The Revolution of '89 Witnessed in Warsaw, Budapest, Berlin, and Prague* (New York: Vintage, 1993); and Robert Darnton, *Berlin Journal, 1989-1990* (New York: W.W. Norton, 1991).

73. For more on this, see Padraic Kenney, *A Carnival of Revolution: Central Europe 1989* (Princeton: Princeton University Press, 2002).

74. See the "Preface" by Stephen Kotkin in his *Uncivil Society: 1989 and the Implosion of the Communist Establishment* (New York: Modern Library, 2009), xiii–xvii.

75. Alexei Yurchak, *Everything Was Forever Until It Was No More,* 146.

PART I

Concert Halls and Estate Museums

CHAPTER 1

Instrumentalizing Entertainment and Education

Early Cold-War Music Festivals in East Germany and Poland

David G. Tompkins

Youth of the cities, youth of the countryside,
Join together in an ensemble
And in harmonious chorus raise
A joyful and happy song:

Of work, of future dreams,
Of happiness already forged
And of beautiful days of freedom
Conquered together with Bierut.[1]
Tadeusz Sygietyński, *Song about Bierut* (*Piosenka o Bierucie*)

For the communist parties of Central Europe in the early Cold War, the arts were a key tool for influencing their populations and implementing political goals. Music occupied a particularly important position in German and Polish cultural life, and cultural officials accorded it an unusual power to affect worldviews. As seen in the song lyrics above, communists and their sympathizers considered music to be a powerful, unifying force that would mobilize their citizenries behind the leadership and aims of the party.[2] Music festivals in particular served as an entertaining break from everyday life and a way to shape the perceptions and passions of citizens. In the Stalinist decade after World War II, cultural officials in East Germany and Poland organized music festivals on a breathtaking scale in order to produce an enjoyable and meaningful leisure activity that would promote party ends.[3]

The music performed at these festivals was to be socialist-realist, the aesthetic ideology mandated for all the arts under Stalinism.[4] In the musical realm, socialist realism meant that music should be straightforward and melodic, and accessible to untutored audiences. Text-based music, such as the ubiquitous mass song, should communicate a political message and also be catchy and appealing. Music was to build on the national traditions of the country; consequently, socialist cultural authorities encouraged folk themes and works by composers who could be included in a progressive view of historical development. Both the East German and Polish communist parties sought to promote a nationalism infused with socialist ideals, and music mixing folk motifs, national traditions, and party messages fit this goal well.[5]

Music festivals functioned as escapes on two levels through the mid-1950s. For a population emerging from war and facing the daunting task of rebuilding, music festivals offered a simple break from an often difficult quotidian reality, although they were greatly influenced by the pervasive Stalinist ideology of the decade. In both countries, composers and audiences often and increasingly pushed for them to be an escape on another level, an escape from ideology as either autonomous artistic events or as uncomplicated entertainment. This chapter first explores the East German case, where the Socialist Unity Party (SED) maintained its political influence over music festivals with only minor concessions, even after Stalin's 1953 death and the subsequent thaw, or loosening of party control, throughout the Soviet Bloc. Here, music festivals were escapes only in this first sense. After initial success around 1950, the SED's Polish counterpart, the Polish United Workers' Party (PZPR), gradually lost influence over musical festivals in the context of the post-Stalinist thaw, and they thereby became true escapes in both senses. After an examination of different types of music festivals in East Germany and then Poland, a final section will look at two international youth festivals with a strong musical component, held in East Berlin in 1951 and Warsaw in 1955, to further illuminate the nature of these musical escapes in these two initially similar, then increasingly divergent national contexts.

East German Music Festivals: Ideology-Filled Escapes

A wide array of music festivals took place in the German Democratic Republic (GDR) during the decade following the devastating Second World War.[6] In this era of rebuilding, hard work, Stalinist ideology, and deep Cold War tensions at the epicenter of the superpower conflict, music festivals provided an escape for the people, albeit one strongly marked by the vision of East Germany's SED. During the post-Stalinist thaw, embodied as a "New Course" of greater openness and less political control in the GDR, officials made some concessions to composers' wishes for more experimentation and to audience desires for less politicized entertainment, but these were minor, and overarching ideological control of music festivals remained largely with the party and its sympathizers in the musical world.[7]

East German music festivals, which occurred with astonishing frequency in an area with a longstanding tradition, took three broad forms in the first post-war decade. First, there were small but prestigious festivals often associated with the East German Composers' Union and attended by the educated, middle- and upper-class concert-going public, and occasionally by workers. Secondly, local festivals in towns of varying sizes were also a common variety of festival that workers often attended. Finally, the festival format that offered the most common musical escape from the everyday was that of amateur festivals, which included ensembles of nonprofessional performers playing for a diverse audience. The SED maintained considerable ideological control over all three of these festival types. While it made some limited concessions to composer and audience demands for less ideology and more simple entertainment, especially during the post-Stalinist and consumer-oriented New Course, the SED continued to maintain considerable influence throughout the thaw of the mid-1950s and beyond.

Several small but high profile music festivals of the first type took place in Berlin and Leipzig during the first half of the 1950s, nearly all of which exhibited strong SED influence. Two of these festivals were linked to regular congresses of the Composers' Union, an institution that grouped all professional composers together and that existed in all Soviet-Bloc countries. The festivals in 1952 in Berlin and in 1954 in Leipzig reveal musical events that were a festive break from the everyday for composers and audiences, but that were nonetheless dominated by the SED and thus not an escape from pervasive ideology.

In the fall of 1952, the Festival of Contemporary Music in Berlin was organized in conjunction with the first regular congress of the newly formed Composers' Union. This festival functioned as a showpiece event, and party and government officials, as well as the composers themselves, placed great stake in the selection of the pieces to be performed. Roughly twenty concerts, including dozens of new works by GDR composers, offered an overview of the new music of the era, from politically themed mass songs to large-scale choral works. For East German officials focused on creating a new socialist culture from above in the early 1950s, bringing music to the masses proved less important than the nature of the music itself, and most concerts took place in traditional concert halls for the usual concert-going public. Nonetheless, one concert featuring contemporary mass songs and cantatas by East German luminaries Hanns Eisler and Paul Dessau, and sung by the legendary communist singer Ernst Busch, was organized on the grounds of the Bergmann-Borsig factory. Eisler and Dessau succeeded as two of the most adept composers at creating melodic and accessible music with a politically light touch celebrating peace, workers, and socialism. According to one observer, workers in the audience responded positively.[8] Workers here and in other official reports seemed receptive to some of this socialist-realist music, especially if the ideological message was relatively subtle. In general, however, workers did not attend most of these concerts at the 1952 festival, a concern addressed at the 1954 version held in Leipzig.

To the surprise of party officials and musical elites, urban workers rose up in June 1953 throughout the GDR to protest higher work norms and dissatisfaction with the SED more generally. Officials responded initially with concessions both to ordinary citizens and to artists, although these were limited and gradually scaled back in succeeding years. Organizers accordingly focused more on catering to the masses at the 1954 music festival in Leipzig than during the previous festival. Although the post-Stalin New Course had led to some relaxation of ideological control in many areas of East German life, musical and otherwise, this important festival continued the SED's push to politically influence society. Party officials desired socialist-realist music, and particularly emphasized the potential effects of this music on the rest of the population.[9] During the discussion at the related Composers' Union Congress, participants frequently mentioned the links between music and society. For example, leading musicologist and composer Ernst Hermann Meyer stated in reference to one of the festival concerts, "Music has an important function in shaping [peoples'] consciousness." Other leading composers called on their colleagues to compose for the masses in order to win them over to the SED's program, as well as to lift their cultural level in general.[10]

In light of these sentiments, 1954 festival organizers made a significant push to invite workers to the various concerts, which took place in traditional concert venues and thus provided an escape from the everyday for workers largely unexposed to music in this context. Furthermore, composers met with ordinary audience members after the performance and encouraged them to take part in post-concert discussions connected to the festival. One such discussion was about a concert of more serious, recently-composed works, including Günter Raphael's *Sinfonia breve* (1949), Rudolf Wagner-Régeny's Suite from the opera *Persische Episode* (*Persian Episodes,* 1951), Helmut Riethmüller's *Divertimento* for Piano and Horns, and Ottmar Gerster's Symphony No. 2 *Thüringische* (*Thuringian,* 1949–52). Female workers from a Leipzig factory found most of the music, "Dreadful! Horrible!" but were pleased by Gerster's symphony, the program's one unambiguously socialist-realist work with traditional harmonies, clear melodic lines, and uncomplicated local patriotism.[11] Most other audience members also seemed to enjoy the Gerster, but the other, more complex works came under heavy criticism from a broad cross-section of audience members.[12] One official claimed that most audience members disliked the music and regretted attending, and another noted that a large portion of the audience left the concert hall after the first half.[13] This was an escape that clearly did not satisfy. Despite the general distaste for most of this more serious and demanding music, the positive reception of Gerster's socialist-realist symphony motivated cultural officials both to pressure composers for similar works and to continue to reach out to a broader audience.

The interaction between workers and composers culminated in the appearance at the Composers' Union Congress of two men from the nearby Leuna factory. They had attended a different concert of serious new works by both younger and older GDR composers, including Max Dehnert's *Heiteres Vorspiel für Orchester* (*Cheerful Prelude for Orchestra,* 1949), Paul Kurzbach's *Divertimento für kleines Orchester* (*Divertimento for Small Orchestra,* 1954), Dieter Nowka's *Konzert für Oboe und Orchester,* Jean Kurt Forest's "Three Arias" from the opera *Patrioten* (1951), and Max Butting's *Sixth Symphony* (1945). These works by East German composers attempted to fulfill the postulates of socialist realism while still allowing for challenging and sometimes more complicated music. One metalworker expressed his disappointment with this concert in strong terms, and encouraged composers to write music that would be more accessible and enjoyable upon the first hearing, asserting that he and his comrades would not come back for another unpleasant experience.[14] Another metalworker, serving as the factory choral director, reported on the long post-concert discussion he had organized among workers, musicians, and composers. He described the active musical life at the factory, and urged composers to write for these workers.[15] Audience members embraced the opportunity to attend such concerts, thus clearly exhibiting an appetite for such diversion. Their reactions, however, demonstrate that these escapes fell short of satisfying workers; while many were open to socialist-realist music, they also wanted to be entertained. Both composers and cultural officials took such comments seriously, debated how best to write for such audiences at this and other meetings, and even formed personal relationships with individual factories in order to be in contact with and help musically educate workers. These composers, who chose to live in the GDR rather than moving to West Germany, felt a more significant connection to communist political aspirations than their counterparts in Poland.[16] These two high-profile festivals provided well-attended escapes from everyday routines in the GDR, but they were also events that manifested the vision and influence of the SED. Thus, while presenting something new and unusual, they did not offer an escape from official ideology.

The second type of East German festivals largely followed this template. Local and amateur festivals provided an opportunity for composers, diverse audiences, and ordinary citizens as performers to step outside of the everyday, while remaining in an atmosphere that the SED essentially determined. East German officials built upon preexisting music festivals to promote hundreds of events in small and large towns across the country. Starting in 1948, the typical example of the Dresden Music Days lasted about a week each year (see Figure 1.1). Similar to other local festivals, this event promoted contemporary socialist-realist music from East Germany and the other Soviet Bloc countries, and reached out to a broader audience in the early 1950s. For the twenty concerts in the representative 1953 iteration, organizers featured a variety of new music by East German composers, a discussion evening with the Composers' Union, music linked to Bertolt Brecht, a concert dedicated to model, overachieving Stakhanovite workers, and one of Dresden's first *Estradenkonzerte,* an ideologically-inclined stage revue incorporating political music and texts. The main essay in the festival program booklet focused on how the festival was reaching out to workers.[17]

By the mid-1950s in the more critical light of the moderate post-Stalinist thaw and New Course, officials cited numerous ways this festival could be improved to achieve party aims. One local notable wrote to Culture Minister Johannes Becher to encourage better organization for a festival of such importance.[18] Local cultural officials praised the 1955 Dresden festival as "an important contribution to the cultural-pedagogical mission," but also, in a self-critical manner, pledged more interesting and accessible programming in an effort to draw in more workers in addition to the usual concert-going public. The desire to shape a broader segment of the population through music is particularly striking here.[19]

Another example of this second, local music festival format was the Thuringian Festival of Contemporary Music, held in Weimar in 1952, 1954, and on an annual basis thereafter. Festival planners sought out like-minded composers from West Germany to promote the idea that the socialist-realist artistic currents in the GDR appealed to composers all across Germany, and to try to convince all Germans that a vibrant culture not only existed in the East, but was superior to that in the West. Organizers divided concert programs equally between works by composers from the GDR and left-leaning colleagues from West Germany. The possibility of hearing music from the West attracted healthy audience numbers.

The Weimar festival organizers made great efforts to bring wider sectors of the population to the concert venues. In the festival program booklet, the mayor of Weimar, Dr. Hans Wiedemann, stated: "Through the introduction of the broadest circles of the working people to the musical compositions of

Figure 1.1. Poster for 1952 Dresden Music Days, featuring music from around the bloc. Permissions from German Bundesarchiv (B 285 Plak-048-029 / graphic designer: Nürnberger).

the present, we will make an essential contribution to our political task of including the entire populace in cultural life, so that our new cultural flowering will in reality be carried and supported by all the people."[20]

The festival organizers engaged a popular local conductor, Kurt Müller, to publicize the festival among the workers of the area. He had minimal success, thus prompting the proposal that the composers themselves visit the district's factories and workplaces to drum up support for the following year's festival.[21] According to one report, these local events presented the best example of the Ministry of Culture's goals for music festivals, "to introduce the broadest possible circles of the population to music, while at the same time introducing artists to the people."[22] These events, however, while an escape from daily routine and an East-West encounter, did not afford a break from pervasive SED ideology.

The extensive East German festival landscape also offered a third festival format, that of amateur music festivals featuring nonprofessional musicians presenting music to diverse audiences. Various associations and workers' institutions in the GDR organized such festivals and competitions related to them. The festivals that best incorporated the SED's goal of mobilizing broad sectors of society were the German Festivals of Folk Art held in 1952 and 1954. These festivals aimed to have amateur musical groups perform politically acceptable folk music, as well as newer socialist-realist works like Hanns Eisler's *Neue deutsche Volkslieder* (*New German Folk Songs*) or Ernst Hermann Meyer's *Mansfelder Oratorium.* Over six thousand groups competed in a series of contests in the provinces, and the festival culminated in several days of concerts by the best groups.[23] The first festival of 1952 took place in Berlin and featured a handful of performances over a long July weekend that ended with a large concert in the center of town.[24] Cultural officials viewed the festival in these typical terms: "This bursting forth of the creative power of our people … is mirrored in the creative work of our professional and amateur artists, and will be, along with the cultivation of our cultural heritage, the content of the German Festival of Folk Art."[25] The festival provided an ideal opportunity for the party to link the population's energy, or perhaps the simple desire to have fun, to its goals. Furthermore, by including the works of great German composers, the party tried to show that it was the true guardian of a progressive German culture, in contrast to the allegedly depraved, Americanized culture in West Germany. For the second German Festival of Folk Art in 1954, officials expanded the competition among amateur groups throughout the country, leading to the Festival in Park Sanssouci in Potsdam. Such festivals in the GDR embodied the SED goal in which artists worked with ordinary people in a party-approved project of creating a new and socialist culture. They provided an escape, but one the party carefully coordinated to preserve and promote its influence and aims.

Such amateur festivals were the truest examples of the circumscribed musical escapes available to average individuals in Stalinist East Germany. Many thousands could join ensembles and perform music that, while usually having a political cast, could provide an entertaining distraction from daily life. Audiences made up of their peers attended concerts at traditional performing halls, factory clubrooms, and outdoor venues, enjoying a break from the routines of work. The local and higher-profile music festivals also supplied welcome diversions to composers, professional music ensembles, more traditional audiences, and workers, even if the content of the concerts remained largely under party influence throughout the period, and were thus an escape only in the basic sense of a break from the everyday. East German cultural officials proved open to the input of composers and audiences, but worked hard to maintain ideological influence over festivals.

Polish Music Festivals: Composers and Audiences Push for Escapes

In Poland, at the peak of the Stalinist era around 1950, music festivals shared many similarities to their counterparts in East Germany. They were certainly an escape from daily realities, but as in the GDR, the vision of the Polish United Workers' Party (PZPR) dominated. Gradually, however, both composers and audiences demanded a more meaningful escape—one that also offered a venue free from party ideology—and thus acquired more agency than their GDR counterparts. Poland lacked East Germany's extensive festival tradition, and thus the party needed to expand a weaker infrastructure and, in some cases, create from scratch. These new festivals initially afforded the party an opportunity to gain control over festival organization, but as an unintended consequence of the promotion of festivals, the post-Stalinist thaw allowed composers and audiences to craft musical escapes that were largely absent of ideological influence. Polish composers, while initially sympathetic to the PZPR's goals, increasingly turned against the party in the context of the thaw and forged their own festival culture. A weaker party, but also less interest in communist ideals and a stronger sense of group autonomy, allowed Polish composers to achieve a more complete escape than their East German counterparts. Audiences, both elite and popular, increasingly turned to Western modernist and popular music, respectively.[26]

Two large festivals dominated the musical landscape of Poland during the first half of the 1950s, and their differing outcomes reflect a political and musical liberalization in Poland that went much further than that in the GDR. These elaborate festival events lasted for months with concerts in towns all across Poland. The first Festival of Polish Music occurred in 1951 and the second in 1955; the differences between the two reveal much about the crisis of party authority in Poland after Stalin's death in 1953. The PZPR pursued nearly identical goals and aims as the more powerful SED, but experienced increasing resistance to an overly ideological agenda from composers and audiences. The 1951 festival shared many broad similarities with GDR festivals, while the second in 1955 was significantly distinct as composers acted with greater autonomy. The still-politicized escape of 1951 became far less so by 1955, portending a Polish music festival culture mostly freed from party interference after the watershed 1956 Polish October.

The first Festival of Polish Music in 1951 represented the closest the PZPR came to realizing its ideal musical event. It sought to engage composers and a broad cross section of the population in a party-sanctioned cultural activity that propagated its values and reinforced its legitimacy. Starting in April 1951 and ending eight months later, this festival was a nationwide event that comprised hundreds of concerts performed by thousands of professional and amateur groups. In addition to contemporary music, concerts also included works by past composers, though organizers specifically selected these works to show how composers like Frédéric Chopin and Karol Szymanowski contributed to a national and realist tradition in music that logically led to the socialist nationalism of the PZPR. The festival featured a wide range of concerts, from serious classical music performed by symphony orchestras in traditional concert halls for customary concert-going audiences, to programs of politicized mass songs and folk music presented by amateur groups for motley audiences in factory clubrooms.

A handful of party and state institutions took the leading role in the organization of the first festival, and these cultural officials worked together to realize consistent ideological aims. With respect to the crucial decisions on the programs of the concerts, Polish officials formed an advisory council made up of representatives close to the party to decide which works, both contemporary and from the past, fit the PZPR's guidelines on socialist realism closely enough to be included in the festival. The Polish Composers' Union also actively took part in the organization of the festival and exercised some influence on its realization, but party and state institutions had the decisive input.[27] These cultural officials shaped the goals of the first Festival of Polish Music to the party's wishes. The party's primary aim appeared in internal party documents, as well as the official literature about the festival: "The fundamental goal of the festival is to deepen the knowledge of Polish music in society at large, while encouraging further compositional work and linking this to the needs of the broad masses of People's Poland."[28] The twin goals were clearly manifested here: to spread music among the population more broadly and to encourage composers to create music in a style the party considered appropriate for the masses.[29] During a speech to composers at a meeting before the festival, the influential Deputy Minister of Culture, Włodzimierz Sokorski, described his conception of the festival as having "didactic significance for both composers as well as the wide mass of listeners … it will have an ideological-pedagogical character."[30] For cultural officials, the festival was to be an opportunity to escape everyday routines, but only secondarily, for its primary purpose was to promote music that would communicate the ideas and values of the party to all.

With respect to society, the party's goal for the festival was less to entertain than to mobilize a wide section of the population in support of its broader political aims and ideology. Officials pushed composers to write mass songs and other socialist-realist music in order to provide appropriate party-approved music to the thousands of amateur groups that took part. The great majority praised this popular aspect of the festival; the leading composer Witold Lutosławski lauded the inclusion of the large number of amateur groups, and the esteemed Grażyna Bacewicz declared the festival an important aspect of "our cultural politics."[31] Cultural officials frequently stated their view of music's role as an ideological tool, as "a shaping agent for the fundament of life of millions of people."[32] The PZPR also sought to propagate a socialist conception of a progressive Polish nationalism through music that alluded to a union of party and workers building a better Poland, as the song lyrics in the epigraph suggest. In this official view, music was to take an active role in influencing worldviews and winning support for the party, and the inclusion of thousands of amateur groups in this party-sponsored festival supplied an important means to this end.[33] Attendance at the festival concerts was high, thus demonstrating a significant level of interest among the population in this mass form of entertainment.[34] The many concerts offered escape from the everyday, although one heavily influenced by the party and its ideology.

The second Festival of Polish Music in 1955 crystallized in a significantly different form from its predecessor, a situation that reflected the larger political changes occurring at the time in Poland. In an unintended consequence of regime policy, a festival supported by the PZPR became an escape from its ideology. Polish composers had, by this time, achieved a considerable amount of autonomy and resisted the party's push for a festival that embodied only official aims and ideology. By 1954, the thaw was setting in more broadly throughout Polish society, including the arts, and the party undertook a thorough reevaluation of its policies, even as composers pushed for more aesthetic and professional freedom. With respect to music festivals, both elites and the masses demanded and received real escapes, from both everyday routines and ideological influence.

Early organizational efforts in the Ministry for Culture continued to call for the presentation of socialist-realist music to a wide audience.[35] In Decem-

ber 1953, the now Minister of Culture, Włodzimierz Sokorski, still characterized the next festival as a site for "expressing the battle for a new music," but,
as in the cultural world after Stalin's death in March, a weakening of control
took place.[36] Sokorski and many composers agreed that the festival would
feature works from the entire post-war period, which opened the door to
music that did not fit a strict definition of socialist realism or the party's cultural norms.[37] By October of 1954, even the hardliners in the party's Central
Committee agreed that a broader range of works could be performed during
the festival. The majority of composers continued to press for more compositional freedom, and the PZPR was gradually losing control over the cultural
realm, thus providing an opening for an escape not just from the everyday,
but also from hardline ideology.

In a major difference from the overbearing party control of the first Festival
of Polish Music in 1951, the Composers' Union took over responsibility for
the planning of the second festival during the course of 1954. Despite infre-
quent interventions by cultural officials, the state institutions that undertook
much of the work for the first festival played a minor role in the second. For
example, a planned organizational committee staffed by functionaries in the
Ministry of Culture never formed, allowing composers to plan the festival in
a more open manner, one more consonant with the majority's less politicized
beliefs about music.[38] The Composers' Union organizers programmed music
that diverged significantly from the rigid definition of socialist realism pushed
by the PZPR in previous years.

The second Festival of Polish Music ran from mid-January to mid-May
1955, covering a time period less than half as long as that of the first. The
festival comprised 250 performances, including 163 philharmonic concerts,
and had a total attendance of 150,000. The program featured roughly 450
works by 119 composers, including 320 works by 80 living composers.[39] A
major difference from the first festival was the greatly reduced involvement of
amateur groups; festival organizers claimed that these groups were too busy
preparing for the Fifth World Festival of Youth and Students, discussed later
in this chapter, which took place in Warsaw in August 1955.[40] Although certainly true, a significant factor was the desire of most composers to have the
festival focus on the more serious and difficult works they wanted to compose,
works less appropriate for performance by an amateur ensemble. The second
festival emerged as an escape for composers and a more elite audience.

While the second festival shared some of the characteristics with the first,
it was much closer to the openness and experimentation of the Warsaw Autumn Festival that began just over a year later in 1956. This smaller-scale
annual festival devoted to serious contemporary music, which still continues
today, symbolized the final break with socialist realism and an engagement

with the modernist musical trends of the West. Musical ensembles from both West and East performed contemporary music from Polish and Soviet-Bloc composers, as well as musically-challenging modernist works by composers formerly condemned as anathema, like Schoenberg, Berg, and Stravinsky.[41] The Warsaw Autumn Festival attracted a smaller audience made up largely of fans of avant-garde and traditional music.

By the mid-1950s, the PZPR's dreams for a didactic festival culture that would help create a socialist polity lay in shambles. The impressive manifestation of its goals and vision embodied in the first Festival of Polish Music did not last. The composers who had embraced the party's aims in 1951 had grown disillusioned, and turned away towards more exclusive, international festivals catering to more serious and modernist music. Favoring escapes that entertained without political interference, audiences bled away to newer festivals coming to prominence that focused on popular song or jazz.

The World Youth Festivals: Ideology and Escape for a New Generation

Two final representative examples of musical festival culture in the first half of the 1950s were the World Festivals of Youth and Students. These festivals took place every few years, usually in capitals of Soviet-Bloc countries. Thousands of communist and left-leaning young people came together from all over the world for entertainment and political activism, and host countries mobilized thoroughly to accommodate the influx. After unfolding in Prague and Budapest in 1947 and 1949, the third festival came to East Berlin in 1951 and the fifth to Warsaw in 1955. These festivals included many sporting events and competitions, a diverse array of political and cultural offerings, and random parties and socializing, but concerts, dance performances, and other music-related events arguably formed the backbone of these massive cultural celebrations. Although significantly influenced by ideology, these festivals were important escapes, as young people interacted with their peers from places inside and outside the Soviet Bloc in a fun and unusual context. Similar to the case of music festivals, the 1955 Warsaw Festival proved to be more of an escape given its location and post-Stalinist timing than its East German counterpart four years earlier.

The third festival unfolded in East Berlin from 5–19 August 1951 celebrating the theme "for peace and friendship—against atomic weapons." During these two weeks, an exciting series of events transported East German festival participants, their West German peers, and the rest of the world from everyday realities to an international festival atmosphere. Both state and society prepared extensively for the 26,000 guests from over 100 countries, as well as the two million East and West Germans who flocked to the festival. The regime constructed new buildings and primed and decorated the city in honor of the event. Amateur musical groups prepared and competed for the right to perform, and leading East German musical figures took part by giving talks, including prominent musicologists like Georg Knepler and Ernst Hermann Meyer, as well as leading composers Hanns Eisler, Ottmar Gerster, Eberhardt Schmidt, and the youthful André Asriel.[42]

During the festival, over eight hundred soloists and groups performed from thirty-seven different countries.[43] At this time of the Korean War, a combined Korean choir took first prize in the competition, and a Korean dance ensemble also participated. The Chinese delegation, fresh from the recent communist victory, garnered a great deal of interest, in particular with an opera about fighting injustice that featured both music and libretto written collectively.[44] The Soviet delegation put on a huge main concert that included a choir singing mass songs, many dance groups, soloists, ballet dancers, and even a Kyrgyz soprano performing an aria from *Madame Butterfly*.[45] The official propaganda praised the performances, but reactions were mixed.[46] The main East German concert featured recent popular youth songs, folk songs, and political mass songs such as *Thanks to the Soviet Union*, and a song dedicated to Stalin, as well as a diverse program of Bach, Beethoven, opera arias, and some contemporary "serious" music by East German composers.[47] Poland sent over one thousand young people to Berlin to take part (see Figure 1.2), and its main performance presented the most prominent mass songs of the day, including one by Witold Lutosławski, selections from a cantata on Stalin, and much more ideologically-inflected music, such as part of leading composer Andrzej Panufnik's recently completed *Symphony of Peace*.[48]

The effect of the music on the festival participants is unclear, and it is unlikely that Erich Honecker, the head of the East German youth organization and future leader of the GDR, and his party colleagues completely achieved their goal to create a "worldwide front for peace"—though not for lack of trying. Young people did undoubtedly have fun and adventures during those two weeks, while consuming a steady diet of political music and related messages that had some effect on their consciousness.[49] As with the East German musical festivals more broadly, this festival was not an escape from ideology, but certainly provided a break from everyday routines of work or school.

After taking place in Bucharest in 1953, the Fifth International Festival of Youth and Students came to Warsaw in August 1955 during the Polish thaw. Hence the event bears the hallmarks of the dual nature of the later Polish music festivals as escapes—as a break both from the everyday and from smothering ideology. As usual, in advance of the main festival, many coun-

Figure 1.2. Polish folk dancers at the 1951 World Youth Festival in Berlin. Permissions from the German Bundesarchiv (Bild 183-11500-1228 / photographer unknown).

tries had their own series of qualifying competitions that comprised an even larger festival in and of themselves. In East Germany, the preparations for the 1955 World Festival lasted months and culminated in a Festival of Young Artists, which served as a competition to determine which groups would travel to Poland as the GDR's representatives.[50] Accompanying this flurry of activities, socialist authorities coordinated a related contest for new musical compositions that would "express the life, struggle, wishes, and thoughts of our youth" in the new, socialist context.[51] Several months before the festival, the host Poles organized a sprawling competition across their own country to determine its representatives, and roughly 25,000 ensembles and soloists participated, including about 7,000 workers' groups and a similar number from the countryside, as well as 9,000 from schools and hundreds more from universities. Polish cultural officials placed great emphasis both on quality and repertoire in their decisions, favoring those who performed classical works, folk music, and mass songs, and working assiduously to make certain the judges took into account these ideological considerations, with mixed success.[52]

In a very different context from the 1951 East Berlin festival, and in the period of the growing thaw, the Fifth World Festival proved difficult for the Polish party to contain within a consistent political framework. The festival itself took place in Warsaw for two weeks during the first half of August 1955, with the same main theme, "for peace and friendship," now accompanied by the slogan "against aggressive, imperialist military pacts." Close to 30,000 young people came from 114 different countries, including 2,500 official Polish delegates, plus an additional 140,000 Poles attending the related Rally of Polish Youth, and another 40,000 from other Polish cities. Hundreds of thousands of ordinary Warsaw residents attended concerts, and the whole country could follow along through heavy newspaper and media coverage.[53]

On opening day, Polish ensembles performed on five large, eight medium, nine small, and three mobile stages set in parks and squares all over Warsaw. On the second day, foreign ensembles joined in, and this massive musical cacophony continued for the following two weeks. The festival competition got underway in the Philharmonic building, and nightly gala concerts featuring the official presentations from leading countries began, as for example, the Soviet Union and China on 3 August, and France and the GDR the following evening. Numerous special and themed concert events took place, including one for the tenth anniversary on 6 August of the dropping of the atomic bomb on Hiroshima, which included peace-related songs and music.[54]

Befitting an event organized during the emerging thaw, however, the festival also offered music outside the political repertoire favored by the party. Albeit a small part of the program, Polish and French groups performed jazz, swing, and Dixieland, while public loudspeakers played jazz and rumba at times. Festival participants from the West brought records with boogie and other popular Western music, and these were heard in informal settings, as young people organized their own parties that included dancing and music.[55] These small but significant deviations from official doctrine exhibited a change taking place in Poland, both with respect to festival culture as well as to culture and society more broadly.

Conclusion

Poland's transitional year of 1956 confirmed developments that had emerged over the previous several years, and which revealed growing differences between it and the GDR with respect to these musical escapes from the everyday. Despite considerable success through 1953, the Polish party retreated almost fully in the face of increasing demands from composers and audiences, and thus the music festivals became escapes both from the everyday as well as from politics. During the post-Stalin thaw, Polish audiences also pushed for and received popular music festivals largely devoid of communist ideology. The Polish port city of Sopot hosted breakthrough jazz festivals in 1956 and 1957, and popular music festivals emerged in other Polish cities in the following years.

The East German party proved far more successful than its Polish counterpart in maintaining ideological control over social life, musical and otherwise. This examination of music festivals shows officials working to infuse them with ideology, but in a manner applied somewhat flexibly that allowed for limited societal input. Although it made some strategic and limited concessions to popular and composer demands in the aftermath of the June 1953 Uprising, the SED continued to influence musical festivals to a considerable extent, and they remained escapes from daily routines, but not from ideology. In the late 1950s, cultural officials embarked on the so-called "Bitterfeld Path" to bring artists closer to workers and to encourage workers to undertake creative activity as part of developing a new socialist culture. Closely related, the annual Workers' Festivals, begun in 1959 (biannually after 1972), featured amateur ensembles performing for a broad public. A more significant tradition of workers' festivals, as well as the opportunity to move to West Germany for those who strongly dissented, helped the stronger and more cohesive SED maintain ideological influence over its music festivals through and beyond the Stalinist era.

Through the height of Stalinism to 1953, however, the planning and ideology behind music festivals in Poland and the GDR looked similar, even if the size, scope, and frequency of these festivals differed somewhat. The patterns of composer involvement in the festivals also reveal striking parallels in the early years. With few exceptions, nearly all composers in both countries contributed works that fit into the parties' conception of the festivals, both because of the considerable financial incentives as well as a desire to help cultural officials fulfill their ideological goals. The more left-leaning East German composers consistently worked with the SED, while the less politically sympathetic Polish composers saw the PZPR's vision as increasingly discredited, and were less and less inclined to accept party leadership. In Poland, while the PZPR achieved a notable success with the 1951 Festival of Polish Music, party dominance began to break down after 1953 as a more cohesive cohort of noncommunist composers asserted professional and aesthetic goals against a weakening party. Thereafter, composers carved out a great deal of autonomy and agency with respect to the second Festival of Polish Music in 1955, and then emancipated themselves almost completely with the Warsaw Autumn festival starting in 1956.[56]

In both satellite countries, the parties strove for mass participation in and attendance at festivals of an ideological nature. Cultural officials attempted to orchestrate entertaining musical festivals that manifested their goals, and thus fashion an escape from the routines of everyday life while maintaining political control. Moreover, amateur performers and concertgoers around 1950 proved mostly willing to take part in and attend festivals stamped with the vision of the SED and PZPR. For a few years in Poland, and throughout the period in the GDR, these ordinary citizens sang and listened to party-approved works from the past, as well as contemporary ideologized productions, and the messages expressed in these musical compositions filled the aural space of the concert hall and factory clubhouse. Up until 1953 in Poland, and beyond in the GDR's more limited thaw, the two states largely succeeded in involving society in its political program in similar but not identical ways, though the regimes did not ignore the demands and desires of composers and audiences, and spaces for some negotiation existed throughout the post-war decade. Thus, this analysis of music festivals demonstrates that the East Bloc was not a homogenous whole where individual countries marched in lockstep under strict Soviet command, but instead exhibited national peculiarities that allowed spaces and practices for autonomous cultural expression.

Notes

1. Bolesław Bierut was president, then prime minster of Poland, as well as the secretary general of the PZPR in the Stalinist period. This *Song about Bierut* (*Piosenka o Bierucie*) was printed in the booklet *Zbiorek pieśni rewolucyjnych i masowych do pochodu 1-szo-majowego* (Prasa Stalinogród, 1953) and is by Tadeusz Sygietyński with text by Sabina Doboszówna.

2. Key works on music in the early GDR include: Elizabeth Janik, *Recomposing German Music: Politics and Musical Tradition in Cold War Berlin* (Leiden: Brill Academic Publishers, 2005); Toby Thacker, *Music after Hitler, 1945-1955* (Aldershot: Ashgate, 2007); Uta G. Poiger, *Jazz, Rock and Rebels: Cold War Politics and American Culture in a Divided Germany* (Berkeley: University of California Press, 2000); Daniel Zur Weihen, *Komponieren in der DDR: Institutionen, Organisationen und die erste Komponistengeneration bis 1961* (Köln: Böhlau Verlag, 1999); and Maren Köster, *Musik-Zeit-Geschehen: Zu den Musikverhältnissen in der SBZ/DDR, 1945 bis 1952* (Saarbrücken: Pfau, 2002). For Poland, see Adrian Thomas, *Polish Music since Szymanowski* (Cambridge: Cambridge University Press, 2005) and David Tompkins, *Composing the Party Line: Music and Politics in Early Cold War Poland and East Germany* (West Lafayette: Purdue University Press, 2013).

3. Many excellent studies on culture in the Soviet Bloc have appeared in the last decade. Important works include: Esther von Richthofen, *Bringing Culture to the Masses: Control, Compromise and Participation in the GDR* (New York: Berghahn, 2009); Katherine Pence and Paul Betts, ed., *Socialist Modern: East German Everyday Culture and Politics* (Ann Arbor: University of Michigan Press, 2008); Susan E. Reid and David Crowley, eds., *Style and Socialism: Modernity and Material Culture in Post-War Eastern Europe* (Oxford: Berg, 2000); Paulina Bren, *The Greengrocer and His TV: The Culture of Communism after the 1968 Prague Spring* (Ithaca: Cornell University Press, 2009); Mark Fenemore, *Sex, Thugs and Rock 'n Roll: Teenage Rebels in Cold-War East Germany* (New York: Berghahn Books, 2007); Jan C. Behrends, *Die erfundene Freundschaft. Propaganda für die Sowjetunion in Polen und in der DDR.* (Köln: Böhlau, 2006); and Kimberly Elman Zarecor, *Manufacturing a Socialist Modernity: Housing in Czechoslovakia, 1945-1960* (Pittsburgh: University of Pittsburgh Press, 2011).

4. The origins of the socialist-realist cultural and artistic movement in the Soviet Union date back to the 1930s. The literature, music, art, and film associated with this movement sought to com-

municate political content through accessible artistic means, usually based on folk traditions as well as on approved national culture from the past.

5. For a particularly incisive take on the relationship between national identity and socialism with respect to culture, see Katherine Verdery, *National Ideology under Socialism: Identity and Cultural Politics in Ceaușescu's Romania* (Berkeley: University of California Press, 1991).

6. The German Democratic Republic (Deutsche Demokratische Republik, DDR or GDR) or East Germany was founded on 7 October 1949, from the territory of the Soviet Occupation Zone. For more on GDR concert life more generally, see David Tompkins, "Orchestrating Identity: Concerts for the Masses and the Shaping of East German Society" in *German History* 30/3 (September 2012): 412–427.

7. Important recent works addressing the relationship between state and society in the cultural realm of the 1950s and beyond are Paul Betts, *Within Walls: Private Life in the German Democratic Republic* (Oxford: Oxford University Press, 2010) and Esther von Richthofen, *Bringing Culture to the Masses: Control, Compromise and Participation in the GDR* (New York: Berghahn Books, 2009); more generally see Mary Fulbrook, *The People's State: East German Society from Hitler to Honecker* (New Haven: Yale University Press, 2005). For an overview of the relevant debates: Corey Ross, *The East German Dictatorship: Problems and Perspectives in the Interpretation of the GDR* (London: Arnold, 2002) and Konrad Jarausch, ed., *Dictatorship as Experience: Towards a Socio-Cultural History of the GDR* (New York: Berghahn Books, 1999).

8. "Diese Musik verstehen auch wir!: Ein Rückblick auf die 'Festtage zeitgenössischer Musik,'" (no citation) Bundesarchiv (BArch), DR-1/6128; "Protokolle I. Jahreskonferenz," Deutsches Musikarchiv Berlin (DMA), Verband deutscher Komponisten und Musikwissenschaftler (VDK), 155.

9. Abschrift VDK, Bezirksleitung Leipzig, 10.9.54, Stiftung Archiv der Parteien und Massenorganisationen der DDR im Bundesarchiv (hereafter SAPMO-BArch), DY-30, IV 2/9.06/281.

10. SAPMO-BArch, DY-30, IV 2/9.06/282; ibid., 95 ff., 256 ff.

11. "Furchtbar! Entsetzlich!" 294.

12. Ibid., 297.

13. Ibid., 308–10; ibid., 301–2.

14. Ibid., 336–39.

15. Ibid., 341–43.

16. In Poland, around 15 of the approximately 120 composers in the union held party membership, while 86 of 339 did in the GDR. See Tompkins, *Composing the Party Line*.

17. "Einführungsheft," BArch, DR-1/6161.

18. Letter dated 31 June 1955 from Hans Böhn, Musikkritiker und Dozent to Becher, BArch, DR-1/361. Becher's encouraging reply follows.

19. "Bericht über die Dresdner Musiktage 1955," signed Tränkner, Abt. Kultur, Rat der Stadt Dresden, BArch, DR-1/79.

20. Programm, II. Thüringische Festtage zeitgenössischer Musik, SAPMO-BArch, DR-1/108.

21. Notizen, 61, SAPMO-BArch, DY-30/IV 2/9.06/288.

22. Stiftung Archiv der Akademie der Künste, Hans-Pischner-Archiv, 655.

23. "Der Aufschwung der deutschen Kultur," BArch, DR-1/315, 60.

24. Programm, Deutsche Festspiele der Volkskunst, SAPMO-BArch, DY-30/IV 2/9.06/287.

25. Potsdamer Musiktage pamphlet, article by Lanke, Leiter der Abteilung für Kunstangelegenheiten, 1952, BArch, DR-1/108.

26. For recent studies of state-society relations in early Cold War Poland, see Małgorzata Fidelis, *Women, Communism and Industrialization in Postwar Poland* (Cambridge: Cambridge University Press, 2010); Błażej Brzostek, *Za progiem. Życie codzienne w przestrzeni publicznej Warszawy lat 1955-1970* (Warszawa: Trio, 2007); Katherine Lebow's work on Nowa Huta; and Padraic Kenney's now classic *Rebuilding Poland: Workers and Communists, 1945-1950* (Ithaca: Cornell

University Press, 1996). A useful overview is Błażej Brzostek, "Contrasts and Grayness: Looking at the First Decade of Postwar Poland," *Journal of Modern European History* 2, no. 1 (March 2004): 110–33.

27. See especially Archiwum Akt Nowych (hereafter AAN), Ministerstwo Kultury i Sztuki (MKiS), DIAiO, 41 and 42.

28. "Sprawozdanie Wydziału Muzyki DTA za I kwartal 1950 roku," AAN, MKiS, DTA, 728, 68.

29. This message was consistently emphasized in the press articles linked to the festival; see Związek Kompozytorów Polskich (ZKP), 12/121, esp. Jerzy Jasieński, "Poznajemy polską muzykę," *Sztandar Młodych,* 21 April 1951.

30. ZKP, 12/92, "Protokół z konferencji kompozytorskiej," 4 February 1950, 2.

31. "Express rozmawia z czołowymi laureatami nagród FMP," *Express Wieczorny,* no. 9 (10 January 1952), in ZKP, 12/121.

32. Notatka o Festiwalu Muzyki Polskiej, 22 November 1950, 34-37, AAN, MKiS, DIAiO, 38.

33. "Protokół z posiedzenia Biura FMP," 7 June 1950, AAN, MKiS, DIAiO, 41.

34. Ibid.

35. "Plan pracy CZOFiIM na 1953," AAN, MKiS, CZTOiF, 2738, 1ff.

36. "Protokół surowy obrad rozszerzonego Plenum Zarzadu Glownego ZKP," 16–17 December 1953, ZKP, 12/22, 21.

37. Ibid., 36.

38. Ibid., 32. This was a mixed blessing, as all the work fell on the composers, a topic of frequent complaint.

39. Ibid.

40. "Notatka w sprawie przygotowań do FMP," 11 October 1954, AAN, (Komitet Centralny) KC PZPR, 237/XVIII-120, 53.

41. For an exhaustive study of the Warsaw Autumn Festival, see Cynthia E. Bylander, "The Warsaw Autumn International Festival of Contemporary Music, 1956-1961: Its Goals, Structures, Programs, and People" (PhD diss., Ohio State University, 1989), esp. 87–174; and Lisa Jakelski, "The Changing Seasons of the Warsaw Autumn: Contemporary Music in Poland, 1960-1990" (PhD diss., University of California-Berkeley, 2009).

42. SAPMO-BArch, DY-30/IV 2/9.06/140, 279.

43. Zentralrat der FDJ, Abt. Agitation und Propaganda, *Argumentation für die Auswertung der III. Weltfestspiele der Jugend und Studenten für den Frieden* (Berlin: Zentralrat der FDJ, 1951).

44. Ernst Hermann Meyer, "Die chinesische Oper 'Das Mädchen mit den weissen Haaren,'" in *III. Weltfestspiele der Jugend und Studenten für den Frieden: Bilder und Berichte* (Berlin: Neues Deutschland, 1951), 15–16.

45. Inge von Wangenheim, "Von der Schönheit des Lebens und der Menschen," in *III. Weltfestspiele der Jugend und Studenten für den Frieden: Bilder und Berichte* (Berlin: Neues Deutschland, 1951), 13–15.

46. Michael Lemke, "Die 'Gegenspiele': Weltjugendfestival und FDJ-Deutschlandtreffen in der Systemkonkurrenz 1950-1954," in *Die DDR und Europa—zwischen Isolation und Öffnung,* ed. Heiner Timmerman (Muenster: Lit, 2005), 485.

47. Heinz Luedecke, "Das Nationalprogramm der deutschen Jugend. Erfolgreiche Uraufführung im Berliner Freidrichstadt-Palast. Orchester, Chöre und Tanzgruppen," in *III. Weltfestspiele der Jugend und Studenten für den Frieden: Bilder und Berichte* (Berlin: Neues Deutschland, 1951), 20–21.

48. AAN, KC PZPR, 237/XVIII-89. For more on Panufnik, see David Tompkins, "Composing for and with the Party: Andrzej Panufnik and Stalinist Poland," *The Polish Review,* vol. 54, no. 3 (2009): 271–88.

49. Ina Rossow, "'… alles nett, schön und gefühlsbetont, mit viel Absicht.' Die III. Weltfestspiele der Jugend und Studenten im Kalten Krieg," in *Fortschritt, Norm und Eigensinn. Erkundungen im Alltag der DDR,* ed. Andreas Ludwig (Berlin: Ch. Links Verlag, 1999), 17–37.

50. BArch, DR-1/82.

51. "Plan zur Vorbereitung der Vorentscheide für den Wettbewerb in Warschau," 5 March 1955, BArch, DR-1/80.

52. AAN, KC PZPR, 237/VIII-426, 44–50.

53. Piotr Osęka, *Rytuały stalinizmu. Oficjalne święta i uroczystości rocznicowe w Polsce 1944-1956* (Warsaw: Trio, 2007), 224ff.

54. Andrzej Krzywicki, *Poststalinowski karnawał radości: V Światowy Festiwal Młodzieży i Studentów o Pokój i Przyjaźń, Warszawa 1955r.* (Warsaw: Trio, 2009), 187–206.

55. Ibid., 177, 231, 294; Osęka, *Rytuały stalinizmu,* 236.

56. For more on this broader story, see Tompkins, *Composing the Party Line.* For similar findings with respect to the university milieu, see John Connelly, *Captive University: The Sovietization of East German, Czech, and Polish Higher Education, 1945-1956* (Chapel Hill: The University of North Carolina Press, 2000).

CHAPTER 2

Open Gates and Wandering Minds
Codes, Castles, and Chateaux in Socialist Czechoslovakia before 1960

Cathleen M. Giustino

In June 1950, Milada Horáková and three codefendants were hanged on fabricated charges of treason after they were sentenced to death in socialist Czechoslovakia's first show trial following the communist takeover of the country in February 1948. Horáková had served in the Czech underground resistance against the Nazis during World War II, and then in Czechoslovakia's short-lived, post-war multiparty parliament.[1] At this time alarms were also sounding in newspapers and movie theatres across the country about another fabled "scourge," namely, American potato beetles purportedly sent by the United States government to devour Czechoslovakia's food and starve its people.[2] The tales about Horáková and ravenous capitalist insects—"six-legged ambassador[s] of Wall Street," as party propagandists called them—were part of extensive efforts to create a new socialist reality.[3] In the early 1950s, Communist officials used invented accounts of internal and external enemies to justify the arrest and grim internment of thousands of political opponents, including religious leaders who were perceived as a particular threat to the young regime's authority. Political persecution eased after the 1953 deaths of Josef Stalin and his devoted Czechoslovak communist follower, Klement Gottwald, but continued until the revolutions of 1989.

Just three days before Horáková and her co-defendants were hanged, Czechoslovakia's socialist government ceremoniously opened to the public the Ratibořice chateau, a once private aristocratic residence transformed in 1950 into a state-owned museum filled with carefully arranged displays of art, antiques, and fine furniture (see Figures 2.1 and 2.2).[4] Farmers and factory laborers could now stroll around the estate's well manicured gardens and take guided tours of the chateau's high-ceilinged rooms, built and decorated for the comfort of the estate's lords. Ratibořice is a small baroque chateau located in a picturesque valley in the farming country of northeastern Bohemia,

Figure 2.1. Visitors waiting for their tour to begin outside the Ratibořice chateau. From the collection of the National Monument Institute of the Czech Republic, Central Office in Prague.

Figure 2.2. Inside the Ratibořice chateau after its 1950 public opening. From the collection of the National Monument Institute of the Czech Republic, Central Office in Prague.

one of the four provinces that comprised socialist Czechoslovakia. Božena Němcová, a revered nineteenth-century Czech author and patriot, grew up on the grounds of the Ratibořice estate when Duchess Kateřina Zaháňská, an acquaintance of Prince Clemens von Metternich, spent her summers there.[5] Its buildings, landscapes, and inhabitants, including the duchess, inspired Němcová to write her beloved novel, *Grandmother* (*Babička;* 1855), a fictionalized work which helped bond generations of Czechs into an imagined community. In 1842 the German noble von Schaumburg-Lippe family purchased the estate, which they held until September 1945 when the Czechoslovak state, recently liberated from the Nazis and not yet in Communist Party hands, seized it and all moveable property on it.[6] Starting in June 1950, socialist-era visitors to Ratibořice gazed upon a unique exhibition containing historic interiors that were modeled partly on fictionalized characters in Němcová's novel, informed by a leading Czechoslovak art historian's knowledge of style, and decorated with art, antiques, and period furniture from a variety of other sequestered aristocratic and middle-class properties.[7]

The Ratibořice chateau was one of dozens of confiscated aristocratic residences in socialist Czechoslovakia that the Communist Party converted into estate museums to serve as domestic tourist destinations and diversions from the daily routines of work, school, and home.[8] Each year, millions of Czechoslovaks, who had very limited opportunities to travel outside their home country or the East Bloc, journeyed to these castles and chateaux where state-employed guides conducted them through historic interiors decorated with valuable furnishings once belonging in private hands.[9] Individuals, families, and groups from schools, factories, and party organizations were among these pilgrims. The estate museums established in Ratibořice and elsewhere in socialist Czechoslovakia, all state-owned and state-managed, were part of the Communist Party's efforts to provide workers with "purposeful tourism"—a variety of "virtuous" leisure.[10] As such, they were expected to further two goals: they were to offer Czechoslovak workers breaks from their labors and opportunities for self-realization; and they were to encourage the internalization and naturalization of lessons about new socialist reality, including belief in the power of the Communist Party to secure "the good life" for the people.[11] Significantly, though, as faithful party officials and visitors repeatedly recognized, throughout the 1950s presentations in the confiscated aristocratic residences, including exhibitions, signage and tour-guide narratives, were not encoded with clear, consistent, commanding signs directing visitors to a single dominant message about socialist ideology. This cultural approach, one of the many tools of power employed in the East Bloc to instill lessons about new socialist reality, was not fully effective in the well-visited estate museums.[12] For a variety of reasons, during the 1950s—even in the highly repressive Stalinist period—estate-museum presentations did not regularly or unambiguously present official party dogma. In some cases, tour guides even extolled the aristocratic past and religious belief, both of which were anathema to the party and its teachings.

The estate museums offer evidence of how the goals of high-ranking party functionaries and central-state agencies in socialist Czechoslovakia were sometimes unrealized at the local, grass-roots level. Visitors faithful to the party would have known how to read official ideology into exhibitions, signage, and tour-guide narratives in the former aristocratic homes, despite their lack of clear authoritative ideological codes. However, mixed messages in those presentations provided less committed visitors some agency and autonomy to view the estate museums without party blinkers, thereby leaving the gates open for people's imaginations to wander in a variety of unofficial directions. Czechoslovak bodies remained confined within East Bloc borders but, while walking through and around these domestic-tourist destinations, their minds could meander outside the boundaries of official ideology. Using evidence found in the records of the State Monument Administration (*Státní památková správa*), an important central-state institution devoted to historic preservation, this chapter demonstrates how, for the first twelve years of socialist rule in Czechoslovakia, displays, signage, and tour-guide narratives in the estate museums failed to align art, architecture, and socialism, thus granting visitors breaks from everyday routines and facilitating opportunities to create meaning for their own lives apart from party dogma.[13] Before examining presentations in estate museums, some background information on socialist cultural policy and the history of the creation of the estate museums, including post-war confiscation laws, will be discussed.[14]

Socialist Cultural Policy and New Socialist Reality

The Ninth Party Congress, held in June 1949, was the first important official gathering of the Czechoslovak Communist Party following its seizure of power in February 1948. Like all other party congresses during the socialist era, this meeting presented official party policies guiding economic, political, and cultural decision-making for the subsequent four to five years. Economic policies announced at the Ninth Party Congress included the nationalization of all private property, and emphasis on heavy industrial production rather than the consumer sector. Most important for this chapter, however, was the cultural policy presented at this early post-war assembly of party faithful. The Minister of Information, Václav Kopecký, announced that all culture would be put in the service of building socialism.[15] For Kopecký, a long-time Communist Party member and a leading voice in the creation of cultural policy in socialist Czechoslovakia, this meant that any cultural activity in the country was strictly to follow the principles of socialist realism.[16] To insure that everyone understood what the party was demanding of its artists, writers, teachers, museum directors, and historic preservationists, the Minister of Culture and Education, Zdeněk Nejedlý, organized a special three-day conference devoted to culture. At this conference, Nejedlý, also a long-time Communist Party member and another leader of socialist cultural policy in Czechoslovakia, spoke about art's role in the creation of new socialist reality. This was a conference devoted to the alignment of culture and party ideology.

Nejedlý firmly stated that only socialist realism suited art's educational and psychological functions, because "[it] is understandable to the widest social strata." He discussed how socialist-realist painting and sculpture supported or championed socialism through appropriately selected images depicting the heroic efforts of iconic party leaders, partisans fighting to defend communism, factory workers, miners, and collective-farm laborers. In a nod to pre-war Czech national-patriotic memories, which contrasted with homogenizing Sovietization and upon which socialist leaders built some legitimacy, Nejedlý allowed that socialist-realist art could draw inspiration from those figures in Czech national history that were progressive for their time, even if they were not socialists. For example, he noted, "The Hussites and the Taborites were not socialists in the current meaning of the word, but still we value them for what their movement meant then."[17] The same was true for many members of the Czech national awakening (*národní obrození*), the eighteenth- and nineteenth-century movement of patriots dedicated to raising Czech national consciousness and Czech nation-building. Its members included Karel Havlíček Borovský, Josef Kajetán Tyl, Mikoláš Aleš, and, in addition, Bedřich Smetana and Božena Němcová, both of whom Nejedlý revered.[18] In contrast, socialist-realist art was to present reactionary figures in Czech history, including members of the aristocracy and clergy, as parasites and exploiters of the working class. This ideology-saturated cultural policy did not result in displays of socialist-realist art in the estate museums, or the complete removal of the many portraits of nobles found in the confiscated aristocratic properties. Translating Communist Party principles expressed at its highest levels into reality at the grass-roots level was no simple process of radical replacement or total erasure of the past.

At the gathering devoted to art's role in the construction of new socialist reality, Nejedlý also declared that art had to make people happy. He said that the more difficult times were the more art needed to raise people's spirits.[19] Nejedlý's appeals to happiness bespoke a certain type of escape from the everyday—one in which the imagination rose above the pangs of personal hardship and the routines of home, work, and school, to an emotional plane of joy or peace detached from lived reality. When riveted to clear, consistent, and commanding ideological codes about true champions or enemies of the people, Nejedlý's lessons about happiness through detachment could serve to instill Communist Party dogma and construct new socialist reality. When ambiguously or inconsistently presented, they could suggest paths of escape for the Czechoslovak mind, even while its body was confined inside East Bloc borders. When looking at former aristocratic residences transformed into domestic tourist destinations, we see that during the 1950s, even before Stalin's 1953 death, socialist authorities did not achieve a firm, compelling union of art, architecture, and political education. Messages presented to visitors at Ratibořice and elsewhere were sometimes different from official party code, leaving Czechoslovaks some expanded mental space in which to wander and produce meaning with at least relative autonomy from ideology.

Post-War Retribution and Sequestration

The transformation of Ratibořice and dozens of other former aristocratic residences into domestic tourist destinations belongs to the history of post-war retribution against individuals and groups accused of Nazi collaboration. The expulsion of roughly three million Germans from the country is the best-known chapter of that reckoning.[20] Much less has been written on the retributive sequestration of millions of pieces of private property from so-called "enemies of the people," including castles, chateaux, palaces, villas, apartments, and all of the furnishings, art, antiques, and other objects in them. Confiscation of private property was not new to Czechoslovakia. A small number of castles and chateaux had been confiscated following World War I, particularly those of Habsburg family members, including the Konopiště and Křivoklát castles.[21] These confiscations, however, paled in scope compared to the post-war sequestrations that officially began in June 1945, almost three years before the communist seizure of power in February 1948. Residents of Czechoslovakia were aware that the state was seizing people's homes and personal items, just like they knew about the expulsion of the Germans. These were matters regularly reported in the daily press. Domestic tourists visiting Ratibořice and other estate museums created after World War II knew they were gazing upon sequestered private effects.

The post-war measure that led to the largest number of confiscations was Beneš Decree no. 12/1945, announced in June 1945.[22] It was one of a number of orders promulgated by President Edvard Beneš during the time period between the end of World War II and before the democratically elected, multiparty parliament convened in May 1946.[23] Beneš Decree no. 12/1945 called for the confiscation of agricultural property, including farm land, adjacent forests and parks, castles, chateaux, mills, barns, and stables, as well as all of the content of those buildings, including paintings, porcelain, tapestries, furniture, books, tools, and animals. It did not call for the seizure of all agricultural property, but only that which belonged to Germans, Magyars, and other "unreliable persons," the latter term referring to Czechs accused of Nazi collaboration. A 1929 census provided the information used to judge who was a German or Magyar. It did not matter that the census asked individuals to identify their mother tongue, rather than their national identity, or that some people lived in mixed marriages and did not feel themselves to be exclusively German or Magyar.[24] Courts determined which Czechs were "unreliable persons."[25] Beneš Decree no. 108/1945, promulgated in October 1945, covered non-agricultural, non-rural property.[26] Its terms stated that urban palaces, villas, houses, apartments, factories, and businesses belonging to Germans, Magyars, and "unreliable persons" would be confiscated, along with their contents. Decree no. 108/1945 less directly affected noble residences than did Decree no. 12/1945, but the art, antiques, and fine furnishings seized under its terms did adorn some historic interiors in sequestered chateaux and castles that became socialist estate museums. In quick time, laws calling for the confiscation of Czech aristocratic property were also created. Rather than being decreed, however, they were passed in the democratically elected, multiparty Parliament in July 1947 (again before the communist takeover in February 1948).[27]

All in all, in the five years following World War II, the Czechoslovak state sequestered roughly 1,000 castles and chateaux. More than 100 of these former aristocratic residences received the protected status of State Cultural Property (*Státní kulturní majetek*), a title ensuring their preservation and sometimes resulting in their becoming estate museums open for mass tourism. Hundreds of thousands of moveable goods from inside of the residences, selected due to their value, also received this status. Initially, this special group of confiscated cultural objects was placed in the care of the National Cultural Commission (*Národní kulturní komise*), an important preservation agency that existed from 1946 until the enactment of the first comprehensive Czechoslovak preservation law in 1958.[28] In November 1948, the National Cultural Commission had jurisdiction over 22 confiscated castles and chateaux, including Ratibořice; by the end of 1949, it oversaw 48; and at the end of 1951, it administered 95.[29] The State Monument Administration, a separate pre-war preservation agency that continued to function after World War II, also had a small number of castles and chateaux under its protective jurisdiction. The hundreds of castles and chateaux that lacked protected status went on to serve as retirement homes, elementary schools, orphanages, military barracks, storage sites for winter food supplies, depositories for cultural property confiscated from other sites, and centers for training tractor drivers; some were simply left to decay.

Zdeněk Wirth and the Contingent Origins of the Estate Museums

Zdeněk Wirth, a leading figure in twentieth-century Czech cultural history, played a critical role in the transformation of the sequestered castles and chateaux into estate museums in post-war Czechoslovakia. Although a close friend of Nejedlý, the Minister of Culture and Education who organized the Stalin-era conference on socialist cultural policy discussed above, Wirth was not a fervent Communist Party member; his great passion was the preservation of Czech and Czechoslovak cultural heritage. He remains esteemed as a leading authority on the history of Czech art and architecture. Because he used his extensive knowledge, not in a university career, but rather while serving as a hardworking employee in state offices devoted to the preservation and promotion of heritage, he is also recognized as a leading cultural administrator. During the interwar period, Wirth worked for Czechoslovakia's Ministry of Education and National Enlightenment, and after World War II he served as the first director of the National Cultural Commission and the first director of the Institute of Art History.[30]

Wirth, with his rich knowledge of Czechoslovakia's castles and chateaux and his devotion to heritage preservation, played a critical role in the transformation of the sequestered properties into estate museums and state-owned domestic-tourist destinations.[31] He never had a long-term grand plan for this transformation, but instead shrewdly reacted to contingencies around him that he perceived to be threats to and promises for the protection of heritage. He also drew from his excellent connections with powerful members of the post-war Czechoslovak central state, including his friend Nejedlý, and from his knowledge of laws and institutions for the governing and administering of culture.[32] In the process of creating the estate museums, Wirth also created local sites of power within the socialist system for art-historical expertise. Through the estate museums he established perceptions, procedures, and institutions granting art historians, with their training in the study of high-cultural style, some professional authority.

An early step leading towards the creation of estate museums concerned the creation of the National Cultural Commission. After hearing reports about the vandalizing and stealing of confiscated cultural property in the early post-war months, Wirth initiated legislation to protect the country's sequestered cultural assets and used his connections within the government to gain the support of Beneš and others for the law's passage.[33] That law called into being the National Cultural Commission and the protected status of State Cultural Property to be assigned to important sequestered castles, chateaux, art, antiques, and furniture. Significantly, the National Cultural Commission did not initially seek to create estate museums. Instead, its employees, especially Wirth, spent their long days working on two demanding sets of activities. They completed the legal and bureaucratic negotiations and paperwork for acquiring protected status for select castles and chateaux; and they reviewed thousands of objects within confiscated sites, winnowing out paintings, sculpture, porcelain, glassware, chairs, desks, and many other items deemed to be worthy of state protection. These selected moveable goods were given the protected status of State Cultural Property and often packed for transport to and storage in large depositories (less-valued sequestered chateaux sometimes served as these depositories). Art historians, in charge of designing estate-museum exhibitions, later pulled some of these objects from storage and used them to decorate historic interiors in former aristocratic homes.

Wirth first published a plan for the creation of the estate museums in December 1949 in response to the call of the Ninth Party Congress for the alignment of culture with ideology in June of that year.[34] Wirth's plan called for specially selected castles and chateaux to be integrated into a network of estate museums extending throughout western Czechoslovakia. The network would have examples from major periods of art and architectural history, including the gothic, renaissance, baroque, and empire periods. The interiors of many of these sites were to be transformed into domestic culture (*bytová kultura*) museums, with art historians responsible for the creation of expertly arranged historic interiors exemplifying the artistic style of the period associated with the architecture of a given castle or chateau. A smaller number of estate museums would be devoted to displays of a single type of item, like the porcelain museum in the Klášterec nad Ohří chateau near the Thun porcelain works in northwestern Bohemia, or the fashion museum in the Jemniště chateau, designed in the eighteenth century by baroque architect František Maxmilián Kaňka.

In order to make his vision of a network of estate museums a reality and to insure the protection of heritage in the new socialist order, Wirth had to bear in mind the power of the party and its desire to bring culture into line with ideology.[35] He thus framed his plan within language suggesting that estate museums would be used for the building of new socialist reality. Among other statements, the December 1949 booklet contained a negative description of the aristocracy as insensitive, greedy parasites that exploited workers and forced them to live in miserable conditions. It described former aristocratic homes in the following manner:

> Primitive hygiene kneeled beside pompous, gilded decoration, where collections of exotic animals and weapons from souvenirs of trips showed that this parasitical stratum was simply alienated from the land that granted it its economic foundation.... The expensive, miniature comfort of children's rooms is from an era when children of workers and peasants had no place to sleep. ... Similarly, aviaries, kennels, and stables—extensive, lit buildings, visually arranged and ornamented with ceiling stuccos, and carved, stone work—stand in contrast to a ground-floor, drafty cell without light or a cold attic closet for servants.[36]

This was a vision of the aristocratic past that, if consistently encoded and widely disseminated, could lead estate-museum visitors to see the historic interiors as something more than nicely arranged collections of art, antiques, and furniture, and absorb from them lessons about class conflict, feudal and capitalist exploitation of workers, and the Communist Party as the people's true advocate. The exhibitions, signage, and tour-guide narratives in estate museums, however, were not fully or consistently suffused with official ideology, thereby providing visitors, both party followers and others who might have been resistant or indifferent, opportunities to escape from both daily routines and party dogma, and create some meaning for themselves independent of party goals.

The Case of the Missing Servants

During the 1950s, the estate museums that Wirth helped to create saw a growing number of visitors.[37] This increase especially occurred in the post-Stalinist period when Antonín Novotný, who replaced Gottwald as head of party and state, began paying more attention to consumer experiences, including cars and travel, as a means of bolstering the party's legitimacy after the difficult years of the purges, nationalization and collectivization, and of raising revenues for the state's beleaguered coffers. The increase in visitors occurred despite the facts that some castles and chateaux were difficult to reach, many lacked basic tourist amenities like lodging, restaurants, and public bathrooms, and few offered souvenirs for sale. The National Cultural Commission and the State Monument Administration supported efforts to establish restaurants and other visitor amenities near the domestic tourism sites; and with assistance from Čedok, the official travel agency in socialist Czechoslovakia, the preservationists helped make travel to former aristocratic residences easier and more affordable. They also strove to make "tasteful" souvenirs available for purchase, but shortages of resources and poor distribution networks continually frustrated these efforts. Interestingly, in this atheist state that imprisoned priests and suppressed religious belief, some of the proposed souvenirs were images of the Madonna and Saint Wenceslas.[38]

State guidelines required that each estate museum make visitor books available in which comments about tours could be recorded. The usefulness of these books for ascertaining the popular reception of the former aristocratic residences might never be known, as none can be found and they were probably not preserved. Still, some records from the State Monument Administration, including letters of complaint, provide evidence of what visitors experienced during their tours, including chances for escape from official ideology. The items displayed in the exhibitions of historic interiors inside the museums also shed light on these experiences. Some historic-interior exhibitions contained the same furnishings and arrangements of the aristocrats who owned the castle or chateau before the post-war confiscations, like the Rychnov nad Kněžnou chateau in eastern Bohemia with its valuable picture gallery.[39] Elsewhere, in Ratibořice for example, the historic interiors consisted entirely of objects confiscated from other chateaux and middle-class villas and apartments.[40] In all cases, however, tour guides led visitors through showroom after showroom of thoughtfully arranged, and artfully crafted, valuable objects that spoke to the comfortable—even luxurious—lives of the aristocracy. It is important to note that these historic interiors did little to display the hardship or suffering of the serfs and other laborers whose long working days helped to make aristocratic opulence possible. Kitchens and laundry rooms where servants labored, places where they ate and slept, and implements of their everyday chores were not exhibited. Only rooms in which aristocrats entertained, dined, slept, dressed, smoked, enjoyed music, read, and wrote were shown. In those spaces, some subtle traces of servants could be identified—for example, sometimes bells for summoning them could be found, or the outlines of hidden doors through which they passed were visible—but a careful, searching gaze was needed to pinpoint them among the far more eye-catching art, antiques, and fine furnishings that were the focus of guided tours. In Ratibořice, some effort was made to recreate the lives of estate laborers in the exhibitions installed in the old mill and bleaching house on the periphery of the estate grounds. Even there, though, the displays were happy depictions of the lives of characters from the fictionalized world of Němcová's novel, *Grandmother*, not discomforting portrayals of miserable conditions that peasants endured while their work enriched the aristocracy. The absence of sociological or ethnographic displays depicting the variety of class experiences on aristocratic estates might have resulted from the role that art historians played in the creation of the exhibitions—as experts in the dissemination of knowledge about high-cultural style, not class relations or folk life.

The artfully arranged interiors of the estate museums posed a challenge to Wirth and other central-state administrators in socialist Czechoslovakia. In purely visual terms, the historic interiors did not push visitors to absorb lessons about class conflict, exploitation, and new socialist reality. If Wirth and his colleagues were to align ideology with art and architecture in the estate museums—and do so without shifting the exhibitions' emphasis from style in art history to class conflict in social history—then they had to provide a means for insuring that visitors read party messages into the displays of art-historical style and left the exhibitions with ideology-permeated understandings of these old-world interiors—understandings that promoted the building of new socialist reality. The objects on display were not inherently imbued with socialist code, especially since they only hinted at the lives of servants and laborers on aristocratic estates. Furthermore, due to the objects' attractiveness and persistent fond memories, identities, and experiences from before World War II, some visitors would have been tempted to view them through wistful, romantic, or religious lenses. Unless there was a means for aligning the presentation and reception of the displays—that is, for mediating between the viewers and the exhibitions—then visitors had relative autonomy to glean meaning for their own lives apart from official ideology.[41]

Central-state officials in the National Cultural Commission and State Monument Administration attempted to use brochures, signage, and tour-guide narratives to mediate between the displays and ideology, although much evidence shows that these efforts were unsuccessful. Numerous, nicely illustrated brochures were produced, some of which offered negative portrayals of the aristocracy, thereby promoting ideology-laden narratives about the estate museums. These brochures might have been more successful as communist propaganda had there not been regular shortages of them available for sale in the estate museums. For example, in 1955 the castellan of Ratibořice complained that the chateau had received no copies of the brochure and only 28,000 out of 60,000 promised postcards.[42] Further, some available brochures did not contain political statements about feudal exploitation of workers or class conflict, but instead focused on the art and architectural histories of specific sites.

Another tool of mediation between the intended meanings of museum exhibitions and viewers' reception is signage, that is, the inclusion of written texts in or near displays to provide some basic facts about items shown and narrative statements indicative of wider lessons to be absorbed. A very notable feature of the estate museums in socialist Czechoslovakia in the 1950s was their lack of signage. No written texts were hung in historic interiors to tell visitors basic facts about individual rooms or the artifacts displayed in them; nor were any texts written to situate the displays within a wider socialist narrative. On their own—without textual intervention—the displays could convey a variety of different impressions or messages, or appeal to a multiplicity of memories, identities, and feelings, some hostile to the old order, others sympathetic and admiring. Perhaps if kitchens, servants' quarters, laundry facilities, and cleaning implements were on display along with intarsia tables, libraries containing the *Almanach de Gotha,* carved ivory pipes, Venetian chandeliers, and Meissen china, then the rooms and the items in them would have presented compelling ideological messages. This mixing of privileged and servant lifestyles, though, was absent from the estate-museum displays, helping to leave presentations open to individual interpretation and escape from ideology.

A last common means for aligning an exhibition with an intended message is the tour guide, or docent, who leads visitors through installations and delivers narratives about the works on display. While the estate museums in post-war Czechoslovakia lacked written signs, they never lacked tour guides. No visitor could view any castle and chateau interior without a guide, a lower-level state functionary. The guide insured that everyone stayed together on the tour-route, which was often marked with carpet runners and rope barriers, with no one allowed to venture off alone or fall behind (perhaps lest they be tempted to steal a piece of confiscated cultural property). Inside the former aristocratic homes all information and presentation came solely from the guide. The tour guides mediating role, especially given the absence of signage, made them potentially important agents in the building of new socialist reality. Still, as many discussions within the central-state bodies of the National Cultural Commission and the State Monument Administration show, throughout the 1950s and at the grass-roots level, guides failed to deliver ideology-permeated presentations as they led factory workers, collective-farm laborers, and others through carefully arranged showrooms of aristocratic opulence and art-historical style.

Tour-Guide Liberties in the Stalinist Years

A problem that frequently required the attention of Wirth and other central-state administrators of estate museums involved tour guides who presented visitors with positive assessments of former aristocratic owners and the pre-socialist world. For example, in January 1951 the National Cultural Commission received a complaint from an employee of a district secretary of the Communist Party—an employee who clearly supported the regime. The complaint urged Wirth and others to find a better way to insure that visitors to estate museums were discouraged from thinking positive thoughts about the old order, and instead absorbed correct socialist messages. The complaint's author had visited several estate museums and ascertained, "that the majority of chateaux guides do not know how to politically orient their comments, and [they] even admire how the earlier owners knew how to manage everything and were kind." The letter was especially critical of one guide who expressed fond memories of the former owners, because "at Christmas time they never forgot him with a gift."[43]

Given the political context, Wirth could not be indifferent to this complaint and he and his staff quickly reacted. They produced an ideology-filled speech that every estate-museum guide was required to memorize and deliver at the start of all tours. The speech was to align art, architecture and party dogma, and to counteract possible favorable assessments of the pre-socialist order. The first part of this lengthy speech contained a negative depiction of the aristocracy's exploitative and unjust treatment of ordinary people. It declared,

Honored Visitors!

Before we continue to the actual tour of the present chateau [or castle] it is necessary to remember the following:

After the victory of the glorious Red Army in 1945 and after the February victory in 1948, the parasitical (*příživnická*) caste of the former aristocracy was forever removed. From the foundation, the whole appearance of our state changed; from the foundation, the Consciousness [*sic*] of our people changed.

The builders of socialism are becoming our heroes—our workers and farmers, shock-workers (*úderníci*) and innovators, etc.

From the classes of the former capitalists and from the feudal aristocracy we inherited their estates, manors, and castles, which are filled with valuables of a high artistic and cultural level from past centuries.

Immediately, at the beginning, we must remember that these jewels of architecture, sculpture, and painting, and other items of domestic culture were acquired and collected with the indescribable suffering and hardship of our ancestors, the little (*drobný*) working people.

The second part of the speech valorized the new socialist order, lauding the democracy, freedom and humanity that it was bringing to working people:

Our people's democratic establishment prevents the exploitation of one person by another and [in it] everything is oriented towards the education and prosperity of all.

Thus, in these places every worker can feel not like an exploited slave, [but like] a great self-conscious human—a human working and living in the spirit of socialism.[44]

The speech, designed at the central-state level to instill faith in the new socialist reality, immediately encountered resistance at the local level from tour guides and visitors alike. Wirth received a December 1951 report stating that not all guides were delivering the speech, even though its presentation was mandatory. Further, when some guides tried to deliver it, visitors silenced them with comments like, "Leave that, we heard that, we already know that."[45] This 1951 report is very important, because it shows that visitors to estate museums reacted to the ideology-laden speech with indifference and open hostility. Even during the age of Stalin and Gottwald, policies conceived at the upper level of the state were not smoothly implemented at the grass-roots level—or implemented, at all.

Before Wirth decided that the mandatory speech was a failure, he received another complaint about the tour guides, this time from the Ministry of Internal Trade, concerning the very popular Karlštejn (Karlstein) castle. Holy Roman Emperor Charles IV built Karlštejn around 1350 as a place to store the imperial crown jewels and his extensive relic collection.[46] The Ministry of Internal Trade alerted Wirth to a number of letters sent to the Communist Party's daily newspaper, Red Right (Rudé právo), complaining about the poor attention to ideology in the estate museums. Among them was a letter from regime-conformist students at a workers' school—an arm of the party—who had toured Karlštejn in May. The students complained that their guide repeatedly referred to "the great religious disposition of Charles IV" and "forgot" to mention that structures like Karlštejn "were made by serfs and subjects, over whom the aristocracy was the absolute lord." Overall, the entire narrative failed to place the history of Karlštejn in "the light of class struggle," which the letter writers argued was important to do at a site that hundreds of people "from the countryside" visited.[47]

After the failure of the mandatory speech, and in order to try to insure that all visitors left the estate museums having clear lessons in official ideology, in late 1951 Wirth and other National Cultural Commission employees went about seeking a different means for consistently and compellingly presenting the party line. They decided they would place signs at the spots where visitors were told to gather in the minutes before the start of their tours. Visitors were to read these signs voluntarily while waiting for their guide to appear with keys to the castle or chateau in hand. The signs were to note that the property on display was sequestered, present negative depictions of the aristocracy as exploiters of working people, and applaud the justice that socialism was bringing to Czechoslovak workers. Over a year later—at the end of 1952—these signs were nowhere to be seen. Instead, the administrators of State Cultural Property were researching how much it would cost to make them.[48] Perhaps, if displayed, the signs would have instilled ideology in more estate-museum visitors. Perhaps, though, visitors would have ignored them and the party lessons written on them.[49]

Tour-Guide Autonomy during the Thaw

Shortly before Nikita Khrushchev's 1956 "Secret Speech" at the Twentieth Party Congress of the Communist Party of the Soviet Union, central-state officials in the State Monument Administration, aiming to keep Czechoslovak party leaders happy, examined the political correctness of the estate museums. They found tour guides to be a specific hindrance to the alignment of art, architecture, and socialism. Staff members issued a report calling for changes in the quality of the tour guides so that the full ideological potential of visits to former aristocratic properties could be realized. "The fulfillment of the main goal of culturally enlightened use of state cultural property is dependent on quality guide service," the report stated. The building of new socialist reality through presentations at the estate museums was not being realized due to the "great insufficiencies" of the guides—insufficiencies, the report said, that were "notoriously known." Too many guides lacked the education and capabilities needed for "ideologically demanding work." The report pointed to low salaries as the cause of the guides' inadequacies. Low pay attracted only unqualified candidates, many of whom "[were] former employees of the last feudal owners."[50] Despite this strong call for change in 1955, the shortcomings of tour guides were repeatedly pointed to for the remainder of the 1950s, but no solutions were found. The party was preoccupied with more pressing matters than museums in the countryside. Furthermore, suffering from chronic financial problems, the party did not then have the revenues necessary for attracting better qualified guides through enhanced pay.

In Czechoslovakia, the second half of the 1950s was simultaneously a time of some liberation of cultural expression due to Khrushchev's thaw and mounting anxiety within higher party echelons about revisionism growing among its cadres.[51] In June 1957 the Central Committee of the Czechoslovak Communist Party, worried about revisionism, passed a resolution with the weighty title, "On Several Contemporary Questions about the Ideological Work of the Party." Its primary concerns included "the problem of educating the widest masses in socialist consciousness, [and] the understanding and acquisition of a Marxist world view."[52] The resolution prompted the State

Monument Administration to issue a report on services at estate museums. The report called the quality of tour guides inadequate.[53]

Newspapers articles from 1957 also contained criticisms of the tour guides. One article, entitled "Castle Ghouls (*Hradní strašidla*)," appeared in the *Literary News* (*Literární noviny*) in late 1957. The anonymous author wrote, "I do not believe in the white lady in another feudal apparition, but winter passes, spring comes, and with spring [there is] tourism. Thus, it is already necessary today to talk about the real ghoul at our castles: [that is,] about what some guides say." The article gave examples of guides telling "distasteful" jokes about knights banging their heads, a chubby idol, and a trick played on a sick patient. The author found this content to be objectionable. He concluded that the real ghoul at the castles—the one needing to be "exorcised"—was the poor quality of the guides.[54] What the article did not mention is that the jokes were no doubt popular with some visitors.[55]

Complaints about tour guides continued after a government meeting in June 1958 to discuss ways to expand domestic and foreign tourism in Czechoslovakia. The State Monument Administration wrote a statement about what it needed to help meet those goals, while also promoting "the education of the public in the spirit of communist ideas." Good tour guides were especially needed. The statement said that the "gloomy" characters and personalities of the guides at state castles and chateaux were harming the building of socialism. It reported that the average age of the guides was fifty-eight, making it a cohort with strong generational roots in the pre-socialist past. The statement discussed how guides interspersed their presentations with local stories and legends, and had little expertise and knowledge of foreign languages. Bad pay was again pointed to as the cause of the guides' poor quality.[56]

Two years later, in 1959, socialist officials held the "Meeting of Socialist Culture" to discuss ways to counter growing revisionism within the party. This gathering showed that the problem of guides' inabilities to present ideologically educational tours persisted. Museum managers speaking there reported again that tour guides were not promoting the party line. They argued, "It is certainly necessary to … find new workers [who are] enthusiastic and not encumbered with idealistic education, religious dogmatism, and love of the past (*staromilectví*)."[57] Again, though, the party was preoccupied with more pressing matters than countryside museums, and it lacked the revenues for hiring better paid, more qualified guides.

During the late 1950s and early 1960s, a small measure was instituted to improve the ideological content of tour-guide presentations. Lectures on Marxist-Leninism, atheism, party history, peasant revolution, and the ideological uses of historic monuments were prepared, and estate-museum employees were required to attend them, with the hope that they would better integrate party dogma into museum presentations.[58] The coming of the Prague Spring shifted attention to other matters, including critiques of the physical care of historic monuments.[59] Efforts to strengthen the presentation of official ideology in estate museums were renewed after Soviet tanks invaded Czechoslovakia in August 1968 and the era of normalization began in the 1970s.[60] After the Fourteenth Party Congress in 1971, the Ministry of Education announced that estate museums were now required to have entry-hall exhibitions. These exhibitions were set up in rooms at the start of estate-museum tours, and arranged with carefully selected images and texts providing ideological lessons about class conflict and the sufferings that workers endured before Communist Party rule.[61] After purchasing tickets of admission to the estate-museums visitors waited in these ideology-imbued entry halls before being allowed into the historic interiors. It was hoped that while there they would absorb official lessons from the materials on display, preparing their minds for the correct ideological reception of the tour they were about to experience.[62] The creation of the entry-hall exhibitions was one of the party's discursive responses to the challenges it faced after the Prague Spring.[63] Vandalism to the entry-hall exhibition in the gothic Zvíkov castle, dating from around 1200, provides evidence that visitors continued to shun the party's efforts to align art, architecture, and ideology.[64] Party discourse was out of sync with everyday life and popular meaning, and the state surveillance apparatus, while still repressive and coercive, was not catching everyone in its net. After the Velvet Revolution of 1989, and still today, most estate museums remain state-owned institutions open to the public (a 1991 post-socialist law stipulates that only property confiscated after the communist takeover in February 1948 is eligible for restitution).[65] Socialist ideology plays no role in tour-guide presentations these days, which still give great attention to art-history but, as the growing number of kitchen exhibitions attests, now better depict everyday experiences of servants on former aristocratic estates.

Conclusion: State-Society Negotiations and the Creation of Meaning

The socialist states of post-war Eastern Europe were repressive and coercive, but they were not monoliths in which party functionaries had total political and social control over cowering populations. The history of estate museums in Czechoslovakia during the 1950s shows that there were constraints on party abilities to achieve total domination. Post-1948 Czechoslovak leaders had more urgent matters for which to care than tourist destinations out in the countryside, and chronic economic challenges left them with limited financial resources for related matters, including brochures, signage, and the education and pay of tour guides. Also, while many regime conformists did exist in socialist Czechoslovakia, numerous social groups had values, practices, and priorities apart from party ideology. This was true not only of the tour guides and visitors to the estate museums, but also of the art historians who designed the exhibitions emphasizing historic high-cultural styles of art and architecture rather than official ideology.

Socialist states did have the power to intervene in the lives of their populations, and they often used it in harsh, inhumane ways. Still, it was power that could be not exercised simply through top-down domination, and socialist societies were not merely "a mass of people suffering under authority from the 'state'."[66] The production of meaning in the Eastern Bloc resulted from a multidirectional, mutually constitutive, creative process of interactions and negotiations between various central, intermediate, and local official and unofficial agents. The opening of the gates of former aristocratic residences in Czechoslovakia, like Ratibořice, allowed possibilities for escapes from both the everyday routines of work, school, and home, and from socialist ideology. In the estate museums, where codes and narratives for ensconcing new socialist reality into the hearts and minds of factory workers and farmers were not consistently or substantively presented, Czechoslovaks could produce some meaning in their own lives independent of party intentions. These opportunities for autonomy and agency, limited yet significant, enabled Eastern Europeans to ground themselves in the socialist system and make themselves at home in it. They also posed challenges to the regime's authority, adding threats to it from within.

Notes

The American Philosophical Society and the Fulbright Commission provided funding that made possible research travel for this chapter. The wonderful staffs of the Institute of Art History of the Czech Academy of Sciences, the Museum of Božena Němcová, and the National Archive of the Czech Republic helped me to access important documents. Kristina Uhlíková deserves special thanks for generously assisting me with primary sources and information about historic preservation in post-war Czechoslovakia. Hana Veselá of the National Monument Institute in Prague graciously facilitated my securing of images and permissions. Nancy M. Wingfield, Catherine J. Plum, Florin Poenaru, Hana Rambousková, and our anonymous reviewers helped me to improve drafts of this article. All translations and errors are my own.

1. On the purges see Karel Kaplan, *The Report on the Murder of the General Secretary* (London: I.B. Tauris, 1990); and Jiří Pelikán, *The Czechoslovak Political Trials, 1950-1954* (London: McDonald, 1971). More information on Horáková and her trial is in Melissa Feinberg, *Elusive Equality: Gender, Citizenship, and the Limits of Democracy in Czechoslovakia, 1918-1950* (Pittsburgh: University of Pittsburgh Press, 2006); and Pavlína Formánková and Petr Koura, ed., *Žádáme trest smrti!: Propagandistická kampaň provázející proces s Miladou Horákovou a spol.* (Prague: Ústav pro studium totalitních režimů, 2009). An insightful study of the Slánský show trial is

Kevin McDermott, "A Polyphony of Voices? Czech Popular Opinion and the Slánský Affair," *Slavic Review* 67, no. 4 (2008): 840–65.

2. An examination that brings Horáková's trial and the potato-beetle scare together in an analysis of party propaganda techniques is Pavlína Formánková, "'Vypořádali jsme se s Horákovou, vypořádáme se i s americkým broukem!': Kampaň provázející proces s JUDr. Miladou Horákovou," *Paměť a dějiny* 1, no. 1 (2007): 20–41.

3. Quotation found in Vladimír Macura, "The Potato Bug," in *The Mystifications of a Nation: The "Potato Bug" and Other Essays on Czech Culture*, ed. Hana Píchová and Craig Cravens (Madison: University of Wisconsin Press, 2010), 53.

4. The Ratibořice chateau was opened to the public, with festivities, on 24 June. Horáková and the others were hung on 27 June. Details of Ratibořice's opening are in "B. Němcová v Ratibořickém údolí: K dnešní všenárodní pouti českého lidu," *Svobodné slovo*, 25 June 1950; "Ministr František Krajčír promluvil na národní pouti v Ratibořickém údolí," *Pochodeň*, 30 June 1950; and "Budujeme radostný život v našich vesnicích v duchu odkazu Boženy Němcové," *Rudé právo*, 28 June 1950. The Minister of Internal Trade, František Krajčír, gave a speech praising Němcová as an inspiration for socialism, proclaiming that happy times were coming to the countryside, calling on his largely agrarian audience to work hard to bring in a good harvest, and warning everyone of imperialist efforts to harm peace and progress. Roughly 30,000 people attended the two-day event.

5. More information on the duchess, a wealthy and influential woman, is in Helena Sobková, *Kateřina Zaháňská* (Prague: Paseka, 2007).

6. The owner in 1945, Frederick Prince von Schaumburg-Lippe, was not a Nazi collaborator, but he registered German as his mother-tongue in the 1929 census and held citizenship in Germany, as he did not want to give up his noble title as Czechoslovak law required him to do for Czechoslovak citizenship. During World War II, the Nazis confiscated Ratibořice and used it as a communications center.

7. Cathleen M. Giustino, "Zdeněk Wirth a Ratibořice: Brány otevřené k nostalgii?" in *Zdeněk Wirth: Pohledem dnešní doby*, ed. Jiří Roháček and Kristina Uhlíková (Prague: Artefactum, 2010), 253-272; and Kristina Kaplanová (Uhlíková), "Babiččino údolí—areál spravovaný Národní kulturní komisí," in *Pro Arte: Sborník k poctě Ivo Hlobila*, ed. Dalibor Prix (Prague: Artefactum, 2002), 383-88. See also Vladimír Macura, "Šťastné to údolí," in *Masarykovy boty a jiné semi(o)fejetony* (Prague: Pražská imaginace, 1993).

8. This chapter treats only castles and chateaux in the western part of Czechoslovakia, which included the provinces of Bohemia, Moravia, and Silesia. A separate set of institutions, with a different history and archival record, cared for castles and chateaux in Slovakia, the easternmost province.

9. The Czech language distinguishes between *hrad* and *zámek*. A *hrad* is a fortified residence and is best translated as castle. A *zámek* is a non-fortified aristocratic residence and is most often translated as chateau.

10. Anne E. Gorsuch and Diane P. Koenker, "Introduction," in *Turizm: The Russian and East European Tourist under Capitalism and Socialism*, ed. Gorsuch and Koenker (Ithaca: Cornell University Press, 2006), 2, 5. They recognize that "purposeful tourism" is not unique to socialist society. David Crowley and Susan E. Reid write about "virtuous socialist leisure" in the East Bloc. They say, "It was distinguished from the alienated forms of 'amusement' that prevailed under capitalism in that it was to contribute to the integration of the individual, to allow her full self-possession and realization of her human essence as well as restoring her for the next day's labor." See David Crowley and Susan E. Reid, ed., *Pleasures in Socialism: Leisure and Luxury in the Eastern Bloc* (Evanston: Northwestern University Press, 2010), 30.

11. Regarding the dual purposes of productive leisure in the GDR, see Ester von Richthofen, *Bringing Culture to the Masses: Control, Compromise and Participation in the GDR* (New York: Berghahn

Books, 2009), 215. She writes, "The SED never regarded leisure-time pursuits as a personal affair. Controlling people's activities in their free time was an instrumental mechanism through which the party leaders hoped to turn East German citizens into 'socialist personalities'."

12. Culture's role as a "gentle" means of building socialism—especially the importance party officials assigned to workers becoming cultured—is discussed in Vadim Volkov, "The Concept of *Kul'turnost*': Notes on the Stalinist Civilizing Process," in *Stalinism: New Directions,* ed. Sheila Fitzpatrick (London: Routledge, 1999), 210–230. See also David Tompkins, "Instrumentalizing Entertainment and Education: Early Cold-War Music Festivals in East Germany and Poland," in this volume.

13. There is a rich literature on power and everyday life useful for studying agency and the creation of meaning autonomous from official ideology in socialist Czechoslovakia. Among others, see Michel de Certeau, *The Practice of Everyday Life* (Berkeley: University of California Press, 1984); Thomas Lindenberger, ed. *Herrschaft und Eigen-Sinn in der Diktatur: Studien zur Gesellschaftsgeschichte der DDR* (Cologne, Weimar, and Vienna: Böhlau, 1999); Alf Lüdtke, ed., *The History of Everyday Life: Reconstructing Historical Experiences and Ways of Life* (Princeton: Princeton University Press, 1995); and James C. Scott, *Weapons of the Weak: Everyday Forms of Peasant Resistance* (New Haven: Yale University Press, 1985). A substantive historiographic examination of the usefulness of these works and others for the study of power and everyday life in socialist Czechoslovakia is Vítězslav Sommer, "Cesta ze slepé uličky 'třetího odboje': Koncepty rezistence a studium socialistické diktatury v Československu," *Soudobé dějiny* 19, no. 1 (2012): 9–36.

14. To date, some research has been carried out on the history of historic preservation and estate museums in post-war Czechoslovakia, but few works place the stories of former aristocratic properties into their wider political context. Works analyzing exhibitions in former aristocratic homes include Ivo Hlobil, "K teorii interiérové instalace české památkové péče," in Ivo Hlobil, *Na zakládech konzervativní teorie české památkové péče: Výbor z textů* (Prague: Národní památkový ústav, 2008); Kaplanová (Uhlíková), "Babiččino údolí," in *Pro Arte,* 383–88; and Petr Weiss, "Specializované muzejní expozice na zámku Jemniště" (Diplomová práce, Filozofická fakulta Masarykovy university, Ústav archeologie a muzeologie, 2006). English-language studies of historic preservation in Central Europe include Rudy Koshar, *Germany's Transient Paths: Preservation and National Memory in the Twentieth Century* (Chapel Hill: University of North Carolina Press, 1998); and Michael Meng, *Shattered Spaces: Encountering Jewish Ruins in Post-War Germany and Poland* (Cambridge, MA: Harvard University Press, 2011). I am presently writing a book-length manuscript on memory, museums, and confiscated cultural property in Czechoslovakia from 1918 until 1992.

15. For more on Kopecký, see Jana Pávová, *Demagog ve službách strany: Portrét komunistického politika a ideologa Václava Kopeckého* (Prague: Ústav pro studium totalitních režimů, 2009).

16. In a statement that speaks to socialist efforts to create a new reality, Sheila Fitzpatrick writes that "the superimposition of a better 'soon' on a still imperfect now ... was [a] basic trope of socialist realism." See Sheila Fitzpatrick, "Becoming Cultured: Socialist Realism and the Representation of Privilege and Taste," in *The Cultural Front: Power and Culture in Revolutionary Russia* (Ithaca: Cornell University Press, 1992), 227. Other works treating socialist realism are Thomas Lahusan and Evgeny Dobrenko, ed., *Socialist Realism without Shores* (Durham: Duke University Press, 1997); and Evgeny Dobrenko, *The Political Economy of Socialist Realism* (New Haven: Yale University Press, 2007). Exhibition catalogues devoted to Czechoslovak socialist realist painting and sculpture include Francesco Augusto Razetto, et al., ed., *Socialistický realismus Československo, 1948-1989* (Prague: Nadační fond Eleutheria, 2008); and Tereza Petišková, *Československý socialistický realismus, 1948-1958* (Prague: Galerie Rudolfinum, 2002).

17. Summaries of Nejedlý's speech are in "Umění—nejdůležitější pomocník výchovy lidu," *Mladá fronta,* 25 June 1949; and "Umění je nejúčinnější pomůckou výchovy," *Svobodné slovo,* 25 June 1949.

18. Defense of Czech national traditions was not common among the Stalinist leaders of socialist Czechoslovakia. Vladimír Macura writes that Nejedlý was "perhaps the single exception in the understanding of tradition: he stubbornly defended values considered to be tied with the past … as relevant [*aktuální*] values and capable of creating the correct foundation for new-age art, …." Found in Macura, *Šťastný věk,* 61. A discussion of Nejedlý's blending of nationalism and communism is in Bradley F. Abrams, *The Struggle for the Soul of the Nation: Czech Culture and the Rise of Communism* (Lanham, MD: Rowman and Littlefield, 2004), 95–97.

19. "Umění—nejdůležitější pomocník výchovy lidu," *Mladá fronta,* 25 June 1949; and "Umění je nejúčinnější pomůckou výchovy," *Svobodné slovo,* 25 June 1949.

20. The last days of Nazi power and calls for retaliation against Germans, including the expulsions, are discussed in Chad Bryant, *Prague in Black: Nazi Rule and Czech Nationalism* (Cambridge, MA: Harvard University Press, 2007). See also the many publications of Adrian von Arburg and Tomáš Staněk, including *Vysídlení Němců a proměny českého pohraničí 1945–1951: Dokumenty z českých archivů,* 2 vols. (Středokluky: Zdeněk Susa, 2010 and 2011).

21. For a list of castles and manors that had belonged to members of the Habsburg royal family and other Austrians, including heirs of Metternich, prior to World War I and were turned over to the newly created Czechoslovak state, see Květa Křížová, "Památkové interiérové instalace," *Zprávy památkové péče* 67, no. 6 (2007): 446. Some discussion of post-World War I confiscations, especially as they related to the First Land Reform, is in Eagle Glassheim, *Noble Nationalists: The Transformation of the Bohemian Aristocracy* (Cambridge, MA: Harvard University Press, 2005).

22. The text of Beneš Decree no. 12/1945, "The Decree for the Confiscation of Agricultural Property," is in Karel Jech and Karel Kaplan, ed., *Dekrety prezidenta republiky, 1940-1945: Dokumenty,* Vol. I (Brno: Ústav pro soudobé dějiny AV ČR, 1995), 276–83.

23. Beneš was a member of the Czechoslovak National Socialist Party, a Czech nationalist party. An overview of his career is in Zbyněk Zeman and Antonín Klimek, *The Life of Edvard Beneš, 1884-1948* (Oxford: Oxford University Press, 1997). See also Igor Lukes, *Czechoslovakia between Stalin and Hitler: The Diplomacy of Edvard Beneš* in the 1930s (New York: Oxford University Press, 1996).

24. David Wester Gerlach, "For Nation and Gain: Economy, Ethnicity and Politics in the Czech Borderlands, 1945-1948" (PhD diss., University of Pittsburgh, 2007), 101–102. He notes that measures for determining nationality were relaxed as time passed, although after many people had been expelled.

25. Post-war people's courts and charges of collaboration are discussed in Benjamin Frommer, *National Cleansing: Retribution against Nazi Collaborators in Postwar Czechoslovakia* (New York: Cambridge University Press, 2005).

26. The text for Beneš Decree no. 108/1945 is in Jech and Kaplan, ed., *Dekrety prezidenta republiky,* Vol. II, 848–60.

27. On 9 July 1947 the Parliament passed a law stipulating that all landed property not yet in state hands become nationalized, including the estates of Czech nobles. This was law no. 142/1947. See Jiří Koťátko, *Land Reform in Czechoslovakia* (Prague: Orbis, 1948). Koťátko, a communist, was head of the Resettlement Office which was responsible for moving Czechs into borderland regions formerly occupied by Germans who were expelled and whose property was confiscated. On 10 July 1947 the Parliament passed the *Lex Schwarzenberg,* which confiscated all property belonging to the Hluboká line of the Czech nationalist Schwarzenberg family, including the Windsor-inspired chateau of Hluboká nad Vltavou and the renaissance chateau of Český Krumlov, now a UNESCO world-heritage site.

28. The law creating the National Cultural Commission is "Zákon č. 137/1946 Sb. o Národních kulturních komisích pro správu státního majetku," *Sbírka zákonů a nařízení* (1946). An English translation of the 1958 monument law is "Act No. 22 of April 17, 1958 Concerning Cultural

Monuments," in *Bulletin of Czechoslovak Law* 19 (1980): 139–50. A well-researched discussion of unsuccessful interwar efforts to create a comprehensive monument law is Petr Štoncner, "Příspěvky k dějinám památkové péče v Československé republice v letech 1918-1938, Část 4: Snahy o vydání památkového zákona," *Zprávy památkové péče* 65, no. 3 (2005): 246–52.

29. Kristina Uhlíková, *Národní kulturní komise, 1947-1951* (Prague: Artefactum, 2004), 11–66.

30. The most comprehensive history of Wirth's activities, which focuses on the period before World War II, is Kristina Uhlíková, *Zdeněk Wirth: První dvě životní etapy* (Prague: Národní památkový ústav, 2011). See also Roháček and Uhlíková, ed., *Zdeněk Wirth*.

31. Two of Wirth's popular works on Czechoslovakia's castles and chateaux are Zdeněk Wirth and Jaroslav Benda, *Státní hrady a zámky* (Prague: Orbis, 1955); and Zdeněk Wirth, "Hrad a zámek," *Československo* 5 (1950): 243–55.

32. Due to his friendship with Nejedlý, the first confiscated chateau under Wirth's care to become a museum was the renaissance Litomyšl chateau in eastern Bohemia, presently a UNESCO world-heritage site. Nejedlý was not only a native of the town of Litomyšl, but his favorite Czech composer Bedřich Smetana had been born in the brewery on the chateau's grounds. Reports on the opening and accompanying festivities, which commemorated the 125th anniversary of Smetana's birth, can be found in "Litomyšl ve znamení Smetanových oslav," *Pondělník*, 7 June 1949; and "Smetanův génius ozařuje celý náš národní život," *Zemědělské noviny*, 8 June 1949. Litomyšl had been confiscated under Beneš Decree no. 12/1945 from the Thurn-Taxis family, and the state opened its gates to the masses in June 1949.

33. A discussion of the fate of some property in the hands of "gold diggers" in the immediate postwar months is in Gerlach, "For Nation and Gain," 108–20.

34. Ústav dějin umění, Fond Národní kulturní komise (hereafter ÚDU, NKK), Carton 6, inv. no. 68–69, "Národní kulturní komise: Zpráva o zřízení, činnosti a úkolech," December 1949.

35. Evidence of Wirth's attention to the Communist Party is the "Politická směrnice" for the National Cultural Commission, containing quotations from Václav Kopecký's speech at the Ninth Party Congress, calling for the alignment of all cultural activities with party ideology. See ÚDU, NKK, Carton 6, inv. no. 79–86, "Politická směrnice."

36. ÚDU, NKK, Carton 6, inv. no. 68–69, "Národní kulturní komise: Zpráva o zřízení, činnosti a úkolech," December 1949, 5. In 1950 the popular magazine, *Československo,* reproduced the critical description above, thereby giving it some readership outside of closed official circles. See Ema Charvatová, "Státní kulturní majetek ve správě Národní kulturní komise," *Československo* 5 (1950): 196–98.

37. The number of visitors to Czechoslovak castles and chateaux significantly increased between 1952 and 1957, a time period of significant change in the East Bloc. In 1952 the number was 1,105,000; in 1953 it was 1,195,000; in 1954 it grew to 1,857,000; in 1955 it was 2,100,000; in 1956 it jumped to 3,190,000; and in 1957 it grew to 3,750,000. Statistics found in Národní archiv, Fond Státní památková správa (hereafter NA, SPS), Carton 23, Folder: Hrady a zámky, A. r. 1956, č. 8842/58, "Informativní zpráva o návštěvnosti na hradech a zámcích," 30 June 1958. Novotný's attention to the consumer sector is discussed in Cathleen M. Giustino, "Socialist Industrial Design and the Czechoslovak Pavilion at EXPO '58: Artistic Autonomy, Party Control, and Cold War Common Ground," *Journal of Contemporary History* 47, no. 1 (2012): 185–212.

38. NA, SPS, Carton 18, Folder: Čedok a propagace. A brief introduction to laws relating to confiscations of churches and their property is in *Navrácené poklady: Restitutio in integrum,* ed. Marie Mžyková (Prague: Pragafilm, 1994), 14. Further information on the fate of church property in post-war Czechoslovakia is in Kristina Uhlíková, "Ochrana sakrálních památek v českých zemích v letech 1945-1958," *Zprávy památkové péče* 65, no. 5 (2005): 335–43.

39. Olga Kotková, ed., *Mistrovská díla z kolowratské obrazárny v Rychnově nad Kněžnou* (Prague: National Gallery, 2009).

40. Giustino, "Zdeněk Wirth a Ratibořice," 253–72; and Kaplanová (Uhlíková), "Babiččino údolí," 383–88.

41. Discussions useful for understanding methods of mediation in museums are in Steven D. Lavine, *Exhibiting Cultures: The Poetics and Politics of Museum Display* (Washington, DC: Smithsonian Books, 1991); Timothy W. Luke, *Museum Politics: Power Plays at the Exhibition* (Minneapolis: University of Minnesota, 2002); Igit Rogoff and Daniel J. Sherman, ed., *Museum Culture: Histories, Discourses, Spectacles* (London: Routledge, 1994). Works treating the politics of display in Czech history include Cathleen M. Giustino, "Rodin in Prague: Modern Art, Cultural Diplomacy, and National Display," *Slavic Review* 69, no. 3 (Fall 2010): 591–619; and Alena Janatková, *Modernisierung und Metropole: Architektur und Repräsentation auf den Landesausstellungen in Prag 1891 und Brünn 1928* (Stuttgart: Franz Steiner Verlag, 2008).

42. NA, SPS, Carton 508: Ratibořice, č. j. 112/55, "Letter from Oblastní správa státního kulturního majetku Ratibořice to Ministerstvo kultury: Státní památková správa," 24 October 1955.

43. NA, SPS, Carton 18, Folder, I/m: Čedok a propagace, č. j. 174/51, Dopis "Vážení soudruzi," 2 January 1951. A later complaint from the State Radio charged that the presentations of some chateaux guides were "cleverly oriented towards clericalism." See NA, SPS, Carton 23, Folder: Hrady a zámky, r. 1956, "Letter from Československý rozhlas," 21 August 1957.

44. NA, SPS, Carton 18, Folder, I/m: Čedok a propagace, Příl. k č. j. 7122/1951, "Předmluva průvodců."

45. Ibid.

46. For information on Karlštejn see Petr Bareš, et al., *Karlštejn a jeho význam v dějinách a kultuře* (Prague: Národní památkový ústav, 2010); and Jiří Fajt, ed., *Magister Theodoricus: Court Painter to Emperor Charles IV* (Prague: The National Gallery, 1998). See also the older, but important work of Dobroslava Menclová, *Karlštejn* (Prague: Státní nakladatelství krásné literatury a umění, 1965).

47. NA, SPS, Carton 239, Folder Karlštejn, r. 1951, "Letter of the Ministry of Internal Trade to the National Cultural Commission," 12 July 1951.

48. NA, SPS, Carton 18, Folder, I/m: Čedok a propogace, č. 12889/51, "Propagace stát. zámků."

49. Disinterest in ideology-filled museum signage was a recognized problem during the 1960s, if not earlier. When commenting on a plan for signage filled with quotations from Gottwald, Nejedlý, and Julius Fučík for a new exhibition in Ratibořice, Helena Johnová, director of the National Museum's Ethnographic Section, wrote, "it is ascertained from research with visitors that writings of this sort remain totally unconsidered …" Found in Národní památkový ústav - Pardubice, Carton Scenáře, I: Hrádek, Skalka, Ratibořice, Decka, Helena Johnová, "Přípomínky k scénáři instalaci Babičky v přízemí zámku Ratibořicích," 14 December 1966.

50. NA, SPS, Carton 28, Folder: Hrady a zámky: Průvodci r. 1953–1955, "Důvodová zpráva k návrhu na ustanovení lektorů a odborných průvodců na státních hradech a zámcích."

51. On the liberation of cultural expression during the time of the thaw, see Giustino, "Socialist Industrial Design;" and Adriana Primusová and Marie Klimešová, *Skupina Máj 57: Úsilí o uměleckou svobodu na přelomu 50. a 60. let* (Prague: ART D, 2007). On revisionism see Michal Kopeček, *Hledání ztraceného smyslu revoluce: Zrod a počátky marxistického revizionizmu ve střední Evropě, 1953-1960* (Prague: Argo, 2009).

52. NA, SPS, Carton 23, Folder: Hrady a zámky, r. 1956, č. 11882/57, "Svolání porad na KNV o úkolech vyplývajících z resoluce ÚV KSČ 'O některých současných otázkách ideologické práce strany,'" 20 July 1957.

53. NA, SPS, Carton 23, Folder: Hrady a zámky, r. 1956, "Věc: Rozpracování vládního usnesení č. 851 ze dne 16 srpna 1957 o rozvoji služeb poskytovaných obyvatelstvu za úplatu na úseku památkové péče," 10 September 1957.

54. "Hradní strašidla," *Literární noviny,* 9 November 1957. Another article complaining about the quality of the guides' presentations (and also about the quality of some estate-museum exhibitions) is "Na hradech a zámcích straší," *Zemědělské noviny,* 14 November 1957.

55. The study of jokes and power in Czech history is a serious topic. See Chad Bryant, "The Language of Resistance? Czech Jokes and Joke-telling under Nazi Occupation, 1943-1945," *Journal of Contemporary History* 41, no. 1 (January 2006): 133–51.

56. NA, SPS, Carton 23, Folder: Hrady a zámky, r. 1956, č. 8842/58, "Informativní zpráva o návštěvnosti na hradech a zámcích," 30 June 1958.

57. NA, SPS, Carton 770, Folder: Konference, 1958–1962, "Několik poznámek k současné problematice péče o památky v českých zemích (Příspěvek k referátu na sjezdu socialistické kultury v r. 1959)."

58. NA, SPS, Carton 769, see various documents in this carton.

59. See, for example, Zdeněk Reimann, "Demolice, devastace, destrukce," *Literární noviny* 15, no. 50 (10 December 1966): 16.

60. A history of normalization, told through television shows, is in Paulina Bren, *The Greengrocer and his TV: The Culture of Communism after the 1968 Prague Spring* (Ithaca: Cornell University Press, 2010).

61. A government critique of the ideological usefulness of the estate museums, which called for the creation of the entry-hall exhibitions, is the Ministry of Culture's publication, *Celonárodní aktiv památkové péče: Brno 29-30 května 1972* (Prague: Státní ústav památkové péče a ochrany přírody, 1972).

62. A discussion about best ways to design entry-hall exhibitions is in Jaroslav Petrů "Vstupní síně na památkových objektech," *Památky a příroda* 1 (1976): 605–8.

63. My appreciation of official discursive undertakings in the 1970s and their incongruence with everyday life and popular meaning comes from György Péteri, ed., *Imagining the West in Eastern Europe and the Soviet Union* (Pittsburgh: University of Pittsburgh Press, 2010), 10–11.

64. This information is from a discussion with Dr. Mája Havlová, a director and curator at the National Monument Office in České Budějovice, 21 October 2009. Dr. Havlová told me that photos of the vandalized entry-hall exhibit in Zvíkov had once existed, but they and other documents were most likely destroyed in the 2002 flood.

65. The important 1991 law that has guided many restitution decisions is "Zákon o mimosoudních rehabilitacích;" http://www.czechoffice.org/zakony/87_1991.htm (accessed 15 November 2012). An older, but still useful newspaper article with a map and lists of properties restituted and not restituted to noble families under this law is "Šlechta a její majetkové nároky na území České republiky: Restituce šlechtického majetku," *České noviny,* 26 January 2004; http://www.ceskenoviny.cz/index_view.php?id=46384 (accessed 15 November 2012).

66. Von Richthofen, *Bringing Culture to the Masses,* 11.

PART II

Cabins in the Woods

CHAPTER 3

Encountering Poland's "Wild West"

Tourism in the Bieszczady Mountains under Socialism

Patrice M. Dabrowski

Ranczo Texas (*Rancho Texas*) might seem an unlikely title for a movie produced and shown anywhere in the Soviet-dominated Eastern Bloc during the Cold War. Nevertheless, in 1959, an adventure film with this name debuted in the theaters of the Polish socialist state. Not surprisingly, given the closed borders separating the two spheres of superpower influence, *Ranczo Texas* did not feature the open plains of the wild American West. Rather, it was shot at home in the People's Republic of Poland. Importantly for this chapter, this first Polish "Western" was set in a corner of Poland that previously had been accorded little attention: the Bieszczady Mountains, located in the outer eastern section of the Carpathian Mountain range. With their wide expanses, sparse settlements, and harsh conditions, the Polish Bieszczady stood in for the prairies of the American West, and as a recognizable frontier from a century earlier. Although critics panned this Polish "Western," *Ranczo Texas* encouraged Poles to view the Bieszczady Mountains, previously terra incognita, as their own "Wild West."

The "Wild West" depiction of the southeastern corner of Poland dovetailed with the interests of the socialist authorities, including the leading Council of Ministers within the Politburo of the Central Committee of the Polish United Workers' Party (PZPR). They saw the Bieszczady Mountains, above all, as frontier land to be conquered and tamed. Yet, this was by no means the only vision of the region existing in post-war Poland. Pre-war tourists and hikers came to value the Bieszczady Mountains for their potential as a special kind of restorative escape. This is not to suggest that post-war Poland was ripe for dude-ranch tourism with opportunities to play at being cowboys, much as the protagonists of *Ranczo Texas* had done. Rather, those outdoor adventurers and travelers with pre-war notions of the value of the mountains viewed the lush terrain with its dense forests, canyon-carving streams, and grassy highland meadows as a revitalizing land par excellence—a place where the refreshing highland air and spectacular views could cure whatever ailed post-war Poles.

Just as there was more than one conception of the Bieszczady Mountains in post-war Poland, there were also many ideas of "tourism" (*turystyka*), which, it should be noted, is an ambiguous word in Polish. On one end of the spectrum, tourism reflected the historic use of the term to connote those traveling on foot—in this case, genuine hard-core hikers who carried all they needed on their backs and sought restoration through escape from all signs of civilization.[1] Alternatively, many Poles equated tourism with the easy comforts of full room and board for the duration of a cherished break from the socialist quotidian. Falling between these two extremes was socialist tourism. It came in varied packages—some more leisurely, some more strenuous—but it always incorporated at least a modicum of socialist content. Whereas this last type of tourism was meant to strengthen the attachment of the Polish working classes to the socialist state, the very nature of tourism in People's Poland often highlighted the regime's shortcomings, not its accomplishments. Often tourists would find themselves in what might be thought of as a touristic "Wild West," a situation where tourist "goods" were in short supply and thus were fought over, sometimes literally.

This chapter will demonstrate the transformation of tourism in post-war Poland, both as a concept and an experience, during the decades after 1945. Prior to World War II, tourism was largely an elitist and strenuous endeavor, focused on upper-class enthusiasts attaining the heights of Poland's mountainous terrains—in particular, the peaks of the segments of the Polish Carpathians known as the Tatras and Eastern Carpathians. After 1945 the forces of socialism and the westward shift of Poland's borders turned the attention of many Poles toward the Bieszczady Mountains, the country's new "Wild East."[2] During the socialist period, another shift took place from socialist tourism in the 1950s and the early 1960s to a broader, less ideological mass tourism in the later 1960s and 1970s. This chapter reveals, however, that throughout this progression—and especially during the 1970s—due to a lack of sufficient and appropriate accommodations and consumer goods that vacationers desired, the Bieszczady Mountains more closely resembled a "Wild West" than a successfully integrated socialist East.

The Making of Poland's "Wild West"

The designation "Wild West" connotes many things: open space, pioneer settlements, and a battle with nature waged by rugged individuals, as well as a state of lawlessness or general disorder, where inhabitants meted out their own justice. All of these characteristics were true of the Carpathian Mountain wilderness that was the Bieszczady in the 1950s. In recent memory, the region had presented many challenges to Polish rule, which became part of the myth of the origins of People's Poland. As such, it is important to get a sense of how Poland's "Wild West" was made before considering the way Poles came to experience it.

Before World War II, the Bieszczady Mountains were densely inhabited, primarily by ethnic Poles. Two other ethnic and religious groups had settled in the region: East Slavs and Jews. Jews, mostly traders, shopkeepers, and artisans, tended to live in the towns and larger settlements. Agricultural and pastoral folk, the region's East Slavs were comprised of two highland "tribes," Lemkos and Boikos. Ukrainians claimed these highland peoples as part of their nation, although in the interwar period Poles likewise claimed them as "Polish tribes"—Polishness understood not in ethnic terms but rather in broader, civic terms.[3]

This conflict came to a head during World War II and its immediate aftermath, when both nations fought to gain control over territories that had been part of the southeastern portion of interwar Poland.[4] Units of the Ukrainian Insurgent Army (UPA) gained a foothold in the mountainous region, which, as of 1944, was being emptied of its East Slavic population via population transfers and resettlement; the UPA burned down abandoned villages and terrorized villagers as they sought to stake a claim on these lands for the Ukrainian nation. The Polish deputy minister of defense, General Karol Świerczewski, traveled to the mountains to assess the situation, only to be gunned down by the UPA in 1947.[5] The death of Świerczewski served as a rallying point for the Polish authorities, who then enacted previously formulated plans to remove the rest of the East Slav population from the southeastern territories under the assumption that some of them had sympathized with and lent support to the UPA. Thus, those who had not already been "repatriated" to the Ukrainian Soviet Socialist Republic, in the population exchanges of 1944 and beyond, were dispersed in the west and north of Poland in the course of Operation Vistula (Akcja Wisła), initiated in 1947.[6]

Much of the territory in the Bieszczady Mountain region had already been depopulated by then, as a result of the Holocaust and battles fought during World War II and its aftermath. Soldiers had burned villages, and inhabitants had dispersed, leaving behind the occasional homestead or church, overgrown cemetery, orchard gone wild, half-buried tool, or other remnant of past life. The region was a veritable no-man's-land for the better part of a decade, as Polish socialist authorities routed out the last underground forces from their highland lairs and exerted a modicum of control over the mountains.

A Palimpsest Inscribed Anew

The area reverted to a wilderness. Waist-high nettles and hardy aspen grew unimpeded, while endless mud covered whatever paths remained. To be sure, this wilderness was one sprinkled with relics of former human settlements. One of the first visitors to the region after it was emptied of its former inhabitants wrote movingly of an overgrown well with a bucket left as if only a moment earlier, and of the extensive alpine meadows and forests, canyons, and ravines as a "frighteningly wild paradise." While this "land of elemental and undisciplined nature" may have been cruel and harsh for the Polish settlers whom the communists subsequently tried to lure to the region, it was, in the words of pre- and post-war tourism activist Władysław Krygowski, "beautiful and wonderful for the eye of the tourist."[7]

However, unlike the Tatra Mountain region to the west, with its well-developed network of trails and longer history of mountain climbing, the Bieszczady Mountains were practically unmarked, unknown. Their densely covered and nearly inaccessible landscape nonetheless appealed to Poles who before the war hiked in what was then Poland's highland wilderness: the Eastern Carpathians, interwar Poland's southeastern corner, which had been incorporated into the Ukrainian Soviet Socialist Republic. As Jacek Kolbuszewski writes, "Bieszczady rivers and streams became a symbolic reminder of the murmur of the Prut and Czeremosz" rivers of the Eastern Carpathians; the *połoniny,* or grassy highland pastures, of the Bieszczady likewise reminded Poles of the beloved region that was now lost to them.[8] Given this loss of precious mountain terrain, the time appeared ripe for the terra incognita of the Bieszczady Mountains to come into its own as a tourist destination within the Polish People's Republic, replacing the Eastern Carpathians as the country's premier highland wilderness.

Yet the fate of the newly wild region in the young socialist state was far from certain. Would it serve the purposes of highland tourism, offering fresh air, refreshing waters, lush forests, and beautiful vistas to vacationers? Or would the Bieszczady become an increasingly tamed "Wild West" in accordance with the socialist injunction to develop large-scale agribusiness and industry throughout the realm, to turn wilderness into productive land? Was it possible to achieve a "happy medium" in socialist Poland?

Hatchet-in-Hand Hikers

The priorities of the new socialist state were to rebuild after the devastation of the war and, even more importantly, to construct socialism along the way.

The authorities sought to alter the physical space in keeping with their vision of what a socialist state would be: progressive, industrial, and collectively owned. At the same time, they hoped to change the human material at hand as well, to transform peasants into workers. The challenge represented by the Bieszczady Mountains was twofold: to reincorporate into the state a region that had been off-limits as a result of the continued fighting, and to settle it with new socialist men and women. Interestingly, the former (men) were much easier to come by than the latter, resulting in quite striking gender disparities—again demonstrating similarities with the Wild West of yore.[9] Early on, practically the only people to be found in the region, barring some foresters, were male border guards and leather-jacket-clad security police.

The isolation and lack of inhabitants did not stop some intrepid tourists from gaining access to Poland's new wilderness.[10] Although this border zone was not truly open until 1954, in 1952 and 1953 two experienced hikers led teams from the newly formed Polish Society of Tourism and Local Studies (PTTK). This state-controlled organization replaced the Polish Tatra Society (PTT) and the Polish Local Studies Society (PTK), both of which were tourist organizations with a long history.[11] Toting hatchets and cans of paint, the groups hacked their way through the overgrowth to clear and mark a trail across the Bieszczady.[12] It took them two seasons to open a route from the spa town of Krynica in the west, in the neighboring region of the Low Beskid, to the Bieszczady mountain peak of Halicz in the east, thus preparing the region for tourism.

The experience of the wild mountains inspired these hatchet-in-hand hikers to such an extent that they encouraged others to come and master the challenges that the untamed region presented.[13] The leader of one of the trailblazing groups and author of an early (1958) guidebook to the Bieszczady, Władysław Krygowski, wrote of "the paths and roads not yet trodden, the battle with a space that summons and attracts, that allures and releases the need to battle with difficulty and with highland surprises."[14] Let tourists come to the Bieszczady, he declared: "A journey amazingly rich in new and instructive impressions and experiences" awaited them there.[15] The Bieszczady were clearly the Polish destination for the rugged adventurer.

The lush, barely penetrable terrain of the Bieszczady acted like a magnet upon a new generation, one that had much to gain from interacting with pure untrammeled nature, even of the secondary kind. Their Poland was already on its way to becoming more heavily urban and industrialized; their future, was likely to be dictated by the regimentation of the factory, not the rhythms of village life. University students from Warsaw proved to be particularly enamored with the Bieszczady; they approached the region in an organized way, forming various student hiking clubs in the mid-1950s. "The

Great Brotherhood" and "Club of the Left Pant Leg" ultimately led to the establishment, in 1957, of a club of hiking tour guides.[16] This organization came to be called the Student Club of Beskid Guides, Beskid being another name applied to the Carpathians.

These students, too, were originally tourists bearing axes, tourists that the state authorities came to classify under the rubric of "qualified tourism" (*turystyka kwalifikowana*). In other words, they were fit, trained, and experienced, able to find their way with only a map and compass on unmarked trails, and prepared to carry in all or most of the food they needed as well as their own accommodations in the form of tents and tarps.[17] Thus, the initial push for tourism in the Bieszczady came from the segments of society that had traditionally provided highland tourists before the war: school and university students in particular, not the working classes. Furthermore, this early tourism in Poland's new highland wilderness tended to foster individualism—not exactly what the Stalinist regime viewed as the proper type of leisure for the new socialist man.

Demarcating Socialist Space

A more welcome type of tourism for People's Poland was what might be termed "mass tourism" with a socialist face. The state strove to put its own stamp on the Bieszczady mountain region and the way that its citizens perceived it. For example, the provincial authorities in Rzeszów requested that the presidia of the national councils take care of places that recalled "the martyrdom and heroic battle of the Polish people for national and social liberation."[18] This approach to the history of the region suggests an important way in which the socialist state used the Bieszczady mountain region to buttress and justify the role that the Polish United Workers' Party played in post-war Poland.

The socialist authorities preferred qualified tourism, which had more social and educative value than "unqualified tourism" (*turystyka niekwalifikowana*), or tourism for the masses. The former was seen as raising the intellectual and cultural level of society while breaking down social barriers and increasing patriotism. The Subcommittee on Tourism concluded: "In all its disciplines, qualified tourism demands solidarity, fortitude and endurance ... becoming an ideal method for the physical and moral education of youth. Camping, marches and *rajdy* ... are perfect forms of the indirect preparation of youth for the defense of the country."[19]

It should come as no surprise, then, that the state availed itself of such useful opportunities to fortify its young people physically, morally, and ideologically while providing them with a taste of the outdoors. With these aims in mind, socialist associations organized group tourist excursions called *rajdy*— the Polish term related to the English homonym "ride," although *rajdy* were hiking excursions. The Warsaw student guides' club, branches of the PTTK, and even labor unions sponsored excursions that could have as many as a thousand or more participants.[20] Such *rajdy* could be considered an ideologically-inflected subset of qualified tourism that not only influenced the tourists' health and self-discipline, but also taught them more about the region in which they were hiking and/or about the event being commemorated.[21]

An early example of such *rajdy* in the Bieszczady was the Friendship *Rajd*. Organized by the PTTK in Rzeszów, the Friendship *Rajd* took place for the first time in 1954, on the tenth anniversary of the "independence of People's Poland."[22] The slogan for that week-long excursion was "We are deepening Friendship with the nations of the USSR."[23] Teams comprised of three to six persons aged eighteen or above assembled tents, sleeping bags, backpacks, and food for a minimum of three days, thus making it a serious hiking trip. The PTTK instructed each team to pack a hatchet or axe, as hikers would have to cut their way through various parts of the terrain. They would also need personal documents, as they were to travel in the border zone.

That first year, the Friendship *Rajd* boasted a total of 345 participants, including 97 women, 76 blue-collar workers, and 43 members of the communist-run Union of Polish Youth. A full 160 participants were in the mountains for the first time.[24] Participants took two routes, one leading from Komańcza, the other from Ustianowa, with both groups ending up in Lutowiska. From this location, guides shuttled all participants to Ustrzyki Dolne for the closing festivities. The *rajd* consisted of both strenuous hiking and ideological activities. During the trip, participants sang Polish and Soviet songs around the campfires. The two routes intersected in Wetlina, where both groups took part in conversations entitled "my experiences with Soviet people." Additionally, in Wetlina, a film crew met up with the *rajd* and filmed it through the group's closing festivities.[25]

Organizers planned suitable events to demonstrate Polish-Soviet friendship. For example, on the 1,320 meter-high peak of Halicz, delegates of the Rzeszów province erected "friendship banners," while all teams helped erect a mound out of rocks. Such mounds are a traditional Polish means of commemorating significant individuals or events. They even mounted busts of Lenin and Stalin atop the peak.[26] At the concluding festivities in Ustrzyki Dolne, leaders called upon the participants to "manifest their common feelings for the brotherly nations [of the USSR]" at the foot of the Stalin monument, an inheritance from the brief period when Ustrzyki Dolne, renamed Shevchenkovo, had been part of the USSR.[27]

The Friendship *Rajd* became an annual event. Within a few years, advertisements for the *rajd*, amazingly enough, focused on its vacation aspects:

> Beautiful, wild, attractive routes. Departures from Ustrzyki Dolne, Ustianowa, and Komańcza. Three days of rest in Ustrzyki Górne. Plan [your] vacation for September.[28]

Nonetheless, it was still very much an ideologically-imbued escape—what Dariusz Jarosz would consider as one of the "ritualized political demonstrations" characteristic of much of Polish tourism in the post-war period.[29] For example, the 1959 *rajd* commemorated the fifteenth anniversary of People's Poland and led the tourists around the site where General Walter-Świerczewski perished, a site that witnessed bloody battles with Ukrainian nationalists.[30]

This Friendship *Rajd* was far from the only tourist event that commemorated General Karol ("Walter") Świerczewski. He proved to be an ideal martyr to the communist internationalist cause, and socialist Poland's communist martyr par excellence. The biography of this son of the working class reflected both the internationalist and communist qualities that the new Polish regime sought to propagate. A communist already in the interwar period, Świerczewski fought in the Spanish Civil War on the side of the communists under the pseudonym "Walter," and was immortalized in Hemingway's *For Whom the Bell Tolls*. He subsequently served in both the Soviet and Polish armies and became deputy minister of defense in the new Polish socialist regime.

As noted earlier, Świerczewski died in the Bieszczady Mountains, at Jabłonki, on 28 March 1947. He had been felled by bullets fired by members of the UPA, fighters who post-war Polish lore termed alternately "bandits," degrading what some perceived to be a real war, and "fascists," suggesting that the Nazis were behind the UPA attacks even at this point.[31] Poles of a certain age may remember him, according to the descriptions of children's writer Janina Broniewska, as "a man who did not bow before bullets." Jan Gerhard also depicted him as the internationalist "symbol of revolutionary battle for freedom in our time."[32]

The Bieszczady village of Jabłonki was henceforth connected with the person of Świerczewski. Although some of his supporters erected an obelisk in the village the year he died, socialist authorities replaced it with a more permanent monument, which they unveiled with much fanfare on 15 July 1962 (see Figure 3.1). A speaker at the dedication ceremony told the fifteen hundred persons present, "We have gathered here at the place of the heroic death of a great patriot, the illustrious son of the Polish working class." As

Figure 3.1. A visit to the Świerczewski Monument in Jabłonki during an orienteering competition in the region of Durna, 1970s. From the collection of the editorial board of *Wierchy.*

a soldier, he gave his life "in the battle with the dark forces of fascism—in the name of the great question of the socialist future of our Fatherland."[33] Although not exactly a vacation escape of the restful sort, this highland site figured prominently in organized Polish mass tourism in the Bieszczady, with busloads of tourists from across the state brought to commemorate the death of Świerczewski and the triumph of People's Poland over fascism.[34]

These fascist-fighting, socialism-building characteristics were an important component of the image of the Bieszczady that the regime sought to propagate. Jabłonki functioned as the ideological key, and even as the proper socialist gateway, to the Bieszczady. That is why the 1960s also saw the blazing of a "freedom" trail named after Świerczewski.[35] Already foreseen in the 1959 project for the development of the Bieszczady was a tourist house in Jabłonki to be named after him. The memorial site would serve the needs of qualified tourism, motorized tourism, and ideologically imbued pilgrimages. Yet, delayed like so many other tourist projects, the regime did not construct the museum/mausoleum with housing for tourists until the 1980s, and by this time many pro-Solidarity Poles thought it utterly irrelevant.[36] If tourism was to be an important aspect of a "socialist upbringing," the touristic experience of the Bieszczady was limited in its effectiveness.[37]

Tourism for the Masses

The ultimate fate of Bieszczady tourism could not be foreseen in the early years of People's Poland. Once the socialist state turned its attention to tourism more broadly, it had another kind of tourism in mind. Tourism should be for the masses, not simply for the elites, which the regime declared had been the only kind of tourism in Poland before the war.[38] With his finger on the pulse of the Stalinist regime, and striving to keep the tourist yearbook *Wierchy* [Peaks] in line with Stalinist currents in Poland, Władysław Krygowski wrote as early as 1949 of "mountains for everyone" in People's Poland.[39] The mountains were to regenerate the strength of working-class comrades, of the new socialist man.

Nonetheless, a member of the propaganda office of the Central Committee of the Polish United Workers' Party related a story on the new mass tourism that suggests some of the pitfalls the regime faced.[40] Zbigniew Kulczycki admitted that qualified tourism was the "most advantageous, most valuable," for health, body, and mind.[41] Yet there were different ways of providing such opportunities to the masses, some better than others. Kulczycki himself witnessed an unforgettable scene during a trip to the Bieszczady in the early 1960s. A tour bus from the Silesian city of Katowice in the west of Poland, arrived in Ustrzyki Górne, one of the most remote villages of the region and a jumping-off point for serious hiking. The driver deposited his cargo and drove off. The tour guide then gathered the tourists together and told them that they were going to hike to the alpine meadow known as the Caryńska Połonina and the village of Berehy Górne; the bus would meet them upon their return. Kulczycki was horrified. The hike required a full four hours. The tourists had no idea what they had gotten themselves into. Women were in high heels and all wore regular street clothes. It started to rain during their hike, so they were soaking wet for the all-night ride home. This was, exclaimed Kulczycki, "qualified tourism in unqualified execution."[42]

The Orbis tourist bureau, the bus driver, and tour guide had the right idea: to give workers a taste of the mountains, to let these Silesians from the most polluted corner of Poland breathe the fresh highland air.[43] Nevertheless, this particular experience was bound to discourage them from ever coming back to the Bieszczady. As this anecdote indicates, qualified mass tourism may have been an oxymoron in the late 1950s and early 1960s, a time when workers had not yet had any exposure to the culture of hiking or mountain tourism. Rather, the toiling masses profited more immediately from unqualified tourism, given that few members of the working class had ever experienced mountains or other, less trying, vacation sites.

Projections for the future of the Bieszczady were only beginning to take shape at this time. Socialist authorities first devised a state plan for the development of the Bieszczady in 1959, half a decade after the border zone had been opened.[44] Still, tourism was hardly a priority in the minds of the country's socialist planners. Dancing around in their heads were visions of modern technological progress in the highlands: gigantic lumber mills, powerful dams producing hydroelectric power, and large state farms.[45] These would transform the Bieszczady and southeastern Poland from the most backwards region of the state into something more in keeping with the image the authorities sought to project. Perhaps it should come as no surprise, then, that the state did not even begin to fund the tourism investments planned in 1959 during the five-year period in which they were to be completed.[46]

Even the two biggest investment projects in the region—projects that would catapult tourism in the Bieszczady to unheard of and unimagined heights—were designed not with tourism in mind, but rather for economic development. These developments included the construction of the dams and hydroelectric power plants at Myczkowce (completed in 1962) and Solina (120 megawatts strong, completed in 1968), as well as two highway loops that cut through the highland region (dating from 1962 and 1969).[47] State engineers designed the first, and larger, highway loop to facilitate access to Bieszczady forests for the deficit-running lumber industry; but they clearly provided a road that would make a previously inaccessible region easier to reach, especially for persons who were not inclined to march for several days on foot from the nearest railway station.[48] Now, any tourist could penetrate the heart of the region in only a day's hike from the highway. The dams at Myczkowce and Solina[49] produced surprisingly picturesque reservoirs on the stunningly beautiful San River. These were places where the Polish masses could swim, or sail, or simply enjoy a drink on the shore on a summer's day— that is, once authorities finally granted public access to the reservoirs.[50]

The people's push for highland tourism and the authorities' grudging acceptance of tourism as a money-making venture led to the transformation of the former housing for construction workers near the dams into vacation hotels, some of which became the property of specific Polish factories, industries, or unions. This emphasis on accommodation reflected the needs of a relatively new phenomenon in the socialist East: that of *wczasy pracownicze*, or organized, company-sponsored vacations away from home for workers.[51] These state-sanctioned holidays enabled true mass tourism. No familiarity with hiking, its etiquette, or physical conditioning was required.[52] If a factory or other type of business owned or had access to the vacation site, vacationers did not have to do any planning. These resorts provided both room and board, giving female guests the option to sit around and drink all day or simply work on their suntans and breathe in fresh air.

Or at least air that was relatively fresh, for tourism in the Bieszczady has also been called "exhaust fumes- and alcohol-fueled tourism."[53] This moniker reflects two major pillars of mass tourism: the ubiquity of alcohol consumption by the vacationing workers, and the more modern rise of the automobile in Poland. That Polish workers drank was a truism. Like their peasant ancestors before them, the new Polish working class drank for relaxation—perhaps the only way they knew how to unwind—and this tradition was transported to vacation venues. At the same time, these infrastructural developments in the Bieszczady took place just as Poland started to motorize in the 1960s. Soon the Fiat 126, the car for the masses, would traverse the roads of the Bieszczady, beginning in the early 1970s.[54]

Once Poles had automobiles, they were free to engage in yet another typical activity for holidays: camping. The highways brought tourists all the way into the mountains, allowing them to camp at will. However, a dearth of organized campsites resulted in a proliferation of "wild" camps, with deleterious results for the highland ecology; Poles parked, camped, and hiked wherever they fancied (see Figure 3.2).[55] This was, furthermore, an example of "open"

Figure 3.2. A group of young tourists fording a Bieszczady stream (already occupied by several cars) during a hiking trip, 1963. Photo by Zbigniew Żochowski. From the collection of the editorial board of *Wierchy*.

or individual tourism, something that the authorities had a difficult time both anticipating and satisfying.

The Command Economy and the Tourist

Open or individual tourism developed because of the way the tourist industry functioned in People's Poland in the 1960s and first half of the 1970s, which was the heyday of Bieszczady tourism.[56] Demand for highland holidays was infinitely greater than the supply of hotel rooms, campsites, and provisions. The Bieszczady appealed to over a million vacationers annually, a result of the successful marketing of mass tourism in the country.[57] Yet the state-run infrastructure lagged far behind in caring for the needs of group and individual tourists who somehow expected to find a place to sleep as well as a place to get a hot meal. A great divide existed between the burgeoning demand for tourism and the inadequate tourist infrastructure in People's Poland.

Much of this can be blamed on the nature of the command economy and the regime's priorities. Following the Soviet model, state planners drew up detailed plans and allocated resources for an entire five-year period in advance.[58] The resultant Five-Year Plan was to countenance every aspect of economic life. Creating it was a daunting task: in the realm of tourism alone, the work of around twenty central agencies and offices, local national councils, cooperatives, trade unions, and social organizations had to be coordinated.[59] Whereas such advance planning may have helped the cash-strapped socialist state prioritize and coordinate big investments in industry or infrastructure (such as the construction of the Bieszczady region's hydroelectric dams), the rigidity of the command economy rendered it unresponsive to change. Furthermore, those who sought to encourage tourism failed to anticipate that a surge in interest in highland vacations would require a reallocation of resources if needs were to be met. In a way, tourists in the Polish Bieszczady found themselves to be somewhat like the pioneers of old, struggling to secure a place to spend the night or procure provisions.

Relative to its size and population density, the Bieszczady Mountain region was a disproportionally popular tourist getaway destination, and one that was disproportionally disadvantaged, insofar as its remoteness, lack of infrastructure, and tiny local population were concerned. Furthermore, the local settlers had a love-hate relationship with the tourists who consumed their resources. The region's workers and farmers were often suspicious of outsiders or simply indifferent to the seasonal needs of tourists. Such attitudes persisted even in cases where the local authorities hosted tourists, when one would expect all resources to be mobilized, such as during the Friendship *Rajd* that included comrades from the USSR.

Indeed, organizational problems plagued the 1954 *rajd* described earlier. In Komańcza, one of the few designated places where hikers acquired supplies, *rajd* leaders ran out of bread, the basic staple of hikers. And, while at the train station in Zagórz, the buffet did have 406 portions of hunters' stew consisting mostly of cabbage, vodka was also available for 3.50 zl. Locals were drinking, some making a ruckus until two o'clock in the morning. Organizers then prohibited participants in the *rajd* from patronizing the buffet to prevent further embarrassing incidents. A similar situation developed at the train station in Ustianowa, from which the second group of hikers was to depart. The fighting that ensued was reminiscent of the saloon brawls of the Wild West.[60]

The Friendship *rajd* encountered these problems despite its status as a government-sponsored event of international significance.[61] Most Bieszczady tourists, especially individual tourists, fared much worse in terms of accommodations and provisions. The Bieszczady mountain region had great potential that the tourist infrastructure hardly reflected. In Ustrzyki Dolne, a potential tourist center for the entire country, the only existing tourist lodge was actually a "collapsing barrack."[62] The same conditions held true for other destinations; in 1962, for example, socialist authorities drew up plans to adapt and modernize former barracks for tourist lodges in Sanok, Ustrzyki Górne, Wetlina, and Folusz.[63] It should come as no surprise, then, that the authorities saw the construction of campgrounds as their salvation; there simply was no way for People's Poland to catch up, let alone keep up, with the demand for more permanent tourist accommodations that could be used during the winter season as well. The state could erect fairly inexpensive campgrounds, including some with tiny two- and four-person camping huts, although even then the terrain had to be leveled, sanitary facilities constructed, and a clean water supply guaranteed.

Even basic campgrounds required what seemed to be nearly insurmountable efforts on the part of the socialist state. Take, for example, the construction of a camping center in Myczkowce to the tune of 470,000 zl., which provincial authorities approved in 1961. The Bieszczady Province Tourist Movement Service Enterprise oversaw this project that was due for completion by the end of May 1961.[64] As the sole organization responsible for the execution of such projects in the Rzeszów province, this brand new enterprise encountered many difficulties along the way. For example, the organization was to equip the campground in Myczkowce with twenty wooden two-person "Winnie the Pooh" camping huts.[65] Yet it could not complete this task in time for the beginning of the tourist season, as the huts that were built literally stank. After covering the smelly cabins with plaster and paint, the organization opened the site for use only as of 31 August, well into the tourist season.[66] Thus, authorities criticized the organization for not fulfilling the plan and achieving the anticipated profit.[67] Yet, as one "comrade" noted, "activity in the direction is something new for us. Which is why so far we are experimenting."[68]

The provincial authorities may have been experimenting, but the crowds who traveled to the Bieszczady to vacation suffered in the meantime. The regime seemed to have a chronic inability to provide cold beverages, whether soda, mineral water, or beer, in the summer, despite a nearby beer bottling plant in Komańcza.[69] There appeared to be problems with getting the bottled drinks during the summer months. Sometimes the plant achieved its production quotas, but only after the tourists had gone home. Other issues concerned the various stores and kiosks' hours of operation where such purchases might be made, a problem that the districts eventually resolved.[70] Of course, that meant that store employees had to work what they perceived to be inconvenient hours.

There were difficulties in the gastronomical industry as well. The prospect of consuming a hot meal while on vacation, especially for weekend getaways, was not very good for individual tourists, whose arrival in a given locale could not be predicted with certainty and who often encountered establishments crowded with work groups holding reservations. Even tour groups found it hard to find dining facilities in a region with next to no restaurants, a reason why the authorities sought time and again to mobilize private dining facilities. They viewed private restaurants as the salvation of the underequipped highland region during the tourist season.[71]

In People's Poland, however, there were serious problems with private sector involvement, difficulties that transcended the regime's desire for more large-scale, collectivized enterprises. There were few people living in what had been, in interwar Poland, an overpopulated region, and the new regime found it impossible to raise the numbers of settlers, despite certain financial incentives. This was especially true in terms of the reclamation of the land for farming. One might expect that settlers would be the ones to provide meals privately in season. But few cared to make that kind of investment, doubtless because there were no tax incentives for them to do so. Indeed, local authorities sought to gain tax revenues from services, such as the renting of rooms in private homes. Thus, despite the tourist industry's desire for more private initiative, it was not forthcoming. For instance, in 1963 only two persons in the Bieszczady region answered an advertisement in the local newspaper *Nowiny Rzeszowskie,* expressing interest in providing meals to tourists.[72]

Therefore, as far as meals were concerned, the tourist industry essentially left travelers to their own devices. Many tried to buy foodstuffs in the occasional kiosks or grocery store. Yet, even when goods were within reach, sometimes the locals simply refused to sell them to outsiders.[73] Such an encounter could lead to fist fights as the frustrated tourists, hot and hungry, grappled with the obstinate salesclerk in their quest for loaves of bread or bottles of lemon-flavored soda.

And woe to any tourist whose automobile or tour bus, for that matter, should have mechanical problems, or who simply needed a tank of gasoline. In the whole Rzeszów province gas stations were few and far between, and there was a dearth of automobile repair facilities.[74] Even those gas stations often lacked what they were supposed to sell.[75] While this situation hardly stemmed the flow of tourists, it meant that many did not leave as happy campers.

Negative experiences clearly had implications that far transcended the realm of tourism. One way to reinforce People's Poland's continued existence within the Eastern Bloc was to suggest that this new highland getaway arose thanks to the new socialist state, which had, after all, built the Solina and Myczkowce dams and the highway. Was it not true that, in the 1970s under the leadership of Party Secretary Edward Gierek, according to the slogan of that time, "Poland was to grow in strength and [its] people live in prosperity"?[76] Polish expectations were being ratcheted up, and Poles increasingly believed they were entitled to a better life in all its dimensions, including the realm of tourism. Yet what was relaxing about having to scramble for under-supplied goods while on vacation? In the grand scheme of things, this was, of course, a little inconvenience; but such "microscopic fissures" in the socialist system led, with time, to more serious cracking.[77]

Instead of winning over Poles to socialism, the perils and pitfalls of Bieszczady tourism broadcast the inefficiencies and the ineptitude of the Soviet-style command economy, with its fetish for industrial mega-projects and its inability to plan adequately for the forms of tourism that the authorities themselves encouraged. Recent historiography on tourism emphasizes the fact that the Polish regime never threw its weight fully behind domestic tourism. Tourism officials in Warsaw and elsewhere were always more interested in attracting hard-currency guests from abroad than in meeting the needs of their own population.[78]

Ultimately, the socialist regime appeared powerless to resolve these contradictions so characteristic of the economics of shortage.[79] Only once the state allowed Poles to travel abroad in the 1970s did this function as something of a safety valve, satisfying pent-up desire and drawing away some of the tourists who would have otherwise vacationed in the Bieszczady. However, foreign travel provided Polish citizens with further grounds for comparison, which found the socialist state and the Polish tourist infrastructure wanting yet again.[80]

Conclusion

As we have seen, the word *turystyka* carries many different connotations in the context of socialist Poland—at least as many as reflected in the desires of state authorities and various groups of post-war Poles regarding the potential recreational use of the Bieszczady mountain region. Groups and individuals all found the newly opened space attractive, if for different reasons, and envisioned its use in a variety of ways.

Under socialism, tourism took a back seat to regional economic development. Tourism was often more of an afterthought than an aim, although with time those responsible for tourism in the Polish People's Republic did strive, however futilely, to catch up with the spirit of the times. As the long-time head of the Main Committee for Physical Culture and Tourism observed, the high standard of living and increasing industrialization that characterized the second half of the twentieth century resulted in the rise of tourism; it now had become a "need of the masses," resulting in people "unconsciously desir[ing] to get away from the urban rhythm."[81] This perceived need was particularly visible in the1960s and early 1970s, the heyday of tourism in the Bieszczady. Yet the Poles' push and desire to vacation in the new, and newly discovered, wilderness of the Bieszczady highlighted the inability of the command economy to cope with mass-organized and surging private unorganized tourism, much of it motorized, in this lightly settled region. While this did not stop Poles from setting off for the mountains on holiday, such escapes—to be fully relaxing—required a certain resourcefulness or preparedness on the part of the vacationer, who had to anticipate the shortages of bread or beverages that were all too typical of the "real lived socialism" of the period and pack accordingly. A socialist escape, perhaps—but not an escape from socialism...

Poles increasingly did wish to escape from their gray socialist apartment blocks and polluted cities into a completely different, and more restful, realm. The authorities' promotion of mass tourism with a decidedly socialist content and purposefulness, creating, as Diane Koenker argues in her study of the Soviet Union, a "proletarian tourism,"[82] was not the form of tourism that most resonated with the broader Polish public. The vast majority of post-war Poles, largely unacquainted with the custom of vacations, preferred more leisurely pursuits—a decidedly unproductive tourism. Indeed, it was not the new monuments in concrete, the Freedom *Rajdy,* or commemorations of Świerczewski that excited vacationing Poles in the early post-war period. Rather, they availed themselves of what made the Bieszczady Mountains unique, what made hiking in the mountains so thrilling, the natural beauty of the wild highlands. By "roughing it" or relaxing, vacationing Poles sought to escape the socialist quotidian and bask in highland freedom.

In the end, the shortages and problems tourists encountered while vacationing in the Bieszczady were but a small sign of the growing divide that separated "real lived socialism," as experienced in the Polish People's Republic, from the expectations of the Polish population, which in the 1970s embraced the idea of increasing prosperity promised by Edward Gierek. Gierek's attempts at providing for ill-conceived hard-currency investments in heavy industry, while simultaneously endeavoring to raise the Polish standard of living, took the Polish economy to the brink—at which point Polish dissatisfaction went public. The inability to provide goods, and especially meat, was the regime's Achilles heel; it was the reason why Polish workers rose periodically in protest, beginning in 1956 and culminating in 1980 with the establishment of the Solidarity movement. Before the decade was out, Solidarity protest helped bring about the collapse of communism in the region.[83]

As the head of the country's tourism office admitted in 1963, the Polish People's Republic was thirty years behind the West.[84] What he did not admit was that it was also on a track that would not allow it to catch up, however valiantly it tried. Indeed, when miraculously one could ride horses in the Bieszczady as part of a burgeoning agro-tourism some thirty years later, the watershed transformation of 1989 was responsible, and not a socialist five-year plan.

Notes

Research for this chapter was supported in part by a fellowship from IREX (International Research & Exchanges Board), with funds provided by the United States Department of State through the Title VIII Program. Neither of these organizations is responsible for the views expressed herein. This volume's editors and authors have been unstinting with their advice and assistance, but earlier versions of this chapter profited from comments made by those in attendance at the Polish Studies Conference, University of Michigan, 16–18 September 2010, as well as at a public lecture at the University of Massachusetts Amherst on 1 December 2009. The illustrations come courtesy of Wiesław A. Wójcik, editor of the Polish Alpine journal *Wierchy* (Peaks), whose generous support and assistance have been invaluable.

1. This is akin to the definition of the tourist being "only that traveler who embarked on a purposeful journey, a circuit (tour) using one's own physical locomotion." Anne E. Gorsuch and Diane P. Koenker, "Introduction," *Turizm: The Russian and East European Tourist under Capitalism and Socialism* (Ithaca: Cornell University Press, 2006), 2–3.

2. Previously the Eastern Carpathians, part of the enlarged Ukrainian Soviet Socialist Republic after World War II, served as the wild highland borderlands of the Polish state. With the shifting of Poland's eastern border, the Poles no longer had access to those mountains; thus their attention shifted to the Polish state's new southeast corner, the Bieszczady mountains, on Poland's border with Slovakia and Ukraine.

3. This is something that I discuss in "'Discovering' the Carpathians: Episodes in Imagining and Reshaping Alpine Borderland Regions," a book manuscript. For more on the use and/or applicability of the terms "ethnic" and "civic" to describe Polish nationalism at various times in history, see the works of Andrzej Walicki, especially *The Enlightenment and the Birth of Mod-*

ern Nationhood: Polish Political Thought from Noble Republicanism to Tadeusz Kościuszko, trans. Emma Harris (Notre Dame, IN: University of Notre Dame Press, 1989).

4. The multiethnic and contested nature of the borderlands was typical of Eastern Europe. For their relation to the development of tourism, see the chapters by Alexander Vari and Aldis Purs, "From Friends of Nature to Tourist-Soldiers: Nation Building and Tourism in Hungary, 1873-1914" and "'One Breath for Every Two Strides': The State's Attempt to Construct Tourism and Identity in Interwar Latvia," respectively, in *Turizm.*

5. Some observers claim that the UPA assassinated Świerczewski. This matter has yet to be settled definitively.

6. Close to 483,000 "Ukrainians and Ruthenians" were deported to the USSR, while another 140,000–150,000 (of which Lemkos amounted to 25,000–35,000) were resettled within Poland. See Kazimierz Pudło, "Dzieje Łemkow po drugiej wojnie światowej [Zarys problematyki]," *Łemkowie w historii i kulturze Karpat,* ed. Jerzy Czajkowski (Rzeszów: Editions Spotkania, 1992), 355–6, 360. Tadeusz Andrzej Olszański claims that most of the inhabitants of the highland regions in the Bieszczady escaped deportation to the USSR but, after the UPA had been routed, did not escape Operation Vistula. See *Bieszczady: Przewodnik,* 8th rev. ed. (Pruszków: Rewasz, 2001), 65.

7. The words of Władysław Krygowski, "Przymierze z Bieszczadami," in Archiwum Państwowe w Rzeszowie, Polskie Towarzystwo Turystyczno-Krajoznawcze, Zarząd Okręgowy w Rzeszowie 1950–1976 (hearafter APRz PTTK), 218, 13.

8. Jacek Kolbuszewski, *Kresy* (Wrocław: Wydawn. Dolnośląskie, 1995), 208, here cited after Andrzej Burghardt, "'Przywołaj lato, święty Jurze': Bieszczady Zachodnie jako substytut Karpat Wschodnich w literaturze górskiej," *Wierchy* 67 (2001): 5. See also Olszański, *Bieszczady: Przewodnik,* 45.

9. Even today, there are only 96 women per 100 men in the region at large, with the communes of Cisna and Lutowiska at only 76 and 69 women, respectively, per 100 men. See Olszański, *Bieszczady: Przewodnik,* 34.

10. Among those who actually hiked in the region during the early 1950s was a young clergyman named Karol Wojtyła, better known in a later period as Pope John Paul II.

11. Perhaps it would be more precise to say that the communists liquidated these two pre-war entities and created a new organization that would be subordinate to the new regime. On this issue see, for example, Pawel Sowiński, *Wakacje w Polsce Ludowej: Polityka władz i ruch turystyczny (1945-1989)* (Warsaw: TRIO, 2005), 33.

12. Olszański, *Bieszczady: Przewodnik,* 146, incorrectly dates this to 1954.

13. In Polish, this type of tourism was called "tourism with a hatchet" (*turystyka z siekierą*). See Olszański, *Bieszczady: Przewodnik,* 145.

14. Władysław Krygowski, "Spotkanie z inną ziemią," *Wierchy* 21 (1952): 126.

15. Ibid., 125.

16. Ibid., 147.

17. Poles had yet to encounter the handy invention of the sleeping bag at this point. In fact, for more than one season, students spending the night in Ustrzyki Górne slept in a chicken coop near the border guard station. See Olszański, *Bieszczady: Przewodnik,* 146–7.

18. Uchwała nr 17/65 Wojewódzkiej Rady Narodowej w Rzeszowie z dnia 21 września 1965 r. w sprawie zatwierdzenia sprawozdania z realizacji uchwał rządowych dotyczących zagospodarowania Bieszczadów oraz głównych kierunków rozwoju terenów południowo-wschodnich województwa rzeszowskiego w latach 1966–1970, in Archiwum Akt Nowych (hereafter AAN), GKKFiT 2/168, 88.

19. GKKFiT, Uchwała podkomitetu turystyki w sprawie podniesienia społeczno-wychowawczej roli turystyki (Warsaw, 9 November 1962), 22–30, in AAN, GKKFiT 1/399, 24.

20. Olszański, *Bieszczady: Przewodnik,* 148.

21. See, for example, AAN, GKKFiT 1/397, 63.

22. APRz PTTK 218, 46 verte. They clearly dated "independence" not from the end of the war but from the establishment, in July 1944, of the communist- (and Moscow-) controlled Polish Committee for National Liberation.

23. Capitalization from the original. Per the Regulamin I-go Okręgowego Raidu Górskiego w Bieszczadach, APRz PTTK 218, 1.

24. Sprawozdanie z odbytego Rajdu Górskiego w Bieszczadach Zachodnich w dniach od 13–19 września 1954 zorganizowanego przez Zarząd Okręgu PTTK i Zarząd Woj. TPPR w miesiącu Pogłębienia Przyjaźni Polsko-Radzieckiej, APRz PTTK 218, 89ff.

25. Ibid., 90.

26. Ibid.

27. APRz PTTK 218, 1. The border had been changed in 1951, when Poland exchanged a piece of territory in the Lublin province for this section of the Bieszczady. Although print publications portrayed this transfer of land as a friendly move on the part of the USSR (as in Krygowski's post-war guidebook to the Bieszczady), the Soviets apparently wanted the coal mine that had been rebuilt near Sokal. Both regimes cleared the territories of their respective populations so as not to undo the ethnic cleansing that had already taken place in these borderlands. See Olszański, *Bieszczady: Przewodnik,* 70–71, 76–77.

28. APRz PTTK 218, 15.

29. Dariusz Jarosz, *"Masy pracujące przede wszystkim": Organizacja wypoczynku w Polsce 1945-1956* (Warsaw-Kielce: Instytut Historii PAN-Akademia Świętokrzyska, 2003), 286.

30. APRz PTTK 218, 14.

31. Whether he was assassinated or simply in the wrong place at the wrong time has never been settled (see note 5). On labeling the Ukrainians "bandits," see Olszański, *Bieszczady: Przewodnik,* 68. For the fascist/Nazi connection, see Tadeusz Graba, "Śmierć generała [Karola Świerczewskiego]," *Kamena* 34, no. 6 (1967): 1, 3.

32. The first quotation comes from the title of Janina Broniewska's popular 1948 children's book about Świerczewski, *O człowieku, który się kulom nie kłaniał;* the second, from Jan Gerhard, "O generale Walterze, pomniku i pamięci," *Życie Literackie* 8, no. 14 (1964): 1–2.

33. Words of Aleksander Zawadzki, the chair of the General Polish Committee of Defenders of Peace, cited in Henryk Pasławski, "W Bieszczadach stanął pomnik generała Waltera," *Kamena* 29, no.15 (1962): 2.

34. Problems included buses parking in front of the monument as well as wild camping in the vicinity. See for example, Protokół No. 5/66 z posiedzenia Prezydium Wojewódzkiego Komitetu Kultury Fizycznej i Turystyki odbytego w dniu 20 maja 1966 r., in AAN, GKKFiT 2/170, 184.

35. See Olszański, *Bieszczady: Przewodnik,* 148, for the timing; Artur Bata, *Jabłonki: Miejsce śmierci Generała Karola* Świerczewskiego (Rzeszów: Krajowa Agencja Wydawnicza, 1987), 66–70, provides details on the trail.

36. The 1959 architectural plans are in AAN, GKKFiT 15/28. The guest book of the museum/ mausoleum, found in the archive of the Muzeum Historyczne w Sanoku, conveys the wide range of responses to the place.

37. Words of Comrade Ćwik from a session of the Subcommittee on Tourism on 6 August 1967, in AAN, GKKFiT 1/405, 92.

38. This was clearly the party line already as of the early 1950s. See Walery Goetel, "Turystyka polska na nowych drogach," *Wierchy* 20 (1950–51): 5–41, especially page 32.

39. W. Krygowski, "Góry nasze—góry dla wszystkich," *Wierchy* 19 (1949): 1–12. Those who reminisced about Krygowski after his death in 1998 chose to view him as someone who did not see the mountains as being for everyone, conveniently forgetting what he wrote during the Stalinist period.

40. Often the term used was "universal tourism," even though it became a reward for shock workers and other especially deserving workers or communist functionaries from early on. See Sowiński, *Wakacje*, 59.

41. Words of Zbigniew Kulczycki, Stenogram z posiedzenia Podkomitetu Turystyki GKKFiT 15 XI 1961 r., AAN, 1/398: GKKFiT, Gabinet Przewodniczącego, Podkomitet Turystyki, Posiedzenia Podkomitetu w dniu 15.11.1961, no. 24.

42. Words of Zbigniew Kulczycki, Stenogram z posiedzenia Podkomitetu Turystyki GKKFiT 15 XI 1961 r. (1-99), AAN 1/398, 24–25.

43. Founded in the 1920s, Orbis was the main Polish tourist bureau; the socialist authorities allowed it to resume activity in the 1940s. See Aleksy Chmiel, *Turystyka w Polsce w latach 1945-1989* (Warsaw: ALMAMER, 2007), 389.

44. The law of the Economic Committee of the Council of Ministers (no. 271/59 of 27 June 1959) addressed the "matter of developing the Bieszczady" (*sprawę zagospodarowania Bieszczad*), not only tourism, although it foresaw the construction of tourist lodges to the tune of 15,000,000 zl. during the period 1959–1965. See Wilhelm Dębicki, "Jeszcze wokół problemu zagospodarowania Bieszczadów," *Wierchy* 37 (1968): 169, among other sources. While that may sound like a lot of money, much more investment was directed towards agricultural settlements. Total investment in the Bieszczady region amounted to about 2.5 billion zl. Of the law's four main components, investment in tourism came in as a distant last.

45. State-owned farms and enterprises outweighed privately-owned farms and businesses, a phenomenon which in Poland reflected the fact that the social and economic structure of the pre-war period had been destroyed. There were a total of fifty-three state-owned farms (PGRs) in the Bieszczady region in the 1950s. With time they came to rely on prison labor, indicating the problems of such large-scale farms under conditions of low population density. See Olszański, *Bieszczady: Przewodnik,* 36, 73.

46. Prezydium Wojewódzkiej Rady Narodowej w Rzeszowie, "Realizacja uchwał rządowych w sprawie aktywizacji gospodarczo-społecznej rejonu Bieszczadów oraz wnioski zmierzające do dalszego rozwoju tych terenów," 24 April 1965, in AAN, GKKFiT 2/168, 22.

47. Completed in the fall of 1962, the large highway ran through Lesko, Baligród, Cisna, Ustrzyki Górne, Lutowiska, Ustrzyki Dolne, and back to Lesko. In sum, in the period 1959–64, the state built 143.3 kilometers of state roads and 30.1 kilometers of local roads. See Prezydium Wojewódzkiej Rady Narodowej w Rzeszowie, "Realizacja uchwał rządowych w sprawie aktywizacji gospodarczo-społecznej rejonu Bieszczadów oraz wnioski zmierzające do dalszego rozwoju tych terenów," 24 April 1965, in AAN, GKKFiT 2/168, 14.

48. The authorities admitted as much. See ibid., 15. In the 1970s, it actually cost more to produce the lumber than it was worth. See Olszański, *Bieszczady: Przewodnik,* 35 and passim.

49. With a price tag of 1.5 billion zl., Solina was the largest Bieszczady investment program under the communists.

50. Permission to swim, sail, approach, or even photograph was not originally granted, according to journalist Adolf Jakubowicz, who decried the situation he encountered. See his "Reklamowa pocztówka…z cieniem," *Kamena* no. 19 (15 October 1962): 12.

51. Sowiński, *Wakacje,* 65. Whereas previously the Fundusz Wczasów Pracowniczych had a monopoly over the organization of leaves from work, as of 1958, individual enterprises could develop their own rest facilities for their workers. (Ibid., 92.) For more on the various permutations of *wczasy,* see, for example, Główny Urząd Statystyczny Polskiej Rzeczypospolitej Ludowej, *Statystyka turystyki 1950-1966* (Warsaw: Główny Urząd Statystyczny, 1967).

52. Despite the creation of such vacation homes, never in the Polish People's Republic did the percentage of genuine workers vacationing rise to reflect the percentage of workers in Poland's trade unions. For the situation in the 1950s, see Jarosz, "Masy pracujące," 286.

53. Protokół z XI posiedzenia Prezydium Polskiego Komitetu Ochrony Środowiska Człowieka, 23 October 1971, AAN, GKKFiT 19/7, 35.

54. This can be seen from the observation in 1963 that "tourism in the Bieszczady is limited to automobile and motored excursions." (Words of Leonard Grześkowiak, the chair of the presidium of the WKKFiT, in AAN, GKKFiT 2/163: 138.) He advocated the construction not of campgrounds, but of a permanent tourist base that could be used all year round.

55. Christian Noack's discussion of "wild" tourism is particularly instructive in his essay, "Coping with the Tourist: Planned and 'Wild' Mass Tourism in the Soviet Black Sea Coast," in *Turizm*.

56. Olszański, *Bieszczady: Przewodnik*, 149. New opportunities for traveling abroad starting in the 1970s made domestic tourism less attractive. Recent historiography on tourism in People's Poland underscores the fact that the 1970s represented "the golden decade" of vacationing in the country. Quotation from Sowiński, *Wakacje*, 282; see also Chmiel, *Turystyka*, 395.

57. For 1964, the figure was 1,237,000; the number of tourists had been growing dynamically since 1960, when there were a mere 479,000 tourists. See Sprawozdanie z realizacji zadań w zakresie upowszechniania i rozwoju kultury fizycznej i turystyki w województwie rzeszowskim, 11 March 1965, in AAN, GKKFiT 2/169, 11. See also Informacja o przedsięwzięciach WKKFiT w zakresie koordynacji i zagospodarowania turystycznego miejscowości turystyczno-wypoczynkowych na terenie województwa rzeszowskiego, AAN, GKKFiT 2/166, 156.

58. The initial "five-year plan" in Poland was actually a six-year one. For an example of the state's planning and priorities in the Bieszczady region, see note 44.

59. From a speech given at the plenary session of the Subcommittee on Tourism on 29 March 1961, in AAN, GKKFiT 1/397, 53.

60. APRz PTTK 218, 89.

61. To be sure, it was the inaugural Friendship *Rajd*, which meant that the organizers did not have enough experience to anticipate these problems.

62. Words of the chair of the PKKFiT in Ustrzyki Dolne, per Minutes #2/61, in AAN, GKKFiT 2/161, 138.

63. See the financial plan of the Central Fund for Tourism and Rest for 1962, AAN, GKKFiT 2/162, 14–15.

64. This was the Wojewódzkie Przedsiębiorstwo Obsługi Ruchu Turystycznego "Bieszczady." Per minutes #06 from the session of the Presidium of WKKFiT in Rzeszów on 17 May 1961, in AAN, GKKFiT 2/160, 153.

65. That, indeed, is what they were called—although the name used was "Kubuś puchatek," which is how the pre-war translator of Milne's works (Irena Tuwim) rendered the famous bear's name in Polish.

66. With that said, they had bought some tents, folding beds, and mattresses so as to open the facility, on a limited basis, on 1 July.

67. See the report on the activity of the Bieszczady Province Tourist Movement Service Enterprise, 2 September 1961, in AAN, GKKFiT 2/161, 103–109.

68. Comrade Kazimierz Partyka, from minutes #2 from a session of the WKKFiT in Rzeszów on 4 October 1961, AAN, GKKFiT 2/161, 99. Experimentation seems to be a constant, and one provincial-level organization after another seems to disappoint. For information on the WOSTiW "Bieszczady," the successor to the Bieszczady Province Tourist Movement Service Enterprise, see AAN, GKKFiT 2/165.

69. GKKFiT, Departament Zagospodarowania Turyst., *Zagospodarowanie turystyczne Polski w latach 1961-1965* (Warsaw, March 1961), in AAN, GKKFiT 1/397, 118.

70. Protokół nr 6/63, AAN, GKKFiT 2/163, 137.

71. Ibid. Nonetheless, a person responsible for the provisioning at the provincial level claimed that "meals will always be guaranteed and prepared if an excursion orders them in advance." See

AAN, GKKFiT 2/170, 186. Naturally, many visitors traveled in small groups on their own, and thus had to scramble to be served.

72. Per protokół nr 6/63, AAN, GKKFiT 2/163, 137. The one glimmer of hope was provided by scouts, who organized campgrounds and actually fed their tourists. See Protokół nr 10/63 of the WKKFiT Presidium in Rzeszów from 18 September 1963, AAN, GKKFiT 2/164, 170.

73. See, for example, Jerzy Fałkowski, "W imieniu stonki," *Walka Młodych* no. 41 (13 October 1963).

74. Per protokół nr 6/63, AAN, GKKFiT 2/163, 137.

75. Protokół nr 5/66 z posiedzenia Prezydium WKKFiT odbytego w dniu 20 maja 1966 r., AAN, GKKFiT 2/170, 185.

76. Quotation from Chmiel, *Turystyka,* 395, among other sources.

77. How such fissures ended up contributing to socialism's demise is discussed by Alexander Vari, "Introduction: Escaping the Monotony of Everyday Life under Socialism" in this volume.

78. This preoccupation is all too evident from even a cursory glance at the archives of the period (for example, AAN, GKKFiT).

79. For more on this important aspect of the command economy, see especially the pioneering work of Hungarian economist Janos Kornai.

80. To be sure, Poland compared unfavorably not only with the West but with other countries within the East Bloc, with more opportunities to vacation and better conditions. See the chapter by Mary Neuberger in this volume as well as Sowiński, *Wakacje,* 282.

81. Włodzimierz Reczek, from Stenogram z posiedzenia Podkomitetu Turystyki GKKFiT 15 XI 1961 r. (1–99), in AAN, GKKFiT 1/398, 97. He was the head of the Główny Komitet Kultury Fizycznej i Turystyki (GKKFiT).

82. Diane P. Koenker, "The Proletarian Tourist in the 1930s: Between Mass Excursion and Mass Escape," in *Turizm,* 119–40.

83. For a sense of how important the supply of bread and, especially, meat was to post-war Poles, who often protested over their relative scarcity and/or price hikes, see, for example, Andrzej Paczkowski, *The Spring Will Be Ours: Poland and the Poles from Occupation to Freedom,* trans. Jane Cave (University Park, PA: Pennsylvania State University Press, 2003).

84. The sentiment of Włodzimierz Reczek, from Stenogram z posiedzenia GKKFiT w składzie Podkomitetu Turystyki z 28 czerwca 1963, AAN, GKKFiT 1/400, 38.

CHAPTER 4

Summer Camp for Socialists

Conformity and Escapism at Camp Mitschurin in East Germany

Catherine J. Plum

For many former East German citizens, collective memories of a Cold-War childhood include the delight of unwrapping chocolate, toys, clothes, and other consumer goods in Western packaging. Surprisingly, one story of Western temptation and escapism transpired in a youth camp for future socialist leaders that was controlled by the official communist youth organization, the Pioneers. At Camp Mitschurin in Thuringia, Pioneers hiking in the summer of 1965 saw Western motorists one day.[1] The travelers began to throw candy from their car windows, and the children eagerly collected the treats.[2] Pioneer camp leaders frowned upon such incidents, however, as undesirable diversions. They found it necessary to have more than one discussion with campers to prevent the children from allowing a sweet tooth to trump their political loyalty.[3] As a desirable luxury item, Western candy was indeed poisonous on one level: it called into question a primary propaganda message of youth and leisure policy in the German Democratic Republic (GDR). The East German state claimed that it cared more about its children than its Western twin, and promised families a satisfactory standard of living with occasional luxuries, vacations, and other forms of recreation.

Significantly, this story of an unintended escape within a state-sponsored escape resonates beyond the 1960s due to a curious twist: in the 1980s, the Pioneer Organization actually sold Western chocolate to its campers. How can one best explain the camp's dramatic shift from candy police to candy peddler? The Pioneer Organization caved in during this period by providing Western chocolate and English pop music, while regime leaders attempted to placate the GDR population at large through cultural compromises and stop-gap measures, including foreign films and Intershops.[4] The policy reversal on Western goods and entertainment is only one example of cultural changes and political transformations at Pioneer camps. What weaknesses in loyalty existed if conformist youth required Western dance music to keep them content? Does it suggest that politics had become so unpalatable for young people at camp that the state needed to provide capitalist treats and diversions?

This chapter focuses on Camp Mitschurin, later renamed Hermann Matern, as a model summer camp providing a socialist escape for children aged eleven to fourteen (Thälmann Pioneers[5]) in Raila/Wetteratal from the 1950s through the fall of socialism.[6] The camp afforded select children from the cities and suburbs of Jena and Gera a break from their urban environment, regular routines, and classmates. Traveling to the camp was not a vacation from political propaganda; rather, it was an escape to a place that embraced socialist conformity to a greater extent than most schools and Pioneer troops through its intense, regimental schedule and socialist activities. While staying at the camp for nearly three weeks, Pioneers experienced rare opportunities to advance their leadership skills, engage in scouting games (Geländespiele), and interact with foreign youth.[7] Camp leaders tried to fashion an ideal socialist community, infused with collective identity, similar to a Benjaminian dreamworld.[8] What they created instead was a temporary parallel world, neither immune to the challenges and contradictions of GDR society, nor sufficiently connected to the real world of Pioneer life back home.

In its first few decades, the camp frequently failed as a socialist escape as employees attempted to fulfill their main goals: to promote health, recreation, and relaxation and, secondly, to carry out political education more effectively than in school-based Pioneer groups.[9] Despite a population of predominantly committed counselors and conformist youth, success was elusive due to problems that included employee error and insubordination, limited resources, environmental issues, and youth discontent. Furthermore, as the capitalist candy episode illustrates, cases of nonconformity, dissent, and opposition surfaced as unofficial escapes from socialism. Camp personnel addressed some, but not all, of these problems over the course of the camp's lifespan. After the Pioneer Organization rebuilt and reopened the camp in the early 1980s, camp counselors offered new opportunities for youth escapes and initiative, some inspired by the West, while its political education persisted in a weakened, but predictable, form with unforeseen consequences. This combination of cultural change and political intransigency reflects both the strengths and limits of local agency.

My analysis uses youth recreation as a lens for investigating socialist leisure policy, including the connection between leisure and socialist education and identity formation. By supporting camps and other forms of travel and leisure tourism, GDR leaders cultivated a notion of purposeful escapes, or "purposeful journeys," a term Anne Gorsuch and Diane Koenker use to describe socialist vacations, fieldtrips, and work-related travel that included an educational component.[10] Purposeful journeys thus supported "productive leisure" practices. From early on, the Pioneer Organization and Free German Youth Organization (Freie Deutsche Jugend or FDJ) strongly encouraged their troops to engage in group tourist and hiking adventures under their auspices, and not other leisure organizations, in order to promote a collective socialist identity.[11]

Aside from the work of Leonore Ansorg and a few others, scholars researching GDR youth have devoted little attention to Pioneers and their activities, much less to the central Pioneer camps or the Pioneer Republic on Werbellinsee.[12] The literature focuses more on older teenagers and young adults, including conformist members of the FDJ and nonconformists and resistors who escaped into musical venues and other leisure sites connected to their alternative subcultures, represented by Caroline Fricke's chapter in this volume.[13] Scholars such as Mary Fulbrook argue that we need more research on the vast majority of GDR youths who were conformists, including those who participated actively and those who simply conceded without energy and enthusiasm.[14] Moreover, Juliane Fürst's research on post-war youth in the Soviet Union reveals that youth involvement in state-sponsored activities frequently concealed young people's interests and agendas that were distinct from official goals.[15] By exploring campers and counselors who demonstrated conformity, nonconformist behavior, and noteworthy cases of dissent and opposition in an unlikely place, this chapter supports a suitable balance within GDR scholarship. The mixture of conformity and alternative attitudes exhibited by youth in the 1980s, in particular, helps to explain young people's participation in the citizen protests that contributed to the fall of socialism. In the period since German reunification, one can find nostalgic references to Pioneer camps necessitating an honest and differentiated understanding of the sites and GDR youth cultures more broadly.[16]

Youth Conformists Escaping to Camp Mitschurin, 1951–1972

Regardless of how far they had traveled, young people entered into a new collective community when they entered a socialist youth camp, according to historian Susan Reid, whose research focuses on the Soviet Union.[17] Similar to their Soviet counterparts, the careful selection of enthusiastic and active Pioneers and counselors was essential for the building of a cohesive socialist community at East German Pioneer camps like Mitschurin. The early history of the camp reveals the potential for a collective community and an escape for socialists as seen in the backgrounds of typical campers and counselors and camp activities, which often varied from young people's everyday experiences at home and in their schools and youth organizations. An analysis of both the camp's potential and its weaknesses provides context for understanding the camp's frequent failure to fulfill its primary goals and effectively engage young people.

Using German communist and Soviet interwar camps as their model, the FDJ began organizing summer camps during the years of Soviet occupation.[18] Serious planning for Camp Mitschurin and thirty-nine other central Pioneer camps began in the early 1950s, soon after the establishment of the Pioneer Organization in 1948 under the auspices of the FDJ.[19] This building campaign should be viewed as part of a larger government effort to improve and increase the number of camps, hostels, resorts, and sports and cultural facilities that provided state-sponsored leisure opportunities for workers and their families.[20] At its height, the Pioneer Organization controlled fifty central Pioneer camps that offered summer sessions designed primarily for Thälmann Pioneers.[21] By the mid-1970s, these camps could accommodate approximately one hundred thousand children each summer, allowing one out of every two youths the opportunity to attend a camp as a Thälmann Pioneer.[22] Similar to Soviet youth camps and Western scouting organizations, East German Pioneer camps provided a base for expeditions and activities in nature, as well as a site for rituals and traditions.[23]

An existing campsite in Raila, located in a nature preserve, became a central Pioneer camp in 1951.[24] Soon after its foundation, the camp acquired the name Mitschurin, referring to a Russian scientist.[25] In the early 1970s camp leaders successfully petitioned to change the name to Hermann Matern, honoring a German antifascist activist who became the vice president of the East German People's Council (Volkskammer), the lower house of parliament.[26] All central Pioneer camps had industrial sponsors, a corporatist feature of social organization and leisure in the GDR.[27] In the case of Camp Mitschurin, VEB Carl Zeiss Jena, an optics manufacturer, supported the camp financially and was responsible for its maintenance.[28] This chapter explores some of the complaints camp leaders expressed regarding their facilities that could have been solved with increased funding, particularly in the period through the early 1970s before the Pioneer Organization rebuilt the camp in the early 1980s. The camp required additional investment based on its expansion in key periods. For example, the camp's capacity increased in the early 1960s, accommodating over fourteen hundred children in two sessions.[29]

It is important to differentiate Camp Mitschurin and the other central Pioneer camps from the larger number of camps that factories and other employers in East Germany organized for their workers' children, called *Betriebsferienlager*, without oversight from the Pioneer Organization. The distinction can be confusing because some of the larger companies in the GDR, like Carl Zeiss, also sponsored *Pionierlager* with direct supervision and educational staffing from the Pioneer Organization. Compared to the central Pioneer camps, the company camps tended to be less political in nature, with a few exceptions, and thus offered a different type of recreational escape.[30] The camps also served distinct youth populations. Unlike the youth attending *Betriebsferienlager,* many children who attended Pioneer camp can be considered enthusiastic conformists, because they earned an invitation through their exemplary efforts in school and in their Pioneer troop. An essay by former Pioneer Carsta Nitzer comments on the role parents played in the decision to accept this invitation, linking parental assent with their attitudes towards the Pioneer Organization, their children's interests, and opportunism. Nitzer maintains that many parents viewed the political camps positively. Others let their children attend camp believing that it would be good for their future.[31] The remaining East German youths at Camp Mitschurin were children with parents who worked for the camp's sponsor. This portion of the camp population represented average families and a wider variety of political perspectives. Based on the screening of many of the counselors and children, the atmosphere and group cohesion at camp were distinct from Pioneer troops back home, which could include more children from families with different attitudes towards the regime. Unlike employee-run *Betriebsferienlager,* the Pioneer camp counselors tended to be university students pursuing a career in teaching, current teachers, and Pioneer leaders, most of whom could be relied upon politically, given their training and prior involvement and conduct in the FDJ. Additionally, according to a 1960 report, the camps also hired some secondary-school students, workers, and housewives, categories of employees more common at *Betriebsferienlager.*[32] Given these factors, the camp appeared to be in a fairly strong position to succeed as an instrument of communist youth group socialization.

In its first two decades, the camp offered Pioneers a mixed adventure, from popular hands-on activities and educational programming to political discussions, including some opportunities that youth rarely had at home. Counselors coordinated a variety of common children's activities including sports, arts and crafts, and games. For instance, in 1960, counselors organized different activity clubs (*Arbeitsgemeinschaften*) focused on cultural pursuits such as singing, dancing, a book club, a Russian language fest, and a talent competition. Young people could also further their knowledge of woodwork, metalwork, chemistry, and the science of optics through experiments and projects Carl Zeiss sponsored.[33] Moreover, beginning in the late 1950s, Pioneers could attend an open-air film theater and produce their own radio broadcasts in a radio barrack.[34] The broadcasts reveal a potential for individual creativity and development, but camp leaders could take away this privilege if they disapproved of the content of a radio broadcast. Through announcements of political anniversaries, art projects, book discussions, films, and many other forms, the staff integrated formal and informal political education into traditional camp fare. Political education had a better chance of succeeding if it differed from typical school-based activities and was motivational and engaging.[35]

One of the most formal elements of political education was the Pioneer task (*Pionierauftrag*) for the new school year, which staff introduced and discussed at length. Based on a socialist theme, the *Pionierauftrag* advanced a common political weltanschauung, or world view, and sense of collective pride and national identity through team work. To promote the *Pionierauftrag* and political education in general, counselors often coordinated book discussions and fieldtrips. The Pioneer Organization hoped that campers would also brainstorm ways to integrate the *Pionierauftrag* into their activities in their Pioneer troops back home, and carry through with their plans in the months that followed.

Additional activities at camp included discussions with special guests, such as antifascist veterans and children from other socialist countries. The veterans of the "antifascist struggle" that visited camps included communist activists who had engaged in nonconformity, opposition, and acts of resistance against the Nazi dictatorship decades earlier. While schools and youth groups frequently invited antifascist veterans to their functions, camps offered the perfect ambience—a darkened sky and roaring fire—for tales of partisans and resistance fighters. Some antifascist activists were effective storytellers and motivational speakers, but not all veterans possessed these skills and related well with young people.[36] Communication was also an issue for Pioneers' interactions with foreign children. Campers had a hard time conversing with Soviet Pioneers, who were frequent guests, and they faced even more language hurdles when a youth group from Vietnam visited in 1967.[37] Pioneers also had fewer connections with the Vietnamese children and associations with Vietnam, unlike their exposure to criticism of Russians and Russian culture in some of their families, based on historic tensions and Soviet troop presence.[38] If challenging at times, discussions and group activities with foreign youth were rare opportunities for GDR youth, and camp leaders expected Pioneers to exemplify model behavior.

Another type of activity counselors frequently organized at Mitschurin and other Pioneer camps was a scouting game (*Geländespiel*). *Geländespiele* are outdoor recreational games in which teams compete against each other, as if engaged in battle or in pursuit of a quest. School-based Pioneer and FDJ groups also played these games at home sometimes, but summer camps offered an ideal environment to engage in these outdoor competitions. While popular in both East and West Germany, GDR youths frequently role-played as contemporary or historical figures, pretending, for instance, that they were communist activists fighting against bourgeois policemen in the 1920s, or World War II partisan fighters engaged in combat against German troops. Quests could include stealing the enemy's cache of weapons or freeing imprisoned comrades.[39]

Counselors at Camp Mitschurin designed a *Geländespiel* in 1963, for example, based on the theme "protecting our state border"—the border GDR leaders had recently strengthened after constructing the Berlin Wall in 1961.[40] In preparation for this event, Pioneers first discussed the building of the Berlin Wall and the new security measures at the border. Then with "great excitement" according to one report, the Pioneers created helmets, gloves, pistols, and other kinds of weapons. On the day of the game, an alarm went off and different companies of troops maneuvered to protect parts of a make-believe border. Pioneers dressed and armed as border guards prevented enemy agents from crossing the border.[41] This *Geländespiel* clearly transformed a very serious theme into a children's game with paramilitary and ideological undertones. The preparation and game itself included the transmission of political education and contributed to a sense of team work and collective identity, a primary goal of the camp as an agent of socialization. However, from their families and close friends, children knew that a larger number of GDR citizens had left East Germany in recent years than Westerners had attempted to spy on or move to East Germany. The gap between these facts and socialist propaganda made lessons such as these highly problematic. Moreover, this disjuncture led to even greater frustrations in the 1980s, as Anna Saunders has noted in her revealing monograph exploring youth patriotism before and after 1989 in East Germany.[42]

The excitement of *Geländespiele* is just one reason why some camp leaders believed young people considered life at camp to be more interesting than their experiences in their troops back home. In a summer report from 1965, the camp director wrote, "The majority of Pioneers expressed the fact that it was first in camp that they realized how interesting and varied life in a Pioneer troop can be."[43] The director is referring to conformists who did not know that their experiences could be so diverse and exciting. Youth attitudes varied, but it is important to emphasize that for conformists, troop activities at home paled in comparison to some of the experiences at camp. The special, if imperfect, atmosphere at camp could not be replicated when the Pioneers returned to their school-based youth troops, which likely resulted in disappointment for conformists, whose enthusiasm peaked at camp. These youth awaited challenges fulfilling their *Pionierauftrag* in their home troops.

A Failed Escape: Arsenic, Old Tents, and Alternative Escapism at Camp Mitschurin, 1951–1972

While the camp succeeded in providing some fun and engaging activities for youth, it frequently failed to provide effective political education for future party cadres, or a healthy environment for youth recreation. Based on forces both within and outside their control, camp leaders and counselors had a difficult time overcoming personnel, environmental, and resource supply challenges. Even in areas in which the Pioneers' experiences appeared better than life back home and in their youth groups, the inconsistencies and limited nature of the escape were obvious. Ultimately, Pioneers and some of their counselors exhibited signs of alternative escapism in the form of nonconformity, verbal dissent, and opposition.

Camp leaders occasionally hired counselors whose political perspective and level of involvement left much to be desired. For example, reports from 1968 and 1969 refer to counselors from Carl Zeiss who failed to exhibit proper class consciousness and support political goals. For instance, some Carl Zeiss counselors considered their time at the camp a vacation and refused to become actively involved.[44] Additionally, according to another report, one counselor, who was a teacher and member of the Socialist United Party (SED), failed to support the party line in comments made at the camp during the summer of 1962, influencing other non-SED staff members.[45] These counselors clearly jeopardized the political programming for which Pioneer camps were known by viewing their time at camp as an escape from work and/or an opportunity for nonconformity and verbal dissent. Criticism of camp personnel in 1960 extended as far as the party secretary and the leader for club activities; the latter failed to show up at camp and evidently was not replaced.[46]

The Pioneer Organization also expected group leaders to stay current with the latest news stories and share what they learned with their Pioneers in a manner that supported the state media's interpretive spin, but this did not always happen. According to a report from 1960, group leaders at Camp Mitschurin met every two days to keep abreast of current political events and prepare for discussions with their campers.[47] However, a document written two years later admitted that several counselors failed to conduct the daily political discussion.[48] Another problem concerned the format of the discussions. A report commenting on all of the central Pioneer camps in 1960 stated that political discussions were "dry" and not always very successful during that summer. Evidently, staff failed to initiate discussions about the collectivization of farms in a manner that was convincing, engaging, and appropriate for children. In fact, the document admitted that campers questioned this campaign by transforming the acronym for a collective farm, LPG, into the words "*langsam pleite gehen*"—referring to a farm that would "slowly go bankrupt."[49] Cases of verbal dissent, such as the word play on this acronym, should be considered in the wider context of GDR society where economic complaints and some political jokes were common, according to scholars Andrew Port and Kerry Kathleen Riley, respectively. In his case study of Saalfeld, Port perceives a "grumble *Gesellschaft* (society)," emphasizing the extent of economic frustrations given voice through verbal and written complaints.[50] A wide segment of the population, including conformists and opponents, used jokes, other cynical expressions, and rumors as a necessary release. By "neutralizing the effect of the SED's influence," Riley argues, jokes broke through ideological rhetoric with candor.[51] In addition to questioning the collectivization of farms, young people also verbalized opposition to other SED policies. For example, at Camp Mitschurin in the early 1960s, some youth from Dresden and Jena admitted that they watched Western television. They could not understand what was so wrong with that personal choice.[52]

Nor did all campers comprehend the benefits of inviting Soviet Pioneers to their camp. In fact, camp staff admonished one camper in front of the entire camp in 1960 before sending him home for stealing Soviet flashlights and handkerchiefs.[53] The decision to steal these accessories that were part of the Soviet uniform was probably not coincidental, because stealing from the Soviet youth required more effort based on segregated accommodations.[54] Most young people knew that camp leaders would interpret this breach in discipline as particularly egregious because the victims were Soviet youth, the Pioneers' guests at the camp. This camper's action is an example of nonconformity and dissent, demonstrating a lack of respect for Camp Mitschurin's guests, and a clear rejection of socialist principles. This Pioneer had failed to internalize the constant emphasis on proletarian internationalism and German-Soviet friendship in the Pioneer Organization and at school.[55] Stealing Soviet Pioneer icons constituted both an alternative escape from socialist values, and also a rejection of socialist international identity. Particularly if the student used the items as prestige or exchange goods within his friendship circle, his act was self-defining, casting the Soviet victims in the role of the "other," perhaps as unwelcome foreigners. While this case stands out, there were additional incidents of stealing and vandalism, which similarly reveal that the youths concerned had failed to adopt "socialist personalities," a primary educational goal.[56]

State leaders in the Pioneer Organization were cognizant of the need for staff training and the somewhat heterogeneous population the camps served. In fact, in materials for planning activities during the summer of 1960, the central leadership reminded camp directors that their camps were for young people, and not mature party functionaries. The assistant director of the Pioneer Organization called into question whether children can be strongly influenced through large group assemblies.[57] Despite this warning, political ceremonies and large group functions remained prominent for years to come, suggesting intransigence on the local level.

In collective memories of growing up in the GDR, one of the more negative features of childhood concerns the militarism in schools and the Pioneer Organization, often exemplified in group ceremonies, rituals, and paramilitary games. For example, at Camp Mitschurin, children frequently learned survival and paramilitary skills through climbing exercises and shooting practice.[58] In her memoir describing experiences as both a student and a teacher in East Germany, Sabine Hädicke recalled the militarism of Pioneer camps as an unpleasant memory. She referred to the practice of serving guard duty as part of a guard group (*Wachgruppe*) as representative of the formalistic control and militarism that permeated these camps.[59] Documents from the 1960s and discussions with camp adminstrators from the 1980s suggest that positioning Pioneer guards at the entrance to the camp was a strong tradition at Camp Mitschurin.[60] This practice encouraged select Pioneers to feel a sense of ownership and collective identity connected to the camp. Two former employees of the camp argue that many Pioneers enjoyed the measure of responsibility and authority this assignment bestowed.[61] The position conferred on select youth power over fellow Pioneers and visitors, albeit not necessarily camp leaders. The sense of individual power that could be derived from this experience was arguably as strong, or stronger, than their sense of collective identity as Camp Mitschurin Pioneers. Based on power dynamics and attitudes towards militarism, young people differed in their attitudes towards this tradition.

While Pioneers could not escape some aspects of political education and militarism, self-selection of their small group activities meant that even at a Pioneer camp, young people made decisions about how they would participate in GDR society based on their own self interest and awareness (*Eigen-Sinn*).[62] Their selections varied session by session, but they provide some information on limited political activism. For example, in one 1967 camp session, only 13 campers out of 498 participated in an activity group that discussed current politics (*Zirkel aktuelle Politik*), whereas 44 selected volleyball and 75 pursued volunteer fireman training. The *Zirkel aktuelle Politik* had the lowest number of children of any group.[63] Clearly, there were very few enthusiastic conformists willing to spend more time discussing politics during this summer session than required. These statistics should not be surprising, especially given research and testimonials from adult members of the SED who complained of dry, boring meetings at the local level.[64]

Campers differed in their reactions to camp activities, rules, and goals. In addition to cases of nonconformity and breeches of discipline, some complained when they found certain activities to be boring and meaningless. The 7 AM fitness workout at camp was notoriously unpopular, as statements in Hädicke's memoir and a camp speech reveal.[65] Nor did Pioneers like some of the volunteer service that camp leaders expected them to perform. While campers enjoyed making toys for disadvantaged children, camp reports from 1962 and 1965 document children's verbal dissent and disinterest, particularly when the work they performed in partner villages included pulling weeds from potato fields and collecting apples for the elderly.[66]

In addition to dry political discussions and some unsavory volunteer work, campers and counselors had reason to object to a number of problems with their food, location, and facilities that made their stay less than a delightful summertime escape. Upon arrival, children learned that there was no swimming pool or lake near Camp Mitschurin where they could safely swim. A final cause for concern for many years involved water issues, including problems with flooding, and access to clean and temperate water for drinking and bathing.

Reports from the 1960s address the topic of food at the camp. Despite promises to parents in camp advertisements from the 1950s, reports from Mitschurin indicate that there were not enough vegetables and eggs during the summer of 1963, and a lack of fruit during some of the other summers.[67] Hence, even the Pioneer camps were subject to the East German shortage economy (*Mangelwirtschaft*), from which there was no escape. A camp inspector who visited a number of central Pioneer camps in the early 1960s noted during an interview that the preparation of large quantities of food compromised the quality of meals.[68] While such complaints could be voiced in non-socialist camps, for parents and camp staff in the GDR, providing diverse, quality food was important for fulfilling the socialist welfare promise. The central Pioneer camps generally received a greater variety of food and delicacies than young people were accustomed to at home, in part because the regime sought to impress their foreign guests.[69] However, even in good times, the contrast between the relatively fortunate situation at camp and the problems at home highlighted the regime's problem fulfilling demand.

Additionally, campers and Pioneer guests could hardly fail to notice signs of repeated flooding at the campsite that damaged and compromised their aging tents, facilities, and equipment. Pioneers often found the floor of their tents under water and their sports fields off-limits. In fact, none of the buildings were safe from flooding in the 1950s. Camp architects had essentially positioned the camp in a valley and on a floodplain.[70] Workers installed a floodgate in 1955, but the problem continued to be an issue for years to come.[71]

While their tents were sometimes swimming in water, children did not have the option of going swimming on a regular basis. Swimming in Bleilochstausee, a nearby lake, was forbidden for hygienic reasons, due to chemical pollution from local factories that processed and manufactured leather, fur, and paper.[72] Ironically, the camp was located in a nature preserve, which meant that the Pioneer Organization could not obtain permission to build a swimming pool.[73] Hence, at Camp Mitschurin children could not experience Neptune fests, which were a tradition that many children enjoyed at other Pioneer camps.[74] Since swimming was one of the main activities advertised in Pioneer camp brochures that date back to the early 1950s, the inability to go swimming on a regular basis was highly problematic.[75] At Mitschurin, children could still go on boat rides on the lake and, as a prize in the 1980s, the camp sometimes bused groups to a location called the "Dragon's Hole" to go swimming.[76] In lieu of bathing regularly in nature, campers had to take showers. Problems persisted in this regard, as a report from 1961 reveals, because Mitschurin had problems supplying enough hot water for showering.[77]

Potentially much more serious was a concern representatives from Carl Zeiss expressed regarding the possibility that cyanide-laced water from the Wettera River could pollute Camp Mitschurin's drinking water. A letter from Carl Zeiss confirms that the company had been worried about the issue of chemical pollution for several years, dating back to 1954.[78] A document from 1963 explained the serious threat: an electroplate company in Tanna was releasing water tainted with cyanide into a river that was located just a few meters from the camp's water source. By the end of 1963, Carl Zeiss had already spent 85,000 Marks on water issues since they began sponsoring the camp, and the cyanide threat was still a matter of concern. Camp documents failed to mention this potential danger, although end-of-the-year reports do include information about medical issues.[79] While there is no evidence of poisoning, this case suggests serious government oversight. On one hand, cold showers, flooded soccer fields, and swimming bans tarnished the government's image of a socialist welfare state committed to modern conveniences and children's recreation. On the other hand, the threat of cyanide poisoning in a nature preserve exposes the state's complete failure to monitor environmental hazards and protect some of its youngest citizens.[80]

While cases of poisoning did not materialize, children sometimes required medical attention, which spoiled their overall experience and prevented the camp from fully achieving its goal of promoting health and recreation. One serious example from 1972 suggests poor management and communication on the part of the camp director, Kurt Pfeffer. In a letter of complaint to Carl Zeiss, a mother reported that her son did not come home from camp with the other children. She soon learned that her son had been sent to a hospital five days earlier because staff members suspected that he suffered from dysentery. The mother was very disturbed that her son's illness was so serious, and that he had been hospitalized for so long without her knowledge.[81] A letter from a district Pioneer administrator suggests that the mother's story was accurate. He directed Carl Zeiss's union leadership to inform her that they would critically evaluate Pfeffer.[82] Camp documents prove, however, that Pfeffer remained the camp director for some years to come despite this clear inability to provide proper oversight.[83]

Personnel problems, along with health and recreation hazards, youth discontent, and cases of alternative escapism reveal that Camp Mitschurin frequently failed in its mission. While some camps were better situated in terms of swimming access and flood-free grounds, facility problems and dissent plagued multiple sites. Further investigations may reveal more evidence of the benefits and drawbacks of Pioneer camps, and further qualify Leonore Ansorg's argument that children generally enjoyed their stay at Pioneer camps regardless of the significant amount of political education and militarism in the 1950s.[84] On multiple levels, Mitschurin was a place from which one might want to seek an escape.

A New Escape: Transforming Space, Identity, and Recreation at Camp Matern, 1972–1989

Faced with deteriorating buildings, drainage issues, and a desire to provide state-of-the-art facilities, the Pioneer Organization was forced to make some decisions about the future of Camp Mitschurin to ensure that Thälmann Pioneers could continue to use it as a summertime escape. Despite a new drainage system installed in 1973 and the addition of sixty-six bungalows for flood-proof sleeping accommodations,[85] significant change did not occur until after the camp closed in 1979 and reopened in 1981 for year-round accommodation.[86] Financial investment in Pioneer camps under Erich Honecker[87] provided for the necessary renovations in Raila and other sites. This investment coincided with the new head of state's massive residential building projects in the 1970s, as the state sought to attain popular approval through public expenditures financed with deficit spending. With time, the altered landscape, facilities, identity, and activities the camp offered reveal the staff's changing notions of appropriate modern leisure and greater success with the goal of providing healthy recreation. However, similar to GDR cultural policy, Pioneer leaders and counselors conceded to youth demands by adopting Western patterns of leisure and forms of consumption, ultimately creating an artificial escape from societal problems. They also demonstrated a common failure of Pioneer institutions to fully reform political education in the regime's final years, leaving open the door for Pioneer interest in alternative diversions.[88]

Following in the footsteps of other camps and youth institutions seeking new identities and inspiration, the camp adopted the name Hermann Matern in 1972 and discontinued using its older Russian namesake.[89] The camp also erected a tradition cabinet dedicated to Matern in 1973 to reinforce this altered identity.[90] Increasingly, Pioneer camps, schools, and district FDJ offices featured a tradition cabinet, room, or bungalow—special exhibits dedicated to the Pioneer Organization or institution's namesake and used as a form of political education. However, it is questionable whether or not the memorials and tradition bungalows in camps were more inspirational than tradition rooms constructed in schools, which often faded into the pedagogical landscape and accumulated dust. The days of a formal tradition cabinet were numbered because of plans finally implemented to tear down and rebuild most of the camp.

The Pioneer Organization closed the camp in 1979 and reopened it a few years later at a cost of some twenty million East German Marks.[91] The new facilities included three large houses with sleeping quarters for 540 campers.[92] One Pioneer described the positive changes made to the camp in a letter. The child wrote, "The newly built houses are beautiful—small rooms with new furniture and nice washing facilities. And this year the new dining hall will be finished."[93] With time, staff members also added a petting zoo, an aquarium, and an astronomy center with a planetarium. The camp's new design and engineering resolved all water problems on site, short of the desire for a swimming pool.[94] With respect to facilities and resources, young people now had fewer reasons to want to escape. In addition to these dramatic transformations of the camp landscape, more subtle visual changes reveal shifts in emphasis at the camp. According to two former staff members, instead of using bulletin boards to share the news of political developments, Pioneer groups in the 1980s posted more information about their activities, emphasizing, for example, the results of their recent soccer tournament.[95]

The camp also featured multiple new options and opportunities for Pioneers, including elements of Western leisure and recreation, and opportunities to meet West German youth in the early 1980s.[96] Amateur ham radio transmissions allowed Pioneers to communicate with children in other nations, such as the United States and Japan, using English primarily as a common language. Camp counselors updated their activities by adopting English-language pop music for discos and even television projection of camp information through the one Atari computer the camp possessed.[97] The optics firm Carl Zeiss supplied equipment that made Camp Matern one of the most modern camps by GDR standards.[98] Documents from the camp even reveal an interest in constructing a basketball court, a sport that originated in the United States.[99] Overall, the staff appears to have worked hard to marry new activities and technology with traditional pastimes. Western influence is not surprising, given the GDR's willingness in the 1970s and 1980s to open up economically to firms like Pepsi-Cola and Nestlé, at least in its Intershop stores, and in cultural terms through the importation of more Western movies and rock music.[100]

Similar to the rest of socialist society, but with more resources, the Pioneer Organization reacted to the desire for change and more interaction with foreign cultures by allowing the West into the camp within certain limits. However, the camp's ambivalent policy promoted a confusing message by providing elements of a Western escape within a camp that emphasized the superiority of socialism. Pioneers returned to hometowns where frustrations with consumer demand were obvious, revealing the very real problems socialism faced despite camp propaganda. Ultimately, as scholars such as Sergei Zhuk argue Western cultural concessions and the broader policy of *Ostpolitik* failed because they sent a mixed message and resulted in stronger demand, creating a youth identity strongly tied to the West.[101] A demand for further engagement with the West at the camp can be seen in the critique of one university student who was a counselor in the summer of 1989. Expressing strong dissent, the young woman complained bitterly that East and West German campers did not have enough opportunities to spend leisure time with each other in informal settings. Late at night, she challenged camp rules by trying to spend more time with the Western visitors.[102]

During the 1980s, political education remained important, although camp leaders preserved many traditions in a weaker form. They still organized camp-wide group meetings featuring uniforms and the symbols of the Pioneer Organization at Hermann Matern, but at least in the late 1980s, they restricted these primarily to the opening and closing ceremony for each session which were important for sharing information and introducing the camp staff.[103] According to a former Pioneer who attended multiple central Pioneer camps, the limited amount of political programming was typical for the late 1980s.[104] Camp Hermann Matern's main form of political education continued to be the *Pionierauftrag* or task for the next school year.[105] Themes included "A festival flower for anti-imperialist solidarity—peace and friendship" in 1985[106] and "On the side of party comrades—always ready" in 1986.[107] As Alexander Bolz, Jörgpeter Lund, and Wilfried Poßner have argued, these themes and their corresponding activities remained quite rigid in the Pioneer Organization in the mid-to-late 1980s.[108] Political programming connected to the Pioneer task at Camp Hermann Matern preserved traditions from earlier decades, including visits to factories and historical sites, and discussions with worker-heroes.[109] Nevertheless, like many schools, the camp no longer enlisted as many historical eyewitnesses in its political education because of difficulties finding older veterans still willing and capable of interacting with youth effectively.[110]

The Pioneer Organization also had to be careful with political discussions detailing contemporary socialist successes, given young people's knowledge of Western news media depicting economic realities. A few years before his death, the late antifascist veteran Fred Löwenberg recalled in an interview how youth in the mid-1980s became increasingly brazen with their questions when he visited them in school, after-school, and camp settings for discussions and leadership training sessions. Young people's probing questions about the material status quo in the GDR revealed a dissatisfaction fueled by images they saw on Western television. Löwenberg understood their frustrations because his own children had asked similar questions in earlier years and expressed the same consumer desires.[111] Youth interest in individual expression and consumer gratification made political education and the promotion of a collective identity all the more difficult for camp leaders and counselors.

An example of a child's reaction to a camp *Geländespiel* suggests both the weakness of political education and the self-perception Pioneers developed as individuals, rather than as members of a collective. In a document from the mid-1980s, a Hermann Matern camper named Matthias expressed how much he enjoyed a scouting game in which he role-played a partisan fighter from World War II, but it is clear that he internalized only a vague message. Matthias wrote, "If it were to come to that, that one would have to fight against something bad, I would be there. I enjoy discovering things, I can move without sound, I can cook something myself and would like the commission of a radio receiver or night guard duty."[112] This quotation supports Ansorg's argument that time spent at camp could be both militaristic and fun, as seen in Matthias's enthusiasm for role playing and adventure. Furthermore, Matthias's words suggest that such activities could provide children with a sense of their own power and independence.[113] He focuses on himself and his abilities rather than adopting the plural expression "we," which would suggest a collective identity. At the same time, the political content of the *Geländespiel* appears weak because Matthias fails to refer to his future service in the National People's Army or a contemporary or future enemy, such as Western imperialists. Aside from the reference to a World War II partisan fighter, a frequent figure in East German children's literature,[114] Matthias's statement does not demonstrate an explicitly East German or broader socialist perspective. Rather, his words reveal how he infused personal meaning into a socialist game, exemplifying the individualism prevalent among youth in the 1980s, and arguably earlier in both East and West Germany.[115]

National Pioneer leaders hoped that through identification with a camp's namesake, Pioneers' sense of collective identity and political consciousness could be strengthened. However, camp leaders at Hermann Matern did not erect a major historical exhibit to the new namesake or engage in other large-scale activities to solidify this identity in the 1980s. Some handwritten notes from a meeting in 1983 suggest that the idea came up as a potential project for the summer of 1984. In subsequent years, the camp leadership discussed plans for a future tradition cabinet, and someone drew a design for such a site.[116] In honor of the fifteenth anniversary of acquiring their namesake, the camp was supposed to complete the tradition cabinet by 1987. District authorities of the Pioneer Organization emphasized that this project would increase the socialist work at the camp.[117] However, the plans never material-ized into a concrete site, demonstrating camp leaders' priorities, local decision making, and the limits of hierarchical control. The camp continued to display a bust of Matern and a plaque with his biography, but in terms of new addi-tions and visual symbols, camp personnel decided to construct a playground and commission a sculpture featuring the image of a mother and child. Ac-cording to two former camp employees, staff considered these apolitical em-bellishments to be the most appropriate for the children they served.[118]

These new symbolic features of the landscape and the Western influence the camp exhibited, within limits, appear particularly fitting for a population of youth that was less politically orientated in the 1980s than their peers of the early-to-mid 1970s. According to Karen Henderson, who has used sta-tistical evidence from the Central Institute for Youth Research in the GDR, school children attending polytechnic schools were fifty percent less likely than older FDJ members to identify with the GDR, and twice as likely in a 1988 survey to understand why people would want to escape from East Ger-many. Henderson further notes that between problems in East Germany and new developments in the Soviet Union, about half of conformists exhibited reservations about Marxism-Leninism, and the number of young dissidents who rejected Marxism-Leninism tripled in the late 1980s, with disloyalty par-ticularly high among schoolchildren as compared to older FDJ members.[119]

Conclusion

For more than thirty years, Camp Mitschurin promised a dream world of social cohesion, meaningful political engagement, and health and recreation for youth conformists. However, Pioneers lived a temporary, parallel exis-tence disconnected from their normal youth troops back home and some-times disconnected from the values of the camp itself. Similar to the stadium, museums, and racetracks discussed in this volume, the camp bore the imprint of state planning in its conception and purpose, but also the potential for alternative escapism the state never envisioned. While life at Mitschurin featured some popular activities such as outdoor sports and arts and crafts, many youths failed to have an inspirational socialist escape due to environmental issues and nonconformist counselors and youth. Through political education, camp leaders tried to reinforce a sense of collective identity and the advantages of living under socialism, even as they struggled to provide their campers with enough fresh fruit and vegetables. Political education that was hands-on, such as fashioning weapons and playing *Geländespiele,* constituted some of the most popular activities, albeit often at the expense of meaningful political content. As the camp sought to socialize young people, Pioneers still had opportunities to develop individual interests and identities. As the chapters on Romanian soccer and hitchhiking in Poland in this volume demonstrate, there was still room within socialist organized leisure for independent and alternative enjoyment of recreation and travel, resulting in cases of nonconformity and dissent.

Particularly in its later years, a combination of factors afforded Camp Matern a measure of success in providing healthy recreation, but with some unintended consequences for youth selected as future socialist leaders. With the renovations and transformations of the early-to-mid 1980s, campers experienced an escape with fewer problems and a wider range of unpolitical activities, including more modern and often Western pastimes. A stronger emphasis on youth interests mirrored the attitude and policies of the new leader of the Pioneer Organization in the mid-1980s, Wilfried Poßner. At the same time, the decline in political emphasis exposed the prerogatives and influence of the local camp director and counselors who altered the balance between political lessons and play. Nevertheless the camp could not promise Pioneers a complete escape from routine political education and the pollution that plagued GDR cities, forests, and waterways. Ultimately the story of Camp Matern in its final years reveals both the strengths and weaknesses of socialist leisure policy, and the coexistence of compromise and intransigence in youth programming. Jeannette Madarász has argued that youth of the 1970s and 1980s found themselves positioned between privilege and control, a description particularly fitting for youth conformists at Pioneer camps.[120] Pioneer camp adventures constituted a partial fulfillment of the socialist welfare promise, in part through Western concessions. However, frustrations with consumer demand and limited access to the West within and outside of the camp's grounds appeared all the more obvious to young people after experiencing a Pioneer camp.[121]

Little did campers realize how well their epithet "LPG," to "slowly go bankrupt," would soon apply to socialist states across Eastern Europe: Camp Matern's sponsor, VEB Carl Zeiss, declared bankruptcy soon after German reunification, resulting in the closure of the camp in 1992. Ironically, as

Camp Matern entertained its final guests, news arrived that the camp could finally build a swimming pool.[122] By this point, the concept of swimming among conformists was part of a lost world that had always been a temporary and limited escape, demonstrating some of the contradictions of life in the GDR and alternative escapism.

Notes

I would like to thank Alexander Vari, Cathleen M. Giustino, Caroline Fricke, David Tompkins, and other reviewers for their very helpful commentary on this chapter.

1. The camp was located near one of the few expressways foreigners could navigate.

2. Literature on youth and consumption reveal additional stories from East Germany that may also remind readers of the West Berlin children who greeted the raisin and candy bombers (*Rosinenbomber*) of the Berlin Airlift with enthusiasm. For a discussion of the importance and symbolism of Western luxury goods in East Germany, see Petra Kabus, "Das Westpaket," in *Erinnerungsorte der DDR,* ed. Martin Sabrow (München: CH Beck, 2009), 441–42; Daphne Berdahl, *Where the World Ended: Re-Unification and Identity in the German Borderland* (Berkeley: University of California, 1999), 119–24; Jana Hensel, *After the Wall: Confessions from an East German Childhood and the Life that Came Next* (New York: Public Affairs, 2004), 45–49; 90–92; 110; and Katrin Heinemann and Dörthe Stein, "Sehnsüchte—Verbote—Probleme," in *Erinnerungsreise—Kindheit in der DDR: Studierende erforschen ihre DDR-Kindheiten,* ed. Ute Geiling and Friederike Heinzel (Baltmannsweiler: Schneider, 2000), 170–73.

3. Zentrales Pionierlager (hereafter ZPL) 'Mitschurin' to the Zentralleitung der Pionierorganisation (hereafter PO) Berlin, "Abschlußbericht über den Pioniersommer 1965," 15, Gera, 1 September 1965, Stiftung der Arbeiterparteien und Massenorganisationen der DDR-Bundesarchiv Berlin (hereafter SAPMO-BArch), DY 25/2537, 60.

4. Intershops were stores that featured Western goods; however, customers had to pay for their purchases in Western currency. On social and consumer compromises in the GDR, see Jonathan Zatlin, *The Currency of Socialism: Money and Political Culture in East Germany* (New York: Cambridge University Press, 2007).

5. Named after the German Communist Party leader in the 1930s, Ernst Thälmann, the Thälmann Pioneers strongly resembled their Soviet sister organization, the Lenin Pioneers.

6. During the 1950s, the Pioneer Organization used these camps extensively for younger children, the so-called Young Pioneers, aged six through nine. See Leonore Ansorg, *Kinder im Klassenkampf: Die Geschichte der Pionierorganisation von 1948 bis Ende der fünfziger Jahre* (Berlin: Akademie Verlag, 1997), 115. I identify this camp as a model because in the 1980s, the Pioneer Organization ranked the camp as the third best central Pioneer camp and the strongest in terms of its activity clubs. Interview with Silvio and Manuela Kaufmann, conducted by the author, Tanna, 3 August 2008. Taped copies of all interviews cited in this chapter remain in the possession of the author. Silvio and Manuela Kaufmann are both former camp employees. Silvio Kaufmann first worked at the camp as a student in 1981. In 1984 he became a fulltime employee, serving as the assistant camp director in charge of logistics, transportation, and other aspects of daily affairs. Manuela Kaufmann was an intern at the camp in 1983 and began working there permanently in 1984. Under the auspices of the Ministry of People's Education, she was responsible for camp clubs (*Arbeitsgemeinschaften*). The couple worked at the camp until 1992.

7. "Führungsplan der Lagerleitung des ZPLs 'Mitschurin,'" 3, ca. 1962, SAPMO-BArch DY 25/2537, 32; and "Abschlußbericht des ZPLs 'Mitschurin,'" 7, 22 August 1962, SAPMO-BArch DY 25/2537, 24.

8. Scholars such as Katherine Pence, Paul Betts, and Susan Buck-Morss have applied the Benjaminian concept of a "dreamworld" effectively to the GDR. Walter Benjamin's concept points to modern regimes' attempts to create utopian societies for the masses, referring here to the idealized GDR its leaders failed to create. See Katherine Pence and Paul Betts, "Introduction," in *Socialist Modern: East German Everyday Culture and Politics*, ed. Katherine Pence and Paul Betts (Ann Arbor, MI: The University of Michigan Press, 2008), 10; and Susan Buck-Morss, *Dreamworlds and Catastrophe: The Passing of Mass Utopia in East and West* (Cambridge, MA: Harvard University Press, 2000), xi.

9. Stellv. Vorsitzender der Zentralleitung der PO, "Material zur Vorbereitung der Feriengestaltung 1960," 12, SAPMO-BArch DY 25/134.

10. See Anne Gorsuch and Diane Koenker, ed., *Turizm: The Russian and East European Tourist under Capitalism and Socialism* (Ithaca: Cornell, 2006), 2–3.

11. Scott Moranda provides a useful discussion of how the Socialist Unity Party (SED) cracked down on competing leisure organizations, such as the Friends of Nature, in favor of their own mass organizations, in "East German Nature Tourism, 1945-1961: In Search of a Common Destination," in *Turizm*, 268–72.

12. The Pioneer Republic was the largest camp the Pioneer Organization controlled, the German equivalent of the Soviet Pioneer youth resort Artek in Ukraine. Leonore Ansorg's publications on the Pioneers include the essay, "'Für Frieden und Sozialismus—seid bereit!' Zur politischen Instrumentalisierung der Jungen Pioniere von Beginn ihrer Gründung bis Ende der 1950er Jahre," in *Historische DDR-Forschung*, ed. Jürgen Kocka (Berlin: Akademie Verlag GmbH, 1993), 169–89; and the text noted above, *Kinder im Klassenkampf*. Alexander Bolz, Jörgpeter Lund, and Wilfried Poßner also recently published the short text, *Die Pionierorganisation "Ernst Thälmann" in der DDR: Historische und Theoretische Reminiszenzen* (Berlin: Helle Panke, 2009), coauthored notably by a former leader of the organization. On the specific topic of Pioneer camps, see *Kinder im Klassenkampf*, 109–19; Martin Blumenthal-Barby, "A Vital Feeling of 'Humanist Hatred': Narratives of Sovereignty and Totalitarian Childhood," *Debatte* 15, no. 1 (April 2007): 65–86; and Carsta Nitzer, "Die Pionierrepublik 'Wilhelm Pieck'—Eine Republik kleiner Leute?" 79–91, in *Erinnerungsreise—Kindheit in der DDR*.

13. One can obtain a broader understanding of GDR youth experience including apathy, conformity, and resistance, by exploring literature on the FDJ by Dorle Zilch, Helga Gotschlich, Ulrich Mählert, Gerd-Rüdiger Stephan, and Alan McDougal, and consulting the following texts: Mark Fenemore, *Sex, Thugs and Rock 'n' Roll: Teenage Rebels in Cold-War East Germany* [Monographs in German History Vol. 16] (Oxford: Berghahn Books, 2007); Manfred Stock and Philipp Mühlberg, *Die Szene von Ihnen: Skinheads, Grufties, Heavy Metals, Punks* (Berlin: Ch. Links, 1990); and Ronald Galenza and Heinz Havemeister, ed., *Wir Wollen immer artig sein ... Punk, New Wave, HipHop, Independent: Szene in der DDR 1980-1990* (Berlin: Schwarzkopf und Schwartzkopf, 1999), among others.

14. See Mary Fulbrook, *The People's State: East German Society from Hitler to Honecker* (New Haven and London: Yale University Press, 2005), 116.

15. See Juliane Fürst, *Stalin's Last Generation: Soviet Post-War Youth and the Emergence of Mature Socialism* (New York: Oxford University Press, 2010), page 13, in particular.

16. Regarding contemporary leisure tied to an East German theme, consider the nostalgic Hotel Ostel where travelers can sleep overnight in a room called "Pioneer camp" (*Pionierlager*). See http://www.ostel.eu/ (accessed 28 November 2012).

17. See Susan Reid, "Krushchev's Children's Paradise: The Pioneer Palace, Moscow, 1958-1962," in *Socialist Spaces: Sites of Everyday Life in the Eastern Bloc*, ed. David Crowley and Susan Reid (New York: Berg, 2002), 144.

18. The history of socialist camps during the interwar years is a ripe area for research. Recent scholarship on the professionalization of camps and their promotion of nationalism is a little stronger

for National Socialist and American Boy Scout camps in this period. See Kenny Cupers, "Governing through Nature: Camps and Youth Movements in Interwar Germany and the United States," *Cultural Geographies,* vol. 15, no. 2 (2008): 173–205.

19. Ansorg, "'Für Frieden und Sozialismus,'" 185–86.
20. For an introduction to the history of tourism and travel in the GDR, see Heike Wolter, *"Ich harre aus einem Land und geh ihm fremd." Die Geschichte des Tourismus in der DDR* (Frankfurt am Main: Campus Verlag, 2009); chapter four of Rudy Koshar's *German Travel Cultures* (New York: Berg, 2000); and select essays in Hasso Spode, ed., *Goldstrand und Teutonengrill: Kultur- und Sozialgeschichte des Tourismus in Deutschland 1945-1989* (Berlin: Werner Moser Verlag für universitäre Kommunikation, 1996).
21. "Die ZPL der DDR," list of camps, date unknown, FDJ Bezirksleitung Gera, Thüringisches Staatsarchiv (hereafter Th StA) Rudolstadt, 250, 62–63; Büro des Präsidiums des Nationalrates der Nationalen Front des demokratischen Deutschland, "Frohe Ferientage für alle Kinder," 1952, SAPMO-BArch, PO 25/568, 1–2; and interview with the Kaufmanns.
22. Siegfried Kreher, Stellv. Vorsitzender der PO, "Referat zur Konferenz der zentralen Pionierlager am 26.11.1976 in Eckartsberga," 25, SAPMO-BArch DY 25/2445, 138.
23. Reid, "Krushchev's Children's Paradise," 143.
24. In fact, the Communist Party had used the site in the 1920s. Interview with the Kaufmanns; "Protokoll zur Überprüfung des ZPL 'Mitschurin,'" 27 April 1961, 1 SAPMO-BArch DC 4/1017.
25. Given Mitschurin's work in the field of botany, leaders in the Pioneer Organization must have thought that his name was suitable for a summer camp in a natural setting.
26. Similar to other revolutionary movements and the Soviet example, East German authorities named and renamed schools, factories, clubs, sports leagues, streets, and other sites after East German and Soviet socialist figures. Hermann Matern was a Communist Party functionary in the 1930s; he escaped Nazi imprisonment, fled from Germany, and spent most of the war years in the Soviet Union. In the early 1950s, Matern served as the head of the socialist party's Central Committee Party Control Commission, where he expressed concern about Zionist influence and supported party purges. See Mike Dennis and Norman LaPorte, ed., *State and Minorities in Communist East German* (New York: Berghahn, 2011), 35–36. For more information on his background prior to his leadership role in the GDR, see Wolfgang Benz and Walter Pehle, ed., *Lexikon des deutschen Widerstandes* (Fischer: Frankfurt am Main, 1999), 377.
27. The role of companies is not surprising, given the major function that they and the Free German Trade Union Association (Freier Deutscher Gewerkschaftsbund) played in organizing travel and the establishment and upkeep of hotels and resorts during the Soviet occupation period and the GDR. See Rudy Koshar, *German Travel Cultures,* 176; and Hans-Ulrich Saretzki and Ursula Krohn, "Vom gewerkschaflich organisierten Urlaub zum begrenzten Tourismus—Reisen als Beitrag zur Lebensqualität," in *Im Trabi durch die Zeit—40 Jahre Leben in der DDR,* ed. Egon Hoelder (Stuttgart: Metzler-Poeschel, 1992), 334–37.
28. "Protokoll zur Überprüfung des ZPLs 'Mitschurin,'" 1, 27 April 1961, SAPMO-BArch DC 4/1017.
29. "Abschlußbericht des ZPLs 'Mitschurin,'" 7, 22 August 1962, SAPMO-BArch DY 25/2537, 24.
30. The amount of political emphasis depended on the camp staff at *Betriebsferienlager.* For example, summer camps for the children of workers employed in state institutions like the Ministry of People's Education (Ministerium für Volksbildung) maintained stronger ties to the Pioneer Organization and preserved communist youth group traditions. See Sabine Hädicke's memoir, *Lehrjahre: Erinnerungen an den Sozialistischen Schulalltag* (Jena: Verlag Neue Literatur, 2000), 36–38.
31. Nitzer, "Die Pionierrepublik 'Wilhelm Pieck,'" 79, 85, 91.

32. "Prognoseplan Feriengestaltung," 1969, 5, SAPMO-BArch DC 4/1060, 5.
33. "Abschlußbericht des Pionierlagers 'Mitschurin' Wetteratal 1960," 8, SAPMO-BArch DY 25/2537.
34. "Protokoll zur Überprüfung des ZPLs 'Mitschurin,'" 2–3, 27 April 1961.
35. Anna Saunders contrasts traditional political education taught in schools with more innovative political activities at residential camps and outdoor environmental projects in her discussion of political education in the 1980s. See *Honecker's Children: Youth and Patriotism in East(ern) Germany,* 1979–2002 (New York: Manchester University Press, 2007), 102.
36. Interview with the Irmgard Klaus, an antifascist activist during the Nazi period and retired GDR teacher and principal, Karow, conducted by the author, 27 September and 4 October 2001.
37. ZPL Mitschurin to the Zentralleitung der PO, "Abschlußbericht über den Pioniersommer 1965," 7, Gera, 1 September 1965, SAPMO-BArch DY 25/2537, 52; and "Abschlußbericht des ZPLs—Mitschurin Feriensommer 1967," 6, SAPMO-BArch DY 25/2537, 84.
38. For a discussion of the history of Soviet troop presence and German-Soviet relations from the period of occupation through reunification, see Silke Satjukow's *Besatzer: 'Die Russen' in Deutschland 1945-1994* (Göttingen: Vandenhoeck and Ruprecht, 2008), particularly "(Un)Freiwillige Nachbarschaften," 177–306.
39. See Silke Satjukow, *Befreiung? Die Ostdeutschen und 1945* (Leipzig: Leipziger Universitätsverlag, 2009), 88–92; and Angela Brock, "Producing the 'Socialist Personality'? Socialisation, Education, and the Emergence of New Patterns of Behavior," in *Power and Society in the GDR 1961-1979,* ed. Mary Fulbrook (New York: Berghahn, 2009), 232.
40. Note the euphemistic use of the word "protect" (*schützen*) which emphasizes a Cold-War ideological fear promoted in socialist propaganda. In reality, the border fortifications functioned primarily to restrict the population flow from East to West.
41. Letter from a camper quoted in a speech from 1982, 18, FDJ Bezirksleitung Gera, ThStA Rudolstadt, 1530; and letter from ZPL 'Mitschurin' to the PO Zentralleitung, 3, Berlin, 26 August 1963, SAPMO-BArch DY 25/2537, 40.
42. Saunders, *Honecker's Children,* 68–69, 98, 102. Covering different periods of GDR history, other scholars also refer to frequent contradictions between the discussion of historical themes and current events presented at school and in the public sphere, versus information and interpretations discussed at home, resulting in the use of different terminology and language. See Leonore Ansorg, "Für Frieden und Sozialismus," 189; and Stefan Küchler, "DDR Geschichtsbilder: Zur Interpretation des Nationalsozialismus, der jüdischen Geschichte und des Holocaust im Geschichtsunterricht der DDR." *Internationale Schulbuchforschung: Zeitschrift des Georg-Eckert-Instituts für internationale Schulbuchforschung* 1 (2000): 46.
43. ZPL 'Mitschurin,' "Abschlußbericht über den Pioniersommer 1965," 6, 51.
44. Ibid., 17, 62; "Arbeitsprogramm und Perspektivplan—Zeitraum 1967 bis 1975 für das ZPL 'Mitschurin,'" 15 January 1968, 5, SAPMO-BArch DC 4/1049; and "Abschlußbericht des ZPLs 'Mitschurin' über die Durchführung der Sommerferiengestaltung 1969," 2, SAPMO-BArch DY 25/2537, 129.
45. "Abschlußbericht des ZPLs 'Mitschurin,'" 22 August 1962, 6.
46. "Abschlußbericht des Pionierlagers 'Mitschurin' Wetteratal 1960," 4, SAPMO-BArch DY 25/2537, 4.
47. Ibid, 1,1.
48. "Politische Information des ZPLs 'Mitschurin' Sommer 1962," 3, SAPMO-BArch DY 25/2537, 27.
49. "Abschlußbericht über das Leben in den ZPL während der Sommerferiengestaltung 1960," 8, dated Berlin, 23 September 1960, SAPMO-BArch DY 25/1917. LPG stands for Agricultural Production Cooperative (Landwirtschaftliche Produktionsgenossenschaft).

50. Andrew Port, *Conflict and Stability in the GDR* (Cambridge, MA: Harvard University Press, 2007), 115–22. This term actually originated in the GDR.

51. See Kerry Kathleen Riley, *Everyday Subversion: From Joking to Revolting in the German Democratic Republic* (East Lansing, MI: Michigan State University Press, 2008), 85.

52. "Abschlußbericht über den Pioniersommer 1965," 16, 61.

53. ZPL Mitschurin Freundschaftsleitung, "Bericht nach den von der Zentralleitung herausgegebenen Schwerpunkten," August 1960, 1, SAPMO-BArch DY 25/2537, 16.

54. Separate accommodations remained typical through the 1980s as a letter from a counselor in late summer 1989 reveals. See ThStA Rudolstadt, 1469.

55. Thälmann Pioneers at the camp would soon be inducted into the German-Soviet Friendship Society in eighth grade, regardless of any individual inclinations one way or the other. For a discussion of youth exposure to these themes, see chapter four of Alan Nothnagle's *Building the East German Myth: Historical Mythology and Youth Propaganda in the German Democratic Republic, 1945-1989* (Ann Arbor: University of Michigan, 2002); Saunders, *Honecker's Children*, 78–87; and Satjukow, *Befreiung*, 176–223, in particular.

56. Letter from ZPL Mitschurin to the PO Zentralleitung Berlin, 26 August 1963, 6, SAPMO-BArch DY 25/ 2537, 43; ZPL Mitschurin, "Statistik der Belegung 1965," 1, SAPMO-BArch DY 25/2537, 64; and "Abschlussbericht über den Pioniersommer 1965," 17/62.

57. Stellv. Vorsitzender der Zentralleitung der PO 'Ernst Thälmann,' "Material zur Vorbereitung der Feriengestaltung 1960," 12, SAPMO-BArch DY 25/134.

58. "Abschlussbericht des ZPLs—Mitschurin Feriensommer 1967," 8/86.

59. Hädicke, *Lehrjahre*, 37.

60. "Politische Information des ZPLs 'Mitschurin' Sommer 1962," 3, 27; and interview with the Kaufmanns.

61. Interview with the Kaufmanns.

62. For a useful discussion applying Alf Lüdtke's concept of *Eigen-Sinn* to the GDR, see Thomas Linderberger's "Die Diktatur der Grenzen, Zur Einleitung," in *Herrschaft und Eigen-Sinn in der Diktatur,* ed. Thomas Lindenberger (Köln: Böhlau Verlag, 1999), 21–25.

63. "Abschlußbericht des ZPLs—Mitschurin Feriensommer 1967," 10/88.

64. Consider, for example, Port's discussion of SED party meetings in *Conflict and Stability in the GDR,* 125.

65. Hädicke, *Lehrjahre,* 37, and a camp speech from 1982, 19, FDJ Bezirksleitung Gera, ThStA Rudolstadt, 1530.

66. "Politische Information des ZPLs 'Mitschurin' (I. Durchgang) Sommer 1962," 2/26; and "Abschlußbericht über den Pioniersommer 1965," 9/54.

67. Amt für Information Schwerin, "Frohe Ferientage fuer unsere Kinder," 1952, SAPMO-BArch, DY 25/568; "Antrag der Verleihung des Ehrennamens 'Hermann Matern' für das ZPL Wetteratal," 1972, SAPMO-BArch DY 25/2537; "Abschlußbericht des ZPLs 'Mitschurin,'" 22 August 1962, 1/4, 18/21; Letter from ZPL Mitschurin to the PO Zentralleitung, 8, Berlin, 26 August 1963, SAPMO-BArch DY 25/2537, 45; and "Abschlußbericht des ZPL—Mitschurin—Feriensommer 1967," 16/94.

68. Interview with a former Pioneer camp inspector, conducted by the author, Berlin, 10 August 2008.

69. Interview with Sabine Reiter, pseudonym for a former Pioneer who attended several Pioneer camps in the late 1980s, conducted by the author, Berlin, 9 August 2008.

70. "Protokoll zur Überprüfung des ZPLs 'Mitschurin,'" 1–2, 27 April 1961, SAPMO-BArch DC 4/1017.

71. Report from the director for culture and social issues, "Aufgabenstellung zum Investitionsvorhaben ZPL 'Hermann Matern' Wetteratal," 39, Jena, 30 May 1979, Bezirkstag und Rat des Bezirkes Gera, ThStA Rudolstadt, 7595.

72. "Protokoll zur Überprüfung des ZPLs 'Mitschurin,'" 4. The document does not refer specifically to the chemical pollution, but my interview with the Kaufmanns revealed that this was the root problem. The lake water could cause skin reactions on swimmers with sensitive skin.

73. Carl Zeiss, "Arbeitsprogramm und Perspektivplan—Zeitraum 1967 bis 1975 für das ZPL 'Mitschurin,'" 4–5, 15 January 1968, SAPMO-BArch DC 4/1049; and interview with the Kaufmanns.

74. A former Pioneer who attended multiple Pioneer camps in the late 1980s provided the following description of this camp tradition: "That was always fun for the kids. Sometimes the camp director was actually dressed up as Neptune. Then there was a revolting drink with perhaps peppermint with mustard and pepper and salt and Maggi (a brand of instant seasoning). Earlier the counselors had chosen kids who would be baptized.... They came forward. And sometimes they were also smeared with paint. Then they had to drink this concoction and be very brave, finish it, and not spit it out.... Then Neptune's henchmen threw them in [the water]." Interview with Sabine Reiter.

75. "Rechenschaftsbericht des Freundschaftsrates der Pionierfreundschaft 'Arthur Becker' über die Arbeit im Schuljahr 1959/1960," 3, 9 November 1960, FDJ Bezirksleitung Gera, ThStA Rudolstadt, 836.

76. Pioneer quoted in a speech from 1982, 19, FDJ Bezirksleitung Gera, ThStA Rudolstadt, 1530.

77. Stellv. Sektorenleiter, Sektor Feriengestaltung, "Auswertung der Protokolle von der Überprüfung der ZPL," 1–4, Spring 1961, SAPMO-BArch DC4/1057. The Pioneer Organization still considered this problem to be even worse at some central Pioneer camps as late as the mid-1970s. See Stellv. Vorsitzender der PO 'Ernst Thälmann,' "Referat zur Konferenz der ZPL am 26.11.1976 in Eckartsberga," 30, SAPMO-BArch DY 25/2445, 143.

78. Letter from Carl Zeiss to the Amt für Jugendfragen, 1, 28 May 1954, SAPMO-BArch DC 4/1017.

79. Letter from Carl Zeiss to the Ministerium für Volksbildung, 1, 6 December, 1963, SAPMO-BArch DC 4/1017. Environmental concerns threatened children's health at other youth camps as well. See Mary Fulbrook's 1974 example from the holiday camp of the German Postal Service in her book *The People's State,* 275.

80. In recent years, scholars have contributed to a better understanding of pollution and other environmental threats in the GDR. See for example, Arvid Nelson, *Cold War Ecology: Forests, Farms, and People in the East German Landscape, 1945-1989* (New Haven: Yale University Press, 2005); and Sandra Chaney, "Protecting Nature in a Divided Nation: Conservation in the Two Germanys, 1945-1972," in *Germany's Nature: Cultural Landscapes and Environmental History,* ed. Thomas Lekan and Thomas Zeller (New Brunswick, NJ: Rutgers University Press, 2005).

81. Letter from a mother of a camper to a union representative at Carl Zeiss, 24 July 1972, 1, FDJ Bezirksleitung Gera, ThStA Rudolstadt, 1038.

82. Letter from the director and secretary of the Gera district to the union leadership at Carl Zeiss, 28 August 1972, FDJ Bezirksleitung Gera, ThStA Rudolstadt, 1038.

83. Ministerium für Chemische Industrie, "Protokoll über die ökonomische Konferenz der ZPL," Berlin, 6 May 1974, FDJ Bezirksleitung Gera, ThStA Rudolstadt, 1041.

84. Ansorg, *Kinder im Klassenkampf,* 109.

85. Interview with the Kaufmanns.

86. FDJ Bezirksleitung, untitled document, 1, ca. 1982, ThStA Rudolstaat, 1270, and interview with the Kaufmanns.

87. Erich Honecker became the first secretary of the SED in 1971, and he was also head of state within a few years. He ruled until October 1989 and refused to allow political reform unlike some of his counterparts in Eastern Europe.

88. Bolz, *Die Pionierorganization 'Ernst Thälmann' in der DDR,* 57–59.

89. "Abschlußbericht der Sommerferiengestaltung 1972 im ZPL 'Hermann Matern,'" 2, SAPMO-BArch DY 25/2537, 243.
90. Director of cultural and social issues, Bezirkstag und Rat des Bezirkes Gera, "Aufgabenstellung zum Investionsvorhaben ZPL'Hermann Matern,'" 7, Jena, 30 May 1979, ThStA Rudolstadt, 7595.
91. Bezirkstag und Rat des Bezirkes Gera, untitled document, ThStA Rudolstaat, 7595; and FDJ Bezirksleitung, untitled document, 1, ca. 1982, ThStA Rudolstaat, 1270.
92. Interview with the Kaufmanns.
93. Letter quoted in a speech from 1982, FDJ Bezirksleitung Gera, ThStA Rudolstadt, 1530.
94. Interview with the Kaufmanns.
95. Ibid.
96. Ibid; Leiter des ZPLs 'Hermann Matern,' "Statistik—Anhang," in "Abschlußschätzung des Feriensommers 1983 im ZPL 'Hermann Matern,'" 25 August 1983, and "1. Belegungsplan des ZPLs 'Hermann Matern,'" 1, FDJ Bezirksleitung Gera, ThStA Rudolstadt, 1270.
97. Interview with the Kaufmanns. According to Sabine Reiter, who attended other central Pioneer camps, the dance music played at discos consisted of English songs; they were the songs that kids knew. The acceptance of Western music in the 1980s provides a sharp contrast to FDJ policies in the early 1960s, when leaders directed members to prevent families from tuning in to Western television by vandalizing antennas if they were facing the West. For more on this topic, see Ute Poiger, *Jazz, Rock and Rebels: Cold War Politics and American Culture in a Divided Germany* (Berkeley: University of California Press, 2000), 209.
98. Interview with the Kaufmanns.
99. FDJ Bezirksleitung Gera, "Arbeitsberatung," 5 November 1985, 2, ThStA Rudolstadt, 1270.
100. The state preferred East German rock of course. For a discussion of imported and domestic rock music in this time period, see Michael Rauhut, *Rock in der DDR, 1964-1989* (Bonn: Bundeszentrale für politische Bildung, 2002); and regarding Western food products, see Burghard Ciesla and Patrice Poutrus, "Food Supply in a Planned Economy: SED Nutrition Policy between Crisis Response and Popular Needs," in *Dictatorship as Experience: Towards a Socio-Cultural History of the GDR,* ed. Konrad Jarausch (New York: Berghahn, 1999), 145. It is important to note that concerns of capitalist influence increased with stronger East/ West international relations (*Ostpolitik*) and influence. It is not a coincidence that in the wake of *Ostpolitik*, the numbers of informal collaborators working for the Ministry of State Security increased.
101. Sergei I. Zhuk, *Rock and Roll in the Rocket City: The West, Identity, and Ideology in Soviet Dniepropetrovsk, 1960-1985* (Baltimore, MD: Johns Hopkins University Press, 2010), 314–17.
102. Letter from a counselor, late summer 1989, ThStA Rudolstadt, 1469.
103. FDJ Bezirksleitung Gera, "Konzeption zur Vorbereitung und Durchführung der Kinderferien-aktion 1989 mit der BRD," ThStA Rudolstadt, 1878; FDJ Kreisleitung Gera-Land, "Vorlage für die Sitzung des Sekretariats der Bezirksleitung der FDJ Gera am 1.11.88: Zu Ergebnissen, Erfahrungen und Schlußfolgerungen in der Sommerferiengestaltung," 25 October 1988, 3, ThStA Rudolstadt; and interview with the Kaufmanns.
104. Interview with Sabine Reiter. According to Reiter, limited political activities and propaganda made these camps preferable to the more serious Pioneer Republic outside of Berlin.
105. Interview with the Kaufmanns.
106. FDJ Bezirksleitung Gera, untitled document, 4, ThStA Rudolstadt, 1530.
107. FDJ Bezirksleitung Gera, Abteilung Junge Pioniere/Schuljugend, "Maßnahmen zur Führung des Pionier Auftrages," Gera, 16 June 1986, 1–3, ThStA Rudolstadt, 1530.
108. *Die Pionierorganisation "Ernst Thälmann,"* 59.

109. FDJ Bezirksleitung Gera, Rat des Bezirkes Gera, Abteilung Volksbildung, Abteilung Jugend-fragen Körperkultur und Sport, "Referat zur Bezirksferienkonferenz am 17.1.1985, " 14 January 1985, 4, ThStA Rudolstadt, 1530.

110. Interview with the Kaufmanns.

111. Interview with Fred Löwenberg, conducted by the author, Berlin, 10 December 2001. The increased expression of frustrations among youth has parallels with the voicing of adult frus-trations in the form of citizen petitions (*Eingaben*). See Paul Betts's discussion of decreased deference and increased sarcasm within the growing number of *Eingaben* in the late 1970s and 1980s, *Within Walls: Private Life in the German Democratic Republic* (New York: Oxford, 2010), 189–90, especially. This is not to say that youth questioning of state policy was com-pletely new, but rather, grew in frequency and level of criticism in the last decade of the GDR. Mark Allison explores earlier periods in which young people posed challenging questions, such as in the summer of 1968, in his monograph *Politics and Popular Opinion in East Germany 1945-68* (New York: Manchester University Press, 2000).

112. FDJ Bezirksleitung Gera, untitled document ca. 1985, 7, ThStA Rudolstadt, 1530. Sabine Reiter also commented that *Geländespiele* were popular in the 1980s in an interview cited above.

113. Ansorg argues that children developed these traits in her analysis of central Pioneer camps of the 1950s. See *Kinder im Klassenkampf,* 116–17.

114. For more information on this topic, see Karin Wieckhorst, *Die Darstellung des 'antifaschisti-schen Widerstandes' in der Kinder und Jugendliteratur der SBZ/DDR* (Frankfurt am Main: Peter Lang, 2000), 46.

115. Mary Fulbrook refers to the strength of individualism among East and West German youth during this decade in *The People's State,* 139–40.

116. FDJ Bezirksleitung Gera, "Arbeitsberatung," 2, 5 November 1985; FDJ Bezirksleitung Gera, "Vorstellungen zur Entwicklung des ZPL 'Hermann Matern' 1986," 1, ThStA Rudolstadt, 1270; and FDJ Bezirksleitung Gera, "Möglichkeiten zum Aufbau eines 'Hermann-Matern' Traditionskabinettes," 1–2, ThStA Rudolstadt, 1270.

117. FDJ Bezirksleitung Gera, Abteilung Junge Pioniere/Schuljugend, "Massnahmen zur Führung des Pionier Auftrages, " 6, Gera, 16 June 1986, 1530.

118. Interview with the Kaufmanns.

119. Karen Henderson, "The Search for Ideological Conformity: Sociological Research on Youth in the GDR under Honecker," *German History* 10, no. 3 (1992): 332.

120. Jeannette Madarász, *Conflict and Compromise in East Germany, 1971-1989* (New York: Pal-grave, 2003), 33–35.

121. For an analysis of the regime's economic policies in this period, see Zatlin, *The Currency of Socialism.*

122. Interview with the Kaufmanns. Left abandoned, the former camp in Raila remained in a state of neglect until the city of Saalburg purchased the site in 2001 and oversaw its conservation as a nature preserve. See Fachhochschule Nordhausen and Bauhaus-Universität Weimar and the Bundesamt für Bauwesen und Raumordnung, *Aufbau Ost: Flächenrecycling in suburbanen Räumen insbesondere zum Renaturierungspotenzial* (Bonn: Selbstverlag, 2005), 57.

PART III

Beach Parties

CHAPTER 5

From the Party to the Beach Party

Nudism and Artistic Expression in the People's Republic of Romania

Irina Costache

Throughout the difficult decades of Romanian state socialism from 1948 through December 1989, "2 Mai (May 2)," a small fishing village on the Romanian-Bulgarian border, was a popular destination among Romanians looking for a summer respite from the bleakness of daily life in their country.[1] Far from major cities and the usual circuit of socialist-style resorts, 2 Mai lacked basic tourist amenities, including running water, electricity, restaurants, hotels, or campsites. To get there from the closest railway station, one had to walk or bike for five kilometers while carrying drinking water and basic foodstuffs. To make matters worse, entire areas in the village's vicinity remained strewn with landmines from World War II, when the Black Sea coast had served as a strategic military location. After the war, the state erected a military compound there to secure the territorial and maritime borders of the People's Republic of Romania. To be able to spend some days in the sun, an adventurous domestic tourist had to go through all of the tedious bureaucratic formalities needed for permission to cross a military base. While in 2 Mai, tourists had to put up with the sound of distant military drills, deal with regular border patrols, and routinely have their identification checked by local *militia*.

Despite all these challenges, from the mid-1950s onwards, the village of 2 Mai gained the aura of an oasis of personal freedom and fun in a desert of state brutality and economic scarcity. 2 Mai became a destination to which an important community of artists and intellectuals, some of them members of the Communist Party, escaped summer after summer for hours of socializing in the nude. Indeed, it was the opportunity to mingle au naturel on the sandy beach that drew them to this remote and undeveloped spot. Nudism was not common in socialist Romania.[2] Nor was it very popular in other, less repressive societies in the twentieth century, with a few notable exceptions.[3]

This chapter highlights the paradoxical development in which a political regime known for its censorship of public displays of nudity and sexuality,[4] as well as its surveillance and disposal of regime nonconformists, tolerated throughout its entire history the existence of a nudist beach used by artists and intellectuals. The nudist community at 2 Mai transgressed the state-socialist norms of bodily modesty and sidestepped the customary rules of organized gatherings. The community's endurance invites a rereading of Romanian state socialism—one that accounts for such a structural inconsistency in the workings of the socialist state. This chapter aims to account for the paradoxical existence of 2 Mai by analyzing nudism and the community of nudists as embodying practices of nonconformity. Such an approach is sensitive to localized practices of nonconformity, towards both party dictates and norms, codes of conduct, and socially acceptable lifestyles in a socialist society. Given the general constraints of a socialist state, such as police control, ideological censorship, and traveling constraints, practices of nonconformity were limited and often connected with particular times and spaces. More often than not, acts of nonconformity worked as escapes and were often assimilated into unproductive leisure pursuits, including beer drinking, joke telling, hobbies, or involvement in rarely documented or captured counter-cultural artistic practices.

Initially, nonproductive leisure practices at 2 Mai did not directly challenge official politics: their significance rests in the fact that their very existence provided a small group of people with a temporary zone of freedom, giving them a sense of comfort, autonomy, and a meaningful sense of identity. Gradually, such venues and their associated practices multiplied and, in their turn, spread to other spaces and different generations of socialist youth (increasing some of their transgressive potential in the process). These acts of nonconformity had a lasting impact that challenged socialist norms and thus rendered acceptable certain acts, certain behaviors, and certain forms of escape from daily routine. Moreover, gestures of nonconformity led to alternative socialist lifestyles, one among them illustrated in this chapter in the section describing socialist hippies.

In order to better understand these developments, I begin with an outline of the place of nudism in Romanian public consciousness prior to the socialist takeover. This examination will reveal the mental barriers and societal pressures the group of nudists of the 1950s had to overcome in order to pursue their passion. In addition, this section will pinpoint some similarities uniting the capitalist and socialist periods in their framing of nudism. Then, I will briefly present the nudist community and their escape site, the village of 2 Mai. A further section discusses their activities, interest in art, and their relationship with the wider societal forces of their time. Finally, by looking at the rise of "socialist hippies," the last section will explore the wider societal effects triggered by this group's nonconformist attitudes.

Nudism and Power in Interwar Romania

At the turn of the twentieth century, the modern Romanian state possessed some 250 kilometers of coastline barely charted for tourism. During this time period, medical professionals developed a heightened interest in the therapeutic benefits of natural agents, such as mineral water, sea water, sun, and air, as alternatives to scientific health treatments. In fact, the medical turn to "natural" solutions simply reflected the wider dialectics of modernity, swinging between a belief in unlimited progress and a return to nature. Thoroughly engaged in its most fast-paced period of modernization, the Romanian state followed suit. Thus, in 1897, the state financed the creation of the Romanian Institute of Medical Balneology under the presidency of Dr. Davila. The institute took its role seriously, and in a series of medical treatises and brochures it highlighted the role of sun therapy in curing a host of illnesses caused by the modernization process itself, and affecting the newly urbanized areas: tuberculosis, rickets, and nervous breakdowns. This literature described the sun as an important natural antiseptic, a catalyst for calcium growth and red blood-cell regeneration, and a natural remedy for insomnia or certain symptoms of hysteria.[5] It was not unusual for doctors to prescribe sun exposure together with other similar therapies, such as mud baths, mineral water ingestion, or sea water baths. A properly scientific sun therapy required the patient to bask in the sun fully naked if the treatment were to succeed. However, exposure in public was hardly possible in a country where a newly formed bourgeoisie had strong ties to religion and the Romanian Orthodox Church. According to the Christian Orthodox tradition, the body is a source of shame and sinfulness. Thus, nudism, as a medical remedy, had to be properly framed in order to overcome patients' religious inhibitions.

The concerns for moral decency and medical care united with the entrepreneurial instinct of the Romanian bourgeoisie to shape the spa businesses along the Black Sea coast. The most notorious institution was the Movilă establishment in Tekirghiol, near the Romanian port of Constanța. Indeed, as a Movilă ad announced, "Our most modern and finely organized balneological center" included a hotel and a restaurant, baths, and sunbathing facilities. Here the patients could enjoy their sun therapies based on "modern standards" in individual roofless wooden cabins that simultaneously protected their nakedness from intrusive gaze while allowing the sun to warm and cure their bodies from the diseases of modernity.[6]

By the mid-1920s an increasingly Westernized and cosmopolitan elite started to flaunt its glamorous lifestyle shaped by Parisian tastes. This generation rejected the wooden huts, which spas replaced with spacious wooden or concrete-enclosed areas on strips of beach that were sex-segregated and allowed for same-sex group socialization while sunbathing. Spa-enthusiasts continued to use the solaria during the period of socialism. In addition to the private solaria that entrepreneurs like Movilă offered, the state financed several sanatoria, therapeutic facilities along the coast for treating the veterans, orphans, and widows of World War I. As part of their general health plan, these institutions organized their own solaria catering solely to their patients.[7]

The care and concern given to properly organizing nude sun therapies went hand-in-hand with finger pointing at eccentrics. In a series of half-medical, half-journalistic reports, Dr. Vicol, a balneologist, vehemently criticized Satul Gol (the Naked Village), a strip of land famous for its intermixing of nude men, women, and children sunbathing. Dr. Vicol described the community gathered at Satul Gol as promiscuous, and recommended that local authorities ban this group for breaching public mores.[8] Moreover, he argued that the police should enforce decency on all public beaches in order to prevent the proliferation of nudist groups and to regulate the behavior of swimsuit wearers.

Equally strong and more pervasive political forces supported the concerns of the medical profession, and expressed the need to organize nudism in a morally acceptable fashion. As fascist movements came to power in several European states, Romania was breeding its own variety of fascism that attracted intellectuals, peasants, and politicians. The guiding ideas of fascist "legionaries" echoed the messianic deliverance of Italian fascism and German National Socialism, as well as the latter's anti-Semitic and xenophobic stances.[9] The distinctive and popular feature of the Romanian "legionnaire" movement was its promotion of Christian Orthodox values as part of a national and ethnic heritage. In right-wing revolutionary ideologies, the fear of racial defilement and degeneracy generally reemphasizes the "pure" features of one's own ethnic body and its reproductive capacities. In Nazi Germany, where the nudist movement had been widespread prior to Hitler's seizure of power, the new political order co-opted the existing nudist associations. These organizations effectively detected the unfit and provided a particular physical and theoretical site for celebrating Aryan beauty. For Romanian fascism, the male nude body, featured in the movement's iconography, was imbued with biblical and heroic references to martyrdom. This contextualized embrace of nudism contrasted sharply with Romanian fascists' belief in the frivolousness of nudism as a therapeutic and leisure practice.

The uneasy relationship between promoters of nudism and legionnaire supporters became obvious in the spring of 1933. Vasile Dimitrie Barnoschi, a former conservative-turned-socialist member of parliament, held a public conference titled "Nudism: A Social Revolution."[10] Drawing on Freudian psychoanalysis and Marxist ideas regarding the reform of the family and social equality, Barnoschi argued that social nudity holds the promise of getting rid of obsessions with sex and false hierarchies that create popular resentment and deter genuine human interactions. However, while delivering his speech, a group of theology students, well-known for their fascist sympathies, and several of their seminary professors stormed the room and brought the conference to an unceremonious end. Furthermore, as Barnoschi noted in several press statements, the Romanian Church filed an official complaint accusing him of communist sympathies and the infringement of moral order.

At the time, accusing someone of possessing communist sympathies could result in a prison sentence. The Romanian Communist Party, formed in 1921 and outlawed three years later, remained a small group of approximately four hundred people throughout the interwar period. Members endured political repression and long years of imprisonment. In fact, prison life forged indestructible bonds between future communist leaders, such as the friendship that formed between Gheorghe Gheorghiu-Dej, the first communist leader after the war, and his successor, Nicolae Ceaușescu.[11] However, major political ideologues were not the only "illegals" resisting for the communist cause under the vicissitudes of a fascist regime. Among them, artistically minded people like Nina Cassian mixed political concerns with their pursuit of artistic achievement. For them, the human body and its suppressed potential became objects of reflection and artistic inspiration. Only after the war, when the Communist Party came to power, could Cassian and her like-minded contemporaries finally find the means and opportunity to express themselves via writing as an avenue of meaningfully engaging with the world. However, for most of them, the very methodology of exploration and self-expression is what they claim put them at odds with the political regime that had previously backed their art. The next section of this chapter will explore these paradoxes more closely by examining the trajectory of this group of communist intellectuals that made nudism a part of their everyday lives under a repressive regime.

The Nudist Community in Socialist Romania

The group of artists and intellectuals that first initiated nudism in 2 Mai generally shared a strong link with the Romanian Communist Party. Their story is a tale of gradual disenchantment and dramatic confrontation with the paradoxes and internal inconsistencies of "real existing socialism," specifically in its Stalinist form. As true believers in communism and some of its staunchest supporters, these artists and intellectuals also became some of the first critics of the regime's errors, abuses, and betrayals. Many of the early 2 Mai nudists had communist views or communist party affiliation prior to 1945; for them, the promise of a communist state entailed both a vision of a more egalitarian society and, most importantly, a break with fascist legacies, anti-Semitic state policies, and wartime atrocities.[12] This was an idealistic take on the prospects of a new world order, but a significant and often overlooked ingredient in the appeal of communism to local elites. Nonetheless, the early enthusiasm for a socialist society started to fade away from the very first decade of dictatorship. As some of the 2 Mai nudists recall, there were both internal and external political developments that made them grow colder towards the Communist Party machine. Many mentioned that internal power struggles within the party apparatus made them feel an increased sense of personal insecurity during the time when party purges and mock trials were a preferred method of control over elite party members. For others, the reason for mistrust was more connected to a perceived dependency on Soviet politics that was developing its own imperialist project very similar to the one denounced in its capitalist counterparts. The suspicion over the violent threat that the USSR posed even to its allies gained more substance with the invasion of Hungary in November 1956. For 2 Mai nudists and Communist Party members, this date marked the end of an expectation that the communist system would be a peaceful one. In spite of all doubts and fears, and sometimes because of them, many of the 2 Mai nudists I interviewed remained active in party politics, yet suspicious in regards to the humane dimension of the regime.[13]

The story of this nudist community does not fit the well-known scenario of communist dictatorships in which normal citizens resisted the pressures of coercive party politics. On the contrary, it is a tale in which prominent supporters of the Communist Party and communist ideology tried to escape the very system that they had eagerly and earnestly helped to erect. Similar to other citizens, however, the artists' and intellectuals' form of revolt did not take the form of an outspoken social protest; nor did it coalesce into a coherent political movement. They simply used the resources they had at hand to generate their own lifestyles and forms of expression.

As we have seen, the group that initiated the informal nudist community on the Black Sea coast was composed of well-established party members on their way to becoming accomplished writers. With time, the artists and intellectuals also included university students and well-established painters, dancers, and musicians within their ranks. However, at first, the 2 Mai summer community of nudists consisted of no more than a few dozen people, most of whom were part of the same networks of friendship and artistic collaboration. But the oasis of respite and the unconstrained practice of nudism attracted more and more visitors each summer. Practical information, pleasant descriptions of the village and its peasants, and gossip about outlandish characters in the village traveled by word-of-mouth, a form of communication frequently used in the Writers' Union. As summers went by, 2 Mai nudists grew in number with over a thousand people vacationing there by the end of the 1970s. As Julian Hale mentions in his travelogue of socialist Romania, the reputation of this particular seaside destination was well established by then, and invoked with appreciation by everyone in the Bucharest cultural milieu.[14]

Among the first vacationers to the pristine beach of 2 Mai was Nina Cassian, then a young poet, and her husband, the writer Alexandru I. Ștefănescu, nicknamed Ali. They first traveled to 2 Mai in the summer of 1954 with their mutual friend and companion Vasile Dumitrescu, who had also provided the group with a security permit.[15] All three had been involved in the Romanian Communist Party's underground resistance movement during World War II. They were all intellectuals committed to radical left-wing views out of conviction, who had been persecuted during the war years.[16] As the socialist state was taking shape, all three were assigned privileged positions in the hierarchy of the Romanian Workers' Party.[17]

In 1954, the three friends first visited 2 Mai as part of an occasional excursion to unexplored sites of the Romanian Black Sea coast. They set out to familiarize themselves with secluded sceneries. As Cassian recorded in her diary, this first visit lasted for a week and left her with a memory of total bliss. The empty sandy beaches, its remoteness, nudism, and a rediscovery of her body and that of her companions' made such a lasting impression that Cassian listed this trip among the main events of the year. Moreover, this trip was portrayed as a cathartic experience characterized by a synergy between one's humanness and one's surroundings that led to a boost of poetic creativity. In this way, Cassian overcame one of the writer's blocks that she said resulted from strenuous conflicts within the party structure of the Romanian Writer's Union where she was an active member.

The newly found shelter was described almost as an escape into a paradise-like garden that fostered innocent play, while sentiments such as shame, guilt, and fear lost their meaning. Party quarrels were safely kept at bay by the lack of newspapers, mail, or phones. In this setting poetry was bound to be set free. Beginning in 1955, many of Cassian's Bucharest-based comrades in the writing profession and in party politics took the bumpy road to the 2 Mai nudist beach. For some, the charm and spirit of Cassian were sufficient motivation for setting up summer residence in this remote village. Yet, for the majority of the early campers, the main attraction of the village lay in its secluded beaches where nudism could be practiced freely as an escape from party routine.[18]

Nudist Routine

At the end of the nineteenth century, nudism sprang from a larger socialist attempt at liberation from the ossified manners and prudishness associated with the bourgeoisie. However, this practice endured an uneasy and contradictory relationship with the moral principles of "real existing socialism." Some socialist theorists initially conceptualized nudism as an expression of an emancipated ethos and a basis for new, radical, and revolutionary forms of cultural sociability based on transparency. While advocates believed that nudism supported gender relations, matrimony, and family interactions based on less authoritarian expectations, state socialism supported traditional values and reproductive politics designed to build and modernize the nation according to state-socialist goals. Criticized as decadent bourgeois cosmopolitanism, nudism was also inevitably linked with sunbathing as an unproductive and non-socialist type of leisure practice.

Thus, while nudism was initially envisaged as a tool with which to hammer at conservative ideas about sexuality and the human body, most of the state-socialist regimes, and the Romanian one in particular, retained a conventional attitude towards matters characteristic of the former bourgeois models they tried to replace.[19] Voided by the socialist ideological criticism of bourgeois mores, but tolerated by the party, the nudist communities acted outside the realm of the state and organized their practices around other categories and ideological tenets. From its inception, nudism practiced in 2 Mai articulated the ethos of an alternative socialist cultural elite willing to stand by their own values and assert their autonomy from state-organized politics. Consequently, they designed their physical community and the nudist practice itself as privileged sites where a host of poets, actors, musicians, writers, and intellectuals enacted their distance from state politics as well as from the working masses. In short, they proposed a vision of being different while being indifferent to the official ebb and flow of politics. In 2 Mai this focal point was the life of the community itself, circumscribed by the daily routine of creative work and infused with fun and mockery.

Portraying themselves as the "high class" [*lumea bună*] of intellectuals, artists, and writers, the campers in 2 Mai structured their holiday time according to a clear program. Daytime was reserved for nude sunbathing, while also sometimes painting, writing, or reading, depending on individual interests. The 2 Mai bohemians brought their colorful sand sheets, books, pens, and pencils to the beach, and often, a pack of cigarettes. Early risers or latecomers would either spend time in solitude or join groups of nudists for small talk and jokes, card games, or reading sessions. Some would perform their usual gymnastics, with swimming in the nude as the best part of the experience. In her notes, Nina Cassian described her daily routine in the village, including how she swam and sunbathed naked along with her lifelong lovers Ali and Vasile. Mornings and afternoons seemed to flow from one into the other, and sometimes people would retire to spend the warmest hours of the day in their hosts' vine-covered gardens.[20]

If daytime activities were centered on physical activities and artistic expression, evening routines in 2 Mai were no less engaging. Nighttime was devoted to group activities such as parties, card games, word games, intellectual debates, and excursions. The usual meeting place for an evening excursion was on the hilly coast above the beach. That particular location was the starting point for a leisurely walk towards the most southern point of Romania, the village of Vama Veche. Upon their return, they joined one of the numerous parties, usually held in a village garden. The artists and intellectuals appreciated and enjoyed the large gardens where they could hold parties or enjoy the shade the foliage provided. Indeed, group garden parties were the most frequent evening activity, and they often ended in a collective naked swim under the moonlight.[21]

In 2 Mai a summer visitor could remain in touch with nature in a manner consistent with her own artistic sensibility, in contrast to the officially-endorsed policy of urbanization and industrialization, and distinct from the modern comforts of the beach resorts. Indeed, the houses of 2 Mai reflected the complete poverty in which peasants lived during socialism. The houses usually offered a small room with a low ceiling, a simple bed, and an additional table and chair to complete the setting. Since there was no running water until the fall of Ceaușescu's regime, local residents improvised outdoor showers for the visitors, while the restrooms consisted of simple wooden cabins in the back of the garden. Clearly, comfortable accommodation was not the primary concern of the 2 Mai nudists. A stay in 2 Mai came with all the strings attached to a remote place. The food offerings mirrored the basic characteristics of the accommodations provided. Tourists generally brought their own provisions, which they could supplement with small purchases from the villagers, such as fresh vegetables, fresh fish, eggs, or cheese. On the other hand, some of the hosts did offer full board to their visitors. Even under these circumstances, the culinary offerings were not very generous or diversified. In exchange for money, the host family would cook simple meals composed of vegetables, fish, and meat for special events. Later on, a state-run grill called *bufet* opened in the village to cater to both nudists and military personnel. Nicknamed "Musaret," after the Turkish term for a man who barbecues, this buffet offered steaks and spicy sausages (*mititei*) grilled to order. In 1976, a third-class restaurant called Dobrogeanu opened its doors for summer tourists.[22] The restaurant's cook offered a more diverse menu, as well as alcohol for purchase including Dobrudjan wine, warm beer, and vodka. The restaurant sometimes featured live music performed by holiday visitors. Due in part to its early closing time, the restaurant never replaced garden parties. More importantly, people simply wanted to spend time outside, in the air, drinking their own drinks in a space that they made meaningful for themselves.

Poking Fun as a Socialist Escape

One particular episode in 2 Mai communal life appears in most of the members' accounts and recollections. On 24 August 1968 Ceauşescu, by then leader of Romania, made a political statement that brought him the attention and the support of the "democratic" West. From the main balcony of the presidential palace in Bucharest—the very balcony on which he would deliver his final speech twenty-one years later—Ceauşescu condemned the Soviet and Warsaw Pact invasion of Czechoslovakia and the suppression of the Prague Spring on 21 August 1968. His speech generated both enthusiasm and fear among Romanians. Most expected that after cleaning up in the Czechoslovak lands, Soviet troops would make Romania the next target. During the hot month of August, as the Soviets were crushing "socialism with a human face" in Prague, the nudists were engaged in their usual, everyday routines at 2 Mai. The only difference from previous summers was that, when night came, all lights were off and the entire coast was wrapped in total darkness. The official explanation, as disclosed to the nudists by the head of the military unit stationed near the village, confirmed this was a measure to prevent an imminent Soviet attack from the sea. There were rumors that Bulgarian troops were already at the border, while the Soviet fleet was standing by in Romanian coastal waters.[23]

Since the blackouts disrupted the customary nightly parties, members of the nudist community decided to wait and watch for the Soviet-led intervention. They even brought their beach chairs closer to the shore and tried to attract attention from the sea with their candles and lighters. They punctuated their serious talk concerning the effects of Ceauşescu's speech and the likelihood of an invasion with jokes, ironic remarks, and mock plans of sabotage. Somebody suggested, for example, that the nudists organize a battalion of their most sexually endowed men and deploy them towards the Soviet men in order to shame them and diminish their self-esteem. Others told jokes about Russian backwardness and the last Soviet "trip" to Europe, referring to the long and troublesome Soviet liberation-turned-occupation at the end of World War II.

As history books reveal, the Soviet invasion never occurred, and there probably was not much of a risk of it anyway. However, for the artists and intellectuals who were at 2 Mai that summer, the whole episode is recalled as a highlight of their interaction, and a telling example of their creative stand and humorous exploits. This incident is also highly evocative of the political standing of the nudist community of 2 Mai. Made up of members of the political establishment, the vacationers frequently voiced their criticism of the aberrations of the political regime through irony and jokes. In this case, they were mocking Ceaușescu's paranoid military precautions, as well as his hasty politics that threatened citizens' lives.

Acting from inside the power system, like any trickster, artist-nudists took the liberty to poke fun at the inconsistencies of the system that, to a large extent, enabled their very existence.

In effect, the nudists carved out an open space for creative and meaningful escapes and alternative interpretations of reality. Indeed, the initial members of the 2 Mai beach community were part of the power structure, and their pleasurable nudist and erotic affairs took place while people were still dying in Stalinist prisons and forced labor camps. However, these extravagant gestures and the 2 Mai nudists' nonconformist lifestyle provided grounds on which a subsequent generation of critical artists and socialist bohemians could resist the conformity and idiosyncrasies of a political regime growing ever more absurd.

The "Hippies" of Socialism

By the late 1960s, a new generation was escaping to 2 Mai. The youth cohort born during the dawn of the new socialist order brought with them an artistic ethos signaling a new type of sensibility. Similar to their counterparts in the West, Romanian socialist youth frequently felt alienated from the world in which they lived, and identified with an international hippie attitude mostly recognizable in musical tastes, clothing, a high value attributed to freedom, and a continuous search for out-of-the-ordinary experiences. Many socialist hippies rejected both a political theater that failed to speak to their generation and the materialistic values of the typical socialist consumer. A Romanian youth movement began to form due to mutual support of the Czechoslovak reforms in the summer of 1968. In Bucharest, student demonstrations defended the reforms, and students' organizational efforts triggered the development of large youth groups. Later, the hippie culture found unity in their adoption of Western music, clothing, and poetry. Donning long hair and jeans, these bohemians explored a world of new ideas, strumming on their guitars and searching for a new spirituality.

One group of Romanian bohemians sought a physical escape from socialism by establishing their summer residence at 2 Mai among the older generation of nudists. However, their presence in the village was regarded with concern and was frowned upon. This attitude was a way of maintaining the boundaries of an already cohesive community. Most importantly, it spoke about a deeper generational divide. For the hippie nudists, the older members were very much a part of the problem. They were part of a cultural and political elite (even though its most liberal edge) that had supported and developed a variety of communist rule in Romania, which had turned out to be an isolating police state with little tolerance for any signs of difference. For the early nudists, the intriguing hippies were ignorant and unambitious when it came to party politics, refusing even membership in the Romanian Communist Party, while their aesthetics were considered with indulgence and sympathy and seen as more of a Western fad than an actual cultural movement. No matter how their predecessors tried to maintain their routines and fence off their community, the new bohemians were a presence that could not be ignored or contained. The initial circle of Nina, Ali, Vasile, and their friends ultimately opened a floodgate for people in search of alternative lifestyles, a trend that neither the regime nor more established members of the 2 Mai community could stop.

Forming a somewhat coherent subculture, this new generation of bohemians felt they had nothing to hide or lose as they attended rock concerts, met in pubs and student clubs, played bridge at the Bucharest bridge club, and ignored politics whenever possible. Growing up under the auspices of a full employment policy endorsed by the Romanian state, in which paid work was both the constitutional right of every socialist citizen and her utmost duty, the youth of the 1970s had few career ambitions, since state regulations and impersonal institutions determined their future and immediate financial needs could be met without great effort. The avenue of personal fulfillment for intellectually motivated youth, irrespective of their class background, had more to do with finding creative outlets in milieus at odds with state/party influence. In this context, the students and young intellectuals could invest most of their time and energy pursuing avenues for self-expression, which were in the end gratifying outlets allowing for personal development.

In a recent article, Dan Goanță, a journalist and a participant in these events, compared the hippie movements of the West with those in the East, focusing particularly on the Romanian case. Under the conditions of state socialism, innovative artistic expressions and interventions in the sphere of culture were the sole tangible outlets for a contentious sub-cultural movement. In the West, apart from drugs, music, and community life, a strong criticism of consumer culture and bourgeois manners fueled the hippie movement; in the East, official state discourse had already appropriated these tenets rhetorically. After all, left-wing politics were state policies, theoretically at least.[24]

Thus, revolutionary young Romanians had to rely mainly on the artistic and aesthetic dimensions of the global hippie movement to fully separate and distinguish themselves from state rhetoric.

Another participant, George Stanca, also remembers the synchronization of the Romanian hippie movement and the predominance of aesthetics over official politics. He recalls the summer of 1969 when groups of motorcycle hippies from other socialist countries gathered on the Black Sea coast in locations like Costineşti and 2 Mai. Stanca writes:

> Young people from Bulgaria or Budapest, beautiful Czech women camped out on the beach. We listened to and sang American folk music, Dylan and some Beatles. We bathed naked and had long hair. This was the hippie movement here. The police didn't quite bother us; we were too young to pose any threats—most of us were students so they couldn't charge us with social parasitism. But we occasionally got negative comments because of our hair.[25]

As in many other places, music played a particular role in the self-expression of these young socialist citizens. Romanian hippies did not restrict themselves to Western music, which they did enjoy, but developed their own styles. They drew inspiration from and tapped into their local heritage. One such notorious example is the psychedelic rock band Ceata Melopoică, with lead singer Mircea Florian, which held several ad hoc performances in some of the house gardens of 2 Mai (see Figure 5.1).[26] The band's song lyrics were infused with metaphors and hidden meanings inspired by traditional Romanian folklore and contemporary politics, making their music rich, intellectually challenging, and subversive. Furthermore, the band's sound came from a mixture of traditional instruments, electric guitars, and the oriental resonance of a sitar. Their improvisational concerts were literally unique, since they performed "unrepeatable" acts.[27] Vera Cîmpeanu, one of the young hippies who spent time at 2 Mai, still has

Figure 5.1. Mircea Florian, lead singer of Ceata Melopoică and one of many socialist hippies. Photo courtesy of Mircea Florian.

powerful memories of the deep impact the band's music had on her when she was nineteen. She described her encounter with this music as the beginning of a long internal quest for spiritual enlightenment. Along with her friends, she opted for an alternative track in socialist life. Instead of socialist consumerist dreams centered on the acquisition of a flat and a car, Vera and her group sought something else. They dedicated their college years to the procurement and manufacturing of hippie clothing, reading Mircea Eliade, and practicing yoga as a meaningful addition to an otherwise uninspiring student existence. Advancing on this path took precedence over engagement with their immediate social and political surroundings.[28] In this context, the practice of nudism took on new meanings and forms. If, for the first generation, nudism was a matter of challenging the strict moral and ideological bonds the party imposed on their everyday lives while discovering new ways of poetic expression, then for the new generation, nudism was part of a wider project of a new lifestyle enriched with spirituality.

Conclusion: The Final Escape

Overall, the nudist community of 2 Mai allowed for a temporary escape from the dull and stressful daily life under Romania's socialist dictatorship. Nakedness was full of meanings for those involved. For some, it was an escape from the straightjacket of party politics, the latter being an arena in which many of its initiators were still active. By contrast, nude sunbathing in the middle of a militarized zone looked insignificant in the eyes of the party, and thus allowed for a thriving artistic community to exist and regenerate each summer.[29] Starting with the 1970s, nudism became part of a socialist hippie lifestyle, expressing the ethos of a different generation, which contrary to the initiators of this escape was oblivious to party politics, yet also very much aesthetically oriented.

During the last decade of Ceauşescu's rule, the romance that developed between nudism, art, and free expression in 2 Mai came to a slow but certain death. In this time of state-imposed shortages, the village attracted a larger and more diversified summer clientele for the same reasons that it was once bypassed by regular tourists—it was inexpensive. In this period, however, contrary to the older custom of tolerating nudism on every strip of sand, the newcomers established a clear demarcation between nudist-designated territory and beach areas that required bathing suits. In effect, free nudism was suddenly impossible in the absence of a tightly-knit community able to sustain itself. However, it was not just economic hardship or the radical transformations of propriety standards at 2 Mai that eroded the practices of previous generations of nudists. The main cause for their final escape from Ceauşescu's dictatorship had much more to do with the new developments taking place in the cultural sphere. Despite its ties to party politics, the world of art and culture in socialist Romania constituted a vibrant milieu from the end of the 1950s to the middle of the 1970s. In the final years under socialism, the Ceauşescus's efforts to develop their own cult of personality monopolized all artistic resources, resulting in the slow and painful degradation of cultural life.

Talented artists lost support and sycophants of the ruler became preoccupied with introducing the new nationalist aesthetics called protocronism to all cultural spheres. Literally meaning "before time," protocronism sought to trace back in history Romanian texts and artistic productions that prefigured their well-known Western counterparts. For example, according to the protocronists, the first decades of the twentieth century did not produce the earliest examples of surrealism. Rather, the roots of surrealism were found in the work of a sixteenth-century Romanian writer. Similar preoccupations marked all the fields of cultural production, with artists and intellectuals engaging in a difficult and imaginative bending of historical facts to prove their points. Essentially, the ruling family enlisted their small impoverished country's economic, political, and culture resources for their own personal aggrandizement. The entire world of artistic expression, whether graphic, written, performative, cinematic, or musical, was reduced to tributes and odes celebrating the presidential couple. At the same time, established art critics ignored solid, innovative art work. Protocronism suffocated Romania's cultural life with few options available for truly enriched and enriching expression.

The old generation of communist idealists and summertime nudists, like Cassian, lost many of their privileges and were sidelined from politics.[30] Under the dire economic circumstances, and with no possibility in sight of gaining artistic independence, many members of the 2 Mai community lost hope and defected to the West. For some members of the older generation of nudist artists, an escape across the country's borders was undesirable and much more problematic. They resumed their political fight within the institutional framework of the party. Their course of action was to publicly criticize the restrictions on artistic expression that party leaders imposed on them.

One of the last socialist political scandals that shook the Romanian dissident intelligentsia had as its main protagonist a 2 Mai nudist and close friend of the Cassian group. In 1985, state authorities arrested Gheorghe Ursu, an engineer and occasional poet, for keeping a detailed diary of everyday life under socialism.[31] They detained the tough 58-year-old poet without a trial. He died on 17 November 1985, as a result of severe beatings received during the police interrogation.[32] His death was the most dramatic event in a long series of grim political actions including house arrests, confiscations of manuscripts, and forced firings that Ceaușescu took against his potential opponents during his last decade in power. For Cassian, the death of Ursu was the last stand that triggered her decision to seek political asylum in the United States.[33] For the 2 Mai community of nudists, Ursu's death revealed the hopelessness of their situation. The community had lost its core members, and without them, the now restricted sandy beach lost its charm as an "island of freedom" for artists and intellectuals escaping the restrictions of Romanian state socialism.

Notes

I wish to thank the following people for contributing to this chapter: the former nudists who allowed me to interview them about their experiences in socialist Romania, including Nina Cassian, Ana-Maria Șmighelschi, and Marina Spallas; Mircea Florian for his generous sharing of photos from the socialist era; Cathleen M. Giustino and Alexander Vari for their helpful comments and editing; and, last but certainly not least, Allaine Cerwonka for her mentoring and confidence in my work.

1. A local archive holds a document that officially records the naming of the village in 1887. See Miruna Țîrcă, *Povești de la 2 Mai* (Pucioasa: Antet, 2004). Additionally, older villagers often speak of a legend connected to the village's name. As the story goes, the godfather of the village was the first Romanian monarch, Carol I (1866–1914). In the aftermath of the 1878 Russian-Ottoman War, the newly independent Romanian state received a territory south of the Danube Delta, present-day Dobrudja, which included the Black Sea coastline. As King Carol was inspecting the new territorial additions and its populations, he came across a small cluster of houses; he asked for the name of the place, but no one in his entourage was able to provide him with one. He decided to name the village after the date of his visit, the second of May. The legend illustrates a perceived lack of importance of the village, its poverty, and its remoteness prior to the arrival of tourists. See Andrei Oișteanu, *Mythos și Logos* (București: Nemira, 1997), 134.

2. Following the literature on nudist movements and groups, I use the term nudism to refer to the social practice whereby women and men chose to sunbathe and/or swim in the nude in the company of other likeminded people. Nudism, also referred to as social nudity, departs from other practices involving the naked body such as striptease or pornography because of its emphasis on personal pleasure and well-being. Nudism is nonremunerative, and nudists tend to downplay the sexuality of the naked body. For definitions and a further discussion of nudism and nudist communities in different social contexts, see Ruth Barcan, *Nudity: a Cultural Anatomy* (Oxford: Berg, 2004).

3. Throughout the 1960s, nudism become popular in a number of countries such as France, the United Kingdom, Germany, and Scandinavia. However, its popularity did not last; nor did it attract mass participation. Nudism remained an outlet of nonconformism, or simply a spontaneous holiday activity. See the "nudism" entry in Akira Iriye and Pierre Yves Saunier, ed., *Palgrave Dictionary of Transnational History* (New York: Palgrave Macmillan, 2009).

4. Adriana Băban,"Women's Sexuality in Post-Ceaușescu's Romania: A Psychological Approach," in Gail Kligman and Susan Gal *Reproducing Gender Politics, Publics and the Everyday Life after Socialism* (Princeton: Princeton University Press, 2000).

5. The early literature on the medical effects of sun therapy includes Leo Chador's *Despre efectele soarelui si cura cu băi reci* (București, 1905). See also Emil Max, *Băile de soare și de liman de la*

Odessa (București, 1884) and Ion Dona, *Factorii Naturali care Determină Virtuțile Terapeutice ale Stațiunii Balneo-Climatice Tekirghiol –Movilă* (București: Institutul de Balneologie, 1937).

6. "Plajele Maritime ale Constanței," *Curierul Constanța* (1920): 2.

7. For an article surveying the opening of baths and solaria on the Black Sea coast, see Ion Dona, "Bucureștii se mută la Malul Mărei," *Curierul Băilor, Stațiunilor Climatice și Turismului* Year. II, no. 3 (March 1928): 8–9.

8. See Ion Vicol, "Satul Gol,"*Curierul Băilor, Stațiunilor Climatice și Turismului* Year III, no. 6 (June 1929): 26–27.

9. Legionnaires were members of the Legion of Archangel Michael, a Romanian fascist movement. With time, the term "legionnaires" became a generic term covering different varieties of fascist movements and their sympathizers. See Constantin Iordachi, *Charisma, Politics and Violence: The Legion of the "Archangel Michael" in Inter-war Romania* (Trondheim: Trondheim Studies on East European Cultures & Societies, 2004).

10. Vasile Dimitrie Barnoschi, *Nudismul: Revoluție Socială; Educație și Reeducație Psiho-Sexuală* (București: Cultura Românească, 1933).

11. See chapter two of Pavel Câmpeanu's *Ceaușescu Anii Numărătorii Inverse* (Iași: Polirom, 2002), 27–40.

12. From 1940 to 1944, Romania was an ally of Nazi Germany. It was led by an authoritarian regime that had explicit anti-Semitic politics.

13. I found this interpretation of a growing disenchantement of party politics by members of the communist party particularly convincing in the case of 2 Mai nudists; it is also an interpretation usually marginalized in post-communist, communist historiography because it is considered to imply a sort of personal post-factum justification. However, I think that the case study I offer here is a good illustration of the value of this argument. This point was strongly debated and emphasized especially during my conversations with Nina Cassian and Radu Cosașu; author's interview with Nina Cassian, 23 April 2009; author's interview with Radu Cosașu, 16 March 2009.

14. See Julian Hale, *Ceaușescu's Romania: A Political Documentary* (London: George G. Harrap, 1971), 75–76.

15. Nina Cassian, *Memoria ca zestre*, Vol. I (București: Institutul Cultural Roman, 2003), 56.

16. Nina Cassian came from a Jewish family and directly experienced the effects of the anti- Semitic legislation beginning with 1940. Vasile Dumitrescu was a member of the illegal communist party for which he served time in prison. Alexandru Ștefănescu was a communist sympathizer during the Party's underground years.

17. In 1948, Vasile Dumitrescu became head of the Romanian Press Agency (Agerpres). Alexandru Ștefănescu was a member of the post-armistice commission in charge of purging libraries of fascist writings. He retained a high position in the General Direction for Press and Printing, the institution in charge of censorship up until 1965. Nina Cassian was a party cadre at the Writer's Union, but she did not hold significant decision making positions. For more details see Vladimir Tismăneanu and Vasile Dobrincu et al., *Comisia Prezidențială pentru Analiza Dictaturii Comuniste din România. Raport Final* (București: Humanitas, 2007), 309–11.

18. The transcripts of important Romanian Writer's Union meetings reveal the tense atmosphere in the socialist cultural industry. For a collection of such documents, see Mihaela Cristea, ed., *Reconstituiri Necesare* (Iași: Polirom, 2005); and Mircea Coloșenco, ed., *Conferința (secretă) a Uniunii Scriitorilor din România* (București: Vremea, 2006).

19. Gail Kligman, *The Politics of Duplicity: Controlling Reproduction in Ceaușescu's Romania* (Berkeley: University of California Press, 1998).

20. Author's interview with Nina Cassian, 23 April 2009.

21. Ibid.

22. Third class was the lowest rank the socialist state used to classify restaurants.

23. Author's interview with Marina Spallas and Ana-Maria Şmighelschi, 27 October 2008.

24. Dan Goanţă, "Despre Mişcări," *Dilema,* 9 April 2004, 2. Author's translation of the quote.

25. Doru Ionescu, *Timpul chitarelor electrice: jurnal de călătorie in arhiva TVR* (Bucureşti: Humanitas, 2008), 336.

26. *Ceată* means "gang" in English, while the term *"Melopoică"* is derived from *melos (*music) and *poesis* (poetry), which together convey the concept of musical poetry.

27. Ionescu, *Timpul chitarelor electrice: jurnal de călătorie in arhiva TVR,* 336.

28. Author's interview with Vera Câmpeanu, 10 October and 6 December 2008.

29. This explanation is derived from the answers provided by participants as the secret police files of some of those involved (and that I had access to), but does not mention 2 Mai at all. I refer here to mainly two secret police files concerning Nina Cassian and Gheorghe Ursu, files I was able to trace at the archives of the former secret police archive: Nina Cassian – FOND INFORMATIV, DUI 279; Gheorghe Ursu – FOND PENAL 66142/Bucureşti.

30. For example, state authorities excluded Jebeleanu from the Central Committee of the Communist Party in 1984, during the XIII Party Congress. See Tismăneanu and Dobrincu et al, *Comisia Prezidenţială pentru Analiza Dictaturii Comuniste din România. Raport Final,* 143.

31. Gheorghe Ursu's diary disappeared in June 1990 from the archives of the Romanian Information Service (SRI), never to be found again. It contained sixty-one notebooks and recorded almost forty years of life under state socialism in Romania. A couple of dozen pages (from the first notebooks) were photocopied in the early 1990s and subsequently published in the cultural magazine *Revista 22.* Gabriel Andreescu, a leading Romanian public intellectual and human rights defender, come across the original journal in the winter of 1990 while persuing a personal investigation of the circumstances of Gheorghe Ursu's death. (For a full description of the episode see an extensive file in *Revista 22,* XIV (821): 29 - 04 December 2005. *Cazul Gheorghe Ursu dupa 20 de ani.*

32. Victor Bârsan, *Marea călătorie: viaţa şi moartea lui Gheorghe Ursu* (Bucureşti: Pythagora, 1998).

33. Cassian, *Memoria ca Zestre,* Vol. III, 30.

CHAPTER 6

Smoke and Beers
Touristic Escapes and Places to Party in Socialist Bulgaria, 1956–1976

Mary Neuburger

In August 1964 an article entitled "A Day of Rest" appeared in *Turist*, the Bulgarian socialist journal dedicated to leisure and holiday travel. The author included a photo essay in which a series of photos walked the reader through a carefully crafted parable of leisure, which juxtaposed the industrious, healthy Ivan Markov to the slovenly, lazy Dimitŭr Ivanov. Both were enjoying their "day of rest" in diametrically opposed fashions: Ivan in a properly socialist, "productive" fashion, and Dimitŭr in an idle and ultimately counter-productive manner. On this precious Sunday off, Ivan traveled to an unspecified mountain using an unspecified mode of transportation with his compliant and happy wife, Vania, and their content son, Asko. They hiked, breathing the crisp air, returned home happy and refreshed, slept well, and got up the following morning invigorated and ready for another day of work. In fact, a photo of Ivan and Vania at their jobs the next morning portrayed them working with blissful smiles on their faces.

Dimitŭr, in contrast, first appeared in a photograph in which the clock read 10 AM: Dimitŭr was shockingly still in bed, leaning on one elbow and reading the paper with a bulbous puff of cigarette smoke obscuring his mouth. As the text accusingly elaborated, "his eyes are closing. Why this laziness? From the stale air and the cigarette smoke that is perpetually on his lips!" Meanwhile, Dimitŭr's wife, Dora, banged around the apartment, cleaning and growing progressively crankier, while both parents simultaneously ignored their son, Vanio. After lunch, Dimitŭr sat down to rakia, cards, and cigarettes with a friend, where he remained until late into the evening. Without exercise or fresh air, the family woke up the next morning unrefreshed—feeling "as if they have worked a double shift"—and unready to face the week of labor and the task of "building socialism." If the message of the two pictorial storyboards and their simple texts was not clear enough, the words that followed spelled it out: "Tourism more and more has entered into the life of the nation. Workers and especially manual laborers should spend their rest time in nature, like the Markov family and not like the Ivanov family!"[1]

The promotion of leisure, especially healthy and productive tourism associated with mountaineering, was by no means new to Bulgarian socialist discourse or activities in 1964. Socialist authorities considered the promotion of "productive" leisure to be as central as work to the Soviet model of creating a "new man" that Bulgaria emulated. For Bulgaria, as elsewhere in the Bloc, this meant that in the early post-war decades, and even thereafter, most "tourist" clubs, associations, and periodicals focused on healthy and nature-based "tourist" experiences like hiking and mountaineering.[2] At the same time, socialist thinkers considered sports, visiting museums, and other urban cultural activities similarly "productive."

Although the rhetoric on "productive" and "healthy" tourism certainly continued, by the late 1950s the parameters of socialist leisure became increasingly malleable in both theory and practice. While few Bulgarians could measure up to the standard of Ivan, a variety of state-sponsored tourist "escapes" opened considerable space for a range of leisure practices.[3] The 1960s and 1970s in particular witnessed the rapid expansion of holiday consumption venues, including hotels, restaurants, bars, and resorts. Bulgaria's urbanized, educated, and professional citizens increasingly demanded these sites of leisure and escape from the monotony of everyday life—supplied with state-provided food, alcohol, and cigarettes. The Bulgarian Communist Party (BCP) expended considerable efforts responding to this demand and providing more leisurely tourist holidays that did not require hiking or camping for all of its citizens. Though Ivan the mountain-hiker remained the ideal citizen, the party knew that Dimitŭr was the more common denominator, and they readily catered to his needs. If Dimitŭr wanted to party, the party was not going to stand in his way. In fact, the party continually expanded and stocked venues for leisure consumption—including drinking and smoking—in this period, both within Bulgarian cities and in prime "unproductive" tourist destinations like the Black Sea coast. Even mountain ski resort areas, though not more remote mountaineering areas, became dotted with restaurants, cafes, and bars. The BCP actively provided "unproductive" holiday pursuits in these years. How could this be justified in terms of idealized notions of the socialist "new man," and the larger project of building socialism?

Interestingly, socialist authorities explained such changes in the structure of leisure provision and acceptability precisely in terms of accelerated "socialist progress," to which the making of a "new man" was integral. The 1956 April Plenum ushered in the era of Todor Zhivkov, who ruled until 1989 with the optimistic assumption of the approach of "ripe communism." During the late 1950s, his "April Line" campaign called for a softening of censorship and repression, but also for a quickened pace towards "progress" in all realms of socialist development, which the BCP named the "Great Leap Forward." Indeed, while Bulgaria's cultural "thaw" was somewhat meager and continued to be punctuated by periods of repression, the rhetoric and persistent activity on accelerated "progress" intensified. In part to counter unfulfilled promises of political relaxation, the BCP focused its energies on tracking material progress, namely the rise in the standard of living among its citizenry.[4] The party also recognized that a "new *modern* type of consumption" had emerged, with the growing demands for quality goods and services.[5] The party responded by tracking statistics and boasting about its ability to provide workers with a deserved break from their labor as another indicator of socialist progress. Whereas in the pre-war years, tourist holidays had largely been the purview of the rich, Bulgarian leaders in the socialist period attempted to supply all workers with vacation time and places to relax and rejuvenate.[6] The provision of "unproductive" tourism including venues for leisure consumption, in fact, became part and parcel of state efforts to bolster its own legitimacy and to prove that "ripe communism" was right around the corner.[7] At the same time, the provision of such goods and services and by extension the building of "ripe communism" required revenues, which compelled Bulgaria to rapidly expand tourist sites and services that attracted foreign tourists, both from inside and outside the Bloc. As tourism, in particular the Black Sea coast, was one of Bulgaria's most marketable "products" (along with cigarettes), tourist revenues were critical to fund continued industrialization as well as the post-Stalinist shift from heavy industry to consumer goods. Party formulations on providing for "socialist brothers in the Bloc" or showcasing "socialist achievements" to foreign visitors helped rationalize the hosting of foreigners, which was seemingly sticky in terms of socialist theory. Perhaps these are merely justifications, but I would venture that these shifts in tourism also show the remarkable flexibility of socialist states, like Bulgaria, to respond to the changing demands of their populations, even catering to the "Dimitŭrs" who probably far outnumbered the "Ivans." In short, Bulgarian tourism, though rather capitalist in form, remained, at least theoretically, profoundly socialist in content. Socialist authorities viewed holiday tourist sites and activities as not only compatible with state socialism, but as *integral* to the "building of socialism," enabling and attesting to socialist achievement.

However, the "building of socialism" was a complex and amorphous project fraught with contradiction. While Bulgarians readily took advantage of new tourist opportunities as never before, the ways in which they participated also heightened anxieties among certain state actors. While state agencies provided scores of new restaurants, bars, and cafés in holiday locales across the country for Bulgarian and foreign visitors, official publications increasingly expressed concerns about "irrational consumption," particularly of alcohol and tobacco in these very venues.[8] As portrayed in a 1964 cartoon from *Turist* showing a hiker surrounded by taverns, bars, and restaurants, such temptations could lead one astray from proper and productive socialist leisure pursuits.[9] While in practice authorities expended a fairly limited effort to control such practices in Bulgaria, their attempts to engineer leisure consumption proved to be, perhaps surprisingly, far more rigorous than regimes from the Stalinist period. In fact, as tourist venues like newly-built cafés, restaurants, bars, hotels, and resorts made a strong appearance in Bulgarian society in the 1960s and 1970s, so too did anti-smoking and anti-alcohol campaigns, which emerged with an unprecedented intensity. State-supported abstinence rhetoric expressed concerns about drinking and smoking as "vestiges" of a capitalist past, inimical to a socialist future. In short, while certain state actors approved state-funded watering holes and resting places in addition to overseeing the production of ever more luxurious and tantalizing cigarettes and alcoholic beverages, others criticized the over-consumption of such products, which became emblematic of benign idleness and waste, as well as more deliberate and threatening social deviance.[10] Hence, a variety of state actors worked at cross purposes and with irreconcilable differences. If official formulations are to be taken seriously, Bulgaria's new forms of leisure and tourism were critical to the "building of ripe communism," but also undermined it. In the final analysis, voices in favor of abstinence lost out as the Bulgarian socialist state continued to enable its population to "escape" in more ways than one—through smoke and beers at tourist resorts.

Expanding Tourist Attractions

Tourism was in many ways the pride of socialist Bulgaria. If Bulgaria did not have many other desirable consumer goods, especially outside the Bloc, its golden sands certainly satisfied. Tourism offered a set of services with accompanying goods that could be "sold" to foreigners, both for soft (Bloc) and hard (Western) currencies. As mentioned above, Western currency played a pivotal role in the rapid development of tourist facilities in the post–1956 period. Tourism—along with the cigarette industry—was the most important engine driving economic growth in Bulgaria, which in the 1960s and 1970s enjoyed the highest per capita rate of expansion in the Bloc.[11] In a sense, profits from tourism and cigarettes enabled the Bulgarian state to provide more goods and services to its increasingly urbanized and modernized populations.

But both, along with locally-produced alcohol, also functioned as rewards in and of themselves. State employers and other institutions could easily provide vacations and tobacco products as bonuses for exemplary work, party service, or more generally to the population at large in less luxurious form, even during times of scarcity. These rewards and welfare provisions complemented the new surplus of free time that accompanied the shortened work week introduced in the Soviet Union and then gradually in most states in the Bloc after 1956.[12] Again, socialist leaders presented the change in work hours, where implemented, as evidence of socialist progress resulting from industrialization and mechanization. This technological advancement, party theorists argued, enabled worker leisure, the importance of which was summed up in the official Marxist view that, "Under communism societal wealth would be gauged by free time and not work time."[13]

In Bulgaria, as elsewhere in the Bloc, the modernizing effects of the first decade of socialism delivered not just the technological means for creating free time, but also a rise in expectations for a "better life" under socialism, including leisure venues and escapes from the everyday. De-Stalinization only heightened such expectations and created a market for tourism and urban leisure consumption, to which the regimes across the Bloc readily responded.[14] Bulgarian tourism—in all senses of the word—rigorously expanded in this period, with facts and figures on growth reported in official sources as evidence of "socialist progress." A large part of this expansion and "official encouragement," however, focused on tourism in the traditional sense of the word—that is, mountaineering and outdoor activity. As discussed below, tourist associations, whose origins in Bulgaria date back to the turn of the century, primarily engaged in hiking and mountaineering. In its early years the socialist regime began appropriating these "healthy" approaches to tourism, led by the "progressive" bourgeoisie. But it was only in the period after 1956 that the party turned with renewed energy toward a definition of "tourism" for the Bulgarian masses. Zhivkov's "April Line"—in reference to policies pursued after the 1956 Plenum—encouraged the mass expansion of the mountaineering "tourist movement" and the "healthy" productive forms of leisure.[15] In 1957 the regime established the Bulgarian Tourist Union, and in the years that followed a range of tourist organizations mushroomed across the country with the fiscal and moral support of the regime. Under the umbrella of *Balkantourist*, founded in 1948, specialized associations emerged, such as Orbita, which coordinated youth travel, and Pirintourist, which managed chains of primitive chalets in the various Bulgarian mountain ranges for hikers.[16] These groups enjoyed strong official support for such endeavors, and as Zhivkov stated at a national meeting for the tourist organization Iundola in 1958, the party promised to "continue to persistently work on the development of tourism as a powerful means for the strengthening of the health and strength of will of the people."[17] As a result, local and national chapters of these organizations proliferated, with the Union of Bulgarians Tourists growing from 41,256 members in 1957 to 800,000 in 1965.[18] Nevertheless, as a number of new travel-oriented periodicals like *Turist* revealed, print publication still associated tourism with "healthy" and mostly outdoor pursuits.[19] As the opening anecdote in this chapter illustrated, in 1964 *Turist* clearly idealized Ivan over Dimitŭr. Indeed, the bulk of articles in *Turist* featured pastoral images of natural settings as well as tips or stories on outdoor adventures.

By the early 1960s, *Turist* began to include occasional pictures of hotels, restaurants, and sunbathers, subtly slipped into its pages along with the familiar panoramas of mountainsides and highland lakes. While only nominally promoted within the general population, party sources bragged about the growth of other forms of tourism not generally associated with "productive" activity. Even as the Bulgarian Tourist Union remained essentially a hiking club, official reports on tourist development boasted a 27 percent per annum growth in available tourist services by the mid-1960s, with an entirely different kind of "tourism" in mind. Tourism industry officials tracked the meteoric rise in available restaurants, hotels, and beds as a "socialist achievement" in the same way analysts still noted rising memberships in mountaineering-oriented tourist associations.[20] These sources readily pointed out that even mountain tourism had begun to develop a new "material base," which meant that more hotels, restaurants, and cafes, as well as ski lifts catered to visitors in mountain resort areas.[21] *Balkantourist* in this period coordinated a more impressive range of hotels, resorts, and restaurants from the Black Sea coast to the Bulgarian mountains and cities. Urban tourism also received considerable attention; events like the bi-annual Plovdiv trade fair became jumping-off points to further develop the tourist industry in Bulgaria, as the industry made outings to the coast or mountains more available for growing crowds of foreign visitors from neighboring socialist states and beyond.[22]

More like nonaligned socialist Yugoslavia in this regard, Bulgaria turned to the development of tourism on a grand scale for foreign and domestic visitors. Indeed, tourism industry officials counted and charted with pride the rising number of foreign visitors as "proof" of the efficacy of industry developments, as 1 million in 1965 rose to 3 million in 1972.[23] While these figures represented far fewer tourists than Yugoslavia, which already had 2.6 million tourists in 1965 and 8.4 million in 1985, Bulgaria's statistics are still impressive given the nation's size and resources.[24] While in Yugoslavia the bulk of foreign tourists traveled from the "West," for Bulgaria, 80 percent of all tourists came from the former Bloc, for which Bulgaria was infinitely more affordable and accessible.[25] Bulgaria became an important provider of beach vacations to socialist citizens from across the Bloc, with an expanding network of hotels, resorts, tourist complexes, campsites, roads, and restaurants. Indeed, Bulgaria's development of its Black Sea coast became a critical part of its niche in the Council for Mutual Economic Assistance (COMECON), which coordinated economic activities among East Bloc states. Bulgaria's southern climate and sandy beaches appealed to Soviets and citizens of other Eastern Bloc partners, with their prevalent Northern and/or inland geography. The Peoples Republic Bulgaria increasingly became a "safe" escape for a "captive" audience—that is, locals and Bloc citizens who could have their day in the sun in an ideologically sound setting.[26] Beginning in the 1960s, progressively larger numbers of Bloc visitors poured in on trains, deluxe buses, planes, and Black Sea ships.[27] Although such escapes were firmly behind the Iron Curtain, the presence of Westerners who vacationed there in significant numbers gave these sites the atmosphere of an international party and certainly heightened their appeal.

During the 1960s, the Black Sea coast became a place of East-West encounter, a multicultural carnival amidst the Bulgarian sands, sun, and resort pleasures. The Bulgarian regime, in fact, actively worked to promote Bulgaria as a tourist site to Americans and West Europeans through diplomatic channels. To a large extent, all of post-Stalinist Eastern Europe, including Yugoslavia and the Bloc, experienced this same phenomenon; commercial and political interests made communist states "market" their countries to consuming Westerners.[28] With few products that could be sold in the West, and continued trade restrictions or prohibitive tariffs, tourism was one of the most promising ways to earn hard currency in the short term for Bulgaria. As French journalist Edouard Calic noted, by the 1960s Bulgarian beaches had become "gold mines" with a "long string of resorts with their hotels, casinos, villas, and rest homes" along a newly built panoramic highway, some seven hundred kilometers long."[29] In this period, the Bulgarian state produced pamphlets, books, and periodicals in English and other "Western" languages that sold Bulgaria as a tourist vacation destination, not just because of the Black Sea, but also based on its verdant mountain ranges, mineral baths, and its unique history and architectural monuments. Images of the "velvety sands" of the Black Sea coast and large-scale resort complexes lured Western tourists in search of sun and amenities.[30] Calic likened "Golden Sands," one of the newest beach resorts near Varna, to Cannes or Le Touquet in France, with the Bulgarian resort's "proximity to linden forests, its countless restaurants with dance floors, its one thousand colorful bungalows, its terraces, its pensions, its neon-lit highway, its camels, excuse me!"[31] Indeed, the glitz and glamour of what he called the "Red Riviera" came with camel rides, "folk taverns," Bulgarian folk orchestras, and dance performances, along with excursions to ancient, Byzantine, and Ottoman cultural monuments. And of course, there was the unforgettable pirate ship restaurant-bar, permanently lodged on the sands of the Sunny Beach resort, where one could drink and smoke the night away, served by young Bulgarians dressed in pirate attire.[32] Natural beauty met modern comfort, glamour, and entertainment in this tourist destination that quenched both foreign visitors' thirst for the exotic and Bulgarians' flights into fantasy. The socialist state facilitated the satisfaction of these assorted appetites.

In quick time Westerners began to take notice. By the mid- and late 1960s, travel pieces on Bulgaria began to appear in the *New York Times* and other Western publications, touting Bulgaria as both beautiful and inexpensive. Far from complaining about bad service or low quality goods, travel writers expressed their infatuation with Bulgaria's layered history, its "magnificent beaches," and even its range of accommodations and restaurants.[33] The vacationers included a mix of adventurers, leftists, or working-class members on a budget, who were willing to suffer some discomfort and uncertainty for a taste of the "East," a Cold War adrenaline rush, or just a cheap beach vacation.[34] By 1969, what the *New York Times* called the "sophisticated seaside" of Bulgaria had lured some fifteen thousand Americans, and had impressed visitors with "folk restaurants" and other unusual venues like the "grounded pirate ship" and another resort bar with stools that "hung from the ceiling like swings."[35] With only gentle jabs at the "institution-like" white hotels, articles in the *Times* also marveled at the tolerance for nudism—purportedly initiated by East Germans—as well as the presumed general atmosphere of "free East-West mixing," calling Bulgaria a veritable "coexistence bazaar."[36] Of course, as British traveler Leslie Gardiner noted, the Bulgarians on holiday were relegated to a "sort of barracks accommodation that the tourist authority would not dream of offering to foreigners," but Bulgarians also perceived resorts like Golden Sands as "marvelous, a dream country." As Gardiner reported, the tourist industry segregated foreigners into "national" hotels, with nicknames like the "English Castle," the "Russian Fortress," and the "Turkish Empire," even staking out their "frontiers" on the beach. But as he also noticed that "fraternizing breaks out when you go for a camel ride, a motorboat trip, a meal in one of the folk restaurants which have seized, sterilized, and served up palatable dollops of old Bulgarian ways, from fire-walking to dancing bears."[37] Of course, certain forms of segregation because of socio-economics or fear surfaced. Bulgarian authorities restricted Westerners in their travel, while secret police and informers observed Bulgarians interacting with Westerners.[38] Nevertheless, the Black Sea coast became a kind of meeting ground for citizens of the East and West to listen, to gawk, and even intermingle—with the requisite social lubricants, namely Bulgarian drinks and cigarettes.

By the early 1970s as many West Germans as East Germans vacationed in this region, and the Black Sea coast became a known meeting ground for German families divided by the wall.[39] As Calic noted: "If the inhabitants of East and West Berlin wish to meet, all they have to do is come to these parts. The same sea, the same sand, the same food for the tourists who have come from abroad. … This is no joke either for it is quite true that the Germans of West and East get together on the beaches of Bulgaria."[40]

As Calic opined, the Black Sea coast had "not become socialist, but sociable."[41] The Bulgarian regime in this period readily served up sociability and a limited East-West encounter, at least for those Bloc citizens lucky enough to be awarded a Black Sea vacation.

The Bulgarian state allowed and even fostered this multinational sociability, but with socialist objectives in mind. The regime welcomed foreigners to Bulgaria, both to see for themselves "socialist progress" on display at the Plovdiv fair or in a coastal resort, and to actively contribute to it by spending their money on Bulgarian goods and services. The state built modern tourist facilities in these locales with "global" standards in mind, to impress foreigners and locals as part of Bulgaria's active role in East-West systemic competition.[42] At the same time, real live Westerners served, in a sense, as a kind of attraction for Bulgarian and other Bloc onlookers. For many Bulgarian citizens, the encounter with Westerners and their accoutrements in places like coastal resorts, in Sofia, or at the annual Plovdiv fair functioned as a veritable replacement for an actual trip to the West. At the bi-annual Plovdiv fair, for example, inquisitive Bulgarian and Russian visitors packed the American exhibit. They repeatedly walked through a maze of interactive exhibits where power boats and motorcycles allowed spectators to "restock [their] fantasy world."[43] The political implications of such "restocking" remain unclear, but the fair did provide an "escape" from the everyday, though for socialist citizens the American offerings could have appeared no more "real" than the Sunny Beach pirate ship. But again, in Plovdiv as on the coast, it was the foreign visitors and the opportunities to socialize in the resultant international party that were the most scintillating. As Calic remarked in reference to his 1964 visit to the Plovdiv fair, "Foreigners invade the restaurants and the pleasure haunts, and on the terraces and in the courtyard of my hotel I have seen over two thousand people, foreigners, and local people, mix freely. They even danced the twist."[44] Reporting on a 1972 visit, Gardiner also commented on the general "atmosphere of excitement" as some sixty nationalities gathered in the spacious restaurant of his Plovdiv hotel, including Bulgarians who, like a student from Sofia University, smoked "everyone's cigarettes but his own."[45]

While such tales of "free mixing" probably exaggerated the truth, or could be merely indicative of anecdotal experiences of "sympathizers," they appear to be a common feature of Western travel sources from the period. It is important to remember the reality of restricted Bulgarian and Bloc citizen access to certain hotels, and the surveillance of East-West encounters. Nevertheless, by all accounts, they still took place—indeed, they were part of the attraction for foreign as well as many domestic tourists, seeking pleasure and an "escape" in the Bulgarian tourist party scene. In terms of regime objectives, providing such "escapes" to foreigners resulted in obvious financial benefits, while for its own citizens it was both cheaper and "safer" than sending them abroad for real "escapes" reserved for the elite. Significantly, the development of tourist venues not only provided an ersatz experience of traveling abroad, it brought Bulgaria's socialist citizenry into the public eye, where the police and security agents could watch and critique its leisure practices. Even if Bulgarians could not all be like Ivan, new places to smoke and drink might assure that they would not be like Dimitŭr, who smoked in bed and drank at the kitchen table. New leisure venues could theoretically encourage adults to take such "unproductive" and polluting activities out of the home and the work place into a special leisure environment under theoretical state supervision.

Places to Smoke and Drink

Cigarettes, along with alcohol and food, were an important part of the Bulgarian pleasures and diversions on the coast and at other tourist sites where restaurants, cafes, and bars rapidly proliferated. Bulgaria's agricultural abundance and its consumer production served as an ideal partner to industries to supply the visiting multitudes and vacationing locals with quality food, drink, and smokes. In addition to feeding their addictions at lively kiosk displays on the streets of Sofia and other Bulgarian cities, consumers could purchase cigarettes in cafes, bars, and at Black Sea resorts where kiosks employed "pretty girls" to tend sleek displays that were open twice as long as equivalent city stalls. The tourist gaze feasted on abundant displays of cigarettes for sale, not just for Bulgarian *lev,* but also for more profitable hard currency in the Bulgarian hotels and *Coresta* (hard currency stores) that abounded in coastal resort cities. Manufacturers marketed their cheap cigarettes using increasingly more seductive packaging and branding in these decades. Significantly, the tobacco industry expended a formidable effort both in satisfying the socialist consumer and in producing a quality product that would appeal to the Western buyer.[46] By the 1960s the industry openly declared its ambition to provide a premium product, an object of luxury and desire.

But such abundance, cigarettes and otherwise, could hardly be tolerated or justified wholly in the name of foreign and Western consumption. The fact that a large percentage of the foreigners who traveled to Bulgaria hailed from other socialist sister states certainly made such a state of affairs more palatable.[47] But the fact of the matter is that Bulgaria developed new leisure venues and consumption opportunities particularly for its own citizens, and not just the party elite. Although the latter had the best access to such abundance, gardens of leisure blossomed everywhere and for everyone—from new eating and drinking establishments in urban centers to *pochivni stantsi* (rest stations or resorts) built all over the country. Smoking was within the range of acceptable activities on offer at such resorts. For example, in *Bŭlgarski Tiutiun,* the trade journal of the state tobacco monopoly, *Bulgartabak,* articles and photographs showcased "rest stations" constructed solely for Bulgaria's tobacco workers in some of the most desirable Black Sea locations. One such venue at Sunny Beach, called "Palace among the Dunes," provided guests with "various things according to the tastes of those staying in the room—books, fishing gear, needlework, cigarettes, toys, radios, letters, etc."[48] Given their substantial contribution to the Bulgarian economy, tobacco workers naturally deserved some of the products of their labor. In addition to its employee perks, *Bulgartabak* also openly associated cigarettes with tourism through branding and advertising. Brand names such as Varna, Roptomo, and Stewardess evoked travel and tourist locales, and cigarette advertisements showed seductive images of airplanes, beach umbrellas, and cards, thereby drawing an acceptable and desirable connection between cigarettes and holiday leisure. Even the popular journal *Turist* advanced this theme when it featured a cigarette advertisement on its back cover in 1963, in spite of its critique of lazy, smoking Dimitŭr Ivanov the following year.

In a certain sense, the link between tourism and smoking, as well as drinking, became increasingly natural and unshakable in this period of expanding leisure consumption for tobacco workers, and for all Bulgarians and visiting foreigners. Of course, drinking and smoking had long been associated with leisure and sociability. However, while drinking dominated more in the past, smoking rapidly expanded in this period—among women as well as men, youth, the working classes, and rural populations, at home and abroad. Modernization seemed to inevitably lead to smoking, as to tourism, and the practice became especially imbedded in Bulgaria, a country that was the eighth largest producer of tobacco in the world, and number one, above even the United States, in terms of cigarette exports by 1966.[49] Still, in spite of industrial and some state interests, the seemingly debauched practices that accompanied Bulgarian tourism eventually came under official scrutiny.

Returning to the Ivanov/Markov story, it is telling that in the 1960s, and even later in the 1970s, the pages of the official journal *Turist* continued to favor healthy, active "tourism." While alpinism and hiking remained popular activities in Bulgaria, sites within the natural environment such as the mountains and beaches were also subject to the encroachment of urban-style consumption venues and customs. Publications for foreign consumption foregrounded this modern built tourist environment.[50] In contrast, *domestic* tourist publications like *Turist* constantly stressed the "pure" enjoyment of nature, much like the "bourgeois" pre-war tourist movement. *Turist,* for example, openly co-opted the personage of Aleko Konstantinov, one of Bulgaria's most famous *fin de siècle* authors, who founded Bulgaria's first tourist association in the 1890s. Konstantinov's promotion of healthy domestic tourism, namely hiking and mountaineering, resonated with the socialist promotion of mountaineering as a mass phenomenon that embraced the beauty of the "Bulgarian homeland."[51] Even amidst the *Balkantourist* building frenzy of resorts, restaurants, bars, and cafes, Konstantinov remained a central and revered figure in the socialist tourist movement, which admired him for his presumed rejection of urban idleness and enthusiastic support for hiking in the Bulgarian wilderness.

Of course, *Turist* and other travel publications presented an exceedingly selective reading of Konstantinov that focused on his famous "invitations" to Sofia inhabitants to climb nearby Mount Vitosha. In an 1895 feuilleton, Konstantinov expressed the need to "raise the curtain that divides urban life from our wild nature," admonishing the urban population for their idleness and unhealthy ways: "You worked six days and you secured plenty of bread for the week. On the seventh day don't be diverted to the café or tavern. Don't you hate the horrible monotony: the smoke of the cigarettes, the stupid clinking of the dice and the billiard balls, the vulgar buffoons, the yawn, and the perpetual feel of frustration, this inertia, and this musty apathy—aren't you bored with it?"[52]

As an antidote, Konstantinov issued "invitations" in the newspaper to "Sofia lovers of nature" to join his "club for Bulgarian tourists" for mass climbs to the highest peaks of adjacent Mount Vitosha and other natural wonders. Perhaps *Turist* editors hoped that average Bulgarians would not realize that for all of his rhetoric, Konstantinov himself drank and smoked heavily—part critic, part patron of the Sofia café set of the 1890s. Indeed, he also wrote a famous feuilleton called "*Strast*" (Passion) in which he expressed his yearnings for tobacco and his need to smoke in order to write. Of course, a large segment of the BCP became addicted to nicotine and politics as a product of the same café scene.

The party inherited a rather contradictory orientation towards leisure, tourism, and smoking from the pre–1945 left, which was divided between active believers in "abstinence," and the smokers and drinkers who were deeply entrenched in the establishment. Georgi Dimitrov, Bulgaria's first communist leader, publically admitted that he was a "*strasten*" (passionate) smoker, as was his contemporary Stalin. Of course, this did not stop him from demanding that the new socialist youth enjoy "healthy pleasures." At a 1947 meeting of the communist youth group, the "Septembrists," Dimitrov reportedly announced, "I am a smoker and a passionate one … [but] Septembrists should not smoke! For them there should be a law against it! In everything else, imitate me, but not in smoking—No! … You should choose healthy pleasures."[53] However, a law against smoking never materialized, and after initial concessions and the "achievement" of the 1947 "law on bars/taverns (*krŭchmi*)," party supporters of abstinence failed to push their agenda further. The law of 1947 limited the number of *krŭchmi* in towns or villages under 30,000 people to one bar for every 800 people. In larger communities, the law permitted one bar for every 1,000 people.[54] Interestingly, as with Konstantinov, it was the venue itself—the tavern, like the café—that became the target of moralizing leisure advice and social engineering. Still, as evidence suggests, the law was rarely enforced. Instead, the regime had to face a post-war reality, a pervasive ethos of smoking and drinking not just among the intelligentsia and workers, but also among partisans, soldiers, even many peasants, and certainly the emancipated women that the regime actively courted. With this in mind, the abstinence movement within the party disbanded, facing the more pressing concern of establishing a new system in 1948. In short, while under Bulgarian Stalinism (1947–1956) the state theoretically embraced "clean living" in practice; it adopted a less interested, less critical, and less regulatory stance towards "irrational" leisure practices, like smoking or drinking, than in the years that followed.

On the surface, then, it appears highly contradictory that a state-sponsored abstinence movement reemerged in the 1960s and 1970s in precisely the period when both the Bulgarian cigarette industry and tourism—with its prevalent smoking venues—rapidly expanded. But this shift can be attributed at least in part to Bulgarian de-Stalinization, which allowed for the renewed influence of pre-war abstinence veterans, like Khristo Stoianov, who wrote openly critical accounts of the "Stalinist" suppression of the abstinence movement.[55] By the mid-1960s, state leaders called upon Stoianov and his cohort to spearhead nationwide abstinence initiatives that included plays, brochures, evening events, exhibitions, contests, and lectures.[56] Party organizers appointed a permanent national abstinence committee and launched the organization of youth clubs and regional and municipal committees with a new range of local initiatives and measures. They also worked with and within tourist organizations to promote healthy and active forms of leisure that precluded drinking and smoking. These efforts also spawned a whole abstinence literature, including books and a range of new periodicals, which explored everything from issues of health and morality to the implications of drinking and smoking for the "building of socialism." In these sources, smoking and drinking as "fashionable" and "luxurious" pursuits associated with leisure and tourism came under direct fire, and were equated with "vestiges" of the capitalist past and a failure to "evolve" in a sound and socialist manner. In this sense, the post-Stalinist mood, while marked by the political and high-cultural "thaw," did not necessarily mean an atmosphere of total social "relaxation." While on the one hand, it was a period in which there were more venues of leisure consumption and touristic "escape" than ever before, these very venues brought citizen sociability into the public eye, and under the scrutiny of an official gaze. At the same time the approach of "ripe communism" assumed, a population was rapidly "evolving" towards the ideal of "Ivan."

Any failure to "evolve" was, at its core, about worker behavior both at work and during free time; according to theory, the latter should rejuvenate workers to maximize the former. With this in mind, many sources began to view smoking as more insidious than drinking, because, for the most part, the latter could be confined to after work-hours consumption. On the other hand, smokers lit up from morning to night, at play and at work and home. With "wasted" time at work tied to concerns about worker health and productivity, smoking presented a potential threat to the very project of building socialism itself. Of course, eliminating smoking from socialist society by this period was far from feasible given that half the population smoked, and a fourth of the population worked in the tobacco industry.[57] Still, in 1976 the State Council of Bulgaria issued its first anti-smoking decree with the aim of "curbing and gradually doing away with this Western Imperialist evil."[58] In practice, this meant only measures to limit smoking within the work place, which numerous sources complained were not actually enforced. In fact, the provision of special smoking areas in the workplace seemed to compound the problem of time lost, as one anti-smoking theorist argued, "If one employee smokes 20 cigarettes a day, and spends 10 to12 minutes per cigarette, plus 14 to16 minutes in getting to and from his smoking area, he will lose some 140 to 160 minutes a day!"[59] With this in mind, socialist legislation sought to separate smoking entirely from work, and to locate it firmly in "free time" and more pointedly in leisure places. The expansion of leisure venues provided a potential solution, a way to separate work and leisure, but also a way to draw smoking slackers, like Dimitŭr, out of the home and into the public eye. Ideally, leisure opportunities would be refreshing, regenerative, and allow for workers to return to work productive and happy. If restrained and contained, however, even drinking and smoking could be compatible with socialist leisure. More importantly, their containment within public venues could assure proper public surveillance and critique of such practices.

In reality, however, not only did smoking in the workplace persist and even intensify in the decades of late communism, but tourism and urban socialist leisure practices also became shockingly debauched in the eyes of state actors. The reality of chain-smoking men, women, and youth, as well as rampant alcohol consumption during leisure hours drew harsh criticism from party circles, even as they enabled such practices. Increased smoking among women and youth were clearly central to party anxieties about citizen smokers in late communist Bulgaria—women because of low Bulgarian birth rates, and youth as the presumed future of the socialist nation.[60] As "idleness" and pleasure seeking continued unabated, especially among Bulgarian youth, abstinence and "tourist" literature continually addressed and critiqued these problems. Caricatures and exposés on improper tourist behavior commonly depicted decadent youth. For example, a 1964 "criminal photo story" in *Turist* depicted a group of young hip Bulgarians smoking and drinking in a mountain cabin on Mount Vitosha, located within easy driving distance of Sofia. The story equated a picture of the aftermath of their debauchery with a crime scene—complete with muddy sheets from one of the Sofia hooligan's boots. Cigarette butts and bottles defiled the pretty little cabin nestled on the pristine mountainside.[61] The urban drinkers and smokers had tainted this mountainside place of rest, one earmarked for enjoyment of the environment. Far from leaving behind urban blight in favor of nature's delights, the hooligans holed up and partied in the state-subsidized cabin meant to facilitate communion with nature and productive tourism. A fictionalized feuilleton in a 1974 edition of *Turist* lampooned a similar story in which two young men from Sofia went up to wintery Mount Vitosha to stay at the "*Shtastlivets*" hotel.[62] The young men brazenly parked themselves in the hotel restaurant where they drank Czech beer and smoked, viewing the nature beyond indirectly through a large picture window. One of the pair, a youth named Ivan, retired to his room to sleep some more so they could "meet in the café and bar later." On his way out of the restaurant he looked at the snowy trees through the "glass and cigarette smoke," commenting, "I don't understand what it is that people think is so exciting and romantic in the winter … there is only boredom as in the city."[63] Clearly, the men had a typical "snow-bunny" approach to winter tourism—idly enjoying nature through the smoky glass. Their excessive sleep, intoxication, and boredom represented the opposite of what advocates of "productive" Bulgarian state tourism had in mind. The pages of *Turist* explained that while enjoying leisure and tourist escapes fulfilled part of the socialist ideal, this was not to mean "laziness and licentiousness."[64] This Ivan, conceived ten years later than the original, ideal Ivan, was even more hopeless than our lazy Dimitŭr. The 1974 Ivan not only wasted his day and precious energy, but also the state's generous provision—the opportunity to commune with Mount Vitosha. Clearly, the socialist predicament was how to avail the population's free time and provide the "good life" without encouraging such debauchery and waste.

Significantly, however, this censure of smoking and drinking seemed limited to mountain resorts and urban venues, as well as the home. Both tourist and abstinence publications from the period remained strangely silent about "irrational" leisure consumption and behaviors at the Black Sea coast. Perhaps it was only here that a true carnival of leisure and sociability could be tacitly accepted. Ultimately, in this period of high socialism, the Bulgarian regime continued to recognize the need for mass tourism—at the coast and beyond—in all its various forms and accompanying consumables. Tourism and cigarette sales were not only connected to state economic imperatives, they continued to be critical to appease the growing needs of a modernizing population. Critiques of leisure consumption generally employed light-hearted, comic lampoons that might have invoked a chuckle, rather a fear of laughing too loud. For committed advocates of abstinence, medical or behavioral, the efforts of journalists appeared neither half-hearted or as "smoke and mirrors," but the Bulgarian state was not a monolith. Economic and political imperatives assured that tourism and smoking would flourish in this period. It is quite clear that for a variety of reasons, the state regarded a certain degree of "irrational" consumption as part of the tourist leisure escape to be not only tacitly acceptable, but a requirement for the building of socialism.

Conclusion

Ideological dilemmas aside, the ability to provide vacation venues and quality cigarettes—in essence, physical and pharmacological escapes—became emblematic and critical to Bulgarian socialist progress. With this in mind, Bulgarian "tourists," even those who indulged in a profusion of intoxicants, did not openly defy the state. Instead, they enjoyed the fruits of their own "socialist achievements," and consumed everything that socialism had to offer. After all, though the population increasingly ignored socialist ideals of "productive leisure," they partook in consumer-oriented forms of leisure, like smoking and drinking in bars and cafes, provided by the state itself.

In post-socialist Bulgaria, of course, consumerist models of leisure have rapidly expanded as state propaganda on "productive leisure" disappeared overnight. As elsewhere in the region, however, there is a considerable amount of nostalgia for the order and "security" and even leisure opportunities of the socialist period.[65] Under socialism, most Bulgarian citizens enjoyed long, state-subsidized vacations including, for many, stays on the lavish Black Sea coast.

Now a large number of average Bulgarians cannot afford vacations, especially on the ever more exclusive Black Sea coast.[66] Furthermore, restrictions on the practice of public smoking increased as Bulgaria became a candidate, and then acceded to the European Union in 2008. There is a certain irony that smoking restrictions and proposed bans have been imposed by post-communist governments, a heightened interference in leisure activity that, for many, seems synonymous with curtailed "freedoms." Though new modes of leisure continue to evolve, in a certain sense, the socialist archipelago of "escape" have quickly faded into an irretrievable past.

Notes

1. "A Day of Rest," *Turist* (August 1969): 16–17.
2. See for example, Christian Noack, "Coping with the Tourist: Planned and Wild Mass Tourism on the Soviet Black Sea Coast," in *Turizm: The Russian and East European Tourist under Capitalism and Socialism,* ed. Anne Gorsuch and Diane Koenker (Ithaca: Cornell University Press, 2006), 281.
3. For shifts in Soviet debates and possibilities in the 1920s and 1930s see Diane Koenker, "The Proletarian Tourist in the 1930s: Between Excursion and Mass Escape," in *Turizm,* 119–40.
4. Rositsa Gocheva, *Razvitie na materialnoto blagosŭstoianie na Bŭlgarskiia narod* (Sofiia: Izdatesltvo na Bŭlgarskata komunistichecka partiia, 1965), 2.
5. Todor Iordanov, *Materialnoto-Tekhnicheska basa na razvitoto sotsialistichesko obshtestvo* (Sofiia: Partizdat, 1973), 7.
6. On the Bulgarian system of subsidized holidays see Kristen Ghodsee, *The Red Riviera: Gender, Tourism, and Postsocialism on the Black Sea* (Durham: Duke University Press, 2005), 82–83.
7. The study of leisure and consumption during the period of the "thaw" are still in their infancy. For some initial research in this direction see for example, Susan Reid and David Crowley, ed., *Style and Socialism: Modernity and Material Culture in Post-War Eastern Europe* (Oxford: Berg Publishing, 2000); and David Crew, ed., *Consuming Germany in the Cold War* (Oxford: Berg, 2003). On tourism see Gorsuch and Koenker, *Turizm* (Ithaca: Cornell University Press, 2006).
8. Atanas Liutov, Boris Atanasov, Violeta Samardzhieva, and Katia Stoianova, *Upravlenie na narodnoto potreblenie* (Sofia: Izdatelstvo na Bŭlgarskata akademiia na naukite—Ikonomicheski institut, 1984), 86. See also Veselina Vlakhova-Nikolova, *Problemi na tiutiunopusheneto i alkokholnata upotreba sred mladezhta* (Plovdiv: Nauchnoizsledovatelska laboratoriia za mladezhdta, 1983), 154.
9. *Turist* (August 1964): 15.
10. In this sense, I agree with Anne White that in the post-Stalinist era the state relinquished much of its "control" over leisure, though, like her, I recognize the simultaneous increased surveillance and attempts to direct leisure pursuits after Stalin in Bulgaria as elsewhere. See Anne White, *Destalinization and the House of Culture* (London: Routledge, 1990), 21, 38.
11. Emil Giatzidis, *An Introduction to Post-Communist Bulgaria: Political Economic and Social Transformation* (Manchester: Manchester University Press, 2002), 27.
12. Between 1956 and 1960 the Soviet Union put into effect a shortened work week, from roughly 48 down to 41 hours a week, with Saturdays off. Similar to many other states in the Bloc, Bulgaria eventually followed suit and made more "free time" a new part of socialist reality, but on average most still had 42 to 46 hour work weeks. Bulgarians, for example, did not get Saturdays

off until 1972; see Georgi Bokov, *Modern Bulgaria: History, Policy, Economy, Culture* (Sofia: Sofia Press, 1981), 119. See White, *Destalinization,* 14. See also Paul Byton, *Time, Work, and Organization* (New York: Routledge, 2001), 111. On East Germany reducing the work week to 45 hours see Sheldon Anderson, *A Cold War in the Eastern Bloc: Polish-East German Relations, 1945-62* (Boulder, CO: Westview, 1989), 161.

13. On the Soviet side see Boris Grushin, *Problems of Free Time in the Soviet Union* (Moscow: Novosti, 1969), 24.

14. I tend to agree with Sheila Fitzpatrick who argues that the Soviet state (or in my case the Bulgarian state) responded to consumer needs rather than "dictated" them, as Gronow and Verdery argue. Sheila Fitzpatrick, *Everyday Stalinism: Ordinary Life in Extraordinary Times, Soviet Russia in the 1930s* (New York: Oxford University Press, 1999), 91; Jukka Gronow, *Caviar with Champagne: Common Luxury and the Ideals of the Good Life in Stalin's Russia* (Oxford: Berg, 2003), 8; and Katherine Verdery, *What was Socialism, and What Comes Next?* (Princeton: Princeton University Press, 1996), 28.

15. For the development of tourism in reference to the "April Line" see Petko Takov, *Nov etap v razvitieto na turizma v NRP* (Sofiia: Meditsina i kultura, 1976), 5–7.

16. Ghodee, *Red Riviera,* 82–83.

17. Takov, *Nov etap,* 7.

18. Ibid., 20.

19. The first issues of *Turist* came out in 1956.

20. See for example, Tsentralno statistichesko upravlenie pri ministerskiia săvet, *mezhdunaroden i vŭtreshen turizŭm (1960-1967)* (Sofiia: 1968), 70, 141.

21. Takov, *Nov etap,* 27–8.

22. *Plovdivski panair* (September 1956): 32.

23. Vicho Sŭbev, *90 Godini organizirano turistichesko dvizheniie v Bŭlgariia* (Sofiia: Meditsina i kultura, 1986), 11.

24. David Turnock, *East European Economy in Context: Communism and Transition* (New York: Routledge, 1997), 45.

25. For this figure on Bulgaria see Derek Hall, Melanie Smith, and Barabara Marcisewska, ed., *Tourism in the New Europe: The Challenges and Opportunities of EU Enlargement* (Oxfordshire, UK: Cabi Publishing, 2006), 251.

26. For Soviet travelers to Bulgaria and elsewhere in Eastern Europe as "demi-other," see Anne Gorsuch, "Time Travelers: Soviet Tourists to Eastern Europe," in *Turizm* (Ithaca: Cornell University Press, 2006), 205–26.

27. Edouard Calic, *Life in Bulgaria as Seen by Edouard Calic* (Sofia: Foreign Languages Press, 1964), 173.

28. On the Soviet example, see Shawn Salmon, "Marketing Socialism: Inturist in the Late 1950s and Early 1960s," in *Turizm,* 186–204.

29. Calic, *Life in Bulgaria,* 160.

30. *Plovdivski panair* (September 1960): 3; PODA—(F-1812k, O-1, E-70, L-1).

31. Calic, *Life in Bulgaria,* 161

32. For images of this see Strashimir Rashev and Boyan Bolgar, *Bulgarian Black Sea Coast* (Sofiia: Sofia Press, 1968), 41, 65.

33. See for example, Arthur Eperon, "Tourism Opens Frontiers in Bulgaria," *New York Times,* 2 March 1969; Arthur Eperson, "Following a New Road," *New York Times,* 26 February 1967; and "The Lure of Inland Bulgaria," *New York Times,* 25 February 1968.

34. On the types of Westerners who visited the Bulgarian coast see Ghodsee, *The Red Riviera,* 85–87.

35. *New York Times,* 8 March 1970.

36. See *New York Times,* 28 February 1970; and *New York Times,* 17 October 1965.

37. Leslie Gardiner, *Curtain Calls: Travels in Albania, Romania and Bulgaria* (London: Duckworth Press, 1976), 163.
38. For some discussion of this phenomenon see Ghodsee, *The Red Riviera,* 92–5.
39. Calic, *Life in Bulgaria,* 157.
40. Ibid.
41. Ibid., 156.
42. On the role of tourism in Cold War rivalry, see Anne Gorsuch and Diane Koenker "Introduction," in *Turizm,* 11–12.
43. Leslie Gardiner, "So Long at the Fair," *Blackwood's Magazine* Vol. 313 (February 1972): 97–110; 106 in particular.
44. Calic, *Life in Bulgaria,* 117.
45. Gardiner, "So Long at the Fair," 104.
46. Tsentralel Durzhven Arhkiv (hereafter TsDA) f-347, O-18, E-147, 1983, 1.
47. Before the transition in 1989, for example, Bloc tourists accounted for 70.9 percent of foreign tourists. Ghodsee, *The Red Riviera,* 86.
48. *Bŭlgarski tiutiun* 9 (1963): 47.
49. *Bŭlgarski tiutiun* 2 (1966): 1.
50. For pictures highlighting hotels and restaurants on the coast see, for example, Rashev and Bolgar, *Bulgarian Black Sea Coast.*
51. *Turist* 6 (1964): 29.
52. Aleko Konstantinov, *Razkazi i feĭletoni* (Sofiia: Knigoizdatesltvo fakel, 1937), 49.
53. Paun Genov, *S Fakela na trezvenostta: Momenti ot borbata protiv pianstvoto i tiutiunopushteneto pres 1300-Godishnata istoriia na Bŭlgariia* (Sofiia: Natsionalen komitet za trezvenost, meditsina i fizkultura, 1980), 43.
54. It also included the closing and prohibition of opening new bars in neighborhoods less than two hundred meters from mines, schools, factories, military bases, reading rooms (*chitalishte*), and military clubs.
55. Kristo Stoianov, *Dvizheniie za trezvenost v razgradski okrŭg* (Razgrad: Okrŭzhen komitet za trezvenost, 1983), 56.
56. Stoianov, *Dvizheniie za trezvenost,* 67–8.
57. See Nauchnoizsledovatelska laboratoriia za mladezhdta kŭm HIIM pri TsK na DKMS, *Problemi na tiutiunopusheneto i alkokholnata upotreba sred mladezhta* (Plovdiv, 1983), 59, 83.
58. *Tobacco Reporter* (April 1976): 80.
59. Nikolai Sikulnov, *Za da ne propushat nashite detsa* (Sofiia: Meditsina i fizkultura, 1980), 3.
60. On women see Institut za Zdravna Prosveta, Natsionalen Komitet za Trezvenost, *Besedi za vredata ot tiutiunopusheneto* (Sofiia, 1976), 26. On youth see Ministerstvo na Zdravookhraneniia—NR Bŭlgariia, Institut Sanitarnovo Prosveshteniia, *Shestoi simposium institutov sanitarnovo prosveshteniia sotsialisticheskikh stran* (Sofiia: 1982), 102.
61. *Turist* 6 (1964): 29.
62. Significantly, *Shtastlivets* means the "happy one" in Bulgarian and was also the well-known pen name of the aforementioned writer and "tourist," Aleko Konstantinov.
63. *Turist* 12 (1974): 30.
64. *Turist* 2 (1974): 6–7.
65. See Kristen Ghodsee, "Red Nostalgia? Communism, Women's Emancipation, and Economic Transformation in Bulgaria," *L'Homme: Zeitschrift für Feministische Geschichtswissenschaft* 15 (2004): 3; and Ivailo Znepolski, *Bŭlgarskiiat komunizŭm: Sotsiokulturni cherti i vlastova traektoriia* (Sofia: Ciela Press, 2008), 220.
66. *The Sofia Echo,* 26 May 2009, 1.

PART IV

Roadside Adventures and Bright City Lights

CHAPTER 7

Hitchhikers' Paradise

The Intersection of Mass Mobility, Consumer Demand, and Ideology in the People's Republic of Poland

Mark Keck-Szajbel

When 28-year-old Karin Stanek took to the stage in 1963 performing as the lead singer and guitarist of the band *Czerwono-Czarni*, she attained fame through her song "Let's Go Hitchhiking" (*"Jedziemy autostopem"*), in which she promised that she was:

> Goin' hitchhiking, hitchhiking
> Brother, that way you get across Europe
> Where the roads are unknown, brothers dare to go,
> About what happens next, don't worry
> *Autostop, autostop,* go on and go!
> The cars are goin', they'll pick you up,
> Today that car's gonna take us....

As if fulfilling the prophecy of hitchhiking across Europe, Stanek eventually emigrated from Poland to West Germany in 1976. However, she stayed in Poland long enough to popularize a form of travel that, while common in all motorized countries, was transformed into a unique program of Polish state socialism.

Hitchhiking, or *autostop* in Polish, was incredibly popular in Poland and eventually became an officially sponsored project. For over thirty years, officials permitted thumbing rides during the summer months in what was called the *autostop* program. With the purchase of an *autostop* booklet, the consumer not only received coupons, maps, and rules concerning the legalized hitchhiking program, but also partook in an inexpensive form of travel. After purchasing a booklet, the hitchhiker gave the driver the necessary coupons when receiving a lift. In return, the driver could collect reimbursement for gasoline. Each booklet afforded the hitchhiker one thousand kilometers, and later two thousand kilometers, of coupons (*kupony*). As such, it was virtually the cheapest form of travel in People's Poland.[1]

Autostop was an intrinsically fascinating form of socialist travel to which Poles have devoted only limited (and often nostalgic) attention, and which Western researchers have ignored altogether.[2] The absence of research on this form of mobility is all the more unusual, since internal state documents recorded that thousands of Poles and foreigners flocked to kiosks annually in order to purchase booklets and to participate in the program.[3] This chapter will help to fill the peculiar research gap. Why, in a region otherwise known for regimes with draconian laws and Stalinist practices, did authorities make the unprecedented decision to support *autostop* in 1957, just one year after mass uprisings and brutal crackdowns in Poland and Hungary? Why did it last for over thirty years—continuing through multiple conflicts, ideological ruptures, and even surviving state socialism itself?

Due to the unique environment in which Poland found itself in the immediate post-war era, it would become a country that tolerated—indeed supported—the masses to travel outside the framework of state-organized programs; in contrast to other socialist modes of travel, Polish officials and individuals in semi-official positions created lobby groups to expand the number of unorganized tourist opportunities such as (but not limited to) *autostop*.[4] Crucially, the program was also seen as a unique way to get to know a country with new borders; it catered to the type of nationalistic socialism that Poland's new first secretary, Władysław Gomułka, actively promoted. Additionally, it was a program that catered to a growing movement of youngsters who were already hitchhiking. By promoting the *autostop* program, the regime hoped to control a population that, even if it had funds to purchase a private automobile, could only hope that enough would be produced to avoid endless queues. The *autostop* program, in other words, was a means of controlling a form of mobility potentially independent of the state while promoting independent mobility, which was seen as a hallmark of a modern, industrialized state.

But even with initial government support, the *autostop* program occupied an ambiguous position in socialist Poland. The fact that organizers were not part of the state-run Socialist Youth Union (*Związek Socjalistycznej Młodzieży*, or ZMS), and that individuals who funded the program were not required to be party members helped abet its negative reputation. Youngsters who left home to go hitchhiking were seen as chimera-like creatures of the East and West, consciously imitating shunned Western models while enjoying the pleasures of a socialist state. Even when officials could not document unusually high rates of deviancy or illegal behavior, everyday Poles and pulp magazines depicted *autostop* as an escape into a world of sexual promiscuity, pedophilia, and occasionally—since it was generally an exclusively male pre-occupation—with homosexuality.

On the other hand, *autostop* was a socialist escape on many levels. In the era of economic booms and in the spirit of Cold-War competition, *autostop* promoted socialist citizens' voluntary cooperation on the road. The program brought workers together to reach for a common goal, and equalized travel opportunities. Like other projects across the East Bloc—most notably Khrushchev's still-born car-sharing project in the late 1950s—the legalized hitchhiking program was a uniquely socialist way to promote automobility.[5] Indeed, the Polish socialist regime was motivated to allow *autostop* both as a cheap stop-gap measure to motorize the country, and as an alternative to strictly organized escapes.

Peculiarly, it grew to become an escape from the very system that initially condoned its creation; teenagers and twenty-somethings chose to hitchhike in lieu of other, more politically-oriented programs, and East Bloc citizens flocked to Polish roads for an experience of freedom. For that reason, when young enthusiasts made a case to incorporate similar hitchhiking programs in Czechoslovakia and East Germany in the late 1960s and 1970s, officials scoffed at the notion of supporting and abetting those who they saw as vagrants and individualistic youngsters. This was certainly due in part to what Alexander Vari cited in the introduction as the return to ideological orthodoxy in the 1970s and 1980s: East German and Czechoslovak authorities were fully aware that, with few exceptions, the hitchhiker was not party cadre. In contrast, Polish *autostop* organizers were able to co-opt the state in the brief era of liberalization in 1956, and developed a program that found genuine popularity amongst the population. As one of the only profitable escapes in the tourist industry, and since it gained in popularity with both native Poles as well as foreigners, authorities allowed *autostop* to continue even after its ideological efficacy eroded.

Hitchhiking "Around the World" (Or at Least around Poland)

In the summer of 1956, workers in the western Polish city of Poznań took to the streets to demand bread and wages. When the government sent tanks and troops to the city, killing more than seventy unarmed civilians, hundreds of thousands demonstrated against the repressive actions. In marked contrast to other uprisings, authorities in Warsaw and Moscow decided to remove the Stalinist head of the party, Edward Ochab, and elect the popular Władysław Gomułka to replace him, in what has come to be known as Poznań June. Most Poles viewed Gomułka as a moderate communist and a nationalist; the period that he ushered in was transformative, leading to a general relaxation of hard-line policies and a broad liberalization.[6] For everyday citizens, one of the most salient results of Gomułka's ascension was the founding of new cultural journals and popular magazines, such as *Dookoła Świata* (*Around the World*), which would endorse *autostop*.

Parallel to the cultural thaw, Gomułka's rise to power also signified a new focus on automobility on par with the West, as in almost every East Bloc country.[7] British sociologist John Urry defines the system of automobility as an "autopoietic web," by which he means that it involves not only the availability of a car, but also a vast array of technologies, as well as a culture that comes to understand mobility, environment, and privacy.[8] Poland also eventually adopted an automobility program, but the route officials took was inherently different from other neighboring countries, since it had many more hurdles to overcome in order to attain automobility.

In 1957, the government created a motorization council composed of scientists, public officials, and managers in order to advise officials on the best way to motorize the country. In addition to encouraging the production of cheap personal automobiles for the masses, the council pushed for the development of improved roads, realizing the genuine mediocrity of Poland's transit infrastructure. In 1958, for example, nearly one-quarter of all the streets in Poland were officially considered "unimproved, hard surface streets." East Germans, in contrast, already had over one thousand kilometers of rapid velocity *Autobahn* in their small republic.[9] Complicating matters was the shortage of cars. Even if Poles dared to risk a trip from pot hole to pot hole, attaining a car was virtually impossible. Not only were there just over two hundred thousand privately owned passenger automobiles well into the 1960s (in a country with a population of thirty million), expanding the number of drivers was difficult, since Poland exported nearly one-third of the personal automobiles produced in the country. Additionally, as in almost every Bloc country, cars were exorbitantly expensive for almost any individual.

Polish socialist authorities' chronic inability to advance mass mobility provided the *autostop* movement with a valuable impetus; as long as there were not enough personal automobiles or train connections to tourist locations, the hitchhiking movement could encourage the culture of automobility and alleviate transportation problems. One writer in *Dookoła Świata* responded that the *autostop* program could be a "genius way to motorize the country in the fewest number of years," since it brought people to the road, even when it was not possible to procure a sufficient number of cars or buses, or paved roads.[10] Nevertheless, the legality of hitchhiking was still in question, as journalists in *Dookoła Świata* were quick to note.

"DRIVERS!" began an appeal in a popular youth magazine, "we always thought and still think today that you have feelings deep in your heart for the poor, beaten travelers on foot."[11] The writer of the article was addressing drivers of personal automobiles in the 1950s, and was explaining how frequently he had been left in the dust as a hitchhiker on Polish streets and highways. But he did not lose hope: He was "deeply convinced" that drivers would pick him up, albeit on the condition that there were "no officers or traffic controllers close by."[12] In Poland—as in most countries in the 1950s—hitchhiking was not necessarily forbidden, but not explicitly legal; this legal gray zone made hitchhikers an ambiguous lot, leaving our writer to wait for hours before being picked up.

Since most of the street traffic directly after the war was in the form of state-owned vehicles, and since the state did not condone picking up hitchhikers, drivers frequently came into conflict with the *milicja obywatelska* (the Polish police) for transporting unknown persons in state-owned vehicles.[13] For the drivers of both state-owned and personal vehicles, "*łebkarstwo*" (or "thumbing it") signified a possibility to earn additional money by providing strangers with a lift. They were upset about getting pulled over by the police only to be forced to pay a fine and face reprimand.[14]

It was in this context that Stanisław Lubicz galvanized support to legalize hitchhiking. Lubicz worked for *Dookoła Świata* and received radio coverage from the fashionable radio program, *Muzyka i Aktualność* (*Music and Actualities*).[15] With the combined efforts of numerous individuals and a coalition of organizations—not to mention the stamp of approval from the ZMS—Lubicz was able to convince the minister of physical culture that his program was legitimate and not subversive.[16]

Crucially, organizers argued that the *autostop* program could be used to celebrate socialist Poland while promoting mass mobility. Since Poland lost a third of its territory to the Soviet Union and reemerged much smaller after World War II, post-war authorities were devoted to strengthen their population's belief in the legitimacy and viability of the new Polish borders.[17] They created a network of institutions to scientifically back claims of Polish heritage in Pomerania, Silesia, and Great Poland; religious leaders were brought to declare to crowds that even the "stones spoke ... Polish;" and huge expositions were planned (most notably the Regained Territories Exposition of 1948 in Wrocław) to demonstrate the Polishness of western territories.[18] A decade later, *Autostop* fit perfectly with this type of propaganda: it made the so-called "reincorporated territories" (*ziemia odzyskana*) more accessible to the general public by encouraging young people to go to unknown places and discover the country for which socialist authorities had fought. But in contrast to large expositions and meetings, the program did not require significant state-expenditure.

In publications, hitchhiking routes encouraged travelers to venture to western Poland or to sites reminding young people of the sacrifices made during World War II. In 1961, for example, *Dookoła Świata* combined the two, suggesting that hitchhikers travel from Bolków to Zielona Góra. Avoiding major cities, this route went roughly from Wrocław to Frankfurt/Oder and took the hitchhiker first to Gross Rosen, a former concentration camp. A visit to this site drew immediate attention to the recent violence against Polish citizens and implicit justification for retribution against Germans. The route then took the traveler to Legnica, where "there [was] a mausoleum of five Piasts [ancient Polish kings]," and then to Iława, where "in 1000, Bolesław Chrobry welcomed the [Holy Roman] Emperor Otto III."[19] Where the Piasts were not explicitly noted, journalists presented history without reference to ethnicity: when traveling to a formerly German area, now called Lubusz, one could find "castle ruins from the twelfth century," and in Sulechów, there was a "city hall from the sixteenth century."[20] Wherever possible, the press publicized the historic Polish character of an area; when they were unable to promote national characteristics, they were left with an ambiguous collection of cultural artifacts without references to ruler or usurper.

Reminding youngsters of the rewards generously procured by the socialist state, travel routes tied Polish history into the *autostop* journey. When there was a Red Army monument or memorial on the trek, hitchhikers were encouraged to take a detour. Similar to projects to rebuild old cities across the country (regardless if they once belonged to the German Reich or pre-World War II Poland), the road less traveled brought the next generation of Poles to recognize the new state's tender stewardship of cultural heritage and national legacy. In other words, by suggesting such routes, organizers were legitimizing communist rule in the home country.

There were, however, immediate limits to the program's propagandistic approach. After all, the hitchhiker was not required to follow a strict itinerary, and those who wanted to put back miles would inevitably avoid cultural sites in the interest of a quick arrival. As for the driver—who would intentionally go out of their way to stop at a Red Army monument, especially if it meant a journey across pot-holed roads with their cherished automobile?

Perhaps for that reason, even with official endorsement from the government, the *autostop* program received only minimal financial assistance. As a result, magazines and radio programs had to encourage hitchhiking through enticement rather than obligation. Magazines promised that the "friendliest … most educated driver[s] of Poland" would be rewarded considerably.[21] Depending on the number of miles, one could enter to win anything from a portable radio to a brand new *Syrena* (the Polish equivalent of a luxury vehicle).[22] Officials also began holding annual meetings of hitchhikers at the end of the summer.[23] The meetings—as well as the program itself—were so popular that locals began complaining about the arrival of thousands of hitchhikers. As organizers overcame initial problems related to ideological conformity (that hitchhikers did not have to be members of an organization or other state-run programs) and the necessity to recruit the masses (in order to assure the program's continuance), they had to manage a plethora of issues and problems stemming from the success of their hitchhiking program.[24]

Games, Smiles, and Knives: Conflicting Cultural Images of Hitchhiking in Post-War Poland

New-found state support of *autostop* eased some fears, but the practice of hitchhiking still conjured up both positive and negative connotations in public opinion. Diametrically opposed images of the hitchhiker circulating in popular novels, films, and in the press fed the ambiguity surrounding *autostop*. On the one hand, there was the devious, calculating hitchhiker thief. In Roman Polański's first cinema film, *Nóż w Wodzie* (*Knife in the Water*), the camera followed the successful sports journalist Andrzej and his girlfriend on their way to a beloved tourist getaway in Masuria. When they decide to pick up a lone, mysterious hitchhiker, the young man turns out to be a disturbed recluse à la James Dean. In the end, he provokes a fight with Andrzej, feigns drowning, and seduces the girl while the sportscaster searches for police.[25] The hitchhiker was, to use the official language of the day, an "asocial element" searching for a cheap thrill, meandering the roads without much of a purpose.

Hitchhiking was also strongly associated with danger, rugged youth, and sexuality.[26] As such, people who went hitchhiking for pleasure belonged to the group of "asocial elements;" they consciously imitated shunned Western models, and were as unkempt as their clothes were ragged. One driver complained, "they're dirtier than dirty," continuing that he had seen "how an elegant, clean driver let an entire group of dirty people out [of an automobile] at the market square in Płońsk." In the middle of the pack, he reported, "there was a prototypical example" of a hitchhiker: "He was barely human. Hair like a bat, head [stuck] in a map, pants ripped. The driver said, 'Look at yourself! Get in a bath, not a car; nobody is going to take you!'"[27] Surprisingly, Communist Party first secretary Władysław Gomułka, who ushered in the liberalization that made *autostop* possible, bitterly denounced the development of hitchhiking early on, exclaiming, "*Autostop*! *Bradiazhenie* [Russian: vagrancy], dirty and louse-ridden. They [the hitchhikers] should go hiking, from Kraków to Zakopane, for example; it's healthy."[28] Nevertheless, the average hitchhiker did not exactly conform to Polański's protagonist or the recommendations of official nomenclature, and numerous books and films offered an alternate view of the hitchhiking practice in post-war Poland.

What some saw as aimless wandering, others saw as a meaningful journey: Hitchhikers were adventurous, happy-go-lucky, and valued personal contact. As one parent explained, "I sent and encouraged my [child] to go hitchhiking from the outset. He should learn to get along with other people, to calculate time, money, [and] to wash shirts and socks."[29] In other words, hitchhiking taught important life lessons and skills.

Corroborating this view was Adam Bahdaj's 1962 children's story, *Podróz za jeden uśmiech* (*Traveling on a Smile*), in which two young boys lose their money for train tickets on the way from Warsaw to Gdańsk.[30] The children's story depicts perfect strangers with very different personalities: Duduś is an uptight little boy who follows rules and wears a jacket and tie, even during the summer break, while Poldek is adventurous and open to new ideas. After a long argument, the two penniless children decide to hitchhike across People's Poland. Of course, since they have no idea how to hitchhike, everything seems to go wrong, and they are forced to rely on numerous new acquaintances to get to their goal.

Traveling on a Smile provided a rich catalogue of different views towards hitchhiking that circulated in socialist Poland. Adam Bahdaj wrote that hitchhikers, as well as those who pick up hitchhikers, were like a "band of Mexicans" they were dressed in "clothes from the country of the Aztecs and Incas, broad sombreros made of old Polish straw, tight jeans made of old Polish linen, [and] checkered shirts made of old Polish flannel."[31] On the one hand, there was the lazy worker—like the mining truck driver who takes his time picking up hikers instead of rushing to the job—or Poldek's aunt, who ponders life while listening to the folk musician, Marek Grechuta (Poland's equivalent of Bob Dylan). At the same time, hitchhikers were incredibly communal types, cherishing human contact rather than materialism, and thus reflected ideologically positive characteristics for a socialist audience.

Regardless if observers imagined hitchhikers as naïvely idealistic or a nuisance, drivers viewed them as a danger on the road, if for no other reason than that they distracted people from driving. Likewise, hitchhikers were either upset at the lack of regulation of *autostop* and/or were enamored with the few hitchhikers they had seen on the streets.[32]

"Girls, if Present, Always Stop the Car": Girls, Kids, and Hooligans in Hitchhiking

In the 1972 made-for-TV film *Podróz za jeden uśmiech* (*Traveling on a Smile*), Poldek and Duduś are unexpectedly dropped off in the deserted outskirts of Kraków. Traveling on foot, they meet another hitchhiker on a desolate street.

She is a young, thin female, dressed in what must have been the tightest jeans available at the time, along with a skin-tight, short-sleeved shirt. Her long brunette hair is tied back into pigtails and topped with a fashionable cap. No sooner does she hold out her *autostop* booklet, as was customary in the program, than a male farmer with an empty truck pulls over to pick her up. Although neither Poldek nor Duduś have an *autostop* booklet, the young woman encourages them to join her, along with another half-dozen hitchhikers who suddenly emerge from the bushes when the driver stops.

For a variety of reasons, this fictional scene is indicative of numerous problems organizers had to face over the decades of *autostop*. Not only were the number of female hitchhikers chronically low, but the women who did hitchhike received a disproportionately greater number of rides. "Girls, if present, always stop the car," Andrzej Wróblewski wrote, since "they think that cars will race to pick them up, and they're right." Avoiding any direct statements explaining why men would be so inclined to stop for women, Wróblewski explained that, "so often people are returning tired from a trip, in a bad mood; nothing will distract him, and then he sees a scantily-clad blond [sic.]. He suddenly has a change of heart, thinking that he could do a service for such a daisy."[33] Over-selective drivers were not the only problem, as two parents noted in *Dookoła Świata*: *autostop* created an environment "for looseness [*łajdactwo*], especially for girls," who were exposed to smoking, drinking, and much older drivers.[34]

In addition to female hitchhikers, adolescents continually caused problems for *autostop* organizers. While the number of pre-teens and young teens was certainly a small group, the fact that Poldek and Duduś were able to go hitchhiking—both barely twelve—was a cause of concern.[35] Parents complained that sixteen-year-olds, and sometimes even younger adolescents, were hitchhiking "without their parents' permission."[36] Children unable to purchase a booklet on their own chose instead to "piggy-back" with someone who had bought one.[37] Others forged copies.[38] In response, enthusiasts worked to ensure safety not only through guaranteed insurance, but also through a campaign directed toward female hitchhikers, would-be hooligans, and youngsters.[39]

Using language that was at times paternalistic and at times admonishing, organizers of the program attempted to streamline *autostop* to prevent the program's total cancellation. Editors and journalists informed female riders they would be treated with respect and could count on the state to protect them from incorrigible male hitchhikers and drivers. Along with interviews, images of purportedly typical female hitchhikers appeared prominently on the pages of illustrated magazines (see Figure 7.1).[40] Concomitant with the push to advertise female hitchhikers, organizers admonished any form of bad behavior, maintaining that "enthusiasm" could easily get out of hand.[41]

Figure 7.1. A typical hitchhiker in the People's Republic of Poland? From the cover of *Dookoła Świata*, no. 303, 18 October 1959.

Reporters did not condemn hitchhikers directly, but explained that problems would naturally occur with the growing popularity of hitchhiking. Andrzej Kantowicz wrote that "the lively growth of *autostop* caused problems with accommodations in the most-visited towns. Many young people spent the night under the open sky, outside."[42] Certain excesses could have been prevented with better planning. Organization was also a problem concerning young people; in the first two years of *autostop*, it was unclear at what age travelers could legally hitchhike.[43] Afterwards, *autostop* organizers officially forbade adolescents under the age of eighteen to hitchhike without written permission from parents.

Importantly, however, the nature of hitchhiking, as an escape from both the hometown and from ideology, was not entirely lost through paternalistic articles in the media, and journalists did not shy away from allusions of the unpredictable quality of *autostop*. According to the logic of the day, the sense of adventure in *autostop* often included mysterious, but friendly, encounters between both men and women. Hence, in the international magazine advertising Polish daily life and culture, *Poland*, Waldemar Żukrowski commented on *autostop* and Polish tourism: *Autostop*, according to Żukrowski, was a "river of young people bubbling with joy [which] meanders all over the country, carried from one end to the other free of charge."[44] After a kind motorist gives them a ride, he continued, "they express their gratitude for the lift with a song, a smile and some girls even with a kiss."[45] The commentary is coupled with a variety of pictures of travelers in Poland—one of which is of a young girl in a bikini, to which Żukowski writes provocatively, "Nature is very beautiful here."[46] Żukrowski promised his foreign audience great prospects for a natural encounter in Poland. Not all drivers were worth being kissed, however, as one cartoon revealed, in which an old, scraggly driver sticks his head out of his truck, expecting a little love, only to receive this response from the young, attractive girl: "No, no! Thanks. I changed my mind. I will take a different car."[47] At times, neither the hitchhiker nor the driver declined, as one caricature showed; there, an older man is successful in picking up two young, sexy hitchhikers. Little does he know, while cruising with one arm around the passengers, that the next hitchhiker hiding behind a tree is none other than his own wife, ready to smack him with a rolling pin.[48] Caricaturists and their journalist colleagues were ambiguous about the aims of hitchhiking, but they gave strong evidence that one could expect a romantic, or would-be romantic, encounter.

The press took a vague position towards female hitchhikers, as did Polish women. Even though newspapers and magazines often paraded female hitchhikers in their pages, the campaign to bring women on the *autostop* trail was largely unsuccessful. In the 1960s, no more than 10 percent of travelers were female, despite the attention women received in official magazines and newspapers.[49] In addition, *autostop* remained largely a university student activity: workers, professionals, and high school students never constituted more than thirty percent of travelers.[50]

Additionally, while the success of the program grew throughout the socialist era, the number of citations and cases of law infringement increased as well. As "hooligans" and "blue birds" that joined the movement either officially or unofficially flocked to major thoroughfares in the summer, drivers grew more hesitant to stop.[51] "In 1960," wrote Wiesław Kot, "when 85,000 booklets found their way to young people's hand, it was said that *autostop* was the feeding grounds for homosexuals."[52] Such rumors polarized the community. On the one hand, young people and organizers defended hitchhiking as a safe and inexpensive form of travel. For many others, *autostop* was a code word for impropriety, insobriety, and promiscuity. In response, Andrzej Piwoński later stood up for the *autostop* movement: "I'll say it again … our committee will immediately compensate for every loss caused by the hitchhiker, if the [victim] steps forward. I have been saying that for ten years, and somehow, nobody has come forward, since the entire story about damage and destruction is based on the principle of 'I heard from a friend that ….' It's all made up."[53]

Andrzej Piwoński was reacting to what he saw as fabricated myths about the behavior of young people in the *autostop* movement. Though he was certainly exaggerating in saying that no hitchhiker misbehaved, Piwoński was highlighting a more fundamental problem in the program: rumors—partially encouraged by the press and public media—made what could be considered a very socialist form of travel appear deviant and subversive.

While no major newspaper would criticize young pioneers hiking in the Bieszczady Mountains or scouts camping on Baltic beaches, the hitchhiking movement in Poland was different. Hitchhiking could not shake its association with danger, rugged youth, and sexuality. Not surprisingly, the blue-jeans and sports-jacket-toting hitchhikers consistently drew the eye of suspicious policemen and hometown locals. After an initial surge of public promotion, the program retreated from the spotlight, and journalists treated it with reserve and ambiguity.[54]

"Drunk ... though certainly not from Vodka": International Reaction to Hitchhiking

Even if the *autostop* program vanished from the spotlight of the mass media, it was rarely in need of participants, and the image of the hitchhiker circulated widely throughout the East Bloc. As in Poland, writers perpetuated the tainted image of hitchhiking, all the while declaring Poland a hitchhiking paradise; fascination with the form of travel encapsulated both danger and joy.

As the only country that consistently supported a legalized hitchhiking program, Poland regularly drew on foreigners from the East Bloc. "Ever more registrations are being submitted," noted organizers in 1958, "from foreign tourists who want to 'hitchhike around the world.'"[55] In 1963, another observer noted that "amongst the group of *autostop* enthusiasts, there are more and more foreign guests;" already in that season, he had personally met "two young Hungarians from Budapest [who] traveled the entire coastline, knowing no other language than their native one."[56] Similarly, Jerzy Woydyłło commented on how many East Germans he had come across hitchhiking in Poland in 1961. "One journalist from the GDR," he recounted, firmly stated that "nothing in the world would make him go by train [in Poland]; he only went hitchhiking."[57]

When, in the 1970s, East Germany, Czechoslovakia, and Poland moved to drastically alleviate travel regulations between the three countries, both the notoriety and the popularity of *autostop* grew internationally. Starting in 1972, citizens were allowed to travel to neighboring communist states, merely with a police-issued identification card. No longer required to obtain a written invitation from abroad, not to mention the coveted passport and visa, millions of citizens ventured across what was officially called the "Borders of Friendship." In any given year, a third of East Germans went to Poland or Czechoslovakia, and Poles and Czechoslovaks similarly endeavored to the GDR in the search for relaxation, hard-to-find goods, and to hitchhike.[58]

That foreigners viewed Poland as a hitchhiking paradise is corroborated by Rolf Schneider's 1974 novel, *Die Reise nach Jaroslaw* (*The Trip to Jarosław*), which inspired young East Germans to venture to Poland. In his surprisingly frank account of a teenage girl unhappy with her life—detailing her uninspiring parents, schooling, and accepted mediocrity in society—he contrasts

Poland with the GDR as an oasis of liberal rules and friendly people. After the protagonist crosses the border, she goes hitchhiking, paring with a young, outgoing Pole to traverse the country. Poland was "groovy"; hitchhiking across the country one could get "drunk ... though certainly not from vodka."[59] The book concludes with the protagonist's return to East Germany, refreshed but happy to come back to a structured society where she could "straighten [herself] out" after her hitchhiking adventures across the border.[60] As long as Poland had a legalized hitchhiking program, one can surmise, other East Bloc countries refused to start their own.

There were numerous attempts to encourage similar programs abroad, but state governments were hesitant. In a 1965 interview for a youth magazine in Czechoslovakia, the head of the Czechoslovak Youth Organization (ČSM), Miroslav Zavadil, suggested that Czechoslovakia legalize hitchhiking, since, as he said, "there [were] already many positive experiences from Poland."[61] But even with official visits from youth group officials, not to mention representatives and enthusiasts from the *autostop* program, authorities in Czechoslovakia and East Germany—in contrast to Poland—found the *autostop* movement objectionable for a variety of reasons, and refused to initiate or maintain a transnational (or national) hitchhiking program.

The first, but by no means primary, reason *autostop* could never be initiated in East Germany or Czechoslovakia was pragmatic. While both of the latter countries could promote quick travel via the highway by the early 1970s, Poland was peculiar in only being able to boast two-lane "express roads," which, with their low speeds and broad shoulders, were more amenable to thumbing.[62] Additionally, as opposed to Czechoslovakia and especially East Germany, authorities in Poland did not have to worry about hitchhikers finding a way to escape to the West.[63] Whereas East German and Czechoslovak authorities stayed in close contact about the number of Westerners in their respective countries, as well as the number of infractions against §213 (that is, illegal immigration attempts), authorities in Poland could be relatively certain that their automobiles were not transporting Western-bound dissidents.[64]

The second reason East German and Czechoslovak authorities would not approve of *autostop* was political and ideological: they considered any attempt at self-organization with the greatest caution and suspicion.[65] While Polish hitchhikers were able to successfully utilize the relatively brief window of opportunity after Gomułka's ascension to power, East German and Czechoslovak youngsters were forced to cautiously avoid drawing the attention of officials to this form of travel. Ironically, it became more difficult for youth organizations in East Germany and Czechoslovakia to create a state-sponsored *autostop* program due to the problems that existed in Poland, which were well-known to East Germans and Czechoslovaks. After all, young Poles were not the only readers of magazines like *Poznaj swój Kraj* (*Know your Country*) or *Dookoła Świata.* The relative openness with which the Polish press enunciated problems such as hooliganism and homosexuality acted as a deterrent for other countries to grow more comfortable with legalized hitchhiking.[66] The fact that *autostop* organizers and journalists consistently suggested the program's Western orientation certainly did not abet attempts to make *autostop* a pan-Bloc phenomenon.

While Poland remained an island of legalized hitchhiking, rarely was the program presented as a prototypically Polish, or socialist, example of motorization. Paradoxically, while other countries were moving to limit hitchhiking, Polish writers drew on music, film, and media to portray it as being quintessentially American and modern. As one journalist for the *Express Wieczorny* (*Evening Express*) exclaimed in 1958, "finally we have our own *autostop* [program]. We have caught up with other civilized nations."[67] Additionally, another magazine article from that same year encouraged "amateur travelers" to get out during the summer, when "every form of mechanical transportation—from the old 'Ford' to the super-modern 'Cadillac'—[would] pick up tourists, as long as there [was] a vacant seat."[68] Even though there was a genuine dearth of Western automobiles, especially Ford and Cadillac, in 1950s and 1960s socialist Poland, the hitchhiking program afforded citizens of East Bloc countries a constructed impression of life in the West. Concomitantly, Western travelers were also encouraged to come to Poland to hitchhike.

As one of the few organized tourist offerings that received no state subsidy, Piwoński wrote in the 1980s that over a million booklets had been sold, and more than fourteen thousand had been purchased by foreigners wanting to participate in hitchhiking.[69] Ironically, when the Czechoslovak and East German regimes imposed unilateral restrictions on liberalized travel regulations after the rise of Poland's Solidarity movement—virtually extinguishing East Bloc citizens' possibility to officially go hitchhiking in Poland—the number of Westerners partaking in the *autostop* program grew in proportion to their socialist brethren after 1981, making it increasingly unlikely that socialist neighbor countries would adopt a similar program. Recognizing the program as ideologically questionable and logistically uncontrollable, East German and Czechoslovak officials made sure that Poland remained an island of legalized hitchhiking.

Conclusion: *Autostop* as an Escape

In a fascinating recent paper on socialism's *Schleichwege* (hidden paths), Włodzimierz Borodziej wrote that the late 1960s marked a watershed moment in Polish society.[70] Citing historian Dariusz Stola, he explained the difference between "primary" and "secondary" state socialism. The former represented the adoption of totalitarian norms and foreign Stalinism; "primary" state socialism was brutally repressive and forced citizens to conform to what they or, better stated, their big brother to the East, saw as normative to Communist society. "Secondary" state socialism perpetuated totalitarian form: rulers still had an entire apparatus built to violently suppress dissent. But "secondary" state socialism also represented a fracture, a point at which the monolithic state gave birth to new forms of escape as citizens worked to instrumentalize and redefine the system.[71] As Borodziej argues in his analysis of the inner workings of ORBIS, Poland's state-run international tourist organization, "society … domesticated the system" in the late 1960s, as authorities grew to silently accept at times unorthodox, and at times downright subversive, behavior.[72]

As the legalized hitchhiking program reveals, the process of everyday citizens' co-optation of the state apparatus began much earlier, with the rise of first secretary Władysław Gomułka. It did so for several reasons. *Autostop* complemented socialist, nationalist, and economic values in theory. On the one hand, it could be utilized to make citizens more familiar with a country that had only recently been drastically redrawn in the outcome of World War II. It was intended to bring impressionable youngsters to the "Polish" countryside, much of which was inaccessible by rail or bus. For officials, *autostop* was initially seen as an appropriate escape from the center to the periphery, from the city to the countryside.

At the same time, the program was immensely ideological. What could be more socialistic than opening your car door, sharing your vehicle, and perhaps forming a friendship with a complete stranger? Given the shortage of a reliable transportation infrastructure, and the dearth of personal automobiles well into the 1970s, planners realized the advantages of partially promoting automobility via the *autostop* program. Like other utopian plans across the East Bloc to encourage automobility, hitchhiking was the Polish response to shortages in a society that wanted to experience driving. In other words, *autostop* provided an escape that helped fulfill consumer demand.

Once the regime acknowledged *autostop* as a form of summer travel, officials could hardly justify making illegal such an immensely popular, nonpolitical (as they would call it, "anti-political"), and self-funded organization that was initially associated with the state. It helped that organizers highlighted its nonbiased, classless nature: *autostop* was meant for men and women, young and old alike. *Autostop* organizers advanced the idea that they were protecting individuals who hitchhiked. In the 1950s and 1960s, most hitchhikers were university students who sought either a way to travel faster, or to arrive at a location at all, since trains did not always run on time or serve all destinations. By allowing an organized hitchhiking program, the state was able to monitor otherwise completely uncontrolled travel. In other words, while the *autostop* program could have become problematic for the regime, such as in 1981 with the rise of the Solidarity movement, *autostop* offered at least a minimal degree of control, since hitchhikers were obliged to purchase booklets.

Initially created by enthusiasts in the wake of the Gomułka thaw, *autostop* was an escape from prescription; the program marked the departure from "primary" state socialism. During the summer months, young people would venture out as individuals or in small numbers, and were forced to act according to circumstance. Even if the hitchhiking season was officially organized, travelers could not predict the weather, and could not expect to encounter friendly drivers. In marked contrast to many of the escapes in this volume, the *autostop* program was an escape from organized group vacations. Since it had no strict destination, or designated duration (even the physical space of the car imposed clear limitations on the number of passengers), it was additionally an escape from a plan. Even when the typical hitchhiker had a destination in mind, much of the experience was meant to be the travel and the characters met on the journey. While there were hitchhiker gatherings at the end of the summer, hikers were otherwise left to their own devices. If nothing else, it was an escape from traditional authority figures that young people encountered in their everyday lives. As such, *autostop* was popularly perceived as an escape from responsibility, from inhibition, from society, and—most of all—as an escape from the very party that created it. In other words, the hitchhiker was liberated. For many—especially parents, women, and party functionaries—it was precisely this form of individualistic escape they feared.

The East German and Czechoslovak reaction to *autostop* reflected the ideological efficacy of the program, as well as the marked contrast between nominally identical systems in different nation states. In other countries, it was not only that law enforcement officials and state officials were concerned about the inherent danger of having youngsters hiking on highways, authorities in neighboring countries feared uncontrollability. Especially in East Germany— where Western automobiles sped across the transit highway from the mainland to West Berlin—*autostop* was integrally tied to subversive, enemy behavior. They saw *autostop* not as a socialist escape, but a potential escape from socialism. Polish activists, acting as a virtual lobby within the rank and file, were able to utilize the brief era of political rupture in the 1950s to create a program that garnered popular support among young people for generations.

Curiously, having survived nearly four decades of state socialism, and after only four years of free-market democracy, Andrzej Piwoński and other organizers ultimately decided to discontinue the *Biuro Autostopu,* noting already in 1991 that the number of booklets sold had plummeted.[73] Clearly some of the main practitioners of *autostop* were questioning the tradition in a new world. When reading contemporary accounts of hitchhikers in state socialism, it is remarkable how frequently they speak of feeling relatively safe on the unknown road. Of course, it was "daring," as Stanek noted in her song, but one did not have the same fears as hitchhikers have today with news reports and popular films depicting crazed killers like Charles Manson, whose hitchhiking followers brutally murdered the wife of the director of *Knife in the Water,* or Leatherhead in the *Texas Chainsaw Massacre.* As a young man, author Waldemar Żukrowki who found female hitchhikers to be one of the most beautiful aspects of Polish nature, fearlessly hitchhiked from Poland to Mongolia. Recently, however, this former self-described ruffian (*"chuligan"*) reflected: "After all these years, I drive my own car. Interestingly enough, I seldom pick up hitchhikers. Maybe because times have changed, if I see a boy and a girl on the road, then I stop. I don't pick up individual girls. Never. You never know what they're up to. And outside of that, it wasn't always so easy to get weapons. The entire atmosphere of *autostop* … isn't the best."[74]

For hitchhikers in Polish state socialism, the perceived strength of the police and the security apparatus, not to mention guaranteed insurance and reimbursement for gasoline, helped ensure that participants considered *autostop* to be both a safe and desirable escape, even if parents sometimes complained about their "pups" traveling alone.[75] Hence, while Poles were actively co-opting state programs to pursue private pleasures, they also recognized the positive aspects of "primary" state socialism. Paradoxically, undesired surveillance of state subjects could, at times, be quite comforting.

Notes

I would like to thank Michael Dean, David Tompkins, Cathleen M. Giustino, and Catherine J. Plum for their critical input and editorial assistance, as well as Paweł and Jędrek Szajbel for their assistance. All translations of Polish-language materials are my own, unless otherwise noted.

1. Współpraca Głównego Komitety Turystyki z organizacjami społecznymi z zakresie organizacji turystyki—autostop. Notatki, broszury, sprawozdania, korespondencja. 1979–1983, Główny Komitet Turystyki, Archiwa Akt Nowych (hereafter AAN) 6/142.

2. Almost all recent research on tourism in Poland has only brief mention of the *autostop* program. Paweł Sowiński, *Wakacje w Polsce Ludowe. Polityka władz i ruch turystyczny (1945-1989)* (Warsaw: Wydawnictwo TRIO, 2005), 140–47.

3. In 2005, a collected volume by Jakub Czupryński offered researchers a plethora of contemporary accounts, photographs, and reflections on both legal and illegal hitchhiking in Communist Poland. Jakub Czupriński, ed., *Autostop polski. PRL i współczesność* (Kraków: Wydawnictwo ha!art, 2005).

4. Cf. Mateusz Hartwich, "Das Riesengebirge als mehrfach angeeignete Landschaft. Tourismus und Identität nach 1945" (PhD Dissertation, Europa-Universität Viadrina, Frankfurt/Oder 2010).

5. Concerning Khrushchev's idea of car rentership, see Luminiţa Gătejel, "Privat oder Staatlich? Automobile Konsumkultur in der Sowjetunion, der DDR und Rumänien," in *Comparativ. Zeitschrift für Globalgeschichte und Vergleichende Gesellschaftsforschung* 19 (2009): 16–32.

6. Andrzej Paczkowski, *Pół wieku dziejów Polski* (Warsaw: Wydawnictwo Naukowe PWN, 2005), 203. For a discussion of the liberalization in Poland and Bloc-wide enthusiasm for Polish culture and language, see Jerzy Kochanowski, "Obóz socjalistyczny," *Polityka* 29 (2006): 63.

7. Lewis Siegelbaum, *Cars for the Comrades. The Life of the Soviet Automobile* (Ithaca: Cornell University Press, 2008); and Luminiţa Gătejel, "Waiting, Hoping and Finally Driving: Cars and Socialism in the Soviet Union, the GDR and Romania (1956-1980)" (PhD dissertation, Freie Universität Berlin, 2009).

8. John Urry, "The 'System' of Automobility," *Theory, Culture, Society* 21 (2004): 4–5, 25–39.

9. Zentralrat der FDJ, 46 Sitzung des Sekretariats am 25 Mai 1972. Zum Tagesordnungspunkt Nr. 16., Betrifft: Standpunkt zu Fragen des "Autostop," Stiftung der Arbeiterparteien und Massenorganisationen der DDR-Bundesarchiv Berlin (hereafter SAPMO-Barch), DY/24/8475; see also Główny Urząd Statystyczny, *Mały rocznik statystyczny* (Warsaw: Nakładem Głównego Urze du Statystycznego, 1960), 103; and Staatliche Zentralverwaltung für Statistik, *Statistisches Jahrbuch der Deutschen Demokratischen Republik* (Berlin: Staatsverlag der DDR, 1989), 214.

10. "WOG, WIWAT-STOP!" *Dookoła Świata* (henceforth *DS*), no. 245, 7 September 1958.

11. "Auto-Stop 1958," *DS,* no. 225, 20 April 1958.

12. Ibid.

13. "Mikroankiecie na Pytania," Autostop 1958, *DS,* no. 229, 18 May 1958.

14. Compare, for example, ibid., with Bogusław Laitl, "Pionierzy autostopu," in Czupryński, *Autostop polski,* 13–14.

15. "WOG, WIWAT-STOP!" *DS,* no. 245, 7 September 1958.

16. Of course, it would help that Gałecki would remain chief of transport police well until the 1980s, similar to Lubicz's successor in the *autostop* program. Piwoński, "Więcej utonęło, niż zginęło na drogach," 19–23. See also Anna Druzic, "Historia autostopu w Polsce Ludowej," in *Autostop polski,* 161.

17. In July 1946 the provisional government held what was advertised as a "free" election to decide if the citizens or populace agreed with the dissolution of the senate, the nationalization of private businesses, and the establishment of the western border of the Polish state between the Baltic Sea and the Lusatian Oder-Neisse. Research has shown that only on the last point, the expansion of Poland's western borders, did citizens overwhelmingly vote in favor of the change. Hartmut Boockmann, *Deutsche Geschichte im Osten Europas: Ostpreußen und Westpreußen* (Berlin: Siedler, 1992), 417.

18. Piwoński, "Więcej utonęło, niż zginęło na drogach," 19–23; Gregor Thum, *Die Fremde Stadt* (Berlin: Siedler, 2003), 288; T. David Curp, *A Clean Sweep? The Politics of Ethnic Cleansing in Western Poland, 1945-1960* (Rochester: University of Rochester Press, 2006); and Sowiński, *Wakacje w Polsce Ludowe,* 140–47.

19. "Autostopem dookoła Polski," *DS,* no. 397, 6 July 1961.

20. "Autostopem dookoła Polski," *DS,* no. 398, 13 July 1961. For socialist Poland, the legitimacy of the Polish ownership of the Reincorporated Territories lies partially in the Piast Dynasty, the oldest Polish dynasty that ruled an area of modern-day western Poland from the tenth to the fifteenth centuries. Jan Musekamp, "Szczecin's Identity after 1989: A Local Turn," in *Cities After the Fall,* ed. John Czaplicka, et al. (Baltimore: Johns Hopkins University Press, 2009), 305–34; and Ignacy Rutkiewicz, *Wroclaw. Gestern und Heute* (Warsaw: Interpress, 1973), 303.

21. "Autostop Gazeta," *DS,* no. 239, 27 July 1958, 4.

22. Cf. Karol Jerz Mórawski, *Syrena. Samochód PRL* (Warsaw: Wydawnictwo TRIO, 2005).

23. Anna Druzic, "Historia autostopu w Polsce Ludowej," 161–68; see also *DS,* no. 350, 11 September 1960.

24. Ibid.

25. Roman Polański, *Nóż w Wodzie,* 1962.

26. Such negative examples are not limited to Poland. In Czechoslovakia, for example, Milan Kundera's short story, published in Polish in 1971, about a couple who pretend to simulate a hitchhiker-driver experience ends in unsatisfying sex between a man and a would-be prostitute. Milan Kundera, "The Hitchhiking Game," *Laughable Loves* (New York: Harper Perennial, 1999), 79–106, specifically 93–94.

27. Agnieszka Leszczyńska and Andrzej Wróblewski, "Kierowcy o nas," *DS,* no. 353, 2 October 1960.

28. Mieczysław Rakowski, *Dzienniki polityczne 1967-1968* (Warsaw: Iskry, 1999), 207.

29. Leszczyńska and Wróblewski, "Kierowcy o nas."

30. Adam Bahdaj, *Podróż za jeden uśmiech* (Warsaw: Nasza Księgarnia, 1974).

31. Cited in "Peerelowski autostop w cytach," in Czupriński, 171.

32. Andrzej Piwoński, "Więcej utonęło, niż zginęło na drogach," in *Autostop polski,* 19–23; see also Cezary Gmyz, "Licencja na podróżowanie. 50. urodziny autostopu," *Wprost* 1277 (2007): 24.

33. Leszczyńska and Wróblewski, "Kierowcy o nas."

34. Ibid.

35. "Autostop Gazeta," *DS,* no. 239, 27 July 1958, 4.

36. Leszczyńska and Wróblewski, "Kierowcy o nas."

37. Adabert, "Autostop 1962," *DS,* no. 457, 30 September 1962.

38. Ibid.

39. "Auto-stop," *DS,* no. 225, 20 April 1958.

40. Julian Lawłaski, "On, Ona i Samochód," *DS,* no. 237, 6 July 1958.

41. "Autostop 1960," *DS,* no. 353, 2 Oct 1960.

42. Andrzej Kantowicz, "Stop 10 Lat Autostop," *DS,* no. 706, 9 July 1967.

43. Hence, in some issues of *Dookoła Świata,* readers such as Leszek Stępnicki would publish requests: "Dear Editors! I would like to go 'autostopping' for a tourist vacation. The thing is that I don't have a good partner. Can you help? I would like a seventeen-year-old boy. That is my age." "Autostop Gazeta," 239.

44. Waldemar Żukrowski, "A Shadow, like Green Water," *Poland,* no. 84 (1961): 35.

45. Ibid., 35.

46. Ibid., 34.

47. "Autostop Gazeta," 239.

48. Ibid.

49. Druzic, "Historia autostopu w Polsce Ludowej," 163.

50. Ibid.

51. Ibid.

52. Wiesław Kot, *PRL—jak cudnie się żyło!* (Poznań: Wydawnictwo Publicat, 2008), 244.

53. "Peerelowski autostop w cytach," 170.

54. Jacek Sawicki, "Siadaj bracie, dalej hop," in *Autostop polski. PRL i współczesność,* ed. Jakub Czupriński (Kraków: Wydawnictwo ha!art, 2005), 182; also Druzic, "Historia autostopu w Polsce Ludowej," 163.

55. "Autostop Gazeta Nr. 1," in *DS,* no. 237, 6 July 1958.

56. Andrzej Kantowicz, "Stop 10 Lat Autostop," in *DS,* no. 706, 9 July 1967. Perhaps one of those hitchhikers was Ákos Engelmayer, who became the first ambassador from Hungary to Poland after the change in government in 1990. He was a passionate hitchhiker in Poland as a child, and came to know Poland via hitchhiking in the 1960s. Jacek Sawicki, "Siadaj bracie, dalej hop," 183.

57. Jerzy Woydyłło, "Autostopowe obrachunki," *DS,* no. 408, 22 October 1961.

58. Cf. Mark Keck-Szajbel, "Shop Around the Bloc: Trader Tourism and its Discontents on the East

German-Polish Border," in *Communism Unwrapped: Consumption in Postwar Eastern Europe,* ed. Paulina Bren and Mary Neuburger (Oxford: Oxford University Press, 2012), 374–92.

59. Rolf Schneider, *Die Reise nach Jaroslaw* (Darmstadt: Luchterhand, 1975), 225–30.

60. Ibid, 254.

61. N.a. "Dvě hodiny u předsedy ÚV ČSM Miroslava Zavadila—devatenáct odpovědí na otázky mladého světa," *Mladý svět* (1963): 45; see also "Autostop ochorel," *Smena* 225, 19 September 1965, XVIII. I would like to thank Zdeněk Nebřenský for the reference.

62. Główny Urząd Statystyczny, *Mały rocznik statystyczny* (Warsaw: Nakładem Głównego Urze du Statystycznego, 1960), 103; and Staatliche Zentralverwaltung für Statistik, *Statistisches Jahrbuch der Deutschen Demokratischen Republik* (Berlin: Staatsverlag der DDR, 1989), 214.

63. Zentralrat der FDJ, 46 Sitzung des Sekretariats am 25 Mai 1972. Zum Tagesordnungspunkt Nr. 16, Betrifft: Standpunkt zu Fragen des "Autostop," SAPMO-BArch, DY/24/8475.

64. See especially Monika Tantzscher, *Die verlängerte Mauer. Die Zusammenarbeit der Sicherheitsdienste der Warschauer-Pakt-Staaten bei der Verhinderung von 'Republikflucht'* (Berlin: Der Bundesbeauftragte für die Unterlagen des Staatssicherheitsdienstes der ehemaligen Deutschen Demokratischen Republik, 1999).

65. Zentralrat der FDJ, 46 Sitzung des Sekretariats am 25 Mai 1972. Zum Tagesordnungspunkt Nr. 16, Betrifft: Standpunkt zu Fragen des "Autostop," SAPMO-BArch, DY/24/8475.

66. Ibid. See also "Dvě hodiny u předsedy ÚV ČSM Miroslava Zavadila—devatenáct odpovědí na otázky mladého světa," *Mladý svět* 45 (1963).

67. "Autostop Gazeta," *DS,* 20 July 1958, 3.

68. "Autostop," *DS,* no. 228, 11 May 1958; for 'imaginary West,' see Alexei Yurchak, *Everything was Forever, Until it Was No More: The Last Soviet Generation* (Princeton: Princeton University Press, 2005), 158–206.

69. Współpraca Głównego Komitety Turystyki z organizacjami społecznymi z zakresie organizacji turystyki—autostop. Notatki, broszury, sprawozdania, korespondencja. 1979–1983, Główny Komitet Turystyki, AAN 6/142.

70. Włodzimierz Borodziej, "Pauschalreisen als Staatliche Veranstalthung—das polnische Reisebüro ORBIS," in *"Schleichwege." Inoffizielle Begegnungen sozialistischer Staatsbürger zwischen 1956 und 1989,* ed. Włodzimierz Borodziej, Jerzy Kochanowski, and Joachim von Puttkamer (Köln: Böhlau, 2010), 207.

71. Ibid.

72. Ibid.

73. Piwoński, "Więcej utonęło, niż zginęło na drogach," 19–23.

74. Waldemar Żukrowski, "Multus Chuliganus," in *Autostop polski,* 50.

75. Leszczyńska and Wróblewski,"Kierowcy o nas."

CHAPTER 8

Nocturnal Entertainments, Five-Star Hotels, and Youth Counterculture

Reinventing Budapest's Nightlife under Socialism

Alexander Vari

Neonlit Budapest
It's so wonderful when the night comes
When thousands of lights get lit
[...]
Everywhere you look
How much shiny magic ...
Budapest never had
So much glitz!

With these words, Lehel Németh sang the praises of the new nocturnal appearance of the Hungarian capital in a 1960s hit song.[1] What these song lyrics did not explicitly disclose, however, was that the neon glare in which Budapest now basked was part of an attempt that socialist authorities in the Kádár regime made to revive the city's nightlife.[2] In addition to neon lights, and as part of a concerted effort to catch up with the West, by the mid-1970s Budapest was able to offer visitors luxurious accommodations in five-star hotels, including the Duna Inter-Continental and Hilton, a richer array of culinary experiences, and quality entertainment in bars, cabarets, and nightclubs. Discussions of the societal aspects of life under the Kádár regime by both Western and Hungarian historians highlight that the newfound interest in satisfying consumer desires, which characterized "goulash communism," located Hungary in the vanguard of the post-Stalinist thaw that Eastern European countries experienced.[3] The revitalization of Budapest's nightlife was an important component of goulash communism. However, recent works on everyday socialist experiences and consumption, focusing on tourism, shopping, the spread of Western music, and fashion, have so far failed to pay close attention to the history of nightlife in Cold War Eastern Europe.[4]

The fact that socialist authorities, preoccupied with reeducating the masses in the spirit of useful work, could pay attention to such trifles as improving the quality of nighttime entertainment can appear baffling. Nightlife was, after all, a powerful symbol of capitalism, which was constantly attacked and repudiated during the advent of socialism in Eastern Europe. In Hungary, for instance, beginning in 1948 the state nationalized the restaurants, dance halls, coffee houses, and bars that survived World War II, and regulated their programs so as to conform to the new socialist expectations. It was only after 1956 that socialist authorities moved from repression to the liberalization of nighttime entertainment, a process that gained momentum a decade later.[5] The 1960s were a time when the reinvention of Budapest's nightlife turned into a state-sponsored program closely connected to priorities such as hotel infrastructure improvements and the new economic course.

Although they continued to profess an ambivalent attitude towards the city's bourgeois past, socialist planners embraced the present, as embodied by the spread in Budapest of the type of modern luxury accommodations found in the West. The five-star hotels built during the late 1960s and 1970s provided settings for wealthy foreigners to enjoy the local cuisine and the city's nighttime attractions. Hotels such as the Duna Inter-Continental and Hilton became enclaves of capitalism in the midst of a socialist economy, a development that caused a spatial disjunction between spaces of entertainment reserved for foreigners and those intended for domestic use. Consider, for example, one nocturnal space for native Hungarians, the *Budai Ifjúsági Park* (Buda Youth Park) opened in 1961 by KISZ (the Communist Youth Alliance) on the Buda-side bank of the Danube. Known as the *Ifipark*, this entertainment complex—featuring a large restaurant combined with a stage for outdoor concerts—represented the domestic counterpart of the foreign tourism-oriented five-star hotels, the difference between them being that the latter openly encouraged capitalist consumption, while the former shunned it in the name of socialist ideals and values.

For Hungarians able to cross this divide, the time that they spent in luxurious hotels and their interaction with wealthy foreigners in that setting provided the opportunity for momentarily escaping the ideological rigors of socialism.[6] For those unable to do so, it was their resistance to the rules and norms governing the use of domestic nocturnal spaces that provided such an escape. There were, of course, conformist youth belonging to KISZ who accepted participation in the nighttime activities of the *Ifipark* within the ideological and behavioral boundaries that the regime set for them; but countercultural trends (carefully watched and regulated by authorities) reflected in the spread of beat, pop, and rock music also gained momentum beginning in the late 1960s.

The reinvention of Budapest nightlife under socialism thus led to its highly compartmentalized consumption by foreigners, socialist youth, and counter-cultural audiences.[7] In spite of repeated attempts made by state authorities to instill socialist values and support "civilized" attitudes in the use of nighttime spaces, socialist entertainment faced a dual challenge: from *within* the ranks of its own supporters, a challenge that was embodied in the tourism promoters' attempts to make the Budapest night more attractive for Westerners; and *externally* from countercultural youth increasingly divorced from socialist values. The effects of that dual challenge led to cultural policymakers losing their grip over the ideological construction of the Budapest night, several years before the fall of communism in Hungary.

The Avatars of Budapest's Nightlife: From Capitalist to Socialist Consumerism

During the 1930s, Budapest had been a city known throughout Europe for its vibrant nightlife. Although its fame did not match that of Paris or Berlin, Budapest was well-ahead of other Eastern European capital cities.[8] After World War I, Budapest marketers aggressively promoted the city abroad as "The Queen of the Danube." However, this marketing strategy was not successful until the 1930s when, as a result of the opening of several cabarets and night clubs such as the Parisien Grill, Moulin Rouge, and the Arizona, Budapest started to attract wealthy foreigners from Germany, England, India, and the Middle East. The sounds of its nightlife filled with Gypsy music, American jazz beats, and Hungarian *csárdás,*[9] and the sensuous curves of the dancers on the revolving stage of the Arizona Night Club attracted such famous pleasure seekers as the Prince of Wales, Count Ciano, and several Indian maharajahs.[10]

Several developments put an end to Budapest's rich and diverse nightlife. Jewish contributions to the city's cultural scene witnessed losses of catastrophic proportion in the Second World War, including the loss of artistic talent as a result of the deportation of more than a hundred thousand, and the mass shooting of between ten and fifteen thousand Budapest Jews by members of the fascist Arrow Cross paramilitary units.[11] The losses continued after the war due to massive waves of immigration to Israel, Western Europe, and the United States.[12] Although not all the entertainers in Budapest were Jewish, Jews played an important role in the city's nightlife before the war. Furthermore, the Red Army virtually destroyed the capital city during the siege of the winter of 1944–1945.[13] With the advent of communism, which led to the nationalization of cabarets, coffee houses, and restaurants, the city's nocturnal lights flickered and almost completely went out. As the socialist regime shifted resources to finance the building of new industrial cities, Budapest not only lacked venues for entertainment, but was often in the grip of food shortages and fared worse than Stalin City, the model worker's city built in the middle of Hungary.[14] The country's capital, which up until 1948 still had a lively coffee house culture, became by the early 1950s a city where one could only go out at night for drinks available in cheap cafeterias (népbüfék).[15]

The lively Budapest jazz scene that characterized the immediate post-war years was also forced underground; police conducted periodic raids on the clubs, bars, and dance halls that continued to stay open.[16] The communists' stance on any manifestation of Western music was summed up in a 1948 article published in Népi Ifjúság (Socialist Youth): "The culture of the urban petty bourgeoisie based on the consumption of hit songs gives birth to sick men. It is enough to see that under the impact of the dances, songs, cabarets, and revues brought in from the West what a sick type of man came into being [in our country]," embodied by no one else than "the well known figure of the hooligan (jampec)." Despite the communist ban on Western music, jazz musicians continued to perform in Budapest dance halls up to the 1956 revolution.[17] However, especially between 1948 and 1953, it was more common for people to listen to music in other circumstances. Work brigades frequently required their members to participate in the enforced pastime of pageants held under socialist banners and portraits of Joseph Stalin and Mátyás Rákosi, the Stalinist leader of Hungary during the early 1950s, and in which artists performed dances or sang songs that praised the achievements of the socialist brigades on the work front.

After Stalin's death, the Imre Nagy government, in power in Hungary between 1953 and 1955, started a process of de-Stalinization, which was stalled in 1955 as a result of Rákosi's return to power—a set of developments that ultimately led to the 1956 uprising against Soviet control in the country. As a result of Moscow's prompt military intervention, the 1956 revolution failed in Hungary.[18] Still, despite the crushing of the revolution, the Kádár regime that emerged in its wake was also forced to turn the page. Emboldened by the switch to the development of light industry, housing, domestic consumption, and the rising of living standards taking place in Khrushchev's Soviet Union,[19] and driven by a desire to gather more mass support, János Kádár's policies were based on the introduction of a set of comprehensive economic reforms in the field of agriculture, industry, and foreign exports. Instead of continuing the aggressive policy of forced industrialization that Rákosi pursued during the Stalinist period, the new government supported an economic policy that, according to Ivan T. Berend and György Ránki, sought a more "balanced development."[20] These authors note further, that in order to achieve this goal,

"Economic policy was consistently made to focus on the gradual, moderate, but permanent increase in real incomes and consumption." Indeed, as Berend and Ránki have argued in their volume on the economic development of Hungary in the twentieth century, "the appearance of washing machines, refrigerators and televisions—from 1957 [on]—and the beginning of limited car ownership in the early 1960s, heralded a basic change towards a much greater consumption of durable goods."[21]

Creating the Scene: Restaurants and Neon Lights

With the introduction of Kádár's consumption-oriented policies, the relationship between communist ideology and nightlife underwent a dramatic shift. Instead of running moral condemnation campaigns and raiding the existing nocturnal establishments as they did before 1956, authorities now embraced them with the aim of using nighttime spots to attract foreign tourists. Their overall aim was to increase state revenues and boost domestic consumption through the integration of Hungary in the international tourist market. In Western Europe, the consumerist boom of the late 1950s and 1960s led to the rise of tourism as an extremely profitable branch in the national economies of France, West Germany, Switzerland, Austria, Spain, and Italy.[22] Spurred by such developments in the West, and eager to catch up, tourism in the Eastern Bloc turned into a competitive economic activity among socialist states as well.[23] The Hungarian state officials' interest in creating a tourism industry resulted in the creation of a revamped National Tourism Office (*Országos Idegenforgalmi Hivatal,* hereafter NTO) in 1964.[24] The NTO wanted to attract more tourists to Hungary by improving the accommodation infrastructure and the quality of services provided to tourists in hotels, campgrounds, restaurants, and representative cultural institutions. This new approach yielded immediate results. In 1964 the number of foreign tourists who visited Hungary reached 1.3 million, far surpassing the roughly half million visitors who crossed the country's borders just a year before.[25] During the next decade, tourism officials tried to capitalize on the increased number of arrivals and turn international tourism to Hungary into a profitable business through a wide array of offerings that included theatrical plays, historical pageants, boat parades on the Danube, music festivals, concerts, and industrial exhibitions in Budapest selling Hungarian finished goods, and gastronomic tours highlighting the national cuisine. Although socialist authorities organized some of these events in smaller Hungarian cities such as Szeged, Sopron, or Balatonfüred, they held the majority in Budapest, which along with Lake Balaton was one of the two most prominent destinations that foreign tourists visited during their stay in Hungary. It was within this broader context that tourist professionals voiced their support for the creation of a Budapest nightlife that would further entice visitors to spend more time in Hungary.

Initially, however, things advanced slowly. Even several years after transitioning into the Kádár era with its new emphasis on consumption, tourism, and raising the standard of living, Budapest was still quiet at night with few places to attract foreign visitors' attention.[26] The situation started to improve around 1963, when the marriage between the economic interest of the socialist state and international tourism was consummated. But offerings remained scarce even then. For instance, beginning in May 1963 the guided "Budapest by night" tours took foreign visitors to the Castle Hill, the Fishermen's Bastion, and the Citadel, to drop them off after having enjoyed the city's panorama by night at the Budapest Dance Palace. This venue featured a program of Hungarian folk dances as a final cultural feast.[27] The tours also included a stop at a restaurant that offered visitors Hungarian specialties.[28]

However, there were not many restaurants in Budapest to offer foreign tourists the delights of ethnic cuisine. One place that tourist guides recommended to visitors was the Czardas-Garden in Buda, where they could not only consume Hungarian fare, but also listen to gypsy music and eventually dance to contemporary music tunes.[29] In 1963, three other restaurants opened that also offered Hungarian fare. Reflecting the scarcity of such restaurants, however, guides advised tourists to visit a newly opened self-serve bistro mini-chain that featured surrogate French dishes.[30]

The situation was a bit better in regard to night clubs. By 1963 the Berlin, Duna Corso, and Inner City (*Belvárosi*) bars had become favorite places for nighttime entertainment in Budapest.[31] A few more Hungarian-themed restaurants that opened during the mid-1960s also added to the strength of nocturnal amusements. Some of them offered foreign tourists visiting Budapest the possibility of having New Year's Eve parties.

In order to confer more color to the city's nightlife, officials recommended the inclusion of "national-folkish" (*nemzeti-népi*) songs and dances in its cultural mix of diversion. A contributor to *Idegenforgalom,* the official publication of the National Tourism Office, argued in 1962 that a "'Magyar Night Club' with gypsy music, Hungarian comic sketches, and chansons, unique interiors, Hungarian wines, and peach brandy drinks" was sorely lacking among the local options.[32] Restaurants such as the Bagolyvár, decorated in the medieval style of Hungary's Anjou kings, opened in 1963 in the City Park area, were also singled out as a way to add local color and thus raise the quality of the city's nocturnal life.[33]

Compared to the timid initiatives of the mid-1960s, the late 1960s and early 1970s saw much more significant achievements. Several developments made this possible. The progressive relaxation of foreigners' surveillance, and the increase in their numbers allowed for their freer circulation between various nightlife establishments. As Joachim Schlör pointed out in his study, *Nights in the Big City,* as early as the nineteenth century it was the nocturnal "establishments and the street together [that] constituted 'night life'; the linking elements were the 'stroller' and the 'night-reveller,' who moved from place to place in search of pleasure and according to their whims." In addition to entering and leaving one establishment at any time, *flâneurs* "could also move on from one establishment to another, and in this way make up their own program for the night—though the commercialization of entertainment and the uniformity that this brought with it at the same time contributed to a growing expropriation of enjoyment."[34]

The liberalization and commercialization of Budapest nightlife during the late 1960s and early 1970s was noticeable through such developments as the introduction of musical variété shows, and even strip tease in some of the night clubs (particularly the Astoria, the Savoy, and the Casanova), which targeted Western tourists.[35] Another transformation was the installation of neon lights and signs all over the city. Socialist authorities celebrated neon-lit Budapest as an electric version of socialist modernity. The neon lights made the city look more like Western European capitals, and created a brightly lit stage for the unfolding of nighttime activities.[36] The rise of a youth counterculture in Hungary, and its embrace of beat music, Western hair, and dressing styles—though still marginal and repressed by the proponents of socialist culture—also gave the city a more cosmopolitan flair both by day and night.[37]

Five-Star Hotels

More than visual, culinary, or sensual diversions, the opening of five-star hotels contributed the most to the expansion of Budapest's nighttime escape options. While in 1964 the head of the National Tourism Office still bluntly declared that Hungary "does not need luxurious hotels,"[38] the position of tourism officials on this matter soon radically changed. The state authorized the construction of several new hotels after 1965. The one million foreign visitors the Hungarian capital received in 1966 turned their opening into an urgent matter.[39] Tourists crowded popular attractions such as the Fishermen's Bastion on the Castle Hill day and night as they enjoyed the panorama of the city and the Danube. According to one tourism professional, while the crowds of foreign tourists visiting Budapest were six or seven times higher than the number of guests who visited in 1937, the total accommodation capacity of the city was only half of what it had been three decades before.[40] Comparisons with Vienna also showed Budapest as lagging far behind the Austrian capital in five-star rated accommodations.[41] The scarcity of hotel rooms in the capital turned into an issue that had to be urgently solved if Budapest wanted to maximize profits from international tourism.

The first newly built five-star hotel to open in the Hungarian capital during the late 1960s was the nineteen-story Hotel Budapest. Although the hotel provided a nice panoramic view of the Buda Hills, its location far away from the downtown area and the Danube bridges limited its overall appeal as a luxury residence. Hotel Budapest joined two older hotels, the Royal (opened in 1896) and the Gellért (opened in 1918), renovated during the early 1960s, in the slowly expanding array of luxury accommodations available to foreign tourists. But none of these hotels inspired as many positive reactions among foreigners as the Hotel Duna-Intercontinental, unveiled in 1969. Unlike Hotel Budapest, the terraced rooms of the Duna Inter-Continental, located on the left bank of the Danube in Pest, offered an impressive view of the Buda Castle Hill.

The Duna Inter-Continental represented a groundbreaking departure for the local tourism industry, since its building was jointly financed by a Hungarian state company and the Inter-Continental Hotels Corporation owned by Pan-American Airways. The flow of foreign finance into the Hungarian hotel industry that the building of this hotel made possible[42] continued during the next decade, leading in 1977 to the opening of another five-star hotel, the Budapest Hilton, located opposite the river on the top of the Castle Hill.[43] Between 1953 and 1967 several Hilton hotels were built in Western Europe—for example, in West Berlin, Rome, London, and Paris—and the Middle East. The Budapest Hilton was the first Hilton hotel to be built in the Eastern Bloc. All the hotels owned by Hilton International were built in a modern architectural style. As Annabel Wharton argues, "[i]n the 1950s and 1960s, the modernity of the Hilton dramatically inscribed the cities in which they were built with a monumental sign of anticommunist, capitalist America."[44] Although ownership of Hilton International changed hands in 1967—the company having been bought and then operated by Trans World Airlines (TWA)[45]—the style and spirit of the Hilton hotels stayed the same. The inauguration of Hilton Budapest on New Year's Eve in 1976 was part of a musical celebration broadcasted live on Hungarian TV, and where pop-music icon Kati Kovács premièred *Ha legközelebb látlak* (When I See You Next Time), the first Hungarian disco song. The event proved the extent to which state authorities were willing to go in attracting foreign tourists to Hungary.

Foreign Celebrities and Cosmopolitan Glamour: Elizabeth Taylor in Budapest

The opening of Hotel Budapest, Duna Inter-Continental, and Hilton considerably enriched the Hungarian capital's nocturnal offerings since many of the new restaurants and night clubs that were opened during the late 1960s and 1970s were located in them. The Champagne Bar on the roof of Hotel Budapest, which stayed open until 5 AM, for instance, extended the possibility for nighttime entertainment well past the midnight closing time of other establishments. The hotel also had a bar and a Hungarian-themed restaurant in its basement.[46] But it was especially the bars and restaurants located in the Duna Inter-Continental and the Hilton, and the customers that these hotels attracted that were to boost the appeal of the Budapest night.

Instead of romantically capitalizing on the city's "soulfulness" vaunted in some of the early "Budapest by night" guidebooks,[47] or keeping the nightlife aligned with the ideology-driven principles of socialist entertainment as they did up to the mid-1960s, Hungarian tourism operators now wanted the creation of a Budapest nightlife spiced with cosmopolitan glamour and variété shows that would equal those offered by the Moulin Rouge in Paris. Although Budapest also had a famous cabaret named after the Moulin Rouge, an establishment that had opened in 1930 and had continued to offer musical revues under socialism,[48] it was not there, but in the newly-built luxury hotels where revelers felt the first stirrings of a cosmopolitan spirit.

A peak in Hungarian tourism operators' attempt to make the Budapest nights more glamorous was reached in 1972 when Elizabeth Taylor, while filming the movie *Bluebeard* in the city, rented the Duna Inter-Continental for three months, and also decided to celebrate her fortieth birthday in the Hungarian capital. Elizabeth Taylor's choice of Budapest brought a host of jet set people to the city. Invited as he was to the event, Roger Moore (alias James Bond) flew to Budapest in his private jet.[49] Many other international movie stars and musicians also attended Taylor's private birthday party, such as Princess Grace of Monaco, Raquel Welch, Michael Caine, Ringo Starr, Susannah York and, of course, Taylor's then-husband, Richard Burton.[50] One of Taylor's companions described her and her guests' arrival in Budapest as a seminal event: "'Nothing like this had been seen in Budapest since Emperor Franz Josef's last Hungarian wingding before World War I,' said *Bluebeard* director Edward Dmytryk. 'And it created more stir than the Revolution of 1956.'"[51] According to a recent biographer of Elizabeth Taylor, "journalists flocked to Budapest." Taylor's birthday party attracted newspaper writers from "Japan, India, Sri Lanka, Europe, [and] the [United] States."[52]

Before coming to Duna Inter-Continental, Taylor asked a famous Parisian designer to redecorate her rooms: "Elizabeth instructed the designer to redecorate some of the hotel suites for the more important guests, such as Princess Grace. She even arranged for him to visit various homes throughout Budapest to borrow the antiques and paintings that he would need."[53] In addition to the celebrities noted above, the ambassadors of the United States and seven Western European countries also attended Taylor's birthday party. Her husband, Richard Burton, created quite a stir when he disclosed to the press the birthday gift he had in store for Taylor: "a $50,000 heart-shaped diamond inscribed with a promise of everlasting love." In Burton's own words: "I would have liked to buy the Taj Mahal for Elizabeth' (…) 'but it would have cost too much to transport it." Richard posed for the photographers with the jewels on his forehead. For the rest of the press conference, the precious stone hung around the neck of a seven-year-old Hungarian boy who had walked in the room.[54]

The birthday party proved to be quite special. Before choosing Budapest, Taylor wanted to gather her guests on two supersonic jets and celebrate the party in the air.[55] Her friends expressed even greater excitement at her choice of destination; they enjoyed traveling behind the Iron Curtain. The birthday celebration held in the Duna Inter-Continental lasted into the early morning hours, producing—according to one of Taylor's recent biographers—a dazzling display of cosmopolitan glamour:

> Over two hundred sat down to the birthday supper. Elizabeth wore white cyclamen blossom in her hair and a white Grecian style dress, the Krupp diamond on her finger, her new jewel suspended from a gold chain on her bosom; on one side of her sat Caine; on the other the American ambassador, one of eight envoys present. The Ringo Starrs were opposite. Burton was flanked by Princess Grace, his sister Cis, the British envoy and Stephen Spender. Some 3,500 helium-filled gold balloons hovered above them; a Hungarian pop group played throughout a dinner of chicken Kiev and fruit salad, and an iced chocolate cake with forty candles was cut and devoured. Dancing went on until 4 a.m.[56]

The flocking of other film stars such as Roger Moore, Max von Sydow, Cary Grant, and Sylvester Stallone to the Duna Inter-Continental, and the cosmopolitan fashion shows organized during the 1970s as part of the Indian, Japanese, and Caribbean Weeks or the Turkish and Spanish gastronomic festivals, to name just a few, placed the bars and night clubs located in Hotel Duna Inter-Continental, and later the Hilton, at the epicenter of the city's nightlife. A 300 million dollar Hungarian-Austrian hotel building agreement gave a further boost to the emergence of such luxury accommodations and, as a result of it, several other five-star hotels such as Hotel Forum and Atrium Hyatt opened their doors in Budapest during the early 1980s.

The developments described above led to an increasingly noticeable spatial separation and compartmentalization of the Budapest night. The arrival of international celebrities such as Taylor, Burton, and Moore in 1972, followed by von Sydow, Grant, and Stallone in 1980, among others, turned downtown Budapest into a destination for droves of visitors from the West who sought a few nights or weeks in a locale that they perceived as exotic because of its location behind the Iron Curtain. However, visits by foreign celebrities and glamorous birthday parties, such as the one held by Elizabeth Taylor at Duna Inter-Continental, represented an exclusive fringe, rather than a mainstay of Budapest nightlife. Socialist authorities wanted Hungarians use and consumption of Budapest by night to take place in different settings and circumstances than those reserved for celebrities and wealthy foreigners.

Between Socialist Norms and Counterculture: The Ifipark

During the early 1960s, after the Kádár regime consolidated itself in the guise of a soft dictatorship in Hungary, Western music did not appear as threatening to party officials as it did to those who built socialism under Rákosi. Hence, they progressively relaxed restrictions against jazz, for instance. By the early 1960s, jazz came to be accepted and even allowed in public spaces. Student clubs such as the Egyetemi Színpad, managed by KISZ, turned into venues where Hungarian jazz musicians could now perform.[57] The audiences of these clubs were too small, however, for them to have a major impact on the domestic construction of Budapest nightlife. Socialism was, after all, an ideology that spoke in the name of the masses, and wanted to reach out to large numbers of people. Conforming more to these expectations was the previously mentioned *Ifipark* (Youth Park), which opened in 1961 under the aegis of KISZ within the precincts of a late nineteenth-century historical arcade and monumental flight of stairs (built initially for the private enjoyment of Empress-Queen Elizabeth of Austria-Hungary) on the Danube-facing slopes of the Buda Castle Hill. From 1961 until its closing in 1984, *Ifipark* was the experimental site that gave birth to a type of nightlife meant for domestic consumption.[58]

Ifipark was a large entertainment complex, which included an eight hundred-seat restaurant, combined with a dance floor and stage. As an internal document from 1972 reported, the KISZ owed a large amount of its disposable revenue to the operation of this establishment.[59] Due to its attractive location on the banks of the Danube, *Ifipark* trumped similar entertainment parks operating under the aegis of KISZ in the outer districts of the capital.[60] Being able to accommodate a total of twenty-five hundred people, the establishment turned into a mega-venue for those seeking entertainment. However, since *Ifipark* was meant to be a socialist model for "civilized" entertainment, communist authorities strictly regulated the behavior and physical appearance of the youth admitted within its precincts. Although tickets were cheap, boys had to wear short hair, neckties, and a suit, while girls were expected to wear decent skirts. In addition to offering contemporary dance music, *Ifipark* hosted concerts that often drew an audience of several thousand spectators. Socialist expectations played an important role in regulating the content of the songs performed by musicians. György Aczél, the deputy minister of Cultural Affairs in the Kádár regime, and a gray eminence in the field of cultural politics, summed up the principles governing the relationship between the party and cultural workers; regarding the creations and initiatives of the latter, he stated "we support, accept, are patient, but, if necessary, we forbid."[61] Spurred, however, by the liberalization of Hungarian media outlets that took place during the late 1960s, alternative pop and later rock bands could perform on the stage of the *Ifipark*, with the texts of their songs occasionally censored. It was there that Béla Radics, a legendary figure of Hungarian art-rock, started his career as the lead vocalist for a band called Sakk Matt. Many other Hungarian pop and rock music bands such as Kex, Omega, Illés, Metró, Piramis, Korál, P. Mobil, and Hobo Blues Band also became famous after they performed at the *Ifipark*. During the late 1970s, the establishment played the same role for newly formed heavy metal groups such as Edda, Karthago, and Dinamit.[62]

In addition to providing a musical escape to the tunes of Western music for those admitted inside, the concerts performed at *Ifipark* attracted droves of nonconformist Hungarian youth to whom security personnel refused entrance because of their long hair and Western-looking dress. Not willing, however, to sacrifice their keen interest in the music performed on its large outdoor stage, many of them camped in *Ifipark*'s immediate vicinity. During the 1970s, groups of disgruntled teenagers drinking beer, wearing head bands, and dancing to the rhythms of the music occupied several spots ranging from a big tree located higher up on the slopes, to the entrance of an underground pass near the *Ifipark*. The *Nagyfa galeri* (Big Tree gang) included a large group of teenagers and young adults who, as a result of their iconoclastic behavior, had several encounters with the police.[63] The spatial islands that they occupied became offshoots of a different nocturnal universe which was at odds with the other two types of nightlife communist authorities supported, one for foreigners and the other targeted at socialist youth. While in the 1960s it was pop music that inspired their interest, by the 1970s as the establishment transitioned to supporting new musical genres, rock and heavy metal fans replaced pop enthusiasts.

Developments at the level of youth behavior matched these spatial and musical challenges. As the increasing acceptance of the bands performing at the *Ifipark* suggests, socialist authorities exercised lenience towards pop and rock music; however, they forbade behaviors that they perceived as disruptive or dangerous. The wearing of jeans by performers, as well as by members of the concerts' audience, was a hotly debated topic throughout the early 1970s.[64] It was only after 1974, after the dismissal of László Rajnák, a former heavy boxer turned *Ifipark* manager, that the authorities' attitude became more flexible in this regard. According to a journalist who recently wrote about the *Ifipark,* while park officials resisted and repressed the Hungarian youth's rhythmic dancing and waving at concerts during the late 1960s, such practices spread and gained more public acceptance by the 1970s. Initially, it was only a few people who dared to physically respond to the increasingly aggressive tunes emanating from the bands performing on stage. Later, however, at concerts such as those performed by Piramis in 1976 and 1977, "the atmosphere was ecstatic."[65] It was in the same spirit that thousands moved their bodies in unison while listening to the hard rock tunes of Omega, Hobo Blues Band, and P. Mobil. The last decade of state socialism saw the creation and mushrooming of punk and heavy metal groups in Budapest and many provincial cities, and their appeal to youth was now a phenomenon that socialist authorities could not ignore.

Supporters of a new musical fashion, dressed in nail-studded leather jackets and pants, carrying brass knuckles and chains, and wearing heavy boots, turned into a conspicuous presence in Budapest subway passages, and especially in the alleyways of the grim and poor block building neighborhoods surrounding the city center. According to sociologist János Kőbányai, who wrote about them in 1979, the working-class youngsters roaming the streets and known as *csövesek* (the Hungarian equivalent of punk) represented the antithesis of the jeans-wearing and Western-connected socialist middle-class. For *csövesek,* unemployed as they were and coming from a socially distressed background, going to expensive concerts or disco dance halls was off limits; instead it was their consumption of live and underground music that united them and gave cohesion to their rebellion. According to one contemporary observer, it was in badly lit and dingy music clubs that they could fully express themselves by "jumping hysterically, taking to the stage as an assaulting wave, and twisting their bodies in gestures reminding one of sexual acts."[66]

Denied entry to *Ifipark,* the numbers of punk rockers gathering outside equaled those dancing inside.[67] Similarly significant, as the 1980s dawned, the band playing on the stage, Beatrice, with musicians dressed up in punk outfits, voiced "social dissent in a crude and straightforward manner."[68] Those in charge of *Ifipark* tried throughout the 1970s to bridge the cultural gap between pop and rock—musical genres now supported by the regime—and countercultural audiences, by also including folk music, disco tunes, and jazz in the weekly offerings of the establishment.[69] Despite these efforts, by the early 1980s, youth counterculture, with its embrace of punk and heavy metal, was winning its uphill battle against the ideologically imposed limits on nighttime entertainment.[70] The youth counterculture of those years became the third component of the city's nightlife—the one that created its own version of nightlife, challenging its official constructions by offering youngsters an escape from the ideological controls the party state imposed.

The Countercultural Takeover of the Three-Tiered Structure of Budapest Nightlife

Budapest by night in the 1980s differed substantially from the city's nocturnal life during the 1960s and 1970s. Although by the mid-1970s the five-star hotels, and the night clubs that they operated, had commercialized local nightlife and turned Budapest into a destination for many members of the international jet set and many other Western tourists, enthusiasm for further boosting mass tourism and improving socialist leisure facilities was receding quickly in Hungary. The reason for this was the slow-down and outright failure of many of the economic policies the Kádár regime launched more than a decade earlier, and the inability of the socialist state to keep up with and match Western standards of consumption for the Hungarian population at large.[71] As a result of the disparities this created in buying power between Westerners and locals, the nighttime establishments operated by the luxury hotels in Budapest turned into economic enclaves reserved for hard currency-paying foreigners who were out of the financial reach of the average Hungarian citizen.

What was left for the latter were spaces such as those within the precincts of the *Ifipark*. Administered initially with an eye on socialist morality, *Ifipark* offered youth growing up during the 1960s and 1970s nighttime entertainment tailored to suit their status and purse. Although with its embrace of pop and rock music the establishment transformed itself into a state-supported escape from the dreary socialist every day, its relevance was questioned by the rise and spread of a second generation youth counterculture in Hungary that represented more than just a mere escape from socialism, embodying, in fact, an ideologically-grounded challenge to the officially sanctioned spaces of the Budapest night.

The new youth counterculture was heralded by the embrace of punk rock by bands such as Spions and Beatrice. Access via a friend's subscription to the *New Musical Express,* a British music news journal (published from1952 to the present), and LPs sent home by Hungarians living abroad allowed a group of musicians led by László Najmányi to form in 1977 the band Spions (Spies)—the first punk band in Hungary. What brought Najmányi to punk was not his interest in music, but his appreciation of punk as "a type of conduct, stance and attitude (*magatartás, hozzáállás-attitűd*)." As a brief presentation published in the Hungarian samizdat press characterized the band: "Spions is made up of artists who play rock and roll not because they enjoy it but coercion. It is not show-business for them but training. The Spions is not made up of stars but soldiers. They do not care about spectacle but action. They are not individualists but surfers of the moment." Socialist authorities reacted immediately to the creation of Spions. The band was able to stage only three concerts in 1977 and 1978 (two in Budapest and one in Pécs) in student clubs before its members were forced in March 1978 to leave Hungary for France.[72]

Beatrice, led by Feró Nagy, was another Hungarian punk band. The band already existed, in fact, as a female beat band created in 1969, but it was Nagy—who was married to the band's female vocal soloist—who refounded it as a punk rock band in 1978. Initially, the band was allowed to perform only in Nyíregyháza, outside of Budapest. Later, however, it was able to play as a start up band in Budapest concerts, staging popular rock and roll bands such as Omega and LGT. Unlike Spions, Beatrice was not influenced by foreign models. According to Ádám Pozsonyi, the author of a recent history of the Hungarian punk movement, the mix of "hard rock, cabaret, punk, commercialized Hungarian folk music, [and] topical song (*kuplé*)," spiced up with a heavy dose of "party jargon" was a "specifically singular phenomenon which had no foreign correspondent."[73] It was due to this less challenging mix that Beatrice was able to survive official reactions against the spread of more openly anti-regime punk songs, and combative attitudes such as those heralded by Spions.

The spread of punk music and fashion, and its embrace by Hungarian youth in the 1980s opened a new chapter in the history of nocturnal entertainments under socialism. During the 1980s, the former spatial centrality of the five-star hotels and *Ifipark* in the construction of the Budapest night receded; Budapest's nightlife now unfolded in underground student clubs. In addition to hosting Beatrice, the Kassák Club, the Aula of the Budapest Economics University, and the *Fiatal Művészek Klubja*—the Young Artists' Club (YAC)—staged concerts by new punk and heavy metal bands with unorthodox names such as *Bizottság* (The Committee), Petting, T-34,

Elhárítás (Spy Defense), and *Vágtázó Halottkémek* (Galloping Morticians). The song lyrics that youngsters listened to in these places openly challenged ideological orthodoxies. For instance, the group Beatrice sang about "waiting for an apartment, relating to one's boss, official peace demonstrations, and the economy" while symbolically throwing bags of milk at the audience, according to scholar Sabrina Ramet.[74] The songs of another music band, the Coitus Punk Group (CPG), were even more escapist and provocative. While singing songs suggestively titled "Our King is a Puppet," "Pigsty," and "Everyone is a Louse," "the CPG would tear apart live chickens on the stage and throw the bleeding chicken parts at the audience."[75] Moreover, while singing a song whose lyrics ended with the words "Rotten stinking communist gang/ Why has nobody hanged them yet?" the leading soloist "tore up the familiar chicken and slashed his own face and arms with a razor blade."[76] Both Beatrice and CPG suffered the consequences of their actions. While Beatrice was unable to release any albums and folded as a band in 1981, members of CPG were tried in 1984, receiving jail sentences stretching from eighteen months to two years.[77]

Authorities' continuous use of force against the spread of ideological dissidence and punk counterculture showed that earlier policies aiming to impose a model of socialist entertainment widely accepted by Hungarian youth had by now became less and less effective. Instead of destroying the punk movement, such official reactions just strengthened and broadened its relevance. In places such as the YAC, supporters of punk counterculture often came in contact with members of the intellectual dissident movement.[78] It was due to these developments that by the mid-1980s the three-tiered structure of the Budapest night, based on its consumption by foreigners, socialist youth, and supporters of the underground counterculture, became tilted in favor of the latter. The city's nightlife gained its substance more and more from the iconoclastic music blasted at punk and heavy metal concerts, in underground spaces, or at the home parties (*házibuli*) of now increasingly dissident Budapest youth.[79]

Conclusion

The history of Budapest's nightlife under socialism illustrates the complex dynamic between the authorities' desire to open up the night for foreign capitalist consumption, while separating the venues fulfilling this role from the spaces reserved for the entertainment of domestic youth, which had to stay within the limits of socialist culture and moral decency. Attempts made by Hungarian youth during the 1960s and 1970s to challenge these boundaries were met with mixed responses from the Hungarian Socialist Workers' Party (MSZMP) and KISZ officials, which stretched from regulation, forbidding, and repression on the one hand, to toleration, co-optation, and support on the other. Such responses were due not only to internal divisions among state authorities regarding the policy to follow, but also to the more liberal atmosphere of the thaw, the need for foreign currency, the greater permeability of borders (allowing for the spread of fashions, music, and living style trends from the West), and the needs and desires voiced by a new generation that did not experience the ideological rigors of Stalinism.

Taming this generation without resorting to the physical and psychological torture of the Stalinist years was as important for the legitimating goals of the Kádár regime as the taming of the rest of the population through the promotion of the consumption of household goods, cars, and weekend homes—including the attempts it made to reform and decentralize the socialist economy through the New Economic Mechanism and compete with the West and other socialist states to bring more tourists to Hungary. However, the attempt to do all this without giving up the party's political, moral, and ideological monopoly over Hungarian society produced a highly noticeable spatial division between entertainment venues reserved for foreigners and those opened for domestic use, which led to a state-endorsed compartmentalization of Budapest's nightlife. A further split (neither envisaged nor wanted by state authorities) between conformist and nonconformist uses of domestic entertainment venues (foremost among them the *Ifipark*) led to a three-tiered compartmentalization of the capital's nightlife under socialism.

During the late 1970s, the spread of punk music and lifestyles from Britain to the US and Western Europe,[80] and from there to socialist states such as the GDR and Hungary,[81] exacerbated this division. It turned previous popular escapes from the grayness of socialism—signified by the wearing of jeans, and the listening to jazz, beat, pop, and rock music, which authorities slowly but progressively were willing to accept, tolerate, co-opt, and support— into escapes (jumping "hysterically" on the rhythm of howling sounds or chanting lyrics that openly mocked and challenged the party), which were now again harshly criticized. As sociologist Ferenc Hammer pointed out in a recent article on the role of nightlife in the construction of the popular public sphere under socialism, "from the point of view of socialist publicity and its normative drive entertainment [was] a crucial field," which in Kádár's Hungary served as a "litmus test" both for the regime's legitimation and lack of support among the country's citizens. As Hammer emphasizes, in socialist Hungary, the use of this "litmus test" turned into "an instrument in the [daily] exercise of power."[82] The public debate conducted in the Hungarian journal *Kritika* in 1979 presented punk both as an extreme left and right cultural phenomenon, the critics distancing themselves from its domestic supporters on the grounds that punk was a "pseudo-left" artistic style, being allied with political and cultural terrorism. Four years later, another article published in the same journal described Hungarian punk bands as fascists, traitors, enemies of socialism, and contributors to the spread of a musical "scum-wave," urging authorities to take immediate measures to stop it.[83] As I have argued here, the call to do this came too late;[84] by the mid-1980s it was nonconformity and open transgression of the party-enforced scenarios of Budapest's nightlife that captured the imagination of Hungarian youth—turning youth's nocturnal pastimes into daily escapes from socialism.

Notes

1. See Győző Hadai and László A. Németh, "Neonfényes Budapest," interpreter Lehel Németh. Full text of the song is available at http://www.zeneszoveg.hu/dalszoveg/ 37042/nemeth-lehel/ neonfenyes-budapest-zeneszoveg.html (accessed 5 July 2009).
2. Sándor Horváth, "Csudapest és a frizsiderszocializmus: a fogyasztás jelentései, a turizmus és a fogyasztáskritika az 1960-as években," *Múltunk*, no. 3 (2008): 60–83.
3. See Robert V. Daniels, *A Documentary History of Communism,* vol. 2: Communism and the World, 2nd ed. (London: I.B. Tauris, 1986), 318–23; Mark Pittaway, *Eastern Europe, 1939-2000* (London: Hodder Arnold, 2004), especially 73 and 122–26; and Tibor Valuch, "A gulyáskommunizmus" in *Mítoszok, legendák, tévhitek a 20. századi magyar történelemről,* ed. Ignác Romsics (Budapest: Osiris, 2002), 361–90.
4. Diane Koenker and Anne Gorsuch, ed., *Turizm: The Russian and Eastern European Tourist under Capitalism and Socialism* (Ithaca: Cornell University Press, 2006); Andreas Ludvig, ed., *Konsum: Konsumgenossenschaften in der DDR* (Köln: Böhlau, 2006); Ina Merkel, "From Stigma to Cult: Changing Meanings in East German Consumer Culture" in *The Making of the Consumer: Knowledge, Power and Identity in the Modern World,* ed. Frank Trentmann (Oxford: Berg, 2006) 249–70; Daniel Hyder Patterson, *Bought & Sold: Living and Losing the Good Life in Socialist Yugoslavia* (Ithaca: Cornell University Press, 2011); Paulina Bren and Mary Neuburger, ed., *Communism Unwrapped: Consumption in Cold War Europe* (Oxford: Oxford University Press, 2012); Mark Fenemore, *Sex, Thugs and Rock 'n' Roll: Teenage Rebels in Cold War East Germany* (New York: Berghahn Books, 2007), especially 132–154; Judd Stitziel, *Fashioning Socialism: Clothing, Politics and Consumer Culture in East Germany* (Oxford: Berg, 2005); and Djurdja Bartlett, *FashionEast: The Spectre that Haunted Socialism* (Cambridge, MA: The MIT Press, 2010).
5. A brief period of liberalization, however, occurred earlier during the Imre Nagy government in power between 1953 and 1955. For more on this see Karl Brown, *Dance Hall Days: Jazz and Hooliganism in Communist Hungary, 1948-1956,* Trondheim Studies in Eastern European Culture and Society, no. 26 (October 2006).
6. Some of these escapes were of a sexual nature. For a Western perspective on promiscuity in Budapest during the early 1970s see Mickey Knox, *The Good, the Bad and the Dolce Vita: The Adventures of an Actor in Hollywood, Paris and Rome* (New York: Nation Books, 2004), 283–84.
7. It should be noted here that there also was a fourth component of Budapest nightlife, which was hidden from public view, being neither publicly supported nor repressed by the state: that of state officials and high party functionaries as they dined and entertained each other in their compounds and private villas. Examination of it, however, goes beyond the purposes of this chapter.

8. See Vilmos Tarján, *A pesti éjszaka* (Budapest: Author's edition, 1940). Some other Eastern European capital cities that were also known for their happening nightlife during this time period were Warsaw and Bucharest. See Ron Nowicki, *Warsaw: The Cabaret Years* (San Francisco: Mercury House, 1992) and Aurel Storin's *Teatrul de revistă Constantin Tănase, 1919-2000* (Bucureşti: Editura Virtual, 2011) on the Cărăbuş variété-theater and music hall directed and managed by Constantin Tănase, an establishment that had a deep impact on the fashioning of Bucharest's nightlife during the interwar period.

9. A Hungarian national dance.

10. Ella Megyeri, *Budapesti notesz* (Budapest, 1937) and Róbert Rátonyi, *Mulató a Nagymező utcában* (Budapest: IPV, 1987). See also my chapter "From 'Paris of the East' to 'Queen of Danube': Transnational Models in the Promotion of Budapest Tourism, 1885-1940," in *Touring Beyond the Nation: A Transnational Approach to European Tourism History,* ed. Eric G.E. Zuelow (Aldershot: Ashgate, 2011), 103–25.

11. Raphael Patai, *The Jews of Hungary: History, Culture, Psychology* (Detroit: Wayne State University Press, 1996), 589–90.

12. See Tamás Stark, *Hungarian Jews during the Holocaust and after the Second World War, 1939-1949: A Statistical Review,* trans. Christina Rozsnyai, East European Monographs (New York: Columbia University Press, 2000).

13. Krisztián Ungváry, *The Siege of Budapest: One Hundred Days in World War II,* trans. Ladislaus Löb (New Haven: Yale University Press, 2006).

14. See Sándor Horváth, *A Kapu és a Határ: mindennapi Sztálinváros* (Budapest: MTA, 2004).

15. Gergő Havadi, "Az új 'népi szórakozóhely': a 'hosszú' ötvenes évek Budapestjének életvilága a szocialista vendéglátásban," *Fons,* XIII, no. 3 (2006): 315–54, especially 345, and György Majtényi, "Kávéháztól a népbüféig: A vendéglátóipar államosítása" in *Archivnet. Történeti források,* available online at http://www.archivnet.hu (accessed 18 February 2011).

16. See Brown, *Dance Hall Days,* and Gergely Havadi, "Állámbiztonság és a vendéglátás szigorúan ellenőrzött terei a szocializmusban" in *Mindennapok Rákosi és Kádár korában: Új utak a szocialista korszak kutatásában,* ed. Sándor Horváth (Budapest: Nyított Könyvműhely, 2008), 172–86.

17. Ibid.

18. For more on this see György Litván, ed., *The Hungarian Revolution of 1956: Reform, Revolution, and Repression, 1953-1963,* trans. János M. Bak and Lyman H. Legters (London: Longman, 1996); Charles Gati, *Failed Illusions: Moscow, Washington, Budapest, and the Hungarian Revolution of 1956* (Stanford: Stanford University Press, 1996); and Paul Lendvai, *One Day That Shook the Communist World: The 1956 Hungarian Uprising and Its Legacy* (Princeton: Princeton University Press, 2008).

19. See the essays in Melanie Ilič, Jeremy Smith, ed., *Soviet State and Society under Nikita Khrushchev* (New York: Routledge, 2009).

20. Ivan T. Berend and György Ránki, *The Hungarian Economy in the Twentieth Century* (New York: St. Martin's Press, 1985), 236. It is significant to note though that while forced industrialization gave way to new consumption-oriented policies, collectivization continued apace throughout the late 1950s and early 1960s.

21. Ibid., 235. For more on the politics of socialist consumption in Hungary see Tibor Valuch, "A bőséges ínségtől az ínséges bőségig. A fogyasztás változásai Magyarországon az 1956 utáni évtizedekben," in *Magyarország a jelenkorban/1956-os Intézet Évkönyv,* ed. János M. Rainer and Éva Standeiszky, X, no. 1 (2003): 51–78.

22. For West Germany see Ernst Bernhauer, *Der Fremdenverkehr im Gemeinsamen Markt: Eine Untersuchung über die möglichen Auswirkungen der wirtschaftlichen Integration aus dem Fremdenverkehr* (Frankfurt am Main: Universität Institut für Fremderverkehrwissenschaft, 1963) and "Fodor's Germany" in Rudy Koshar, *German Travel Cultures* (Oxford: Berg, 2000), 161–202,

while for similar developments in France, Italy and Spain see Luciano Segreto, Carles Manera, and Manfred Pohl, ed., *Europe at the Seaside: The Economic History of Mass Tourism in the Mediterranean* (New York: Berghahn Books, 2009). West Germans also flocked in large numbers to the Spanish beaches, cf. Anne-Katrin Becker, "Sonne, Strand und Meer: Spanien und der boom turistico" in *Viva Espana! Von den Alhambra bis zum Ballermann: Deutsche Reisen nach Spanien,* ed. Anne-Katrin Becker, Margarete Meggle-Freund (Karlsruhe: Badisches Landesmuseum, 2007), 97–116.

23. Kasimir Libera, "A szocialista országok idegenforgalmának helyzete és perspektivái," in *Idegenforgalmi Kollokvium* (I), 23–25 November 1964 (Budapest: Országos Idegenforgalmi Hivatal, 1966). See also Hannes Grandits and Karin Taylor, ed., *Yugoslavia's Sunnyside: A History of Tourism in Socialism* (*1950s-1980s*) (Budapest and New York: Central European University Press, 2010).

24. The mission of the new agency was to coordinate the activity of county and municipal tourism offices, and cooperate with already existing travel agencies such as IBUSZ and EXPRESZ, the touring section of the Hungarian Auto Club, the newly created MALÉV (The Hungarian Air Travel Company), and a score of trade unions in the service sector represented by the Alliance of Trade Unions in the Restaurant Industry (*Vendéglátóipari Szakszervezetek Szövetsége*). For more on this see "Az Idegenforgalom új szervezete," *Idegenforgalom* 6–7 (1964): 4.

25. László Kovács and János Takács, *Az idegenforgalom alakulása és fejlődése Magyarországon, 1945-1965* (Budapest: Panorama, 1966), 76. To put the development of Hungarian tourism in a wider European perspective it is important to note that around the same time, eleven million people visited Spain, while Italy attracted more than twenty-three million foreign tourists. See György Lantos, "Néhány adat az europai országok idegenforgalmáról," *Idegenforgalom,* 8 (1964): 9–10. For more on the rise of the Spanish tourism industry see Sasha D. Pack, *Tourism and Dictatorship: Europe's Peaceful Invasion of Franco's Spain* (New York: Palgrave Macmillan, 2006).

26. Ferenc Bodor, "Eszpresszók 1945 es 1957 között," *Budapesti Negyed,* no. 2–3 (1996): 279–86.

27. See Károlyné Kovács, "Új városnéző körséták Budapesten," *Idegenforgalom,* 3 (1964): 10; and "Budapesti vásárprogram," *Idegenforgalom* 5 (1963): 13. The launching of the "Budapest by Night" tours was connected to the opening of the Budapest Industrial Fair, which in 1963 had been upgraded into an international fair. For more on the connections between the Budapest International Fair, economic activities under state socialism, and the topic of tourism in general, see Ottó Gecser and Dávid Kitzinger, "Fairy Sales: The Budapest International Fairs as Virtual Shopping tours," *Cultural Studies* 16, no. 1 (2002): 145–64.

28. Konrád Nemesi, "Vendéglátás a vásáron" *Idegenforgalom* 5 (1963): 17.

29. "Budapesti vásárprogram," *Idegenforgalom* 5 (1963): 13.

30. Nemesi, "Vendéglátás a vásáron," 17.

31. See their graphic advertising on the interior back cover of *Idegenforgalom,* no. 3 (1963): 23.

32. Zachar Gyuláné, "Magyar vendéglátás—külföldi szemmel," *Idegenforgalom,* no. 2 (1962): 14.

33. See Miklós Rózsa, "Magyar vendéglátás—külföldi szemmel," *Idegenforgalom,* no. 1 (1963): 15.

34. Joachim Schlör, *Nights in the Big City: Paris, Berlin, London, 1830-1940,* trans. Pierre Gottfried Imhof and Dafydd Rees Roberts (London: Reaktion Books, 1998), 252–57.

35. According to a tourism industry official the night clubs offering such shows were kept open especially for the sake of Western tourists. For more on this see Konrád Nemesi, "A pesti éjszaka fényei és árnyai," *Idegenforgalom,* no. 12 (1967): 12–13.

36. See http://www.iz.webzona.hu/neon0.htm (accessed 10 July 2009) and Horváth, "Csudapest és a frizsiderszocializmus," 76.

37. For more on this see Sándor Horváth, "Hooligans, Spivs and Gangs: Youth Subcultures in the 1960s," in *Muddling Through in the Long 1960s: Ideas and Everyday Life in High Politics and the Lower Classes of Communist Hungary,* ed. János M. Rainer and György Péteri, Trondheim Stud-

ies on East European Cultures and Societies, no. 16 (May 2005), 199–223; Dénes Csengey, "A magyar beatnemzedékről," *Életünk,* no. 3 (1983): 258–74; Tamás Fricz, "A hatvanas évek és a beat-nemzedék," *Ifjúsági Szemle,* no. 4 (1982): 43–52; Tibor Valuch, "A lódentől a miniszoknyáig. Az öltözködés és a divat Magyarországon az 1950-es és az 1960-as években," in *Magyarország a jelenkorban/1956-os Intézeti Évkönyv,* IV, ed. János. M. Rainer and Éva Standeiszky (Budapest: 1956-os Intézet, 2002).

38. See András Vitéz, "Most rajtunk a sor, hogy az előlegezett bizalomra méltóak legyünk," *Idegenforgalom,* no. 6–7 (1964): 5–10. Quote from page 9.

39. János Rőczey, "Beszámolók az 1966-os évről: Budapest," *Idegenforgalom,* no. 1 (1967): 1–10.

40. See Mihály Viszket, "A budapesti fürdők," *Idegenforgalom,* no. 11 (1966): 3–4.

41. András Bolgár, "Az 1970 utáni időszak szállodafejlesztésének kategóriak szerinti igénye," *Idegenforgalom,* no. 7 (1967): 14–15.

42. See János Erdei, *Nemzetközi szállodaláncok és tagszállodáik Magyarországon* (Budapest: Belkereskedelmi Továbbképző Intézet, 1983). For more on the role of foreign investment in supporting the Hungarian hotel building program see David Turnock, *The Economy of East-Central Europe, 1815-1989: Stages of Transformation in a Peripheral Region* (London: Routledge, 2006), 349.

43. Géza Baróti, "Budapest Hilton," *Idegenforgalom,* no. 1 (1977): 5.

44. Annabel Jane Wharton, *Building the Cold War: Hilton International Hotels and Modern Architecture* (Chicago: University of Chicago Press, 2001), 197.

45. Ibid., 196.

46. See "Hotel Budapest," *Idegenforgalom,* no. 2 (1968): 6–7.

47. See Iván Boldizsár, "Preface," in Lajos Czeizing, *Budapest bei Nacht/ by Night/ la Nuit* (Budapest: Corvina, 1965, 1ˢᵗ ed. 1961), xi–xv.

48. During the socialist period, however, the establishment had its name changed to "Vörös Malom," a literal translation into Hungarian of the French Moulin Rouge. See Zsuzsa Kaán, "Újra forog a Vörösmalom," *Táncművészet,* no. 1 (2000): 18–19.

49. Roger Moore, *My Word is my Bond: A Memoir* (New York: Harper Collins, 2009), 168.

50. *Szálloda a Duna-parton. 20 éves a Hotel Duna-InterContinental* (Budapest: Hotel Duna Inter-Continental, 1989), 35–36. See also Sándor Ják, "Kiknek épült az Intercontinental?" *Idegenforgalom,* no 4. (1972): 13.

51. Kitty Kelley, *Elizabeth Taylor, the Last Star* (New York: Simon & Schuster, 1981), 244.

52. Sam Kashner and Nancy Schoenberger, *Furious Love: Elizabeth Taylor, Richard Burton and the Marriage of the Century* (New York: HarperCollins, 2010), 333.

53. Kelley, *Elizabeth Taylor, the Last Star,* 244–45.

54. Ibid., 245. For the veracity of this episode see also Thomas Thompson, "Happy 40ᵗʰ, Dear Liz," *Life Magazine,* 25 February 1972; and Kashner and Schoenberger, *Furious Love,* 333.

55. Alexander Walker, *Elizabeth: The Life of Elizabeth Taylor* (New York: Grove Press, 2001), 313.

56. Ibid., 314.

57. It was also in 1961 that the *Komsomol,* the Communist youth organization in the Soviet Union, made a similar move by opening several cafes in downtown Moscow, where students could legally listen to jazz. For more on this see Vladislav Zubok, *Zhivago's Children: The Last Russian Intelligentsia* (Cambridge, MA: Belknap Press, 2009), 196–97.

58. János Sebők, *Rock a vasfüggöny mögött: hatalom és ifjúsági zene a Kádár-korszakban* (Budapest: GM és Társai Kiadó, 2002).

59. See "Jelentés a KISZ Budapesti Bizottság 1971.évi gazdálkodásáról," Budapest City Archives, MSZMP Budapesti Végrehajtó Bizottságának ülései (XXXV.1.a.4.), 373. őe. (27), 10 March 1972.

60. It should be noted that, although the most successful, the Ifipark was just one out of 270 youth entertainment centers KISZ operated in the country. For more on this, see Budapest City Ar-

chives, MSZMP Budapesti Végrehajtó Bizottságának ülései (XXXV.1.a.4.), 402. őe. (32), 25 May 1973.

61. He reiterated these principles on several occasions: at an address given at the Political Academy in 1968, and in a speech (as quoted from) given in 1979. For more on this see Bence Csatári, "A Kádár rendszer könnyűzenei politikája" (PhD diss., ELTE Budapest, 2007), 3 ff.

62. Magdolna Balázs, "Az Ifipark," *Budapesti Negyed,* no. 1 (1994): 137-50. See also János Sebök, ed., *Egyszer volt egy Ifipark* (Budapest: 1984).

63. For more on Great Tree Gang see an article by Sándor Horváth, "Myths of the Great Tree Gang: Constructing Urban Spaces and Youth Culture in the 'Socialist' Budapest" in *Testimonies of the City: Identity, Community and Change in a Contemporary Urban World,* ed. Richard Rodger and Joanna Herbert (Aldershot: Ashgate, 2007), 73–96, and Horváth's recent book: *Kádár gyermekei. Ifjúsági lázadás a hatvanas években* (Budapest: Nyított Könyvműhely, 2009).

64. On the role of blue jeans as signifiers of Western values in socialist Hungary see Ferenc Hammer, "Sartorial Manoeuvres in the Dusk: Blue Jeans in Socialist Hungary," in *Citizenship and Consumption,* ed. Kate Soper and Frank Trentmann (London: Palgrave Macmillan, 2008), 51–68.

65. See Szentesi Zöldi László, "Csápolók és fejrázók," *Magyar Hírlap,* 20 February 2009, online at http://www.magyarhirlap.hu/cikk.php?cikk=160760 (accessed 29 July 2009).

66. János Kőbányai, "Biztosítótű és bőrnadrág," *Mozgó Világ* (1979), reprinted in *Budapesti Negyed* 35–36, no. 1–2 (2002): 193–218.

67. Ibid., 210.

68. See the chapter on the making of the rock underground and the politics of marginality in Anna Szemere, *Up from the Underground. The Culture of Rock Music in Postsocialist Hungary* (State College: Penn State University Press, 1997), 29–72. Quote from page 39.

69. See Balázs, "Az Ifipark," 146. For a perspective on the Communist Youth Alliance's thinking on this matter, which concerned not just the Ifipark but Hungarian youth entertainments habits as a whole, see KISZ Központi Bizottság Kulturális Osztálya, *Tézisek az ifjúság szórakozásának néhány időszerű kérdéséről* and *Javaslat az ifjúsági szórakozási tevékenység fejlesztésének fő irányaira,* MOL XIX-I-9-a 7. D. Művelődési Minisztérium, and the discussion in Rolf Müller, "Diszkórobbanás a KISZ Központi Bizottságában" in *Archivnet. Történeti források,* available online at http://www.archivnet.hu (accessed 18 February 2011).

70. Balázs, "Az Ifipark," 146.

71. See Tibor Valuch, "A 'gulyáskommunizmus' valósága," *Rubicon,* no. 114–15, (2001–2002): 69–76 and Bianca L. Adair, "Interest Articulation in Communist Regimes: The New Economic Policy in Hungary, 1962-1980," *East European Quarterly,* XXXVII, no. 1 (2003): 101–26.

72. László Márton, Interview with László Najmányi in "Tilost csinálni: Jegyzőkönyv: Najmányi Lászlóval a Kolibri pincében," *Balkon,* no. 7–8 (1998), available online at http://www.c3.hu/scripta/ (accessed 21 February 2011).

73. Ádám Pozsonyi, *A Lenin-szobor helyén bombatölcsér tátong: a magyar punk története, 1978-1990,* 2nd enlarged edition (Budapest: Mucsa Könyvek, 2003), 85.

74. Sabrina P. Ramet, *Social Currents in Eastern Europe: the Sources and Consequences of the Great Transformation* (Durham: Duke University Press, 2nd ed., 1995), 258.

75. Ibid.

76. Ibid., 259. However, the veracity of this episode is contested. For more on this see "A csirkedarálás legendája," available online at http://www.urbanlegends.hu/2009/05/csirkedaralas-legenda-nagy-fero-beatrice-cpg/ (accessed 23 February 2011).

77. Ramet, *Social Currents in Eastern Europe,* 259.

78. Szemere, *Up from the Underground,* 40.

79. See István Csörsz, *Elhagyott a közérzetem: Riportok 1982-83* (Budapest: Magvető, 1986); "Minden megy tovább: fe Lugossy Lászlóval, Krizbai Sándorral és Vincze Ottóval a Vajda La-

jos Stúdióról L. Simon László beszélget," *Szépirodalmi Figyelő*, no. 2 (2003): 65–73; and Béla Szilárd Jávorszky and János Sebők, *A magyarock története: A Beatkezdetektől a kemény rockig* (Budapest: Népszabadság, 2005). For a discussion of home parties in 1980s Budapest by a foreign observer see the chapter "Hungarian Confusions," in Hans Magnus Enzensberger, *Europe, Europe: Forays into a Continent* (New York: Pantheon Books, 1989).

80. For the early history of punk in Britain and the music's impact on and spread to the US, see Phil Strong, *Pretty Vacant: A History of UK Punk* (Chicago: Chicago Review Press, 2008), while for Western Europe see Rémy Pépin, *Rebelles: Une histoire du rock alternatif* (Paris: Éditions Hugo, 2007) and Ronald Galenza "Zwischen 'Plan' und 'Planloss': Punk in Deutschland," in *Rock! Jugend und Musik in Deutschland,* eds. Barbara Hammerschmitt and Bernd Lindner (Berlin: Ch. Links Verlag, 2005), 96–103.

81. See Anna Szemere, "The Politics of Marginality: A Rock Musical Subculture in Socialist Hungary in the early 1980s," in *Rockin' the Boat: Mass Music and Mass Movements,* ed. Reebee Garofalo (Cambridge, MA: South End Press, 1992), 93–114.

82. Ferenc Hammer, "Az éjszakai élet mint populáris nyilvánosság a szocializmusban," *Médiakutató* (Winter 2009): 89–107.

83. See József Havasréti, *Alternatív regiszterek: a kulturális ellenállás formái a magyar neoavantgárdban* (Budapest: Typotex, 2006), 52–56.

84. As was the case in the GDR (see Gareth Dale, *Popular Protest in East Germany, 1945-1989* [London: Routledge, 2005], 95), repression of punk music in Hungary backfired, turning a sub-cultural trend that was not intrinsically anti-establishment into something openly oppositional. For a discussion of the fading of KISZ's relevance in matters of enforcing musical styles and policy in Hungary after 1985 see Bence Csatári, "A KISZ könnyűzenei politikája," *Múltunk,* no. 3 (2007): 67–103, especially 103.

PART V

Sports and Stadia

CHAPTER 9

Getting off Track in East Germany

Adolescent Motorcycle Fans and Honecker's Consumer Socialism

Caroline Fricke

With spring fever in the air, some seventy thousand motorcycle enthusiasts hit the road on Pentecost weekend for the famous Bergring tracks, home of the longest natural grass racetrack in Europe.[1] The year was 1988, and as some youthful fans sputtered along in their Trabants, the new hit song "Bergringrennen" by the East German heavy metal band Crystal could be heard on the radio.[2] In the background of the song, motorcycle gears roar; it quickly transitions into heavy drumming followed by an electric guitar riff. A coarse voice sings, "When the sun rises higher and the days get longer everyone knows, it is going on again, time to get off work. It is *'Bergringzeit'* (time for the Bergring)."[3]

The annual motorcycle race Bergringrennen in Teterow was one of the most popular public escapes of the 1970s and 1980s in the rural northern region of the German Democratic Republic (GDR), especially among young people. In an area with few public events, many adolescents camped out for a weekend of races, outdoor revelry, and a break from everyday routines (see Figure 9.1).[4]

Many traveled with large groups of friends and stayed together at one of the surrounding campgrounds; they lit campfires, listened to music from their portable tape recorders, danced, and drank. Given their exposure to almost constant political influence in school, at work, and often during their leisure time, young people looked forward to a weekend free of parental control and institutional oversight. However, not all youth gained admittance to the races or the nearby campgrounds near the Bergring towards the end of Honecker's reign. While the security forces at motorcycle races remained relatively inconspicuous in the 1970s and early 1980s,[5] by the end of the GDR regime they imposed more restrictions to prevent unaligned youth from reaching the racetracks. Furthermore, fearing unruly fans, the authorities denounced

Figure 9.1. Youths gathered to watch the Bergring races, 1983. Permissions from the Roger-Melis Estate, Berlin.

many of the celebrations at local campgrounds as exhibiting "decadent behavior," taking measures to prevent the youth from going to the races and hanging out at the campsites.

This chapter explores the political and cultural history of the Bergring and the popularity of this escape during the Honecker years. The Bergring races and related festivities are an example of how the regime's concept of "consumer socialism," the new course that East German authorities introduced in the beginning of the 1970s, was implemented. Instead of delaying the benefits of the envisioned socialist lifestyle, the new course proposed "real existing socialism" and the fulfillment of consumer desires in the immediate present, including entertainment and leisure demands. To satisfy the youth in particular, the regime hosted public events such as rock concerts and athletic competitions like the Bergringrennen. The popularity of the Bergringrennen symbolized the success of this new cultural and economic policy, and the authorities took precautions to ensure that nothing would spoil the ideal image of this leisure site. The Bergringrennen can be seen as an example of how the regime used public events, which seemingly offered an escape from the ubiquitous political indoctrination, to simultaneously satisfy the masses' desire for escapes from daily routines, and to control those who did not align themselves with the norms imposed on the society. Such "apolitical festivities" as a method of engineering society implied several layers of political consideration, and they ultimately relied on the exclusion of certain societal groups. Despite promises to the contrary in the 1970s, security forces at the Bergringrennen relied upon superficial judgments of appearance to assess youth and their political reliability at public venues such as sports stadiums. This chapter reveals the rational, criteria, and techniques that security forces used to exclude specific groups of adolescents from official public events like the Bergringrennen in the final years of socialist rule. The foundation of a parallel, private escape at a campground a few kilometers from the Bergring demonstrates just how difficult it was for the East German regime to control alternative youth and the private escapes they established. Although outdoor camping fit within the concept of productive leisure activities,[6] the adolescents' conduct at this particular campground defied regime expectations. This example illustrates the subversive appropriation of public venues to escape the conformity demanded of youth; this perspective also sheds light on the state's ambivalent reaction toward such escapism.[7] In order to keep official public festivities free of demonstrations of noncompliance, the regime reluctantly tolerated spaces of escapism outside of public view.

The history of racetracks like the Bergring thus contribute to an understanding of the controversies connected to leisure and official public escapes in Eastern Europe, and the manner in which state socialist policies functioned and malfunctioned on a local level in the area of youth politics. The excluded fans of the Bergring provide a case study of popular dissatisfaction within youth cultures, and opportunities for individual and group agency under a repressive regime.

The History of the Bergringrennen before Honecker's Consumer Socialism

The popularity and political significance of the Bergring races in the 1980s can best be understood in the context of the longer history and tradition of this motorcycle rally. The Bergringrennen dates back to the 1930s, when authorities prohibited wild motorcycle rallies on the streets and racing enthusiasts laid out what was and still is the largest natural grass track in Europe in the Mecklenburg heath. The course traverses over wells and narrow curves, requiring highly skilled drivers who maintain total control of their machines. The first race in 1930 drew more than seven thousand spectators. The track's fame quickly spread and attracted more bold drivers and spectators from all over Europe.

But politics soon cast a grim shadow on this success story. When the Nazis came to power, the motorcyclist clubs experienced *Gleichschaltung*, an enforced political synchronization, like other German institutions. Nazi authorities forced all motorcyclists to join a political umbrella organization, the *Nationalsozialistisches Kraftfahrkorps* (National Socialist Automobile Society), which organized both clubs and races. Nazi "racial laws" excluded German "Jews" from the contests, and eventually from the audience as well.[8] German "Aryans" and international drivers and spectators enjoyed several races per year until Pentecost 1939. A few weeks later, German troops invaded Poland and unleashed the Second World War. Local authorities closed down the track for the duration of the war years.[9]

In the wake of wartime destruction, the daily struggle for survival outweighed thoughts of entertainment, and local residents used the grounds of the track for growing potatoes. As early as 1948, however, the new socialist local authorities decided to reconstruct the track. They celebrated the twenty-first Bergringrennen in August 1949—two months before the foundation of the GDR in October of that year. Due to travel restrictions between the German occupation zones, most of the seventy thousand spectators were from Mecklenburg and other parts of the Soviet Occupation Zone.[10] In the 1950s, international drivers returned to Teterow to race alongside their East German counterparts, allowing for international contests once again.[11] Although West German racing fans experienced problems trying to cross the border, they were still able to attend the races. However, the building of the Berlin Wall and the tightening of border controls in 1961 further divided the racing community. Drivers and spectators from non-socialist countries faced severe difficulties entering the GDR, and the East German government prevented their citizens from attending races in non-socialist countries. East German drivers were well-aware that they were viewed suspiciously, especially when they went to non-socialist countries.[12] Although political and travel limitations hindered the Bergringrennen from gaining its pre-war importance within the European racing community, a chronicle of the Bergringrennen published after 1989 describes the 1960s as the "golden years" in GDR motorcycle sports.[13] East German motorcyclists could still compete with some West Germans, Australians, English, and Dutch drivers at the Bergring.[14] However, these so-called "golden years" ended in the beginning of the 1970s.

The year 1972 marked a sudden end to the careers of many elite athletes from the GDR, including motorcycle racers. In order to foster a competitive East German advantage in select international contests, the regime compelled the socialist umbrella sports association, *Deutscher Turn- und Sportbund* (DTSB), to impose the notorious "resolution on elite sports." This directive restricted GDR participation in contests with non-socialist competitors, and allocated financial support predominantly to those fields that rewarded East German athletes with the most fame and recognition in international competitions due to the prestige they conferred. Those sports that required the maintenance of a whole team, but pledged only one potential trophy, received less financial support than individual athletes.[15] Under the terms of the "resolution on elite sports," motorcycle rallies merited little state support. There was only one manufacturer of motorcycles in the GDR, and the limited funding further hampered technical development. Drivers from other socialist countries such as Hungary, Czechoslovakia, and even Cuba imported Japanese motorcycles, but East German drivers were compelled to ride motorcycles of socialist production, which they carefully transformed into competitive racing machines. In 1986, the motor sports section of the DTSB *Allgemeiner Deutscher Motorsportverband* (ADMV), which organized the Bergringrennen, had eighty thousand members, but only three hundred officially licensed motorcycle racers.[16]

As with many other political resolutions, GDR leaders did not disclose this new course in sport politics to the public. East German sportsmen simply ceased to participate in many international contests, and authorities halted Western competition within East Germany's borders. It became apparent afterwards that 1971 had been the last traditional Bergringrennen; the races of 1972 had to be interrupted due to heavy rainfall, and in 1973 the ADMV tacitly excluded drivers from non-socialist countries.[17] Because of the conspiratorial silence about the new course, rumors regarding the reasons for the withdrawal from international competitions quickly spread. Even today, many people are convinced that the GDR retired from international motor sport events because of an incident at the Grand Prix motorcycle race in 1971 on the Sachsenring, another East German race track. Although it was not the true reason, the rumor, like many explanations that circulated among GDR citizens, contains a kernel of truth.[18] The regime was preoccupied with Cold War rivalry and took precautions to ensure that no Western drivers gained glory on GDR race tracks, or that audiences would be able to cheer for them. The fear of German nationalism was prevalent not only in the GDR, but also in its socialist brother states where it was often associated with memories of Nazi notions of German superiority. However, in 1971, the West German motorcyclist Dieter Braun won the race at the Sachsenring, despite the efforts of the ADMV to disqualify him. The organization later dismissed the referee responsible, but Dieter Braun remained the 1971 winner. To avoid any demonstration of sympathy for West German citizens, the ADMV ordered that loudspeakers be turned off during the victory ceremony. The predominantly East German audience nevertheless loudly sang the West German anthem, thwarting the regime's ban. The next year witnessed the last Grand Prix races on the Sachsenring until 1996; in 1973, the event essentially vanished from the international racing calendar.[19]

In 1973, the first season without Western participation, fans boycotted the GDR tracks. At the Bergring, the number of spectators shrank drastically to a fraction of the 1972 audience levels. Several drivers left the country in reaction to the "resolution on elite sports."[20] Racing enthusiasts who insisted on world-class competitions now had to travel to Czechoslovakia to attend the Grand Prix races in Brno. In 1972, visa-free travel between the GDR and Czechoslovakia came into effect, and this new freedom facilitated the boycott of East German tracks, as many East German fans took advantage of the new regulation and made the annual pilgrimage to Brno.[21]

To win back the support of racing enthusiasts, the ADMV tried to offer new attractions. In 1974 it began to award another trophy—the Golden Helmet—in addition to the traditional Bergring trophy, to drivers, including competitors from other socialist countries. However, until 1990 and 1991, when more international drivers returned to the tracks, only GDR motorcyclists won the two trophies, indicating that the races failed to draw the best drivers from socialist countries. Moreover, publicity ads favored the speedway races in Güstrow, another small town about eighteen miles from Teterow. Since 1963, Güstrow featured speedway races on Pentecost, but the *Pfingstpokal* (Pentecost trophy races) were only accessible to drivers from socialist countries. Until 1973 the Bergringrennen had overshadowed the *Pfingstpokal* because the races at Güstrow lacked Western international competition. Eventually, the efforts of the ADMV appeared to be successful, and by the end of the 1970s, the number of spectators continued to increase. Given the few official public events in the rural north of the GDR, the audience simply accepted the limitations of GDR motor sports and returned to the Bergringrennen.[22]

GDR Youth, Caught Between East and West

Youthful East German motorcycle enthusiasts witnessed and embraced the symbolic power of the Bergringrennen from the early years of the GDR, before the construction of the Berlin Wall and the tightening of border security, and into the Honecker years. The East German state was conscious of the potential power of Western influence over a population group it considered to be very significant for the future of socialism. The maxim "trust in the young generation" is one of the most common tenets found in documents on youth and youth politics, but the party leadership lacked trust and expected adolescents to fit the mold of the "generally cultured socialist personality."[23] The special leadership role assigned to youth helps to explain leading party politicians' notorious and contradictory mistrust of young people; because adolescents had not experienced class struggle themselves, the authorities were

apprehensive that they might underestimate their "class enemies" and the enemies' subversive techniques to gain influence. GDR authorities considered
the capitalist use of entertainment to be particularly dangerous, referring to
such Western entertainment as political-ideological diversion or PID.[24]

Since the Second World War, the music, dress codes, and habits of the
new popular cultures from the US and the United Kingdom had excited
adolescents in East and West Germany. These new teenager cultures shocked
parents and authorities in East and West alike. But whereas in the Federal
Republic these new forms of cultural expression were soon tamed by commercialization, GDR authorities interpreted cultural influences from Western
countries as a form of psychological Cold War warfare.[25] The erection of the
Berlin Wall in 1961 physically cut off GDR citizens from the sites of Western
popular culture, but the wall did not hinder Western-inspired popular and
teen cultures from invading the GDR through the air waves and other forms
of mass media. The socialist regime perceived such influence to be PID, designed to undermine the class consciousness of precarious minds.[26] In their
eyes, the youth especially were a target of PID, and since the late 1940s, GDR
authorities had been monitoring youth who sought an escape into Western-
inspired youth cultures.[27]

Characteristic for this perception of the young were the notorious order
11/66 and its enforcement provision, DA 4/66, which the state security
(Ministerium für Staatssicherheit or Stasi) enacted in 1966, and enforced until 1989.[28] By way of introduction, the order states that the regime and East
German youth share the same interests, one of the chief presumptions of all
socialist youth policy. According to the order, only a few juveniles subject to
Western influence were not yet convinced of the advantages of the socialist
order and required Stasi surveillance. However, the enforcement provision
then broadly defined who belonged to this unreliable group: pupils, trainees,
students and adolescents with relatives in West Germany, religious teenagers, those who preferred solitude to collective activities, partygoers, Western-
inspired rock bands and their fans, and consumers of Western mass media. In
short, all East German adolescents fell under general suspicion. Sites requiring
surveillance were likewise unlimited; they included schools, universities, factories, city centers, collective farms, clubs, housing estates, and official public
sites like sports stadiums.[29] Thus, the order documents a fundamental distrust
regarding youth, contradicting official statements affirming the state's belief in
the youth population. GDR authorities expected the young to focus on "meaningful leisure activities" and adopt a "generally cultured socialist personality."
They applied the concept of "productive leisure activities" to young people as
well as adult workers. "Meaningful leisure activity" was ideally maintained
under adult surveillance and under the auspices of the socialist youth organi-

zation, the Freie Deutsche Jugend (FDJ).[30] The annual Pentecost meetings of the FDJ can be seen as a model for the desired entertainment at official public sites for adolescents. Every year at Pentecost, the political youth organization sponsored public festivals throughout the republic. These festivals not only included political programming, discussions, and sometimes athletic competitions, but also concerts with popular music bands and dancing.[31]

After the Eighth Party Congress, the official perception of "meaningful leisure activity" broadened in the era of Honecker's consumer socialism. This term was coined in hindsight to describe a social-political concept the communist party of the Soviet Union enacted during the Twenty-fourth Party Congress in April 1971, and which the German Socialist Unity Party (Sozialistische Einheitspartei Deutschlands or SED) adopted while convening their Eighth Party Congress in the same year. At the German party congress, Honecker revealed an outline of the government program he envisioned. In the context of the need for cultural reforms, Honecker specifically referred to the regime's strict youth policy, which had been a primary obstacle to popular support in previous years.[32]

The overt pressure of conformity appeared to diminish along with open political repression and compared to earlier decades, youth culture became more colorful and differentiated. While the special surveillance of adolescent behavior remained, the regime did not react as harshly to undesirable appearances, especially compared to the extreme cases of forced haircutting in public earlier. But the regime displayed no consistency in policies towards musical tastes and dress codes, alternating between more tolerance in the early 1970s and stronger restrictions at the end of the decade. The regime's tolerance was rather limited, however, and nonexistent when the outer appearances proved to be inspired by youth cultures of Western origin. These youth cultures were interpreted as a form of PID and their adherents denounced as "negative-decadent."[33]

Under consumer socialism, the FDJ also expanded leisure opportunities and events at least in larger towns, which included sporting events, dances, educational programs, and political instruction. GDR officials credited the people's compliance to the politics of consumer socialism with the increased number of spectators at events such as the Bergringrennen.

Youth Motor-sports Fans and Alternative Cultures under Consumer Socialism

Under consumer socialism, adolescent activities without adult supervision also remained suspect, and to engage reluctant juveniles to spend their leisure time on FDJ activities, other mass organizations intensified their youth work. The motor sport sections of the paramilitary Association for Sport and Technology (*Gesellschaft für Sport und Technik,* GST), were particularly popular among adolescents, because they offered opportunities to attend sporting events and attain driver's licenses. However, GST authorities often used youth interest in motor sports to discipline unaligned juveniles with the threat of exclusion.[34] Local sports clubs of the ADMV usually perceived adolescent self-expression more tolerantly. However, the ADMV often experienced financial difficulties limiting local opportunities. Economic shortcomings along with general concerns about appropriate entertainment often hampered authorities' plans for controlled leisure activities for young people that would support societal integration. By the mid-1980s, GDR youth had largely turned away from societal participation within the established institutions, such as the FDJ, despite the initial success of the new political course of consumer socialism. Opinion polls surveying adolescents documented a decreasing identification with the political system.[35] Furthermore, security forces consistently complained that adolescents refrained from FDJ work as soon as they left school, and had to be urged to prolong their membership and lured to engage in activities of the FDJ.[36]

The regime reacted to its continuously declining credit of trust in two ways. On one hand, the state continued its attempts to organize attractive public events to regain youth support. On the other hand, it sought to enforce compliance by excluding the politically unaligned from public escapes. At the Bergring the authorities were very concerned about motorcycle fans involved with groups such as the so-called *Blueser* (named after their favorite kind of pop music) and heavy metal fans.

The *Blueser* scene emerged in the 1970s, when the hippie youth culture invaded the GDR. These adolescents provoked the regime (and many older citizens) purely through their outer appearance; they wore long hair and beards and dressed in worn-out jeans, a parka, and sandals or workers boots, thus departing from the desired ideal of the "socialist personality," in a pressed FDJ uniform shirt and with hair neatly parted. Even more than outer appearance, the nonconformist lifestyle of the *Blueser* and its obvious non-socialist origins provoked authorities. Many *Blueser* traveled regularly around the republic and even to the socialist sister states, attending official and unofficial public escapes, like sporting events, wherever they had the chance. Whenever *Blueser* met on such occasions, they listened to music and consumed large quantities of alcohol.[37]

Heavy metal fans then began to appear in the early 1980s in the GDR. Their outer appearance was even more striking than the *Blueser's*. Heavy metal fans also wore long hair, which was by now more acceptable, but many also sported tattoos, which the regime not only judged to be offensive and rebellious, but the result of a criminal act of self-mutilation.[38] Heavy metal fans were easy to spot at sporting events because of their signature black leather clothes, which were usually not even available for purchase in the GDR. Those who did not have the connections to obtain leather clothes from the Federal Republic or Hungary decorated jeans and jean jackets with large emblems of music groups and rivets.[39] Like the *Blueser,* heavy metal enthusiasts traveled around the GDR and neighboring socialist states to attend their favorite public events, such as rock concerts, motor cycle rallies in Brno, and folk festivals like the dark beer festival in Prague. The heavy metal fans' common interests focused mainly on heavy metal music, motor sports, and alcohol.[40]

Initially, the majority of the security force teams were unable to detect and distinguish these groups' stylistic conventions from other more tolerable fashion trends. Hence the state security compiled profiles of the different groups, often utilizing photographs of arrested delinquents that they could use at the Bergring and elsewhere. These profiles portrayed the different styles, their visual features, their preferred music, and their assumed political disposition. The Stasi drew its conclusions about the political beliefs of members of these youth cultures solely from phenomenological preconceptions; when a juvenile dressed in a specific way, he was assigned to a certain group with assumed political beliefs.[41] All Western-inspired youth cultures, *Blueser,* punks, goths, heavy metal fans, and skinheads alike were ultimately suspected of fascist activities. This assumption led to misconceptions, as the case of heavy metal fans at a Grand Prix motorcycle rally in Brno illustrates.

In 1985, Stasi agents at the international motorcycle races in Brno, Czechoslovakia noticed a group of twenty-eight heavy metal motorcycle fans from the GDR. They were dressed in heavy metal outfits, which the Stasi interpreted as uniforms, and wore an "eagle-like entity" on their backs.[42] The eagle, the traditional German heraldic symbol, was generally associated with Nazi sympathizers. Although the "eagle-like entity" turned out to be the trademark of Honda, the so-called "Honda-Wing," the Stasi arrested five members of the group.[43]

This harsh treatment provides context for later developments near the Bergring, and must be viewed in light of other tense incidents during previous races, such as the violent clashes said to have broken out between East and West German spectators and the Czechoslovakian security forces on the sidelines of the Brno Grand Prix race in August 1981. That year about sixty thousand predominantly young spectators from the GDR arrived in Brno. Many of them spent the night on the campgrounds near the tracks, where fans from West Germany also tented. The lively celebrations of the West German world champion Anton "Toni" Mang and shouts of "Deutschland!

Deutschland!" provoked Czechoslovak security forces, which started scuffling with German fans to suppress the nationalist enthusiasm. Unperturbed, East and West Germans sang the West German national anthem and waived flags of the Federal Republic, whereupon a drunken East German teenager was instantly arrested. The situation escalated at a campground near the Mysliva-curve when the kiosks closed and the crowd ran out of alcohol. About one hundred and fifty juveniles started rioting; they burned paper cups and trash bins and threw stones at the police cars that arrived at the scene. The crowd temporarily increased to about three hundred people; two kiosks were set on fire, and a fireman and three policemen sustained injuries. The motorcycle fans experienced the policemen's arbitrary use of bats, tear gas, and water cannons.[44]

The next day, no alcohol was sold and the police increased its presence at the track, but rioting sparked anew. Some youth erected barricades and stole about sixty beer crates from a nearby beer depot. The Czechoslovak or-gans then combed through the campground, arrested eleven of the so-called "rowdies," ascertained personal data from numerous citizens of the GDR, and returned ninety-three of them to the Stasi for preliminary investigations. Based on lack of evidence, the Stasi could only convict thirteen of them for participation in the riots and report sixteen other suspects to the local Stasi-departments for further controls. Two hundred and twenty-eight East Ger-man adolescents, who had simply been present at the campground, were later identified as sport enthusiasts who often went to the races and otherwise led an inconspicuous life.[45]

According to the Stasi, the reasons for the riots of 1981 were, besides al-cohol abuse, "demonstrative utterance of German-German commonness, the glorification of Toni Mang as German world champion, and a gener-ally hostile-negative attitude against socialist organs of security."[46] Other than what the Czechoslovakian police reported, the Stasi found no evidence of fascist activities. Erich Mielke, Minister of State Security, added in writing, however, that the Stasi did find evidence of "nationalist and antisocialist ca-bals."[47] Expressed through a common hero and the West German anthem, East/West camaraderie laced with alcohol incited a violent reaction to the security forces. East German authorities viewed this incident as a case of anti-socialist behavior, and adopted stricter methods to screen revelers in future years at sporting events.

This incident in Brno provides a backdrop for a series of incidents at and near the Bergring, and the development of a more coherent alternative cul-tural scene that banned youth created on local campgrounds. Similar to the youth in Brno, security forces would suspect adolescent Bergring fans of in-ebriation, inappropriate nationalism, and fascist sympathies. The Bergring case study reveals the comprehensive and successful use of surveillance techniques at the public racetracks and railway stations, but an initial failure on the part of local authorities to react to and contend with the private alternative youth scene.

Youth Surveillance at the Bergring and the Campgrounds near Krakow am See

The story of the Bergringrennen in the 1980s begins with a post-war high of seventy thousand spectators in the audience.[48] As the song "Bergringrennen" by the East German heavy metal band Crystal hit the GDR music charts in 1988, the popularity of the races among adolescents was patently obvious.[49] The authorities perceived the enormous popularity of the races with ambivalence. On one hand, the success of the official event promoted the concept of consumer socialism. In 1986 the West German television channel ZDF even produced a report on the Bergringrennen.[50] On the other hand, a large crowd was a challenge for the security forces, which not only aimed to avoid alcohol-induced violent clashes near the tracks in 1981, but were also prepared should the audience act out beyond the limits of acceptable behavior according to the regime's understanding of socialist entertainment. West German attention intensified the regime's eagerness to prevent any spoiling of the image of socialist races (see Figure 9.2).

The authorities heavily promoted the races for ordinary people, while at the same time they carried out restrictive measures to prevent certain suspected groups, such as *Blueser* and heavy metal fans, from appearing at the Bergring. Some of their efforts went unnoticed as youth suspected of rowdy behavior were given special assignments at work or were prevented from traveling, while others underwent police questioning and were forced to promise they would not attend the races in Teterow. In some cases, the police confiscated personal documents and issued provisional identification cards, which either prohibited them from leaving their domestic district, or banned them from entering certain districts.[51] Furthermore, the authorities ordered the ADMV to offer organized tours to monitor and control fans. If ADMV representatives witnessed inappropriate behavior, they could impose discipline by threatening to exclude youth from the motor sports club. Moreover, the campgrounds in close vicinity to the tracks accepted only pre-registered fans, facilitating control of the lists in advance and allowing authorities to ban suspicious campers.[52]

Policemen used a more public form of exclusion on the Pentecost weekend when they formed a human chain that surrounded the train station of

Figure 9.2. Young race enthusiasts near the Teterow racetracks, 1983. Permissions from the Roger-Melis Estate, Berlin.

Teterow to pick out *Bluesers*, heavy metal fans, and other unwanted persons. The policemen were quick to use their batons on those who tried to escape the cordon. They singled out juveniles and arrested them in a nearby sports hall; the young people had to stand, hands up to the wall, until the police transported them back home in the evening. To outwit the policemen, *Blueser* and heavy metal fans disguised themselves on their way to the tracks. In particular, they hid their typically long hairstyles. Some jumped off the trains before they reached Teterow and headed to the Bergring on foot. Others evaded authorities by traveling to other surrounding towns, and trying to make their way to the Bergring from there. Soon the police controlled the country roads leading to Teterow as well. The banned youth had to stay at home or to try to make the best of the weekend and organize their own entertainment, taking matters into their own hands.[53]

For several years, a campground near Krakow am See became a meeting place for *Blueser* and heavy metal fans from all over the republic who wanted to celebrate, drink, and listen to music with others at Pentecost. Located near a small town about twenty-one miles from Teterow, the campground served as a base for youth heading to the Bergring and avoiding the controls at the Teterow railway station. As the police controls tightened, many youth spent Pentecost at the campground and made it a private escape in a public setting. Annually, about thirteen hundred juveniles from all districts of the GDR arrived at the train station. Local adolescents welcomed them and transported them on motorbikes and pushcarts to the campground, where chaos prevailed for the next two days. The young people celebrated day and night, drank lots of alcohol, listened to loud heavy metal music, and danced emphatically with head banging, which was strictly prohibited in most areas of the GDR.

For several years, the crowd celebrated their event without a major incident, annoying other campers with their tremendous noise. The frustrated leaseholder of the campground was powerless to maintain order. The policeman on duty showed up occasionally, but saw neither reason nor means to intervene. At night the juveniles headed to a tavern situated between the town and the campground. Every year they demolished glasses and furniture, but the local police refused to intervene despite the complaints of the manager of the establishment. The leaseholder of the campground and the tavern manager repeatedly appealed to the mayor of Krakow to impose an alcohol ban for the weekend, but the mayor refused to take any action. On the contrary, he reminded the tavern manager of his legal duty to serve the campers; moreover, the tavern made a third of its annual profits at Pentecost. Actually, the town authorities feared the youth might invade the town if they were not distracted on their way. Up until then, only small groups of *Blueser* and heavy metal fans hung around in town, annoying the inhabitants with music from their portable tape recorders. Many citizens regularly left town for Pentecost.[54] Although the annual gatherings began in 1983, only in the aftermath of Pentecost 1986 did the council deal with the unofficial party at the campground for the first time. The year before, the campground had even been designated as a "zone of exemplary order and security" in a contest the state-owned trade association (*Handelsorganisation*) oversaw.[55]

The annual parties came to an end when a neo-Nazi incident captured the attention of the Stasi at Pentecost 1986. An adolescent group from Potsdam posed, mimicking the Hitler salute on the campground. Although other teens had quickly stopped the unwelcome nationalist display, the state security accidentally found out about the incident, and the investigation that followed finally forced the local authorities to take stricter measures. Beginning in 1987, the campground only accepted registered visitors, and for the weekend of Pentecost, the local government imposed a ban on alcohol. The authorities excluded *Blueser* and heavy metal fans once again, and they had to seek out other sites for unsupervised entertainment.[56]

The long-lasting and surprising tolerance towards some aspects of the otherwise strictly constrained youth cultures was partly due to the primacy of local interests and the fact that alcohol played a tremendous role in GDR society as a legal drug. Although it was officially branded as "alien to socialism" and a "relic of capitalism," alcoholism was very common in the GDR, which was among the top three nations in the world in per capita consumption of alcoholic beverages in 1982. Alcohol abuse was widespread and a concomitant feature of public escapes.[57] In most of these cases, the suppliers of alcohol ignored the strict rules to protect youth. Often the enterprising managers of taverns in the province specifically organized dances for alternative youth that set aside the norms of "socialist order and security" to increase their profits.[58] In the case of Krakow am See, however, it was the contrary: the local authority responded to the complaints of trade professionals with the reference to the enormous profits the excesses of the Pentecost weekend provided. The mayor of Krakow was ultimately responsible for maintaining order, but he was eager to safeguard his residents from the chaos the young people caused with their drunken revelry. The community policemen were well aware of the limits of their authority. Both local authorities were reluctant to concede their impotence by asking their superiors for assistance. The security forces of the district were overcommitted, monitoring the two motorcycle events at the Bergring and Güstrow.

The political benefits and expediency of public events for the masses like the Bergringrennen made it more important to hide the "negative-decadents" from public sight than to establish flawless socialist order throughout the province. This alternative youth getaway is an example of the many compromises the socialist authorities were forced to make on a small scale to maintain their power. Thus, the attempt to ban a repressed group from a sports venue for the masses in turn gave way to nonconformist adolescents carving out their own self-determined escape for several years.

Conclusion

Ultimately, the Bergringrennen outlived the Weimar Republic, the Nazi era, and the German Democratic Republic (GDR) as a popular motor sports competition and escape for the masses. The history of the Bergringrennen as narrated in this chapter reveals the strong influence of political developments in German sporting events. Historical influences such as the Second World War and post-war division resulted in serious repercussions for motorcycle enthusiasts. The exclusion of certain fans and spectators like German "Jews" during the Nazi era, and Westerners and specific groups of adolescents in the GDR reveals the socio-political controversies this site witnessed in the twentieth century. Both dictatorships sought to engineer German society based on their respective ideologies; they exercised firm control over the "public sphere," and attempted to transform and manipulate mass leisure sites like the Bergring by excluding certain groups, while still trying to appeal to the masses and retain popular support.

In the 1980s, socialist authorities used the Pentecost races at Bergring as evidence of the success of consumer socialism, promoting the weekend of races as a festival for the people, including the youth. Adolescents celebrated and drank on campsites near the tracks, a common feature of motorcycle rallies that did not generally conflict with accepted forms of behavior. Many campsites around Teterow witnessed parties similar to the one in Krakow. The opportunity for adolescents to celebrate without adult supervision was a break from the required conformity to given norms in daily life. The regime often tolerated drunken excesses at public getaways to pacify citizens. The reasons why authorities excluded *Blueser* and heavy metal fans were independent from their actual conduct, and rooted in the stylistic influence of Western youth cultures. In official literature, youth cultures in capitalism resulted from the political and social deprivation of the young. Their emergence in the GDR contradicted the regime's fiction of the "developed socialist society," and therefore had to be hidden from public sight. The intensity of surveillance and restriction lessened over the years, and varied in different parts of the GDR. While the East German capital Berlin hosted a distinct heavy metal youth club by the mid-1980s,[59] the social control in rural Mecklenburg was more severe. Local authorities there prohibited the heavy metal band Crystal from playing based on their fear of local fans, although fans across the GDR could tune in to the song "Bergringrennen" on the radio airwaves.[60] In the end, the authorities' attempts to exclude *Blueser* and heavy metal fans from official public escapes did not result in their desired compliance with required norms, but rather the opposite: nonconformist youth who sought out their own unobserved spaces and advanced subcultures that were even more alienated from the social and political system.

Notes

1. See the specialized journal *Illustrierter Motor Sport* (*IMS*) for visitor statistics.
2. See "Die DDR—Hitlisten 1975—1990 mit Platten- und CD—Hinweisen," http://www.ost beat.de/1988.htm (accessed 25 November 2012).
3. Crystal, "Bergringrennen," self recording, 1988.
4. See the local party newspaper *Neue Erde* and *IMS*, 4, 1983, 73, for statistical information.
5. "Bißchen Remmidemmi," *Der Spiegel* 33, 11 August 1986, 65.
6. Scholars such as David Crowley, Susan Reid, Anne Gorsuch, and Diane Koenker refer to leisure activities as productive and purposeful. See David Crowley and Susan E. Reid, "Style and Socialism: Modernity and Material Culture in Post-War Eastern Europe," in *Pleasures in Socialism: Leisure and Luxury in the Eastern Bloc*, ed. Susan E. Reid and David Crowley (Evanston: Northwestern University Press, 2010), 30; and Anne E. Gorsuch and Diane P. Koenker, "Introduction," in *Turizm: The Russian and East European Tourist under Capitalism and Socialism*, ed. Anne E. Gorsuch and Diane P. Koenker (Ithaca: Cornell University Press, 2006), 3, 5.
7. See the chapter by Catherine Plum in this volume, which illustrates the ambivalent policy towards acceptable leisure activities even in state-run Pioneer camps.

8. Dorothee Hochstätter, *Motorisierung und "Volksgemeinschaft." Das Nationalsozialistische Kraft-fahrkorps 1931-1945* (München: Oldenbourg Verlag 2005), 176.

9. Horst Baumann and Willi Peterss, *Der Teterower Bergring im Wandel der Zeiten* (Neubranden-burg: Bezirksdruckerei "Erich Weinert," 1986), 9.

10. Horst Baumann and Willi Peterss, *Die Gipfelstürmer des Bergrings. Bergringpokal- und Gold-helmgewinner auf einen Blick* (Stavenhagen: Khs. Verlag, 1998), 16.

11. *Motorsport Spezial: Die Sachsenring-Story* (Berlin: Sportverlag der DDR, 1987), 7.

12. Manfred Woll, *Heinz Rosner ... startet für MZ* (Chemnitz: HB-Werbung u. Verlag, 2006), 93.

13. Allgemeiner Deutscher Motorsport-Verband, *Chronik 1957–1992* (self-published, 1992), 10.

14. Baumann and Peterss, *Die Gipfelstürmer*, 18, 72.

15. Beschluss des Präsidiums des DTSB vom 22 April 1969: Die weitere Entwicklung des Lei-stungssports bis zu den Olympischen Spielen 1972, Stiftung der Arbeiterparteien und Mas-senorganisationen der DDR-Bundesarchiv Berlin (hereafter SAPMO-Barch), DY 12/926, 6. Soccer, the traditional German national sport, was the only exception.

16. "Bißchen Remmidemmi," *Der Spiegel* 33, 8 November 1986, 65.

17. Baumann and Peterss, *Die Gipfelstürmer*, 20.

18. Stefan Wolle, *Die heile Welt der Diktatur. Alltag und Herrschaft in der DDR 1971-1989* (Berlin: Links Verlag 1998), 156.

19. The English-language version of Wikipedia accepts the rumor that the public singing of the West German national anthem in the GDR caused the regime to retire from international sporting events. See "Sachsenring," http://en.wikipedia.org/wiki/Sachsenring (accessed 25 No-vember 2012).

20. *Chronik*, 25. Statistics revealing the exact number of fans are unavailable. State officials sought to conceal the loss of fans.

21. Thomas Kochan, *Den Blues haben. Momente einer jugendlichen Subkultur in der DDR* [*Berliner ethnografische Studien Vol. 3*] (Münster: Lit Verlag 2002), 74.

22. See the announcements of spectators in the according numbers of *IMS*.

23. For an example, see Erich Honecker, *Bericht des Politbüros an die 11. Tagung des Zentralkomitees der Sozialistischen Einheitspartei Deutschlands. 15.-18. Dezember 1965* (Berlin: Dietz Verlag, 1966), 66.

24. Margot Honecker, "Zu einigen Fragen der Bildungspolitik der Partei nach dem VIII. Parteitag der SED," in *Zur Bildungspolitik und Pädagogik in der Deutschen Demokratischen Republik. Aus-gewählte Reden und Schriften*, ed. Margot Honecker (Berlin: Verlag Volk und Wissen, 1986), 349–76, 350, in particular.

25. Uta G. Poiger, *Jazz, Rock, and Rebels: Cold War Politics and American Culture in a divided Ger-many* (Berkeley: University of California Press [Studies on the History of Society and Culture Vol. 35], 2000), 90.

26. Mark Fenemore, *Sex, Thugs and Rock 'n' Roll. Teenage Rebels in Cold-War East Germany* [Mono-graphs in German History Vol. 16], (Oxford: Berghahn Books, 2007), 78. The phenomenon was not entirely new; before the end of World War II, American swing music and the subculture it was a part of inspired some adolescents, despite the severe punishment they faced if caught. Nevertheless, swing music and culture were not a mass phenomenon. See Detlev K. Peukert, *Grenzen der Sozialdisziplinierung: Aufstieg und Krise der deutschen Jugendfürsorge von 1878 bis 1932* (Köln: Bund-Verlag 1986), 145.

27. Dorothee Wierling observed the 1960s. See Dorothee Wierling, *Youth as Internal Enemy: Con-flicts in the Education Dictatorship of the 1960s*, in *Socialist Modern. East German Everyday Cul-ture and Politics*, ed. Katherine Pence and Paul Betts (Ann Arbor: The University of Michigan Press, 2008), 157–82.

28. The Stasi order cited above is entitled, "Zur politisch-operativen Bekämpfung der politisch-ideologischen Diversion und Untergrundtätigkeit unter jugendlichen Personenkreisen der

DDR," Bundesbeauftragter für die Unterlagen des Staatssicherheitsdienstes der ehemaligen Deutschen Demokratischen Republik (hereafter BStU): Zentralarchiv MfS: HA VIII 1074.

29. DA 4/66, 15 May 1966, BStU: Zentralarchiv MfS: HA VIII 1074: 15 et seq. Published in Heinrich Sippel and Walter Süß, *Staatssicherheit und Rechtsextremismus* (Bochum: Universitätsverlag Brockmeyer [Kritische Aufarbeitung der DDR und Osteuropas Vol. 2], 1994), 52–59.

30. Margot Honecker, *Zu einigen Fragen,* 373.

31. SED Bezirksleitung: Pfingsttreffen der FDJ, 16 April 1982, Landeshauptarchiv Schwerin: 10.34-4/10, E 164.

32. Peter Borowsky, *Die DDR in den Siebziger Jahren, Informationen zur politischen Bildung 258,* no. 1 (1998), available online at http://www.bpb.de/publikationen/05049451825358354051 911907431409,2,0, Die_DDR_in_den_siebziger_Jahren.html#art2 (accessed 25 November 2012).

33. Michael Rauhut, *Rock in der DDR 1964 bis 1989* (Berlin: Bundeszentrale für politische Bildung, 2002), 12.

34. Interview with Roberto Schallnass, conducted by the author, 2 March 2006, in Schwerin, 21.

35. Zentralinstitut für Jugendforschung: Politisch-historische Einstellungen der Jugendlichen 1988, SAPMO-BArch: DC 4, 303, 18.

36. KD Hagenow 5282: Bericht zur politisch-operativen Lage unter jugendlichen Personenkreisen im Jahr 1984, 29.01.1985, BStU: MfS BV Schwerin, 44.

37. Rauhut, *Rock in der DDR,* 46; Kochan, *Den Blues haben,* 65.

38. Karin Hartewig, "Botschaften auf der Haut der Geächteten. Die Tätowierungen von Strafgefangenen in Fotografien der Staatssicherheit," in *Die DDR im Bild. Zum Gebrauch der Fotografie im andern deutschen Staat,* ed. Karin Hartewig and Alf Lüdtke (Berlin: Wallstein, 2004), 125–44.

39. Interview with Roberto Schallnass, conducted by the author, 2 March 2006, in Schwerin, 14.

40. Information zu aktuellen Erscheinungsformen gesellschaftswidrigen Auftretens und Verhaltens negativ-dekadenter Jugendlicher sowie Ergebnisse und Wirksamkeit der politisch-operative Arbeit zu ihrer Unterbindung und Zurückdrängung, 10 April 1989, BstU: Archiv der Zentralstelle MfS—HA VII 2969, 6.

41. MDI Informationen—Kriminalpolizei, Sonderheft 1/1988-II, BStU: Zentralarchiv MfS—HA IX 10711,12.

42. HA XX: Information zu aktuellen Erscheinungsformen gesellschaftswidrigen Auftretens und Verhaltens negativ-dekadenter Jugendlicher, so genannter Punker in der DDR [1986], BStU: Zentralarchiv MfS—HA VIII 1082, 5–13, 18.

43. AKG: Untersuchungsergebnisse zur Einschätzung ausgewählter politisch-operativ zu beachtender Erscheinungen unter jugendlichen Personenkreisen im Zeitraum vom 1.1.1985 bis 31.3.1986, 9 June 1986, BStU: Archiv der Zentralstelle MfS—HA IX 285, 58.

44. HA IX/2: Abschlußbericht über die Ergebnisse der Untersuchungen zur Aufklärung der rowdyhaften Ausschreitungen von Bürgern der DDR während ihres Aufenthaltes zum Weltmeisterschaftslauf in Brno/ČSSR, 28 October 1981, BStU: ZA MfS: HA IX 18559, 49.

45. Ibid.

46. Ibid.

47. Various documents on the rioting in Brno/ČSSR 1981, see BStU: ZA MfS: HA IX 18559.

48. Discussed in *IMS,* 1980, et seq.

49. See "Die DDR—Hitlisten 1975—1990 mit Platten- und CD-Hinweisen," http://www.ost beat.de/1988.htm (accessed 25 November 2012).

50. BStU, BV Neubrandenburg, MfS, Abteilung II, 424.

51. Nichtstrukturelle Arbeitsgruppe Jugend: Erkenntnisse 1981 und Schlussfolgerungen 1982, 6 November 1981, BStU: BV Schwerin, Abt. XIX 10061: 34.

52. *IMS* 4, 1983, 83.

53. Interview with Thomas Tost, conducted by the author, 10 January 2006, in Schwerin, 18.

54. VPKA Güstrow: Bericht über das Ermittlungsergebnis zu den bekanntgewordenen Vorkomm-nissen im Raum Krakow über die Pfingstfeiertage 1986, BStU: MfS BV Swn: Abt. XII: Aop. 357/87, 69.

55. Ratssitzungen Güstrow 27 August 1986, Kreisarchiv Güstrow (hereafter KA Güstrow): 2265.

56. Ratssitzungen Güstrow 27 May 1987, KA Güstrow: 2267.

57. Literature on this subject is still relatively sparse. For an introduction see Thomas Kochan, "Alkohol und Alkoholrausch in der DDR," http://www.stiftung-aufarbeitung.de/downloads/pdf/KOCHAN.pdf (accessed 25 November 2012); or Thomas Kochan, *Alkohol und Alkohol-rausch in der DDR* (Berlin: Bundesstiftung zur Aufarbeitung der SED-Diktatur, 2007). See also Mary Neuburger's contribution in this volume, which discusses the consumption of alcohol in Bulgaria.

58. Rauhut, *Rock in der DDR,* 66.

59. Susanne Binas, *"Rockmusik—kulturelles Medium Jugendlicher. Eine Untersuchung zur Praxis und Theorie kultureller Formen im Symbolsystem von Rockmusik"* (PhD diss., Humboldt-University, 1991), 104.

60. BStU Archiv der Zentralstelle MfS—HA VII 2519, 12.

CHAPTER 10

Power at Play
Soccer Stadiums and Popular Culture in 1980s Romania

Florin Poenaru

We have to organize the fun, the life, the play.
Nicolae Ceauşescu, 1968[1]

Some people believe soccer is a matter of life and death. I am very disappointed with that attitude. I can assure you it is much, much more important than that.
Bill Shankly, Liverpool soccer legend[2]

On 26 June 1988, in front of a crowd of approximately fifty thousand spectators, the archrivals Dinamo (Dynamo) and Steaua (Red Star) Bucharest met in a Soccer Cup final at the Romanian National Stadium, which was called "23 August" to commemorate the Soviet army's liberation of Romania in 1944. One minute before the game's end, the teams were level with one goal scored by each side, and then Steaua made a further push and managed to score. The referee, however, denied the tie-breaking goal to the team, calling it offside. This call set Steaua's players and supporters on fire. They suspected that Dinamo rigged yet another game by bribing the referees. After a brief physical altercation with the referee and the Dinamo players, Steaua's players left the field, resulting in the game's cancellation. Significantly, before retreating to his locker room, one of the Dinamo players went to the officials' stand and angrily raised his middle finger, pointing it in the direction of Valentin Ceauşescu, the protector of Steaua and also the son of Romania's leader, Nicolae Ceauşescu, one of the most notorious of Eastern Europe's communist rulers. The tension mounted both on the field and in the stands, but football officials and the police intervened, calming down the players and their fans.[3] Two days later, Steaua was proclaimed the de facto winner of the game, while the Dinamo player who made the offensive gesture received a life suspension.[4]

How does one make sense of this sudden outburst of obscenity and insubordination in a political regime that is usually portrayed as ruthlessly oppressive, dictatorial, and neo-Stalinist? How is one to explain the player who gave the finger to a prominent figure of the Romanian communist regime, when such a gesture was officially labeled a "decadent bourgeois" symbol? How was it possible that a soccer referee had the nerve to make an obviously flawed decision against the team Ceauşescu's son supported, if everything was supposed to be under the spell of his father's totalitarian control? This chapter explores these questions by engaging soccer stadiums as strategic sites, revealing the complexities and paradoxes of the late years of Ceauşescu's rule in Romania. During the 1980s, the centrality of the stadiums in the country's public life is quite striking. The state co-opted these sites for both popular soccer matches and huge state-organized celebrations. Within the confines of the soccer field, the official face of the regime met with the more casual, mass-cultural activities of the sports competition.

Traian Ungureanu, a Romanian author, claims that the popularity of soccer in Romania during the 1980s was an accepted, officially sanctioned, and apolitical Romanian equivalent of Roman circuses, albeit without the bread, which castrated viewers of political will and action while offering a cheap distraction as a palliative for the regime's brutality.[5] According to this logic, the stadiums and soccer games constituted a safety valve, a channeling of negative emotions and frustrations that ensured the proper functioning of the socialist subjects. In contrast to this view, advocates of everyday-life experience and its disruptive potential emphasize that stadiums and leisure places were sites supporting covert, hidden, and small-scale forms of resistance against the regime.[6] In a regime that deployed a vast arsenal of surveillance tactics, these particular acts were the only means possible for people to disrupt and resist the system without being annihilated. Thus, the advocates of this perspective argue that people managed to introduce a gap between their beliefs and practices and the official ideology, a space that then constituted a foundation for freedom.[7]

The ongoing binary thinking that opposes total control to generalized resistance should be transcended in order to better understand the role and function of such sites during state socialism. The first step to do so is to claim the obvious: stadiums (and other leisure destinations) functioned *both* as safety valves—that is, as tools in the hands of the regime—*and* as places of resistance. However, this simple point, while seeking to bridge the gap between power and resistance, still frames the realities of state socialism as a dualism of two politically and ideologically constructed categories instead of grasping their "circular" relationship.[8]

One further shortcoming of the power-and-resistance paradigm, as it is applied in studies of Eastern European state socialism, stems not necessarily from the theoretical inadequacy of conceptualizing social reality in dual terms, without at least noting its mutually constitutive relations, but from an utterly political and ideological bias. As Alexei Yurchak rightfully pointed out, the persistence of binary divisions in grasping Soviet-style socialism is a result of "the particular situatedness of much critical knowledge about Soviet socialism: it has been produced either outside of, or in retrospect to, socialism, in contexts dominated by antisocialist, non-socialist or post-socialist political, moral, and cultural agendas and truths."[9]

What is missing is a proper understanding of the internal paradoxes, contradictions, and gaps constitutive of the power edifice that shaped the lives of people experiencing real-existing socialism in creative, productive, and positive manners. As one Romanian writer and football commentator put it, people during socialism died not only because of political repression and harsh living conditions, but also "because of love, jealousy, and passion."[10] It is the love and passion for soccer, expressed by so many on the soccer stadiums, that this chapter seeks to explore, pinpointing the meaningful and creative aspects of life under socialism. Thus, I will focus on various productive and meaningful activities developed around the soccer games that emerged not necessarily in spite of the regime, but because the regime enabled them.

"23 August": By the People, For the People

I will limit my case to an analysis of one particular soccer stadium, the national stadium "23 August." Built in the first decade of communist rule in Romania, and modernized during the mid-1970s, the stadium cogently expressed the regime's sports ideals and political ambitions.[11] It was the site for both the most important national and international sports events, and for the famous state pageants that fostered Ceaușescu's cult of personality (see Figure 10.1). Thus, the stadium was situated at a critical junction between politics and fun, between the state's ideological rhetoric and people's creative capacities and leisure-time activities.

The idea of building a national stadium and its subsequent construction embodies a typical socialist success story. At the beginning of the 1950s, the recently established communist regime started its grand modernizing plans by implementing the first of the well-known Five Year Plans. Since no aspect of life was to be left untouched, sports were part and parcel of the scheme. Youth volunteers built the "23 August" stadium in less than half a year. It was meant to be a truly national stadium, constructed by the people, for the people. The regime opened the arena, with a capacity to hold eighty thousand, with twenty-one training fields, a lake, and a pool, in 1953 when Romania

Figure 10.1. The state pageant in the "23 August" Stadium on 23 August 1978. Courtesy of the National Archives of Romania, Online Communism Photo Collection (ANIC, Scînteia), BA539 (accessed 29 September 2011), 309/1978.

hosted the World Youth Festival.[12] Situated on the outskirts of Bucharest, the stadium was located at the end point of a long boulevard traversing a neighborhood of new working-class apartment buildings. Throughout much of the 1950s and 1960s, it served exclusively as a sports site, hosting the most important games of the national soccer and rugby leagues, and also international matches of the Romanian National Soccer Team.

During the mid-1970s, Ceauşescu's regime's hyper-modernizing plan to restructure the urban texture of Bucharest affected the stadium as well.[13] The administration introduced modern floodlights and replaced the stadium's old seats. During this time period, the stadium started to be used not only for sports events, but also for hosting the mass gatherings that supported Ceauşescu's cult of personality. Throughout the 1980s, the regime used the stadium more often for this kind of activity than for athletic competitions such as soccer.

A problem with the current literature on the mass propagandistic gatherings, such as National Day or May Day, the International Workers' Day organized at the "23 August" stadium, is not only that it privileges a totalitarian interpretation according to which the individuals were simple cogs in a vast machine, but that it ignores the inseparable counterpart of these gatherings, namely, the soccer games.[14] One cannot separate the two types of events, because the public's participation in the performance of these seemingly contrasting activities was never a simple matter of reproducing a pre-established, officially designed form.

Alexey Yurchak's work on late Soviet socialism could enable us to better understand their complex intertwining. Following in the footsteps of John Austin, Jacques Derrida, and Judith Butler, Yurchak identified two modes of the discourse: the constative mode (speech acts that describe a reality) and the performative mode (speech acts that perform a change in the surrounding reality).[15] Yurchak's thesis argued that what characterized Soviet socialism was people's repeated enactment of the form of the regime's authoritative discourse, without attending to its constative meaning. The repeated performance of these fixed forms, however, opened ways for the emergence of various meaningful and creative activities, communities, beliefs, and social networks. In other words, while the spatial, ideological, and symbolic form of mass gatherings (related to specific meeting places and expressed through ideological rhetoric, choreography, and the display of banners and slogans) remained the same throughout the years and was performed always following the same rules, the very performance of these fixed forms allowed unintended and often unexpected social practices to emerge.[16]

To clarify this point, consider the following recollection of a football aficionado during the 1980s, who was also a young party member.[17] Contrary to the customary view that portrays party gatherings as coercive and degrading episodes in the lives of individuals, in an interview he described them as enjoyable, almost leisurely moments. He explained that because the routine of the parades and gatherings was so well-known in advance (everybody knew what to do without giving much effort and attention to the overall ceremony), the parade days were considered free days. For a little effort in the morning, workers enjoyed the afternoon off as a reward. Consequently, the evening before a parade, my informant would invite friends over for an all-night party of poker games and drinks. They would go to the parade straight from the poker table and take short naps between the performance acts. After the parade, properly refreshed, they would spend the rest of the day drinking in one of Bucharest's beer establishments.

A further example reinforces the point that such officially decreed public gatherings opened up relatively autonomous creative spaces. Recently, a Romanian publishing house came out with the photo album of a well-known Romanian photographer.[18] The album consists of a series of photos depicting everyday life in Bucharest from the mid-1980s until the regime's collapse. While most of the photos illustrate the hardships and humiliations people had to endure during those times, notably due to the food shortages and massive urban rearrangements, one particular image contrasts with the album's overall bleak mood and tone. The photo was taken in August 1982, during one of "Cântarea României's" state-sponsored pageants held in the "23 August" stadium.[19] A huge mass of people holds variously colored placards, which together, and seen from the official tribune where Ceauşescu sat, turned into a meaningful picture or representation (the ruler's figure, a slogan, etc).[20] However, what strikes the eye in this picture is not the number of people sitting in similar postures and holding meaningless cards, but the activities that they engaged in while holding the cards and performing the choreography for the event. Most of the people were absorbed with books and newspapers, which they read under the placards they held; others played with things taken from their pockets; and one man yawned, seeming to prepare for a short nap, while two others took a deep look into the camera with a casual pose. The photographer himself became part of this array of leisurely and creative activities enabled by the very enactment of the official discourse: he pursued his hobby of taking photos in urban contexts while holding his placard.

What these examples suggest is that the customary image of the regime-orchestrated parades and gatherings as times of oppressive and humiliating experiences is inaccurate, because it neglects the multiple and meaningful personal activities that these events enabled. In other words, while the regime staged these pageants with the purpose of constantly accentuating the grandeur of the ruler and the party, the actual performance of this staging produced a series of effects that went beyond its original purpose, eluding the regime's grasp or control. When attending the parade, people simply tried to make the best out of a situation that they considered to be a mere formality. If this was the case during official gatherings, which were supposed to be highly regulated by strict formal procedures, how elusive and creative were the proliferating effects of performativity at soccer matches officially sanctioned as leisure time? The next sections will address this question, while stressing a further characteristic of the regime that enabled the development of meaningful social realities against its very logic: the fragmentation of power at the top of the ruling echelons.

Soccer During Socialism: The History of a Cold Embrace

Romanians imported soccer in the early days of the sport. Initially introduced at the end of the nineteenth century by German and Dutch entrepreneurs, the game soon became popular among Romanians. During the interwar period, teams located in Transylvania, inspired by and connected to the highly successful Austrian school of soccer, dominated the local league. Typically, for worldwide developments of this sport, the teams that the middle-class progressive entrepreneurial strata supported and financed mixed with proper working-class clubs. After World War II the new political and ideological realities swept away the former institutional arrangement, and supporters' affiliations were forced to keep up with the new requirements. While the regime disbanded old soccer clubs, strongly linked with interwar capitalist and bourgeois enterprises, new sports and soccer clubs formed around various working professions. This period witnessed the formation of the army and militia sports clubs, including soccer, as an attempt to offer some legitimacy and popular connection to two powerful, systemic institutions (see Figure 10.2).[21]

The regime's ambivalence towards soccer throughout the 1950s and 1960s, coupled with specific laws and regulations that kept sport an amateur activity, brought few notable international results achieved by Romanian clubs, and only moderate support for the sport.[22] The 1970s saw the beginning of a change towards more visibility for soccer. However, the dominant sport was still gymnastics, with Nadia Comăneci's gold medals turned into the epitome of the regime's success. The unexpectedly dignifying defeat of the national soccer team against Brazil (3 to 2) during the 1970 Mexican World Cup brought Romania some international attention, and convinced people at home that further progress could be achieved. While the national team had to wait another two decades before playing again in a World Cup, the clubs rose in prominence with performances that culminated during the mid-1980s with Steaua winning the most important European club trophy—the European Champions Cup.

Figure 10.2. Gheorghe Gheorghiu-Dej and future top-echelon party cadres at the first post-war soccer game in Romania (Romania versus the Soviet Union). Courtesy of the National Archives of Romania, Online Communism Photo Collection (ANIC, Scînteia), HA186 (accessed 29 September 2011), 186/1945.

It is worthwhile to explore what prompted an increased interest in soccer, especially among the higher echelons of the regime. First, it has to be noted that the ambiguity regarding soccer persisted throughout state socialism, until the very end of the regime. Ceauşescu himself was "not a fan," sporting positive feelings only for chess and gymnastics.[23] As a proper communist, Ceauşescu did not believe in the distinction between working and leisure time, dismissing it as a bourgeois and capitalist fallacy. He repeatedly stated that his hobby was "building socialism in Romania"—a statement that signifies a total identification between the man and socialist ideology.[24] He actually considered soccer a cheap distraction for the masses, but tolerated the sport and sometimes watched some of the national team's matches.[25]

Because of the official reluctance to fully endorse soccer as a popular activity, the broadcasting of soccer matches on the national television was limited to matches of the national team or some very important international games that featured Romanian soccer clubs.[26] For example, almost half of the European matches Steaua played in 1986 before reaching the final were not broadcast on television. What is more, the media did not even plan to broadcast the team's game in the final since important announcements and speeches were to be made that evening regarding the Day of the Party, which was celebrated the next day.[27] After intense pressure from the football club and other officials, Ceauşescu finally agreed to allow the broadcasting. This type of official limitation of soccer games on TV produced the unintended and unexpected result that stadiums became highly popular, and the number of spectators sky-rocketed. Being at the stadium was often the only possibility to see one's favorite team playing. Thus, what seemed to be a rational decision on the regime's part to limit people's exposure to soccer via television gave a huge boost to soccer stadiums' attendance.

In an interview with Radu Cosaşu, one of the most famous and influential soccer commentators during socialism, I asked him about the regime's sudden interest in soccer in the 1980s.[28] He pointed to the need for legitimacy and foreign recognition, which Ceauşescu's regime constantly sought. If during the 1970s, Ceauşescu's role on the international scene benefited from the ability to break away from Soviet policy (the public denouncement of the invasion of Czechoslovakia by Warsaw Treaty troops in 1968 being the most well-known example), the political actions that followed, notably an embrace of neo-Stalinism, so uncharacteristic for the rest of the socialist Bloc and even for the USSR, put the regime in an uncomfortable position. Being successful in sports remained an avenue to remind the world of the regime's "exceptionality," and of the innate physical qualities of the Romanian population. Thus, after worldwide recognition in gymnastics and handball, soccer became the next state-supported sport for winning international trophies.

It is worth noting, though, that the international context of soccer played its part in this new orientation as well. During the 1980s, soccer was reorganized on more powerful neoliberal bases in North America and Western Europe, with revenues from advertising and broadcasting on the rise. In a country plagued by severe shortages, Romanian officials could not remain insensitive to such financial incentives.[29] Thus, ideological and financial interests united to form a powerful alliance that sought to score high on the international soccer scene. However, the rise in soccer's popularity during the 1980s was linked with yet another powerful cause. Not only was the regime itself seeking international recognition through this sport, but various branches of the government were also aiming to express their supremacy in internal affairs through the victories of their own soccer clubs.[30]

Internal Cracks: How to Play Soccer with the Generals

The Romanian soccer scene of the 1980s was largely dominated by four teams—Steaua, Dinamo, Rapid, and Sportul Studențesc—all from Bucharest. While other teams managed to achieve comparable successes and produce impressive results, the "only game in town" was between these four teams. The competition between them reached a peak during the confrontations between Steaua and Dinamo. All were institutionally positioned in relation to centers of power within the regime. Their rivalry grew with the sport and reached a climax in the 1980s. Furthermore, their rivalry was fueled by the fact that these teams were highly symbolically charged and could thus reach out to nationwide audiences compared to other teams.[31]

Steaua Bucharest, formed by and dependent on army support, was the only club in which Ceaușescu seemed to express any interest. Though always close to and fond of the team, his son Valentin openly took charge of it only around the mid-1980s with Ceaușescu, predictably, reproaching him for wasting his time on such trivial matters.[32] After a late start, Steaua dominated the domestic competition in the 1980s by winning most championships and domestic cups. Most importantly, the team achieved an unprecedented European success. In 1986 it became the first and only team from the Eastern Bloc to win the European Champions Cup (ECC), before the fall of the Berlin Wall. In 1989, just a few months before the collapse of the regime, Steaua made it again to the final of this competition, only to be soundly defeated by Silvio Berlusconi's AC Milan. This game was the last important moment in the history of the club; the end of its European success coincided with the end of the regime itself.

Ceaușescu's younger son, Nicu, was also involved with soccer. He was in charge of Sportul Studențesc, the Bucharest students' club, which organized the youth and students' leisure activities. Capable of attracting the best young talents in the country, Sportul gained some recognition on the domestic scene and was always among the top teams in the league. At the international level, however, its achievements were much more modest.

Rapid Bucharest shared some features with Sportul. Although always on top in the domestic championship, the club was unable to win any titles during this period and had modest results in international matches. Nonetheless, it was portrayed and celebrated as the team of the working class, a representation sustained and popularized by Ceauşescu's "court poet," Adrian Păunescu, through a series of propagandistic songs and poems.

The Ministry of Internal Affairs (the police) and Securitate, the repressive wing of the regime, supported and managed the team Dinamo Bucharest. Dinamo was Steaua's fiercest competitor, and the only team in the soccer league capable of balancing its influence. In fact, during the 1980s, the entire championship was a competition between these two teams. Due to their institutional affiliations, they had no problems winning most of the matches of the season, either because of genuine superiority, or due to pressure and rigged games.

It was the rivalry between Dinamo Bucharest and Steaua that best represented the cracks developing in the edifice of power. Despite a general and superficial view rendering Ceauşescu as the country's omnipotent leader, the practice of everyday politics registered a fundamental split between the Securitate and the army, which shaped the regime's entire field of force.[33] Consequently, the confrontation on the soccer field between these two teams was a performance of a more fundamental, pervasive split in the edifice of power. Every soccer game between Steaua and Dynamo was an overt-covert confrontation between the army and the Securitate in their search for symbolic assertion. So, the real stake of every game was not only the result per se, but also the extent to which it indicated and symbolized the capacity of these two branches of state power to outrun and outwit the other at a societal level.

What I would like to stress here is that knowledge of this split in the system was not hidden information available only to insiders of the regime, but was made public through every game. Thus, the soccer stadium was simultaneously a locus for asserting the imaginary unity, grandeur, and omnipotence of the regime, through the various parades and propagandistic events that it hosted, and a site where the internal divisions, struggles, and fundamental cracks of the regime became fully apparent. Consequently, during the 1980s, the national stadium was the meeting place not only between the official ideology of the system and citizens' meaningful practices, but more importantly, the meeting point between the official ideology of the system and its obverse, constitutive cracks. Here might be the proper place to reformulate the relationship between politics and soccer during Ceauşescu's regime: far from being just an ideological tool for rendering subjects governable through occasional cheap distraction, various branches of power employed soccer as a powerful symbolic device to assert their own supremacy. Thus, the soccer stadium connoted not only the place of struggle and negotiation between the state and its citizens, but at the very same time connoted a place for the struggles inherent to the power edifice itself.

Cuplaj—The Long Day of Soccer

Both Steaua and Dinamo had their own friendly "satellite" teams in provincial cities forming an all encompassing web of interests, connections, and dependencies.[34] A match between one of the two leading Bucharest teams and a rival satellite was worth watching. The real interest of the game was related, again, to watching how the army and the Securitate would manage to outwit each other. Essentially, someone bribed the referee who invented fouls and penalty kicks and sent off undesirable players. If none of these tricks worked, a referee prolonged the game until victory was secured.

The most interesting fixtures, however, unfolded when the aforementioned four teams from Bucharest met together. One of the matches would be scheduled in the afternoon, while the other immediately followed. Thus, spectators paying for a single ticket would get admitted to two soccer games in a row, including the opportunity to watch a fierce clash between the competing branches of power. On these particular occasions, the stadium usually hosted between eighty thousand and one hundred twenty thousand people.[35] Bucharest's traffic system was paralyzed on the routes to the stadium because various people, and even visitors from neighboring cities, traveled to the capital to see these "*cuplaje*" (couplings).

Despite focusing solely on Steaua, in a recent book Andrei Vochin captured with great care the overall atmosphere of the Romanian clubs of the 1980s. For example, the manner in which managers assembled teams and transferred players suggests the existence of a vast web of interest and co-dependencies that shaped the soccer scene. The popular belief has been for many years now that soccer players were coerced to join the clubs, especially those from the big four. Undoubtedly, this strategy was part of the story. However, based on interviews with the players and coaches that won the European Cup, Vochin manages to show that coercion and outright pressure were limited and only used in exceptional cases. The customary practice involved the sporting director of the club approaching the player, or his parents if he was underage, with an offer for a transfer. Once the player received the offer, he was expected to voice his demands. Usual demands included a good monthly salary, a certain amount of cash bonuses for wins, a car, a house in Bucharest, and a comfortable sinecure for his wife if he was married. The club tendering the offer usually accepted most demands, even unusual ones. For instance, one of Steaua's coaches asked for 150,000 Lei (the equivalent of one hundred monthly salaries for a high school teacher), and the renovation of his summer cottage by the army—demands which the club ultimately accepted.[36]

Consequently, when dealing with offers tendered to them by the clubs, most players had significant space for maneuvering, which they did either by mounting incredible demands or by negotiating at the very same time with one of the other four big clubs. To add to the system's vagaries, securing the services of a certain player did not entail the end of headaches for a club. Nobody was totally sure whether a player would do his best in all games and not sabotage them when people were least expecting it. Bribing the referees went hand in hand with bribing the players of the opposing team in order to ultimately secure a win.

Far from being simple puppets in the circus that the regime orchestrated, players and coaches enjoyed a degree of autonomy and freedom that enabled them to express themselves, both on and off the field, in various creative and meaningful ways. People regularly attending the games knew that perfectly well. Consequently, although the soccer games, especially *cuplaje*, were staged clashes between various branches of power, their outcome remained unpredictable because of the soccer players' autonomy to express themselves creatively. Thus, *cuplaje* were times of "total" socialist soccer,[37] with their strange mix of predictable political interests and arrangements, and unpredictable outbursts of creativity. In other words, people attending *cuplaje* knew very well that a match between Steaua and Dynamo was highly politicized and orchestrated, but the encounter between the most talented twenty-two players of the country produced a show that went beyond political sensibilities.

At the peak of its domestic success, when scoring more than four times in a match was more commonplace than exception, Steaua devised a rule aimed at strengthening the club's relations with its "satellites." Once the victory was secured by scoring one or two goals, the coaches advised players to slow down in order not to damage the goal difference of their "friendly" team. However, during one full house match in Bucharest on 7 December 1988, the players, goaded by their supporters, decided to ignore the rule and trounced the opposing team 11 to 0. The audience was asking for more after every goal and the players kept delivering.[38] This sudden symbiosis between the players and the supporters nicely illustrates the capacities for autonomous moments and creative expression enabled by the very rules organizing the game. Is it not safe to assume that while soccer was indeed heavily entrenched between various political interests and struggles that both the players and the audience managed to use these very divisions to positively inscribe soccer as a meaningful, exciting, and open-ended activity? Was not the very negativity on which soccer was premised—political interests, limited TV access, stigmatization as lowbrow mass entertainment, etc.—the basis on which positive personal and collective significations could be formulated?

But how did this positive expression shine through, apart from sudden outbursts of magnificent playing and/or outright obscenity? The most fitting example is the star system that soccer, and life around stadiums, generated. As noted before, the authorities restricted TV broadcasting to a handful of carefully selected matches. Consequently, the local heroes—the soccer stars—emerged from the direct interaction between the viewers and the players unfolding at the stadiums through a series of informal networks imbued with lived stories, histories, and memories. In his interview, Radu Cosașu warned against the simplistic overlapping of soccer with the weekly visit to the stadium. Other meeting places and communities prepared and prolonged the stadium experience.[39] Beer gardens, pubs, and the Pronosport offices[40] were essential in shaping and coloring the life of a soccer enthusiast. Together with the stadiums, these were places where people heatedly debated past games, expressed opinions about players and teams, and commented on the latest news concerning their favorites. It was precisely in these contexts that the star system was created and sustained, supporting with it a vast array of meaningful communities, friendships, and cordial rivalries. A significant circular relationship is discernable here: the communities of supporters created and sustained a soccer star system that, in turn, further shaped and sustained such communities by allowing them to debate the last games and performances. Thus, meaningful interactions took place among various informal networks of people brought together by a positive and creative investment in soccer.

The emergence of this star system produced a series of additional effects, however. First, it created a passionate divide in the soccer audience. People coming to the stadium were not simply a homogenous mass, hoping to make the most out of their leisurely time so they could happily go back to building socialism on Monday morning after a "brainwashing experience." The very attachment to certain local heroes transcended the purposes of productive leisure as officially staked out. Thus, the soccer stadium and the game became a place and a time to celebrate one's own freely chosen or constructed idols; they provided opportunities to assert one's real distance from the regime's star system by producing an alternative one. The construction, appropriation, and celebration of soccer figures signaled an active stance, a form of productive assertion on the part of viewers. The audience itself created a network of passionate affiliations and identifications outside of the ones proposed by the regime. Thus, while the regime was proposing a form of concrete universality restricted to the values and institutions designed by it, identifying with a particular soccer team and with a constellation of soccer players represented a form of seeking an abstract universality, a way of transcending the straitjacket of the regime, by referring to something outside its logic, though enabled and organized by it.[41]

One example that is often forgotten is the fact that during soccer games the supporters of the opposing teams were separated in different sectors of the stadium.[42] It would not make sense to presuppose that this separation stemmed from the fact that some people liked the army's team more, while the Securitate particularly inspired others. On the contrary, the already pre-existing split of the audience, according to the different abstract universalities embraced, was spatialized, inside the stadium. What is even less known and acknowledged is that occasionally there were confrontations, sometimes involving violence, between the opposing supporters. Thus, people's creative investment in and passionate affiliation with soccer ranged from violent physical clashes to collective beer drinking—and poetry.

Soccer Poetry

While stadiums are sometimes associated with collective outbursts of vulgarity and obscene language aimed to fulfill cathartic functions—*especially* during socialism when there was plenty of need for catharsis—it is perhaps paradoxical to note that one rarely heard vulgar language and chanting in the Romanian socialist stadiums. Fear of repression and genuine civility both played their part, since perhaps no one actually dared to curse the teams of the Securitate or the army. The most people did was to shout ironically, "This is Dinamo" or "This is Steaua," when one of the teams was involved in foul play.[43] This particular constellation of factors obliged people to inscribe their chanting with positive content, to compose meaningful songs and verses, and to adapt their singing to wining or losing moments, to home or away games—in short, to generate a complex form of expressive culture.

An in-depth study of the slogans and songs heard on the soccer stadiums during socialism would be highly revealing of the symbolic complexities the game reached throughout the 1980s. The problem is that most of the lyrics are so cryptic and so imbued with obscure meanings that make little sense even for Romanian soccer fans today, not to mention for an international audience. In a sense, just like the political jokes and literature of the time, most of these songs are untranslatable without losing their barb. Of course, there were officially sanctioned and written songs, most notably those written by court poet Păunescu for Universitatea Craiova and Rapid, while others were so naïve and clumsy that they went unnoticed. Most of the songs bore witness to the creative collective efforts invested in their composition and reproduction. Apart from fostering the passionate identification with a respective team, these songs signaled the viewers' active stance as they experienced the soccer game, on and off the field. The customary push to win was supplemented, in these cases, by almost carnival-like, ruthless, ironic commentaries on the part of the audience. For example, a soccer player known for his alcoholic escapades had a special song that played with this theme. Whenever he touched the ball, the crowd would immediately begin to sing it. No one was immune to this ironic celebration; from referees to officials, everybody might have a chant addressed to him.[44]

Irony and creativity went even further, in the same burlesque and carnivalesque manner. Sport fans around the world are familiar with the "question and answer" technique. Somebody from the crowd of fans, usually the leader, asks a banal question such as: "who's gonna win today?" Then the rest of the fans shout their team's name or something to that effect. Those in attendance often used this technique at Romanian socialist stadiums with a particular twist. While the answers were correct, the questions were "wrong." For example, supporters of a small team would shout, especially when losing, "Ceaușescu, PCR"—a perfectly legitimate, officially sanctioned slogan. But the question that prompted such an answer was "Who decided our relegation?"[45] Consequently, the whole mechanism relied heavily on periphrastic constructions and allusive, hidden meanings, which, in turn, meant that only fans really involved in the soccer life understood the dynamics and messages of chants heard during a game. In other words, one had to rely on a preestablished, preexisting web of meanings to fully participate in the soccer spectacle.

Still, the life of a genuine Romanian soccer supporter was no walk in the park, particularly in the 1980s. The shortage economy made a significant impact on the soccer experience. Following state efforts to save energy, officials scheduled soccer games early in the afternoon, if not at noon, during the winter periods. The timing was indeed a major blow for many since they had to be at work, and getting permission to leave to watch a soccer game was not easy to obtain. Furthermore, more measures led to severe restrictions on public transportation. Thus, traveling throughout the country to accompany one's team was a rare event that transformed the participants into local heroes. Perhaps the most visible and frustrating deficiency for a soccer fan was the virtual lack of any professional paraphernalia. Drums, confetti, trumpets, fireworks, and torches were all part of a distant dream. While supporters living in cities near the border with Yugoslavia managed to sneak over a handful of second-hand torches from time to time, most of the others had to rely on their own imagination.[46] And usually, that is what they did. The most common replacement for the professional torches was a newspaper. Fans rolled up sports and political newspapers, set them on fire, and waved them to celebrate their team's hard-won victory. Of course, one may be tempted to interpret these gestures as low-scale resistance, since most of these papers had pictures of the ruling family or some political messages on their front pages. It might have been the case on particular occasions, but, as a rule, the act of burning newspapers as celebratory torches was simply an available gesture for expressing pleasure with a performance, a creative gesture that turned objective material conditions into productive resources. Newspapers were just part of the possibilities at hand. During one game in the early 1980s that saw Universitatea Craiova advance to the semi-finals of the European Champions Cup, a crowd of over seventy thousand celebrated the winning goal by throwing their hats into the air. The game resumed only after the field was cleared.[47]

Conclusion: Organized Escapes

This chapter has discussed supporters, not of state socialism per se, but of soccer as it was played and organized in 1980s Romania. Far from illustrating the roles ascribed to them by anti- or post-communist social scientists as hidden resisters and/or depoliticized viewers, soccer aficionados took soccer seriously and invested it with personal and collective meanings, significations, and passions. Furthermore, because of the political forces that shaped the soccer field, fans managed to develop and practice creative strategies to transform their genuine passion into a form of leisure that escaped the logic of the regime that enabled it.

Soccer stadiums were at the core of the Romanian public life during socialism, particularly during the 1980s. On these sites, the staged activities meant to affirm the grandeur of the regime overlapped with the casual, leisurely activities of sports, soccer chief among them. This intersection of contrasting registers, ranging from the utterly official and mandatory to the ironic, mocking, and even subversive, generated a series of unintended consequences that escaped the logic and grasp of the regime that made this intersection possible in the first place. While acknowledging the fixed form of the official script that regulated everything from the economy and state pageants to the teams' crests and game commentary, I maintain that precisely this fixity of the regime enabled the emergence of various social worlds of meaning outside its control and intentions. Soccer stadiums and soccer-related activities more generally represent a prime example of how alternative worlds, meanings, and communities could be developed, not despite the regime, but because of its initiatives. Thus, I aimed to reexamine the old dichotomy between power and resistance, or between structure and agency, not by seeking for an improbable middle point, but by casting it aside altogether. The strategic maneuvers of the state and soccer enthusiasts reveal the complexity of power relationships in Ceauşescu's Romania, at a time when Securitate surveillance, coupled with poor political and economic decisions, brought the country to the brink of collapse and forced people to endure long spells of severe misery in the 1980s. Surely, people protested, resisted, and disobeyed, maybe not in the outright, organized form called "dissidence," but rather at the micro-level of the every-day. But such an observation is valid for any power regime in history: in one way or another, people always resist and subvert power. Thus, my claim is that in order to actually grasp the particularities of state socialism, this framework is not enough. I suggested instead a more dialectical and performative ap-proach that focuses on people's various interactions, and their unexpected, surprising. and often contradictory outcomes, unfolding within the various social contexts organized, accepted, or even encouraged by the regime itself. In so doing I was able to discover a series of social worlds, with their own people, histories, solidarities, and emotions that offer a more complex under-standing of what East European state socialism was, and how it functioned beyond the immediate level of top official politics and party bureaucracy.

Like state socialism, those worlds are now gone. After the regime collapsed in 1989 the soccer scene went through dramatic changes, just like the rest of the society—most of them highly predictable and usually contradictory. While people were finally able to travel again, both at home and abroad, few of them could afford it in the new economic setting. The old rivalries between clubs lost their political edge, but the supporters radicalized to the extent that most soccer games between Dinamo and Steaua—to name just the most conspicuous example—are now marred by severe violent clashes. Torches, finally available, quickly became trademarks of the most violent sections of the supporters, and are now mostly used for destructive purposes, rather than for celebration. While more money became available for soccer, usually fol-lowing massive investments by shady local businessmen, all of the best Ro-manian players are now abroad playing for better-ranked teams. With all the power in the hands of the club owners, who ultimately seek to maximize their profits with little investment, coaches and players are left with little space for negotiation and must learn how to survive in a volatile context, at least until they manage to secure a contract abroad. Increasing acts of violence, both physical and verbal, coupled with the full coverage of games on TV channels emptied the stadiums. Like me, most soccer fans I talked to while researching this chapter gave up the habit of going to the stadium more than a decade ago, mainly due to the violence around the stadiums, but also because of poor games. Only special games, usually involving international teams, offer a compelling reason for such a leisurely escape, while for the rest, watching TV has become the norm.

In this context it is always very easy to fall into nostalgic discourses and idealize the past in pristine images. While there is some truth to that, the radical point here is different: what soccer lost after the Wall fell was its creative underside, its potential for generating unexpected social outcomes. Under the new socio-economic and political conditions, soccer is often nothing more than a cheap distraction, an easy escape for the impoverished and desperate masses. Thus, Ceaușescu was perhaps right when he said, "We have to organize the fun, the life, the play[,]" if people are to really enjoy themselves.

Notes

This text was greatly improved by the comments of Cathleen M. Giustino and Alexander Vari to whom I am grateful. Completing it would have been impossible without the useful knowledge that my various informants provided me and I thank them all. All remaining errors are entirely mine. I dedicate this text to Radu Cosașu, one of Romania's best and most charismatic writers. His knowledge and cerebral passion for soccer are contagious.

1. Quoted in Traian Ungureanu, "Jocul englez," *Secolul 20,* 462 (2002): 401.
2. Ibid.
3. See also Jonathan Wilson, *Behind the Curtain. Travels in Eastern European Football* (London: Orion 2006), 203–4, for a slightly different version of the same event.
4. Apparently, Valentin Ceaușescu's appeal to his father, in which he claimed that he took no offence from the gesture, removed the player's penalty, and he was thus able to play again after some official apologies.
5. Traian Ungureanu, *Manifestul fotbalist* (București: Humanitas, 2005).
6. See James C. Scott's classic text, *Weapons of the Weak: Everyday Forms of Peasant Resistance* (New Heaven: Yale University Press, 1985), for a formulation of such arguments, albeit in a different political context.
7. See on this point Robert Edelman, *Spartak Moscow: A History of the People's Team in the Workers' State* (Ithaca: Cornell University Press, 2009).
8. On this point, see Torben Bech Dyrberg, *The Circular Structure of Power* (London: Verso, 1997).
9. Alexei Yurchak, *Everything Was Forever Until It Was No More: The Last Soviet Generation* (Princeton: Princeton University Press, 2005), 6.
10. Author's interview with Radu Cosașu, 13 March 2009.
11. For the link between socialism and sports, see James Riordan and Arnd Kruger, *The International Politics of Sports in the 20ᵗʰ Century* (New York: Routledge, 1999).
12. I rely here on the excellent special issue published by the Romanian sports daily, *Gazeta Sporturilor,* at the time of the stadium's demolition on 27 November 2007.
13. Derrick Danta, "Ceaușescu's Bucharest," *Geographical Review* 83, no. 2 (1993): 170–82.
14. See for example, Ioan Stanomir, Paul Cernat, Ion Manolescu, and Angelo Mitchievici, *Explorări în Comunismul Românesc* [Explorations in Romanian Communism], Vol. I–III (Iași: Polirom, 2004–2009).

15. The discussion becomes thoroughly complicated if one notes that these discursive modes are in fact ideal-types. No speech act is simply constative, meaning that every "neutral" description is actually a performative act, while every performative act has to rely on some previous constative knowledge in order to perform a change.

16. Yurchak, *Everything was Forever Until It was No More,* 121.

17. Author's interview with T.P., 1 September 2008.

18. Andrei Pandele, *The Surprise Witness* (Bucharest: Compania, 2008).

19. This was the name of the most important cult-building mass gathering. People sang songs celebrating the country and its ruler, followed by overly complicated choreographed dances. It was simply a mixture of nationalist worship and praise for Ceauşescu.

20. The fascist (*Führerprinzip*) core of Ceauşescu's regime is discernable in this celebratory manner. Only the ruler, from his privileged position, is capable of seeing the entire message andinterpreting its meaning, whereas the ordinary people in this ritual view random pieces of the message. Indeed, while it takes the entire people to convey the message of communism, it is only the ruler who can have a proper, global understanding of it.

21. Ioan Chirilă, "Un veac de fotbal românesc," [A century of Romanian Football] *Secolul 20* no. 20 (1998): 146–74.

22. The ambivalence stems from a paradox. In its early days, the regime aimed at popularizing sports, and at transforming it into a mass leisure time activity. However, this popularity was about people practicing sports, not just simply watching. Under Ceauşescu, the popularity of sports, and football in particular, came to be regarded as a problem, rather than as a goal for the regime.

23. Michael Janofsky, "Ceauşescu Was Not a Fan," *The New York Times,* 11 February 1990. Available at http://www.nytimes.com/1990/02/11/sports/ceausescu-was-not-a-fan-official-says.html ?pagewanted=1 (Accessed 29 March 2010).

24. Daniel Barbu, *Republica absentă* [The Absent Republic] (Bucureşti: Nemira, 1999): 91–94.

25. Andrei Vochin, *Supersteaua,* Vol. I (Bucureşti: Gazeta Sporturilor, 2009), 11–12.

26. Strange as it may seem today, this situation was not a feature unique to the Romanian socialist state. In England for example, things were similar at the time, with the first league games shown on TV only as late as 1982. For a broader discussion, see Simon Kuper, Stefan Szymanski, *Soccernomics* (London 2009), 206 and ff.

27. Andrei Vochin, *Supersteaua,* Vol. II (Bucureşti: Gazeta Sporturilor, 2009), 64–65; 115.

28. Author's interview with Radu Cosaşu, 13 March 2009.

29. For example Steaua, under the leadership of Valentin Ceauşescu, was the first Romanian team to sign a commercial deal with Ford, which entailed that the players had to wear the logo of the company on their shirts. See more details of this capitalist mixture with state socialism in Jonathan Wilson, *Behind the Curtain. Travels in Eastern European Football* (London: Orion, 2006), 205. This practice, however, was not singular across the Eastern Bloc. During perestroika, Dynamo Kiev, under the leadership of famous Valery Lobanovsky, became a private entity able to trade and secure funds for players' wages and sportive infrastructure. The neo-liberalization of sports, as well as other aspects of life during late state-socialism, has remained a topic under-researched throughout the "transition" years.

30. A situation that was similar across the Eastern Bloc, the army and secret police teams were in fierce competition for domestic supremacy.

31. Ioan Chirilă, "Un veac de fotbal românesc," *Secolul 20,* no. 20 (1998): 146–74.

32. Interview with Valentin Ceauşescu in *Gazeta Sporturilor,* 11 August 2009.

33. The dimension of the split between the Securitate and army forces is yet to be properly researched, especially since many archival documents concerning these socialist institutions are still not publicly available. As with many aspects of socialism, particularly regarding the 1970s and 1980s, the competition between these two branches of power is usually assessed based on

oral sources. However, many scholars have already identified this split at the core of the success of the Romanian revolution: the moment the army stopped backing Ceaușescu, he had to flee, with some sections of the Securitate and police still on the side of the regime. Mutatis mutandis, this was a comparable situation in Egypt with Mubarak's ousting in February 2011: from the moment the army forces backed the demonstrators, the fate of the dictator was sealed.

34. For example, Flacăra Moreni was a team formed and sustained by the Interior Minister himself, to represent Ceaușescus's birth city. Consequently, the team turned into a satellite for Dinamo. At the opposite end, FC Olt, representing the county where Ceaușescu was born, was a good ally for Steaua.

35. It is evident that there was no real concern with the physical security of the spectators. An audience of 120,000 turned out in March 1985, when some authorities were up for reelection the following day, and allowed free entrance to the stadium to remind people of the generosity of the regime. However, by the end of the game, supporters clashed with the police, and the incident led to the decision to ban the *cuplaje* altogether. See *Gazeta Sporturilor,* 27 November 2007, 5.

36. Vochin, *SuperSteaua,* Vol. I, 153.

37. This, of course, is an ironic reference to the "total football" style of play developed by the Dutch in the 1970s.

38. Author's interview with A.C., 8 February 2009.

39. Author's interview with Radu Cosașu, 13 March 2009.

40. State-owned offices where soccer fans could place bets on the results of the upcoming matches.

41. In a sense, the regime itself paved the way to supporters' identification with abstract universalities on the soccer field. How else can one explain the creation of Army and Securitate soccer teams if not as an attempt to sever people's previous concrete identification with local teams, based on class, ethnic, or neighborhood associations' identification, by replacing them with more general-universal identifications from which the concrete social distinctions, with all their imbued modes of exploitation, were removed. The People's Army defending socialism was therefore seen as a large enough umbrella, under which various people could be united.

42. Alin Buzarin, Romanian sports journalist, interviewed for "The best of Steaua—Dinamo," DVD, 2010.

43. This chant and other similar ones were audible in the recordings of football games I could find and watch. The Romanian Television has only recently eased the public access to its soccer games archive.

44. Information provided by Radu Cosașu. The chant in Romanian is "Dobrin, Dobrin/Prietenul sticlei de vin," which means, "Dobrin, the friend of the wine bottles."

45. In Romanian the whole joke rhymes too, so it makes sense. PCR stands for the Romanian Communist Party.

46. Author's interview with C.M., supporter involved in such trafficking, 25 February 2008. European professional sports leagues typically use relegation at the end of the season, allowing for the transfer of teams between competitive divisions based on their performance.

47. Alin Buzarin on "The Best of Steaua—Dinamo," DVD, 2010.

Conclusion
Escapes and Other Border Crossings in Socialist Eastern Europe
Cathleen M. Giustino

In December 1971, Ladislav Bezák undertook a daring plan of escape from socialist Czechoslovakia with his wife and their four young sons. Bezák and his family attempted to flee their native land in a self-built, single-engine monoplane. The 39-year-old pilot had special qualifications for this danger-ous mission; he was the first World Aerobatic Champion, a title honoring his skills as a stunt-pilot and his development of the "lomcovák," a death-defying aeronautic maneuver in which a pilot deliberately tumbles a plane end-over-end while dropping straight down from a high altitude. Despite his flying prowess, escaping from the East Bloc would be no small feat. Fitting his family into the tiny two-seat plane without attracting attention posed special challenges and, very importantly, while in the air he had to avoid being forced to turn around and land, or worse, shot down. Within minutes of taking off and flying at 150 mph, a Czechoslovak air force MiG-17, traveling at 740 mph, was in pursuit of them. After the air-force pilot fired a warning shot at the fleeing family, Bezák put his plane into a steep 4,000-foot drop. The children were slammed against the front of the cockpit and his wife screamed, "It's all up. We better go back." Then Bezák turned his plane slipping into a cloud that shielded the escapees from view. About twenty minutes later, he and his family safely crossed the West German border near Nuremburg.[1]

Ideology and Agency

As the Bezák family's story illustrates, physical escape from the geophysical borders of Soviet-style East Bloc countries was an exceedingly difficult act during most of the Cold War. These were states with extensive systems of po-lice surveillance over society and harsh punishments for disobedience to communist single-party rule. They were also regimes where promises of fulfillment and happiness were, from the beginning, part of ideological claims about socialism's uniqueness and superiority over capitalism.[2] Leisure, entertainment, and tourism were some of the attractions offered for the realization of those promises, albeit often within the limits of struggling command economies. The central questions in this volume, addressed through time off from work, school, and household chores, concern the possibilities for socialist escapes less dramatic than Bezák's, but no less important—namely, breaks away from the routines of everyday life and official ideology in post-war Eastern Europe. When studying life in the East Bloc, can we talk about breaks from everyday life that did not internalize, naturalize, and reproduce official party dogma while people were taking time off from mundane routines? Stated differently, was free time ever truly "free" in these mono-party states with their centrally planned economies? Further, what were the popular receptions, rejections, and (re)interpretations of party ideology embedded within official and unofficial leisure pursuits, and how did those popular reactions affect the nature and workings of socialism?

The authors in this volume present numerous examples of breaks from mundane routines in post-war Eastern Europe, including hours spent at beaches, nightclubs, camp sites, concerts, castles, and soccer matches. Because socialist states strictly limited traveling, especially outside the East Bloc, these escapes were very often domestic distractions and destinations inside the sealed physical borders of inhabitants' own countries or, increasingly after the start of the 1970s, other nearby socialist countries. They were mostly state-driven, state-sponsored activities and sites where official and unofficial, and public and private interests came together in multiple ways, sometimes colliding, clashing, and resisting, and other times blending, assimilating, and reproducing. The outcome of these encounters was contingent on the circumstances and people involved, and not simply determined by the dictates of "rule from above." Taken together, they demonstrate that Eastern Europeans often creatively consumed the official ideology ensconced in free-time pursuits, not merely internalizing, reproducing, or rejecting party teachings. They actively interpreted and reinterpreted them, building meanings and communities that were partially autonomous from party dogma and also experiencing some of the joy and fulfillment that socialist ideology promised to them. Unlike the military force used to crush the revolutionary attempts in Hungary in 1956 and Czechoslovakia in 1968, official ideology was sometimes negotiable, thereby opening up small spaces for the creation of individual identities and group solidarities within state-provided free-time activities—spaces that Eastern Europeans were adept and comfortable at identifying, maximizing, and even openly enjoying.[3] As articles in this volume reveal, leisure, entertainment, and tourism provided Eastern Europeans with gratifying activities that could be performative dialogues and negotiations between long-standing party promises and priorities, and non-party histories, needs, and desires. In free-time activities, the line dividing the official, public, state realm from the unofficial, private, social realm was semi-porous, allowing border crossings and creating, in effect, a borderlands zone, where party dictates encountered and mixed in multiple ways with *Eigen-Sinn* or "doing things one's own way."[4]

Thus, articles here are important for overcoming the limits of old Cold War binary oppositions long applied in studies of the Soviet sphere of influence, including, to quote from Alexei Yurchak, "oppression and resistance, repression and freedom, the state and the people, official economy and second economy, official culture and counterculture, totalitarian language and counter-language, public self and private self, truth and lie, reality and dissimulation, morality and corruption, and so on."[5] Among other problems, these closed categories, conceived as having dense, intransgressible borders, underestimate possibilities East Bloc residents had to create meanings and solidarities that were at least partly autonomous from party ideology, and to "force the authorities to make compromises."[6] By denying possibilities for relative social agency and influence, these binary oppositions, with their sealed boundaries, also fail to illuminate the complex web of power binding and mutually constituting state and society in post-war Eastern Europe, and other modern contexts with single-party rule.

The leisure, entertainment, and tourist escapes analyzed in this volume might not be as immediately spectacular as life-risking flights across closely watched international borders, but they do help make visible the serious, less immediately obvious, but still important local and grassroots power games dotting the landscape of the East Bloc. They show that people living under Communist Party rule did find some moments for practicing agency, exercising influence, and creating unofficial meanings and communities that were important to them. Opportunities for agency and meaning did not necessarily make life easy for large numbers of Eastern Europeans. These occasions did, however, make many of their situations more bearable, fulfilling, and even enjoyable. Furthermore, they signified that the pillars of power rested not simply on physical might and notable examples of a ruthless willingness to use it. While residents of the East Bloc had reasons to fear their regimes, it was not fear alone—or fear at all—that drove each of them.[7] Motivation was also derived from a set of relations resembling a socialist social contract. In this contract, many Eastern Europeans hushed, repressed, or lived with complaints about the loss of far-reaching, inclusive fundamental rights, including freedom of speech and movement. In return, they had state-proffered social-welfare and consumer offerings, including free-time attractions, which provided some possibilities to experience agency, create meaning, and build solidarities. Limited as those consumer offerings often were in the command economies of post-war Eastern Europe, they could sweeten the terms of the socialist social contract. They could also potentially substantiate socialism's ideological promises of bringing fulfillment and happiness to people, although insufficient realization of these utopian party proclamations could and did weaken the contract and the regime's authority.

Time and the West

A comparative reading of chapters in this volume also reveals that, as time passed, Eastern Europeans experienced the spread and diversification of opportunities for socialist escapes and, with those changes, came new possibilities to create unofficial meanings and solidarities. Time was not static in the East Bloc; change did take place, although it was not always marked by dramatic, quickly occurring, easily noticeable moments that are commonly studied. The era of the thaw and much of the 1960s saw the first significant rise in opportunities for socialist free-time pursuits. In those years, the socialist regimes followed the liberalizing cues of Khrushchev in the Soviet Union and sought, like the United States and countries in its sphere of influence, to raise the living standards of their populations and deliver on their promises of happiness and fulfillment, in part, through attention to consumer goods and experiences, including leisure-time distractions and destinations.[8] As this volume shows, Eastern Europeans enjoyed the enhanced relaxation offerings often embracing, negotiating, and reshaping those experiences according to their own contexts and desires, rather than merely absorbing or reproducing party lessons embedded within them. During the late 1960s and the 1970s, following the Soviet Union's military suppression of the 1968 Prague Spring in Czechoslovakia and during the rise of Solidarity in Poland, party officials did undertake efforts to tighten state control over society and reemphasize official ideological discourse in public and private life.[9] Still, none of those efforts resulted in the cessation of popular interpretation, reinterpretation, rejection, and negotiation of official ideology. Nor did they lead to renewed or deepened absorption of official party ideology in mass consciousness on a wide scale. In his 1978 essay, "The Power of the Powerless," former Czechoslovak dissident playwright Václav Havel wrote about a greengrocer during the age of normalization mindlessly placing signs "among the onions and carrots"—signs that read, "Workers of the world, unite!"[10] Like the greengrocer, significant parts of the population never believed much in ideological discourse or the activities involved in displays of conformity. They did, however, believe in the meanings and solidarities that they created and experienced when taking breaks from everyday routines.

Various explanations of the spread, diversification, and creative, unofficial consumption of leisure, entertainment, and tourism in the East Bloc can be gleaned from this volume. One cause concerns the nature of the state in post-war Eastern Europe. Contrary to some old Cold War understandings of the realm under Soviet domination, neither the East Bloc nor any of the individual states in it were monolithic or homogeneous entities. Power within them was fragmented across various central-state, district-level, and local officials and managers who frequently vied against one another for some, if only small, amounts of influence, and often lacked the resources necessary for building socialism.[11] Articles here show various state and social actors negotiating with and competing against one another, rather than marching in lockstep behind a totalistic party order. Further, they reveal how the fragmented state contributed to the partial liberation of society from party dictates, showing that fissures in the edifice of party power provided people with opportunities to create meanings and communities that were autonomous, at least relatively, from official ideology and policy.

Perhaps no explanation of change over time in socialist escapes is more striking than the growing adoration and tightening embrace of tastes, lifestyles, habits, and ideas from the capitalist West, regularly denigrated as "decadent" in official Communist Party ideology. Instead of completely blocking any Western capitalist influences from crossing into the socialist side, the border between the two rival spheres of influence was semi-porous. While Eastern Europeans were physically confined within East Bloc borders, images and sounds of Western consumer goods and mass culture crossed the Cold War divide, providing inhabitants of socialist states with ideas and encouragement for escapes from mundane responsibilities and official ideology. Sociologist David Riesman was an early observer of the semi-permeable nature of the border between socialist East and capitalist West. In 1951 he published a satirical article called "The Nylon War" describing "Operation Abundance," a fictional account of a massive Cold War undertaking in which the United States, working to weaken communism's grip over Eastern Europe, air-dropped cargo loads of Western consumer goods over the Soviet sphere of influence. The "initial forays were small-scale—200,000 pairs of nylon hose, 4,000,000 packs of cigarettes, 35,000 Toni wave kits, 20,000 yo-yos, 10,000 wrist watches, and a number of odds and ends from PX overstock."[12] Time quickly revealed that Riesman's fantastical description of deliveries across the East/West divide, while exaggerated, also touched upon realities of the age of mass consumer culture and post-war preoccupations with living standards.

Through humor, he pointed out that the imaginary, yet real "iron curtain" about which Churchill warned his 1946 audience in Fulton, Missouri, could be envisioned not simply as a dense impenetrable geophysical border across which human escapes were near impossible, but also as a passable "nylon curtain" that allowed for both the transnational and the transsystemic migration ideas, images, tastes, and habits.[13]

Owing first to radio and increasingly to television, some Western ideas and images entered the Eastern Bloc without any encouragement from party officials, who in many cases worked to stop those "decadent" influences from crossing behind their borders. They jammed radios signals, ceased the production of television antennas, and grew nervous about the advent of satellite communications.[14] Still, despite these defensive actions, Communist Party leaders were significantly responsible for Eastern Europeans' romance with Western capitalist mass culture, especially after Khrushchev's thaw began in 1956. Their attention to improving living standards helped expose East Bloc residents to Western fashion, music, domestic furnishings, transportation, gender relations, vacations, and more. Socialist leaders had to generate badly needed revenue, especially hard currencies tied to the international gold standard, to pay for the production of consumer goods and experiences in the struggling command economies, and also have a budget for other state matters including social welfare expenditures. With these pecuniary needs in mind, as chapters here show, they increasingly offered attractive vacations and tourist enticements to Westerners. They hoped that people with marks, francs, pounds, and dollars in their wallets would cross into the East Bloc to travel to Prague, Budapest, the Black Sea coast, or other socialist destinations for their holidays and spend money, thereby raising living standards and propping up communist-party rule. Due to the pressing need to raise revenue and the socialist officials' identification and recruitment of capitalist Westerners as a source of income, Eastern Europeans had regular, and, in some cases (Bulgaria and Hungary to be specific) increasing exposure to Westerners and their tastes, ideas, and habits—despite being forbidden to travel to the West themselves.

This migration of Western tastes and habits across divided Cold War Europe contributed to the spread and diversification of socialist escapes from ideology and everyday routines in the East Bloc. These transsystemic border crossings also challenged official arguments about the uniqueness of socialism and its superiority over capitalism, highlighting instead commonalities between the socialist East and the capitalist West, including shared preoccupations with higher living standards. They also suggest "the deep embeddedness of the socialist project in (capitalist) modernity...."[15] The ideological borders from which East Bloc residents were sometimes escaping through free-time destinations and distractions were never entirely socialist in the first place. Socialism had an innate transsystemic quality due to its historical roots in industrial capitalism.

Nostalgia and the Future

Much has recently been written about nostalgia in the territories of the former East Bloc during the post-socialist period—or "*Ostalgie.*" Nostalgia is a word meaning grief or longing for a lost home or homesickness. When the term has been applied to Eastern Europe since 1989, many people—mainly Westerners—have concluded that peoples living there now have strong desires to return to the socialist past and relive it, in part or in its entirety, as their present and future. It is a term that can be misapplied.[16] What might appear as nostalgia to Western observers of Eastern Europe could be something entirely different to the subjects being labeled. Furthermore, the attribution of nostalgia to post-socialist Eastern Europeans reproduces some older orientalist notions about Western progressiveness and Eastern backwardness. Thus, articles in this volume should not be used to explain post-socialist nostalgia through the lens of socialist-era leisure and tourism, or to say that due to good times and the fond memories that Eastern Europeans had while living under socialism, they presently display symptoms of "*Ostalgie.*" Eastern Europeans have some good memories of the socialist past due, in part, to free-time activities and the meanings and communities that they created and experienced during them. They like discussing those memories with friends and guests, keeping alive old meanings and solidarities, and even attempting to recreate some of those experiences—but they often are doing so while being forward-looking, progressive people with a propensity for autonomous self-rule expressed in everyday, local, grassroots arenas that are not always obvious, transparent, or interesting to foreign observers.

Thus, the authors in this volume present important lessons that can be learned from socialist escapes to the beach, summer camps, and motorcycle rallies; visits to museums, concerts, and nightclubs; and experiences of thumbing a ride and cheering at soccer games. There are a great many sites, activities, and topics related to leisure, entertainment, and tourism in various parts of post-war Eastern Europe that are not developed or touched upon here. Among others, they include movie theaters, amusement parks, houses of culture and pubs, or women's free time, factory outings, child's play, hobbies, and official and unofficial days of observance, including religious holidays. Such additional studies would enhance the panorama of offerings and findings in this book. So would more research on the early 1950s before the thaw occurred, and the late 1950s when consumer experiences and access to Western mass culture were first being expanded. As chapters here show, oral-history interviews provide valuable evidence for this work, as does researching in central-state, regional, and local archives. Investigations of free-time pursuits before 1945 could illuminate important continuities and changes in Eastern Europe after World War II. By deepening our knowledge of how residents of the East Bloc spent their time off from work, school, and domestic duties, we can gain a more authentic knowledge of life under socialism and Communist Party power. Through the further exploration of agency in post-war Eastern Europe, we can advance knowledge about state-society relations in the East Bloc, deepen critical reflection on the usefulness of terms like dictatorship and totalitarianism for this historical context, and enhance understanding of the real and potential possibilities for official and unofficial power in a variety of world contexts with single-party rule.

Notes

I have a number of scholars to thank for help with the writing of this conclusion, including Alan Meyer, György Péteri, Catherine J. Plum, David Tompkins, Alexander Vari, and Nancy M. Wingfield. Florin Poenaru deserves special acknowledgement for the very substantive critical comments that he generously took the time to share with me.

1. "Czechoslovakia: A Do-It-Yourself Escape," *Time,* 3 January 1972. The lomcovák is, in part, named after a drunk person's weaving walk.
2. Socialism was to achieve "future fulfillment and abundance" and "the greatest happiness for the greatest number in the radiant future." See David Crowley and Susan E. Reid, ed., *Pleasures in Socialism: Leisure and Luxury in the Eastern Bloc* (Evanston: Northwestern University Press, 2010), 3–4.
3. On negotiable and non-negotiable areas in post-war Eastern Europe, see Esther von Richthofen, *Bringing Culture to the Masses: Control, Compromise and Participation in the GDR* (Oxford: Berghahn Books, 2009), 216.
4. Paul Betts, *Within Walls: Private Life in the German Democratic Republic* (Oxford: Oxford University Press, 2010), 14. Betts' book provides a valuable discussion of the private sphere in socialism and the semi-porous border between it and the public sphere.
5. Alexei Yurchak, *Everything Was Forever, Until It Was No More* (Princeton: Princeton University Press, 2005), 5.
6. Konrad J. Jarausch, "Beyond Uniformity: The Challenge of Historicizing the GDR," in Jarausch, ed., *Dictatorship as Experience: Towards a Socio-Cultural History of the GDR* (New York: Berghahn Books, 1999), 9.
7. The motivating power of fear versus leisure and "the quiet life" is discussed in Paulina Bren, *The Greengrocer and His TV: The Culture of Communism after the 1968 Prague Spring* (Ithaca: Cornell University Press, 2010), 201–8.
8. Diane Koenker writes, "But socialism perhaps distinguished itself, especially in the early years of socialist regimes, in emphasizing the consumption of experiences rather than things." See Anne E. Gorsuch and Diane P. Koenker, ed., *Turizm: The Russian and East European Tourist under Capitalism and Socialism* (Ithaca: Cornell University Press, 2006), 6.

9. György Péteri, ed., *Imagining the West in Eastern Europe and the Soviet Union* (Pittsburgh: University of Pittsburgh Press, 2010), 10.

10. Václav Havel, "The Power of the Powerless," in *The Power of the Powerless: Citizens against the State in Central-Eastern Europe,* John Keane, ed. (New York: M.E. Sharpe, 1985), 23–96.

11. Katherine Verdery illustrates the fragmented nature of the East Bloc states when discussing the non-centralized nature of "centralized planning" in "What was Socialism, and Why did it Fail?" in Verdery, *What was Socialism, and What Comes Next?* (Princeton: Princeton University Press, 1996), 19–38.

12. David Riesman, "The Nylon War," in Riesman, *Abundance for What* (New Brunswick: Transaction Publishers, 1993), 69. I first encountered Riesman's fascinating piece when reading Victoria de Grazia, *Irresistible Empire: America's Advance through 20th Century Europe* (Cambridge: Harvard University Press, 2005), 350–51.

13. See György Péteri, "Nylon Curtain: Transnational and Transsystemic Tendencies in the Cultural Life of State-Socialist Russia and East-Central Europe," *Slavonica,* 10, no. 2 (2004): 111–13.

14. The popularity of the American television show "Dallas" is the subject of Nick Gillespie and Matt Welch, "How 'Dallas' Won the Cold War," *The Washington Post,* 27 April 2008. Information on party responses to antennas and satellite broadcasting is in Bren, *The Greengrocer and His TV,* 120–21.

15. György Péteri, "Sites of Convergence: The USSR and Communist Eastern Europe at International Fairs Abroad and At Home," *Journal of Contemporary History* 47, no. 1 (January 2012): 5. See also Susan E. Reid, "The Soviet Pavilion at Brussels '58: Convergence, Conversion, Critical Assimilation, or Transculturation?" Cold War International History Project, Working Paper #62, December 2010; http://www.wilsoncenter.org/sites/default/files/WP62_Reid_web_V3sm.pdf (accessed 15 November 2012).

16. See the essays in Maria Todorová and Zsuzsa Gille, ed., *Post-Communist Nostalgia* (New York: Berghahn Books, 2010). In the book's postscript, Gille writes, "post-Communist nostalgia is not simply a shorthand: it is a misnomer" (286).

Selected Bibliography

The following bibliography includes a number of conceptual works and memoirs along with a wider array of empirical studies. Reflecting the volume itself, this resource strives to bring East German history into dialog with the histories of other Eastern Bloc countries. A few texts on leisure in post-war Soviet, Yugoslav, and Albanian history have also been added for scholars with interest in Eastern European countries not treated in this volume. Additional titles related to socialist escapes, including article titles, can be found in the notes of individual chapters.

Conceptualizing State, Society, and Everyday Life

De Certeau, Michel. *The Practice of Everyday Life.* Berkeley and Los Angeles: University of California Press, 1984.

Havel, Václav. *The Power of the Powerless: Citizens against the State in East-Central Europe.* New York: M.E. Sharpe, 1985.

Konrad, György. *Antipolitics.* San Diego: Harcourt, Brace, Jovanovich, 1984.

Kott, Sandrine. *Le communisme au quotidien: les enterprises d'état dans la société est-allemande.* Paris: Belin, 2001.

Lüdtke, Alf, ed. *The History of Everyday Life: Reconstructing Historical Experiences and Ways of Life.* Princeton: Princeton University Press, 1995.

Miłosz, Czesław. *The Captive Mind.* New York: Vintage Books, 1990.

Scott, James C. *Weapons of the Weak*: *Everyday Forms of Peasant Resistance.* New Haven: Yale University Press, 1985.

Shove, Elizabeth, Frank Trentmann, and Richard Wilk, ed. *Time, Consumption and Everyday Life: Practice, Materiality and Culture.* Oxford: Berg, 2009.

Memoir Literature

Ash, Timothy Garton. *The File: A Personal History.* New York: Vintage Books, 1998.

Brucan, Silviu. *The Wasted Generation: Memoirs of the Romanian Journey from Capitalism to Socialism and Back.* Boulder, San Francisco and Oxford: Westview Press, 2008.

Drakulic, Slavenka. *How We Survived Communism and Even Laughed.* New York: Harper, 1993.

Djilas, Milovan. *Conversations with Stalin.* New York: Harcourt Brace, 1963.

Gorokhova, Elena. *A Mountain of Crumbs: A Memoir.* New York: Simon & Schuster, 2011.

Hensel, Jana. *After the Wall: Confessions from an East German Childhood and the Life that Came Next.* New York: Public Affairs, 2008.

Kassabova, Kapka. *Street without a Name: Childhood and Other Misadventures in Bulgaria.* New York: Skyhorse Publishing, 2009.

Klima, Ivan. *The Spirit of Prague.* London: Granta Books, 2000.

Klemperer, Victor. *The Lesser Evil. The Diaries of Victor Klemperer, 1945-1959.* London: Orion, 2004.

Margolius-Kovaly, Heda. *Under a Cruel Star: A Life in Prague, 1941-1968.* New York: Holmes & Meier, 1997.

Messana, Paola. *Soviet Communal Living: An Oral History of the Kommunalka.* New York: Palgrave Macmillan, 2011.

Rusch, Claudia. *Meine Freie Deutsche Jugend.* Frankfurt am Main: S. Fischer Verlag, 2003.

Secondary Works on the State, Society, Leisure and Tourism in Postwar Eastern Europe

Allan, Sean, and John Sandford, ed. *DEFA: East German Cinema, 1946-1992.* New York and Oxford: Berghahn Books, 1999.

Apor, Balázs, Péter Apor, and E. A. Rees, ed. *The Sovietization of Eastern Europe: New Perspectives on the Postwar Period.* Washington, DC: New Academia Publishing, 2008.

Arnold, Klaus, and Christoph Classen, ed. *Zwischen Pop und Propaganda: Radio in der DDR.* Berlin: Ch. Links Verlag, 2004.

Bek, Mikuláš, Geoffrey Chew, and Petr Macek, ed. *Socialist Realism and Music.* Praha: KLP, 2004.

Betts, Paul. Within Walls: Private Life in the German Democratic Republic. Oxford: Oxford University Press, 2010.

Boym, Svetlana. *Common Places: Mythologies of Everyday Life in Russia.* Cambridge, MA: Harvard University Press, 1994.

Bradley, Laura. *Cooperation and Conflict: GDR Theatre Censorship, 1961-1989.* New York: Oxford University Press, 2011.

Bren, Paulina. *The Greengrocer and His TV: The Culture of Communism after the 1968 Prague Spring.* Ithaca: Cornell University Press, 2010.

Bren, Paulina, and Mary Neuburger, ed. *Communism Unwrapped: Consumption in Cold War Eastern Europe.* New York: Oxford University Press, 2012

Brenner, Christiane, and Peter Heumos, ed. *Sozialgeschichtliche Kommunismusforschung. Vergleichende Beiträge zur sozialen Entwicklung in der Tschechoslowakei, DDR, Polen und Ungarn, 1945-1968.* Munich: Collegium Karolinum, 2005.

Brown, Karl. "Dance Hall Days: Jazz and Hooliganism in Communist Hungary, 1948-1956." *Trondheim Studies in Eastern European Culture and Society,* no. 26 (October 2006).

Buchli, Victor. *An Archeology of Socialism.* Oxford: Berg Publishers, 2000.

Buck-Morss, Susan. *Dreamworld and Catastrophe: The Passing of Mass Utopia in East and West.* Cambridge, MA: MIT Press, 2002.

Connelly, John. *Captive University: The Sovietization of East German, Czech and Polish Higher Education, 1945-1956.* Chapel Hill: University of North Carolina Press, 2000.

Crew, David F., ed. *Consuming Germany in the Cold War.* Oxford: Berg Publishers, 2003.

Crowley, David, and Susan E. Reid, ed. *Pleasures in Socialism: Leisure and Luxury in the Eastern Bloc.* Evanston, IL: Northwestern University Press, 2010.

———, and Susan E. Reid, ed. *Socialist Spaces: Sites of Everyday Life in the Eastern Bloc.* Oxford: Berg Publishers, 2002.

Davidson, John, and Sabine Hake, ed. *Framing the Fifties: Cinema in a Divided Germany.* New York: Berghahn, 2008.

Davis, Belinda, Thomas Lindenberger, and Michael Wildt, ed. *Alltag, Erfahrung, Eigensinn: Historisch-anthropologische Erkundungen.* Frankfurt am Main and New York: Campus, 2008.

Dessewffy, Tibor. "Speculators and Travellers: The Political Construction of the Tourist in the Kádár Regime." *Cultural Studies* 16, no. 1 (2002): 44–62.

Dobrenko, Evgeny. *The Political Economy of Socialist Realism.* New Haven: Yale University Press, 2007.

Eastern European Quarterly. Special Issue on Alcohol Consumption in Eastern Europe. Vol. 18, no. 4 (1984).

Edele, Mark. *Stalinist Society, 1928-1953.* Oxford: Oxford University Press, 2011.

Edelman, Robert. *Serious Fun: A History of Spectator Sports in the USSR.* Oxford: Oxford University Press, 1993.

———. *Spartak Moscow: A History of the People's Team in the Workers' State.* Ithaca: Cornell University Press, 2009.

Fitzpatrick, Sheila. *Everyday Stalinism: Ordinary Life in Extraordinary Times, Soviet Russia in the 1930s.* Oxford: Oxford University Press, 1999.

Fenemore, Mark. *Sex, Thugs and Rock 'n' Roll: Teenage Rebels in Cold-War East Germany.* New York and Oxford: Berghahn Books, 2007.

Fulbrook, Mary. *The People's State: East German Society from Hitler to Honecker.* New Haven: Yale University Press, 2005.

———, ed. *Power and Society in the GDR: 1961-1979.* New York and Oxford: Berghahn Books, 2009.

Furst, Juliane. *Stalin's Last Generation: Soviet Post-War Youth and the Emergence of Mature Socialism.* New York: Oxford University Press, 2010.

Galenza, Ronald, and Heinz Havemeister, ed. *Wir Wollen immer artig sein … Punk, New Wave, HipHop, Independent: Szene in der DDR 1980-1990.* Berlin: Schwarzkopf und Schwarzkopf, 1999.

Gecser, Ottó, and Dávid Kitzinger. "Fairy Sales: The Budapest International Fairs as Virtual Shopping Tours." *Cultural Studies* 16, no. 1 (2002): 145–64.

Ghodsee, Kristen. *The Red Riviera: Gender, Tourism, and Postsocialism on the Black Sea.* Durham, NC: Duke University Press, 2005.

Gorsuch, Anne E. *All This is Your World: Soviet Tourism at Home and Abroad after Stalin.* Oxford: Oxford University Press, 2011.

Gorsuch, Anne E., and Diane P. Koenker, ed. *Turizm: The Russian and East European Tourist under Capitalism and Socialism.* Ithaca: Cornell University Press, 2006.

Grandits, Hannes, and Karin Taylor, ed. *Yugoslavia's Sunny Side: A History of Tourism in Socialism (1950s-1980s).* Budapest: Central European University Press, 2010.

Hall, Derek. "Albania's Changing Tourism Environment." *Journal of Cultural Geography* 12, no. 2 (1992): 35–44.

Hammer, Ferenc. "A Gasoline Scented Sindbad: The Truck Driver as a Popular Hero in Socialist Hungary." *Cultural Studies* 16, no. 1 (2002): 80–126.

Hilton, Marjorie L. "Retailing the Revolution: The State Department Store (GUM) and Soviet Society in the 1920s." *Journal of Social History* 37, no. 4 (2004): 939–64.

Horváth, Sándor. "Myths of the Great Tree Gang: Constructing Urban Spaces and Youth Culture in the 'Socialist' Budapest." In *Testimonies of the City: Identity, Community and Change in a Contemporary Urban World,* ed. Richard Rodger and Joanna Hebert. Aldershot: Ashgate, 2007: 73–86.

Jakovljević, Branislav. "Human Resources: June 1968, Hair, and the Beginning of Yugoslavia's End." *Grey Room* 24 (Winter 2008): 38–53.

Jarausch, Konrad H., and Thomas Lindenberger, ed. *Conflicted Memories: Europeanizing Contemporary History.* New York and London: Berghahn Books, 2007.

———, ed., and Eve Duffy, transl. *Dictatorship as Experience: Towards a Socio-Cultural History of the GDR.* New York and London: Berghahn Books, 1999.

Johnson, Molly Wilkinson. *Training Socialist Citizens: Sports and the State in East Germany.* London: Brill, 2008.

Johnston, Timothy. *Being Soviet: Identity, Rumour and Everyday Life under Stalin, 1939-1953.* Oxford: Oxford University Press, 2011.

Kenney, Padraic. *A Carnival of Revolution: Central Europe 1989.* Princeton: Princeton University Press, 2002.

———. "Remaking the Polish Working Class: Early Stalinist Models of Labor and Leisure." *Slavic Review* 53, no. 1 (1994): 1–25.

Kligman, Gail. *The Politics of Duplicity: Controlling Reproduction in Ceaușescu's Romania.* Berkeley: University of California Press, 1998.

Koshar, Rudy. *German Travel Cultures.* New York: Berg, 2000.

Landsman, Mark. *Dictatorship and Demand: The Politics of Consumerism in East Germany.* Cambridge, MA: Harvard University Press, 2005.

Lahusen, Thomas, and Evgeny Dobrenko, ed. *Socialist Realism without Shores.* Durham, NC: Duke University Press, 1997.

Lindenberger, Thomas, ed. *Herrschaft und Eigen-Sinn in der Diktatur: Studien zur Gesellschaftsgeschichte der DDR,* Cologne, Weimar, and Vienna: Böhlau, 1999.

Ludwig, Andreas. *Fortschritt, Norm und Eigensinn. Erkundungen im Alltag der DDR.* Berlin: Ch. Links Verlag, 1999.

Luthar, Breda, and Marusa Pusnik, ed. *Remembering Utopia: The Culture of Everyday Life in Socialist Yugoslavia.* Washington, DC: New Academia Publishing, 2010.

Madarász, Jeanette Z. *Working in East Germany: Normality in a Socialist Dictatorship, 1961-1979.* London: Palgrave Macmillan, 2006.

Maxim, Juliana. "Mass Housing and Collective Experience: On the Notion of *Microraion* in Romania in the 1950s and 1960s." *The Journal of Architecture* 14, no. 1 (2009): 7–26.

McDermott, Kevin, and Matthew Stibbe, ed. *Revolution and Resistance in Eastern Europe: Challenges to Communist Rule.* Oxford, New York: Berg Publishers, 2006.

McLellan, Josie. "State Socialist Nudism: East German Nudism from Ban to Boom," *The Journal of Modern History* 79, no. 1 (2007): 48–111.

Moran, Joe. "November in Berlin: The End of the Everyday." *History Workshop Journal,* no. 57 (2004): 216–34.

Naimark, Norman. "The Sovietization of Eastern Europe, 1944–1953." In *The Cambridge History of the Cold War,* vol. I: *Origins,* ed. Melvyn P. Leffler and Odd Arne Westad. Cambridge: Cambridge University Press, 2010: 175–97.

Neuburger, Mary. *Balkan Smoke: Tobacco and the Making of Modern Bulgaria.* Cornell: Cornell University Press, 2012.

Palmowski, Jan. *Inventing a Socialist Nation: Heimat and the Politics of Everyday Life in the GDR, 1945-1990.* Cambridge: Cambridge University Press, 2009.

Major, Patrick. *Behind the Berlin Wall: East Germany and the Frontiers of Power.* New York: Oxford University Press, 2009.

Patterson, Patrick Hyder. "Dangerous Liaisons: Soviet-Block Tourists and the Temptations of the Yugoslav Good Life in the 1960s and 1970s." In *The Business of Tourism: Place, Faith, and History,* ed. Philip Scranton and Janet F. Davidson. Philadelphia: University of Pennsylvania Press, 2006: 186–212.

Pence, Katherine, and Paul Betts, ed. *Socialist Modern: East German Everyday Culture and Politics.* Ann Arbor: University of Michigan Press, 2008.

Penn, Shanna, and Jill Massino. *Gender Politics and Everyday Life in State Socialist Eastern and Central Europe.* London: Palgrave Macmillan, 2009.

Péteri, György. "Streetcars of Desire: Cars and Automobilism in Communist Hungary, 1958-1970." *Social History* 34, no. 1 (2002): 1–28.

———, ed. *Imagining the West in Eastern Europe and the Soviet Union.* Pittsburgh: University of Pittsburgh Press, 2010.

Píchová, Hana. "The Lineup for Meat: The Stalin Statue in Prague." *PMLA* 123 (2008): 614–30.

Pittaway, Mark. *Eastern Europe, 1939-2000.* London: Hodder Arnold, 2004.

Poiger, Uta. *Jazz, Rock and Rebels: Cold War Politics and American Culture in a Divided Germany.* Berkeley: University of California Press, 2000.

Potocki, Rodger P. "The Life and Times of Poland's 'Bikini Boys.'" *The Polish Review* 39, no. 3 (1994): 259–90.

Rainer, János M., and György Péteri, ed. *Muddling Through in the Long 1960s: Ideas and Everyday Life in High Politics and the Lower Classes of Communist Hungary.* Trondheim and Budapest: Institute for the History of the 1956 Hungarian Revolution and Program on Eastern European Cultures and Societies, 2005.

Rauhut, Michael, and Thomas Kochan, ed. *Bye bye, Lübben City: Bluesfreaks, Tramps und Hippies in der DDR.* Berlin: Schwarkkopf und Schwarzkopf, 2009.

Reid, Susan E., and David Crowley, ed. *Style and Socialism: Modernity and Material Culture in Post-War Eastern Europe.* Oxford: Berg Publishers, 2000.

Richthofen, Esther von. *Bringing Culture to the Masses: Control, Compromise and Participation in the GDR.* New York and Oxford: Berghahn Books, 2009.

Risch, William J. "Soviet Flower Children: Hippies and the Youth Culture in 1970s L'viv." *Journal of Contemporary History* 40, no. 3 (2005): 565–84.

Roubal, Petr. "A Didactic Project Transformed into the Celebration of a Ritual: The Czechoslovak Spartakiads, 1955-1990." *Zeitschrift für moderne europäische Geschichte* 4, no. 1 (2006): 90–113.

Rubin, Eli. *Synthetic Socialism: Plastics and Dictatorship in the German Democratic Republic.* Chapel Hill: University of North Carolina Press, 2008.

———. "The Trabant: Consumption, Eigen-Sinn and Movement." *History Workshop Journal* 68 (Autumn 2009): 27–44.

Ryback, Timothy W. *Rock around the Block: A History of Rock Music in Eastern Europe and the Soviet Union.* Oxford: Oxford University Press, 1990.

Schwandner-Sievers, and Bernd J. Fischer, ed. *Albanian Identities: Myth and History.* Bloomington: Indiana University Press, 2002.

Siegelbaum, Lewis, ed. *The Socialist Car: Automobility in the Eastern Bloc.* Ithaca: Cornell University Press, 2011.

Spode, Hasso, ed. *Goldstrand und Teutonengrill: Kultur- und Sozialgeschichte des Tourismus in Deutschland 1945-1989.* Berlin: Werner Moser Verlag für universitäre Kommunikation, 1996.

Stitziel, Judd. *Fashioning Socialism: Clothing, Politics, and Consumer Culture in East Germany.* Oxford: Berg Publishers, 2005.

Stock, Manfred, and Philipp Mühlberg. *Die Szene von Ihnen: Skinheads, Grufties, Heavy Metals, Punks.* Berlin: Ch. Links, 1990.

Švab, Alenka. "Consuming Western Image of Well-Being: Shopping Tourism in Socialist Slovenia." *Cultural Studies* 16, no. 1 (2002): 63–79.

Taylor, Karin. *Let's Twist Again: Youth and Leisure in Socialist Bulgaria.* Vienna and Berlin: Lit Verlag, 2006.

Tismaneanu, Vladimir. *Stalinism for All Seasons: A Political History of Romanian Communism.* Berkeley: University of California Press, 2003.

———. *Stalinism Revisited: The Establishment of Communist Regimes in East-Central Europe.* Budapest: Central European University Press, 2009.

Todorova, Maria and Zsuzsa Gille, ed. *Post-Communist Nostalgia.* New York: Berghahn Books, 2010.

Tomlinson, Alan, and Christopher Young, ed. *German Football: History, Culture, Society.* London and New York: Routledge, 2006.

Verdery, Katherine. *What was Socialism and What Comes Next?* Princeton: Princeton University Press, 1996.

White, Anne. *De-Stalinization and the House of Culture: Declining State Control over Leisure in USSR, Poland, and Hungary, 1953-1989.* London and New York: Routledge, 1990.

Wilkinson, Molly Johnson. "The *Friedensfahrt*: International Sports and East German Socialism in the 1950s." *The International History Review* 29, no. 1 (2007): 57–82.

Williams, Allan M., and Vladimír Baláž, ed. *Tourism in Transition: Economic Change in Central Europe.* London: I.B. Tauris, 2001.

Wolter, Wolter. *"Ich harre aus einem Land und geh ihm fremd." Die Geschichte des Tourismus in der DDR.* Frankfurt am Main: Campus Verlag, 2009.

Zatlin, Jonathan. "The Vehicle of Desire: The Trabant, the Wartburg and the End of the GDR." *German History* 15, no. 3 (1997): 258–380.

Zhuk, Sergei I. *Rock and Roll in the Rocket City: The West, Identity and Ideology in Soviet Dniepropetrovsk, 1960-1985.* Washington, DC: Woodrow Wilson Center Press, 2010.

Notes on Contributors

Irina Costache is a PhD candidate in comparative gender studies at the Central European University in Budapest, where she focuses on Eastern European history and feminist philosophy. In 2007 she received a master's degree from the same department for an ethnography of women's soccer in Romania. Her most recent publication is "Sociologia corpului gol: istorii şi ideologii ale nudismului" in *Introducere în sociologia corpului: Teme, Perspective şi Experienţe Întrupate,* ed. Laura Grumberg (Polirom, 2010). She is currently completing her doctoral dissertation provisionally entitled "On the Socialist Body: Exploring the Carnalities of Real-Existing Socialism," a rereading of everyday life under Ceauşescu's dictatorship through the trope of the body. She was awarded a Fulbright scholarship to study in the United States during 2011–12.

Patrice M. Dabrowski (PhD Harvard University, 1999) is the author of *Commemorations and the Shaping of Modern Poland* (Indiana University Press, 2004). Her most recent articles (several of them prize-winning) have appeared in *Austrian History Yearbook, Centropa, East Central Europe, L'Europe du Centre-Est: Eine wissenschaftliche Zeitschrift,* and *Slavic Review.* She has also authored chapters in a number of edited volumes, including *Capital Cities in the Aftermath of Empires: Planning in Central and Southeastern Europe* (Routledge, 2010). Dabrowski has just completed the text of a popular history of Poland. She is currently working on another book-length project, tentatively entitled *"Discovering" the Carpathians: Episodes in Imagining and Reshaping Alpine Borderland Regions.* She has taught at Harvard, Brown, and the University of Massachusetts-Amherst. She also has served as director of the Harvard Ukrainian Summer Institute.

Caroline Fricke (PhD University of Potsdam, 2012) wrote her dissertation on "Jugendliche im Bezirk Schwerin 1971 bis 1989." She has published "Einweisung zur Umerziehung: Vom Umgang mit sozial auffälligen Jugendlichen," in *Zeitschrift zur kritischen Aufarbeitung der SED-Diktatur,* "Negativ dekadent? Jugendkulturen im Bezirk Schwerin in den 1980er Jahren," in *Zeitgeschichte regional,* and "Heavy Metal in der DDR-Provinz" in *Metal Matters: Heavy Metal als Kultur und Welt,* ed. Rolf Nohr and Herbert Schwab (LIT Verlag, 2011).

Cathleen M. Giustino (PhD University of Chicago, 1997) is the Mills Carter professor of history at Auburn University, where she teaches modern Central and Eastern European history and visual culture. She is author of *Tearing Down Prague's Jewish Town: Ghetto Clearance and the Legacy of Middle-Class Ethnic Politics around 1900* (East European Monographs, 2003). She has published chapters in edited volumes and her journal articles include "Municipal Activism in Late-Nineteenth-Century Prague: The House Numbered 207-V and Ghetto Clearance" in the *Austrian History Yearbook,* "Rodin in Prague: Modern Art, Cultural Diplomacy and National Display" in *Slavic Review,* and "Industrial Design and the Czechoslovak Pavilion at EXPO '58: Artistic Autonomy, Party Control, and Cold War Common Ground" in *Journal of Contemporary History.* She is currently writing a book manuscript on confiscated cultural property, museums, and memory in Czechoslovakia from 1918 to 1992, and an article on women's work and Czechoslovak bijouterie during socialism.

Mark Keck-Szajbel is a specialist in twentieth-century European history, an academic research fellow with the Center for Interdisciplinary Polish Studies at the European University Viadrina, and a PhD candidate in history at the University of California, Berkeley. He has also been a visiting scholar at Univerzita Karlova (Prague), Europa-Universität Viadrina (Frankfurt/Oder), Uniwersytet Adama Mickiewicza (Poznań), and Eberhard Karls Universität (Tübingen). A Fulbright scholar during 2010–11, he is currently completing his dissertation on everyday experiences of the open border between East Germany, Czechoslovakia, and Poland, 1972–1989. He is the author and translator of numerous articles in *Kritika, Global Studies,* and edited volumes.

Mary Neuburger (PhD University of Washington, 1997) is professor of history at the University of Texas, Austin, where she teaches courses on the history of modern Eastern Europe. She specializes in southeastern Europe and has interests in urban culture, consumption, gender, and nationalism. She has published *The Orient Within: Muslim Minorities and the Negotiation of Nationhood in Modern Bulgaria* (Cornell University Press, 2004) and, more recently, *Balkan Smoke: Tobacco and the Making of Modern Bulgaria* (Cornell University Press, 2012). She has published articles in *Slavic Review, Nationalities Papers, Centropa,* and numerous edited volumes. She co-edited a collection of essays with Paulina Bren entitled, *Communism Unwrapped: Consumption in Cold War Eastern Europe* (Oxford University Press, 2012).

Catherine J. Plum (PhD University of Wisconsin, 2005) is associate professor of history at Western New England University, where she teaches courses on modern European and German history. She is currently writing a book on antifascist education and commemoration in East German schools and extracurricular activities. She published "The Children of Antifascism: Exploring Young Historian Clubs in the GDR," in *German Politics and Society* and "Contested Namesakes: East Berlin School Names under Communism & in Reunified Germany," in *History of Education Quarterly*. Her article, "Feminine Heroes, Masculine Superheroes? Contradictions within Antifascist Youth Education in the German Democratic Republic (GDR)," appeared in *Témoigner. Entre Histoire et Mémoire Revue interdisciplinaire de la Fondation Auschwitz* (Zeitschrift der Auschwitz-Stiftung Brüssel, Éditions Kimé, Paris).

Florin Poenaru (PhD Central European University, 2013) recently completed his dissertation examining the class politics of writing history in post-socialist Romania and connected practices of memorialization, museumification, and forgetting in a context marked by struggles to rearticulate new labor politics. He received a Central European University PhD research grant for his fieldwork, a doctoral research support grant at the Graduate Center of the City University of New York, and a Fulbright scholarship for study in the United States during 2011–12. Currently, he is researching changing structures of feelings in the context of the ongoing crisis of global capitalism.

David G. Tompkins (PhD Columbia University, 2004) is assistant professor of history at Carleton College, where he teaches courses on modern Europe, in particular Central Europe. His book, *Composing the Party Line: Music and Politics in Early Cold War Poland and East Germany,* is forthcoming from Purdue University Press in 2013. He has published "Orchestrating Identity: Concerts for the Masses and the Shaping of East German Society" in *German History* and "Composing for and with the Party: Andrzej Panufnik and Stalinist Poland" in *The Polish Review,* as well as several articles in edited volumes. He is working on a second book project on everyday life in communist Central Europe through the prism of images of friends and enemies. For his work, he has received funding from numerous sources, including Fulbright, DAAD, ACLS, IREX, SSRC, and the Mellon Foundation.

Alexander Vari (PhD Brown University, 2005) was an Andrew W. Mellon postdoctoral fellow at Carnegie Mellon University (2005–06) and is currently associate professor of modern European history at Marywood University in Scranton, Pennsylvania. His research interests relate to the history of the Austro-Hungarian Empire and the Habsburg successor states under capitalism and socialism. He has published articles in *Austrian History Yearbook, Journeys, Budapest Review of Books, Journal of Contemporary History,* and *Urban History.* He has book chapters in *Turizm: The Russian and Eastern European Tourist under Capitalism and Socialism,* ed. A. Gorsuch and D. Koenker (Cornell University Press, 2006), *(Im)permanence: Cultures in/out of Time,* ed. J. Schachter and S. Brockmann (Penn State University Press, 2008), and *Touring Beyond the Nation: A Transnational Approach to European Tourism History,* ed. Eric G.E. Zuelow (Ashgate, 2011). Currently, he is working on a book manuscript on the impact of globalization and nation-building on turn-of-the-century Budapest, and has started a new research project on histories of nightlife under socialism.

Index